Bombing the City

Second World War is enshrined in our collective memory as the good war – a victory of good over evil. However, the bombing war has always troubled this narrative as total war transformed civilians into legitimate targets and raised unsettling questions, such as whether it was possible for Allied and Axis alike to be victims of aggression. In *Bombing the City*, an unprecedented comparative history of how ordinary Britons and Japanese experienced bombing, Aaron William Moore offers a major new contribution to these debates. Utilising hundreds of diaries, letters, and memoirs, he recovers the voices of ordinary people on both sides – from builders, doctors, and factory workers to housewives, students, and policemen – and reveals the shared experiences shaped by gender, class, race, and age. He reveals how the British and Japanese public continued to support bombing elsewhere even as they felt first-hand its terrible impact at home.

AARON WILLIAM MOORE is the Handa Chair of Japanese-Chinese Relations at the University of Edinburgh. His research has received support from the British Academy, the Arts & Humanities Research Council, and the Leverhulme Trust. In 2014, he was awarded the prestigious Leverhulme Prize for his work in comparative history.

Studies in the Social and Cultural History of Modern Warfare

General Editor

Jay Winter, *Yale University*

Advisory Editors

David Blight, *Yale University*

Richard Bosworth, *University of Western Australia*

Peter Fritzsche, *University of Illinois, Urbana-Champaign*

Carol Gluck, *Columbia University*

Benedict Kiernan, *Yale University*

Antoine Prost, *Université de Paris-Sorbonne*

Robert Wohl, *University of California, Los Angeles*

In recent years the field of modern history has been enriched by the exploration of two parallel histories. These are the social and cultural history of armed conflict, and the impact of military events on social and cultural history.

Studies in the Social and Cultural History of Modern Warfare presents the fruits of this growing area of research, reflecting both the colonization of military history by cultural historians and the reciprocal interest of military historians in social and cultural history, to the benefit of both. The series offers the latest scholarship in European and non-European events from the 1850s to the present day.

A full list of titles in the series can be found at:
www.cambridge.org/modernwarfare

Bombing the City

Civilian Accounts of the Air War in Britain and Japan, 1939–1945

Aaron William Moore

University of Edinburgh

CAMBRIDGE
UNIVERSITY PRESS

CAMBRIDGE
UNIVERSITY PRESS

University Printing House, Cambridge CB2 8BS, United Kingdom

One Liberty Plaza, 20th Floor, New York, NY 10006, USA

477 Williamstown Road, Port Melbourne, VIC 3207, Australia

314–321, 3rd Floor, Plot 3, Splendor Forum, Jasola District Centre,
New Delhi – 110025, India

79 Anson Road, #06–04/06, Singapore 079906

Cambridge University Press is part of the University of Cambridge.

It furthers the University's mission by disseminating knowledge in the pursuit of
education, learning, and research at the highest international levels of excellence.

www.cambridge.org
Information on this title: www.cambridge.org/9781108428255
DOI: 10.1017/9781108552479

First published 2018

Printed in the United Kingdom by TJ International Ltd. Padstow Cornwall

A catalogue record for this publication is available from the British Library.

ISBN 978-1-108-42825-5 Hardback
ISBN 978-1-108-44652-5 Paperback

Contents

Figures

Acknowledgements

The first draft of this book was written during a period of academic research leave funded by the Leverhulme Trust, from whom I have received considerable assistance over the years. While preparing this book for its contract with Cambridge University Press, I received advice from Richard Overy and Keith Lowe. My editor at Cambridge University Press, Michael Watson, has been very patient as I missed multiple deadlines. The book has benefitted from comments by colleagues at every stage, but John Treat and Penny Summerfield gave me excellent critical feedback from the Japanese and British perspective as I was preparing to finally let the book go. Any mistakes in *Bombing the City* are my responsibility alone.

I dedicate the book to Sarah, who was even happier than I was to see it finished.

Note to the Reader

Japanese names appear in the East Asian fashion, with surname first and given name second. Subsequently, the given name will be used for both British and Japanese authors.

This book is based on diaries, letters, and memoirs by citizens of cities in Britain and Japan from 1939 to 1945. *Bombing the City* includes texts such as:

1. commercially published, self-published, and unpublished (manuscript) materials
2. documents from the wartime period, including diaries, letters, and reports
3. single-authored memoirs from the post-war period
4. memoir collections (e.g., *Nagoya kūshūshi*, or *Journal of the Nagoya Air Raids*), although many of these will include reprinted diary accounts as well.

In most cases, I have corrected minor grammatical and spelling errors without indicating this in the book. I will note significant changes with brackets when directly quoting from primary documents. I have replaced the use of '&' and '+' in original documents with 'and' for readability.

This book generally avoids using the term 'blitz' or 'the Blitz', as it is sometimes overly focused on Britain and London, and usually refers to the limited period of 1940–1941, ignoring the longer-term bombing campaigns over cities such as Hull and the V1 and V2 rocket attacks.

Featured Diarists

Each chapter begins and ends with discussions by six featured diarists, which follow their reactions to the events described within by examining their war diaries.

Kojima Yoshitaka (M), 12 to 16 years old, Nagoya. Diary, 19 November 1941 to 31 November 1945, *Guriko nikki* (self-published, 1995).

> Yoshitaka began the war as a primary school student, where he learned how to write a diary. After graduation, he continued the practice, observing evacuation and the bombing of Nagoya as a middle-school student.

Kenneth A. Holmes (M), 15 to 16 years old, London. Diary, 2 August 1944 to April 1945, Imperial War Museum (London).

> Kenneth left school at 16 to work as a printer's apprentice in Kensington. The diary captures his growing interest in politics and the first use of rocket technology by the German armed forces against civilians in Britain.

Inohara Mitsuko (F), 15 to 16 years old, Osaka. Diary, 8 January 1945 to 18 September 1945, *Tojōryō no shojo-tachi* (self-published, 1991).

> Mitsuko was removed from school by the state at age 16 in order to work in a textile factory. The diary records her experience of being fired upon by Allied aircraft, food shortages, and observing the devastation of Osaka by firebombing.

Dora E. Mockett (F), 22 to 28 years old, Hull. Diary, 1 January 1939 to 31 December 1945, Hull History Centre.

> Dora was a young woman who lived with her friend Mary from 1926 to 1946 in a shared residence on Goddard Avenue, near central Hull. An avid knitter, she worked as a public sector secretary in Britain's most bombed city.

Takahashi Aiko (F), 48 to 51 years old, Tokyo. Diary, 18 February 1942 to 15 August 1945, *Shōwa sensō bungaku zenshū 14: Shimin no nikki* (Tokyo: Shūeisha, 1965), reprint.

Aiko was a well-educated Tokyo urbanite who had spent time abroad in the United States. She kept the diary for her children, who obtained US citizenship and left Japan after the war, and self-published it in 1955. It records the Tokyo firebombing.

Dorothy Hughes (F), 19 to 21 years old, Liverpool. Diary, 24 August 1939 to 4 February 1942, Mass-Observation Archives (Brighton).

Dorothy was a young woman of middle-class background working as a clerk in Liverpool while still living in her parents' home. She witnessed multiple raids on Liverpool and the surrounding coastal areas.

Each diarist was selected for being particularly observant, not only regarding the effects of the war, but also for the moral implications of bombing, and also because they represent a wide geographical spread.

Introduction
Attacking the People: Democracy, Populism, and Modern War

Before the outbreak of the Second World War in Europe, the Irish Republican Army (IRA) carried out a campaign of bombings across England following a January 1939 demand for the total withdrawal of British forces from Ireland. Despite IRA claims to only target city infrastructure, a devastating attack rocked the Coventry city centre on 24 August while war with Germany was looming in continental Europe. In a personal diary, Coventry resident Mary Bloomfield called the IRA bombing 'a terrible crime', and added that 'the horror of it completely took people's minds off the coming war'.[1] The British people, but especially the citizens of Coventry, were obsessed with the IRA terrorist acts; newspaper clippings pepper diaries from 1939 as they followed the case. Ordinary urban citizens were horrified by the idea that an armed force could slaughter non-combatants like themselves to further its political and military goals. Newspapers decried terrorism's inhumanity, and broadsheets in Coventry carried the names of victims as they came to light.

It is incredible to think of the attention British society paid to the dead in Coventry before the Second World War, and the shock displayed at the treatment of ordinary people as targets. By the end of the war, the devastation meted out to Coventry's people was so terrible that Joseph Goebbels described the mass destruction of any British city as being 'Coventried' (*coventriert*). British citizens, in turn, supported reprisals in the form of targeting civilians in Germany, just as the Americans ruthlessly firebombed Japan.[2] The transition from moral outrage over civilian deaths to it being the 'new normal' took place more rapidly, and easily, than we would like to admit. In many cases, even the victims of aerial bombardment accepted the targeting of non-combatants, which would have included their relatives and neighbours, as a normal wartime practice. In his comparative study of bombing in Britain and Germany, Dietmar Süss analysed some remarkable correspondence between Germans in the heavily bombed city of Hamburg. One letter writer speculated that the Allied destruction of his home town was 'retaliation for our treatment of the Jews', and that other 'bombed out' citizens were similarly worried that 'if we hadn't treated the Jews so badly we wouldn't have had to suffer so much from the terror attacks'.[3] Most people in wartime Europe and Asia, despite the proliferation of racial theory, accepted the fact that their enemies were human beings like themselves; thus, attacking the enemy's non-combatants necessarily meant that ordinary people at home would be attacked in retaliation – and this cycle could repeat itself over and over again. Following the firebombing of Takamatsu, Iriye Hisae reflected on how she was no longer able to feel the horror of war, which was, in itself, a new form of war horror:

The stench of burning corpses poured through the streets, but I was not afraid, and I unexpectedly became accustomed to the smell. These days [in the post-war] a person's death is terrible and disgusting no matter what, but back then I think people's hearts were numbed. In war, you're mentally abnormal. It's terrible to think that you can get used to evil.[4]

Hisae's statement shows us that Hannah Arendt's 'banality of evil' was hardly unique to Nazi Germany – in fact, it was a transnational wartime condition. As Hew Strachan argued, the nature of 'total war' was not simply mass mobilisation, but the transformation of civilians into legitimate targets.[5] Nevertheless, the experience of being bombed did not necessarily create a hatred of war, but a desire for more, and more inhumane, forms of it, which arguably culminated in the atomic bombings of Hiroshima and Nagasaki. The bombing war thus made ordinary people willing perpetrators of ever-escalating brutality against other civilians, meaning, as Susan Neiman put it, for us today 'the sources of evil are not mysterious or profound but fully within our grasp'; in other words, by studying the accounts of civilians in the Second World War, we should be able to understand how such a destructive war was made possible by people very much like ourselves.[6]

The war was hardest on non-elites who lived in the city – the builders, doctors, machinists, housewives, students, and policemen – who simultaneously made peacetime urban life possible (even desirable) and supported the machinery necessary for waging total war. Take, for example, the case of Ōmura Seitarō, who was a 37-year-old owner of a cloth-dyeing workshop in Hakata, a city in the northernmost edge of Japan's large southern island, Kyūshū. Because Kyūshū was a significant launch pad for invasion forces heading to East Asia and the Pacific, and Hakata was a major port linking Kyūshū to the main island of Honshū, the city was bombed heavily by the Allies. When the attack began, Seitarō hurried his wife and children into a nearby bomb shelter, following exercises organised by local authorities. Despite his neighbours' calls for help to fight fires, he wrote 'I couldn't let my workshop burn down', so he expended his energies there, albeit ultimately in vain; his business was lost. Meanwhile, his home was also swimming 'in a sea of fire'. Seeing the neighbourhood abandoned and the situation increasingly dire, he tossed away his fire-fighting bucket, fetched his family, and ran to a road that led into the countryside. 'Looking back at Hakata', he recalled, 'it was entirely engulfed in flames. Until then I was going on instinct alone, but I finally had a sense of relief having escaped'. He came upon a rural household, and from the road he could see nets that would keep swarms of summertime mosquitoes away from his children. 'We are refugees', he pleaded with the owners, 'let us rest here'. The owners graciously allowed his wife and children to sleep in peace, and he spoke of the raids while the evening was brightened by the fires consuming his hometown. After his rustic hosts fed the desperate city folk, Seitarō thanked them profusely, and then returned to the family home. It had burned to the ground. 'I wonder if the evacuation supplies that we had left behind are gone', he thought, but soon discovered that 'even the plants in the garden were burnt to cinders'. Then, a mysterious sensation took hold of him:

Strangely enough, just because the house and our evacuation supplies were gone didn't mean that I felt, in any way, it was a great loss or a terribly sad event. What I felt at that moment, I can still vividly remember now: it was like I was cleansed. I hadn't been conscripted, but at the very least I had given everything for the nation, so it felt like I was able to comfort myself by this sense of having shouldered my responsibilities.

Citizens of Britain and Japan felt that giving everything was their duty which, given how casually the state threw away their lives and livelihood, was a mysterious phenomenon indeed. After describing his 'cleansing', Seitarō laconically noted that his sacrifices were still not enough: 'That August, I was drafted into the Imperial Japanese Navy'.[7] Still, while it was easier to see a foreign government, and not one's own, as responsible for personal losses, supporting bombing and then being bombed were linked in the minds of many in Britain and Japan; before the 'blitzes' began on British cities, in late 1939, Liverpudlian Dorothy Hughes watched with some dismay as war fever gripped the country, writing that 'people in England do not realise what we are up against. They think that what has happened in Poland could never happen here, but I sometimes wonder'.[8] Before the war, some citizens realised that supporting the bombing war meant that it could be returned to them and their loved ones in kind. During the war, many no longer cared as long as their side achieved victory.

The terror suffered at home was simultaneously being meted out abroad by one's own, or allied, forces; the context in which the modern world came to embrace area bombing is almost unknown to citizens in Japan and Britain today, where it is considered dishonourable and immoral to attack non-combatants. For example, in critiques of political organisations such as Hezbollah, better-organised, formal armies such as the Israeli Defence Forces point out the 'cowardice' that their enemies display by hiding in civilian areas and using them as a 'human shield'. Further cowardice is revealed, and particularly enraging to observers in the West, when Hezbollah forces fire rockets into Israeli civilian areas, conducting campaigns of terror.[9] Hezbollah retorts that it is the IDF that is 'cowardly', as it wields all of the power of the state against defenceless Muslims. Reading such accusations in the Western mass media, it is easy for us to think that we were never capable of such brutality. Westerners lambast the Islamic State in Iraq and the Levant (ISIL, also known as ISIS or simply IS) as 'barbaric', 'medieval', and 'uncivilised', but it was only in the last century that Allied bombers irrevocably erased historic urban areas in Germany and Japan, including the use of an atomic weapon against Nagasaki, one of the most historically significant cities in the archipelago (including being the centre of Japanese Christianity from the sixteenth century). It was not so long ago, then, that we bombed non-combatants, launched terror campaigns, and destroyed irreplaceable historical sites in what we fervently believed to be a righteous conflict. Then again, the Allies did not start the war, so what else could we do?

The difficulty we have in confronting the inhumanity of our wartime past is exacerbated by the enduring power of remembrance narratives, particularly in former Allied countries. As we have seen in the recent conflicts over historical memory of the Second World War between China and Japan, embracing Manichean 'victim narratives' about the past is very tempting, and more appropriate for contemporary political struggles than understanding the war. Joshua Fogel pointed out that, as how the memory of the Shoah helped the Jewish diaspora find a common identity in the chaos of the post-war era, so too did righteous anger over the Nanjing Massacre promise to elide irreconcilable divisions between Chinese in America, Taiwan, Singapore, and the People's Republic.[10] In the United States and Britain, being part of a heroic anti-fascist force obfuscates our own history of racism, anti-Semitism, imperialism, and acts of mass violence. Consequently, self-serving heroic or victim narratives will always be unsatisfactory for anyone acquainted with the complexities of the wartime past. The Second World War, as a 'total war', put the ordinary person in the uncomfortable position of being an enforced contributor to mobilisation and thereby a 'legitimate target' of enemy aggression, but it did not make civilians more sympathetic toward non-combatants elsewhere. As George Orwell put it in 1943:

... what impressed me [during the Spanish Civil War], and has impressed me ever since, is that atrocities are believed in or disbelieved in solely on grounds of political predilection. Everyone believes in the atrocities of the enemy and disbelieves in those of his own side, without ever bothering to examine the evidence.[11]

Consequently, British citizens chiefly remember the war as one in which they were subjected to enemy bombing campaigns, particularly in the cities; their former 'enemies', however, the Japanese, have come to articulate exactly the same collective memory of the Second World War. Is it possible for both Allied and Axis to be victims of aggression? After the figurative firestorm over David Irving's critique of Allied bombing as a war crime, a close critical examination by historians of the decision to area bomb city centres quickly followed. Frederick Taylor's illumination of Dresden as an actual military target mirrors the problematic way we look at cities such as Hiroshima, which was a major launching point for the invasion of Asia by Japanese forces, but was portrayed as an unwitting, passive recipient of Allied aggression in the film *Black Rain* (Kuroi Ame). During the Second World War, even so-called precision bombing of military targets was problematic: the forced mobilisation of teenagers into Japanese war factories meant that legitimate objects of aerial bombardment would include schoolgirls. In any case, as historians like Yoshimi Yoshiaki showed, the Japanese people were as supportive of the war effort as the British and Germans were, which makes facile victim/perpetrator narratives difficult to defend under sustained scrutiny.[12]

Within the grim cheering of citizens supporting the annihilation of the enemy, there were voices of concern and even dissent, but these remained, unfortunately, comparatively quiet. By 1941, official opposition to the war effort in Japan had been quashed following debates about the 1937 war in China. Military officers like Ishiwara Kanji and Matsuno Hironori, who opposed the escalating conflicts, were either exiled or sidelined in official discussions; in Britain, veterans and officers like Tom Wintringham and Philip S. Mumford did not shift the discourse away from support for total war in Britain. In Liverpool on 3 March 1941, Dorothy Hughes saw a piece of silk parachute, spattered with blood, inscribed with the following bit of anti-German bigotry: 'Another squarehead gone West'. Upon reflection, Dorothy wrote in her diary that she was convinced:

... the only way to stop this business was to cut out all nationalism. All speak one language, and have equal rights. No top dog. No doubt we have been guilty of this all along. Certain American opinion still thinks it serves us right.[13]

In due time, the United States would also enter the war and, as John Dower showed, its government deployed even worse examples of bigotry and racism against their Japanese enemies.[14] Dorothy had grasped an important aspect of the Second World War, however: the dehumanisation of the enemy abetted area bombing campaigns, and justified popular support for the mechanisms of total war. The people's embrace of war in Britain and Japan enabled the massacre of innocent people in enemy nations, but also legitimised the attacks on their loved ones back home. In our rush to support the war, we were killing ourselves. Contrary to wartime propaganda and patriotic post-war memory, this outcome was neither 'normal' nor inevitable in the long view of modern history.

double-side

Mirror, Mirror: The Heyday of British and Japanese Imperialism

Throughout the Second World War, Japanese and British propagandists insisted that East and West were irreconcilably different, but both entered into the era of total war from a shared history of capitalist growth, imperialist expansion, and international cooperation. The new world order that the Second World War created was one that no one could have imagined even a decade prior; after the war, the British and the Japanese empires would totally collapse, and both would share a 'special relationship' with the United States. After the war, Britain and Japan's convergence as peripheral economies, but crucial allies, vis-à-vis American power may seem to be a curious postscript to the Second World War, but in many respects it greatly resembled the mutual admiration the empires expressed for each other prior to the 1930s.

The transformation of Britain and Japan during the Second World War was so total that it left older citizens in a state of shock and disorientation. On the eve of the air war, and his 66th birthday, in September 1940, H. B. Monck reflected on how thorough home front mobilisation had deeply shaken countries like Britain and Japan, which had enjoyed decades of mostly uncritical populist support for imperial violence:

I cannot help thinking what a different world it is to when I was a boy. You could read as I did all about our wars in Egypt and Abyssinia and take a mild interest in them. Our totalitarianism had not yet been invented and yet it seems to be only just that everyone should be involved in such a serious thing as war. You can only be astonished in actual fact what little control individuals have over events which are going to have a vital effect on their lives.[15]

Monck sensed that the city and its people had entered a significantly new historical epoch, and not necessarily a better one. For too long, Britain and Japan had successfully exported mass murder to their empires with little political consequence at home; in the new world, however, bombing wars brought this violence back to the home islands, and in the process remade cities across Britain and Japan (with help from zealous post-war city planners as well). Yokouchi Tomi, who was a factory foreman during the heavy Allied bombing of Kōfu, began his post-war memoir by remarking on how much his home town had changed:

I'm heading out from the south gate of the Kōfu Station, down Peace Street . . . and there is a forest of tall buildings and structures that are impervious to fire. For one such as I, who was born in the Meiji Era [1868–1912] and knew Kōfu before the war, this is a sight that makes me feel like I'm from another world.[16]

Indeed, by the time Tomi was writing in the early 1970s, Japan had transformed from a wartime disaster zone to the second largest economy in the world, while Britain's trajectory seemed irrevocably fixed downward. This post-war reversal of fortunes, from the perspective of the Meiji and Victorian generations, as well as the previous wartime division of Japan and Britain into Axis and Allied powers, was a bizarre historical rupture. For Monck and Yokouchi, the mutually beneficial 'civilised' world of the fin-de-siècle British and Japanese empires had disappeared in a cataclysm of parachute mines and incendiary bombs.

To those who grew up watching 'enlightened' lords and industrial leaders guide their empires to fame and profit, Japan and Britain's collision course was not a foregone conclusion. Both prided themselves on professional armed forces, 'civilisation and enlightenment', monarchy, and a dedication to parliamentary government. By the end of the nineteenth century, 'British financial backing for Japan's imperial ambitions . . . became a central feature of the dawning era of East Asian international relations'.[17] From the 1902 Anglo-Japanese Alliance to the early 1930s, the two countries frequently collaborated in the imperial 'great game', successfully containing Russia, opposing the Communist International, exacting concessions from the Qing Dynasty and Chinese Republic, concluding successful naval arms limitation treaties, and even being allies in the First World War.[18]

Relations were sometimes strained, such as during the failure of the Racial Equality Proposal at the Paris Peace Conference (1919) and the Washington Naval Conference (1921–1922); moreover, post-First-World-War Japanese growth could threaten and rankle British merchants and Commonwealth citizens. While the early period of Japanese expansion was not driven by excess capital and production,[19] from the First World War a second industrial revolution in Japan made their companies equal and direct competitors with Britain's for markets throughout Africa and Asia. Still the Japanese did not see their actions as a direct challenge to the old world order that Britain helped create: Japanese imperialists explicitly compared their annexation of Korea in 1910 to the British occupation of Egypt in 1882, and many British expatriates in Shanghai actually expressed a desire for Japanese seizure of the city because, they believed, it would bring order. Throughout this period the Japanese Imperial Navy and the Bank of Japan worked amicably with, and were inspired by, their British counterparts: British citizens celebrated Japanese 'efficiency' and the elegance of their arts; Japanese scientists and engineers worked closely with their British colleagues in a fairly free and collegial international environment.[20] Alfred Stead and H. G. Wells imagined the present and future importance of Japan for the twentieth century world, sometimes explicitly comparing it to Britain. This positive view of Japanese modernity was not limited to Britain: rediscovered original cuts of *Metropolis* reveal that Thea von Harbou launched the futuristic narrative not in Germany, but Tokyo's Yoshiwara district. While early English views of Japanese visitors to the United Kingdom, in the 1860s, were a mixture of condescending bemusement and appreciation for their earnestness in learning modern engineering,[21] by the 1930s, both British and Japanese aviation experts were working furiously to best each other on equal footing.

Indeed, after the 1929 market crash Britain was mired in the Great Depression and Japanese leaders launched a 'quest for autonomy', which involved describing Japan's former ally as an eternal enemy.[22] The Japanese economy boomed after Finance Minister Takahashi Korekiyo took Japan off of the gold standard and launched aggressive fiscal and monetary policies, which seriously threatened the British position in important Asian markets. Meanwhile, the Japanese civilian bureaucrats, elected officials, and business leaders with whom the British collaborated were intimidated or murdered in a system that wartime commentators described as 'government by assassination'.[23] The Japanese invasion of northeastern China (Manchuria) proved a breaking point. In 1931, the Earl of Lytton headed an exploratory committee to investigate the Japanese seizure of Manchuria, and by October 1932 they determined the new state, Manchukuo to be a puppet regime under the control of the Japanese Army; this directly led to Japan's departure from the League of Nations in 1933. Furthermore, the old guard who had led Japan at the

end of the nineteenth and beginning of the twentieth century, understanding Japan's limitations and the necessity of international cooperation, was quickly passing away.

The new breed of Japanese bureaucrats were not advocates of
Western-style 'civilisation and enlightenment', but staunchly opposed
to 'Anglo-American encirclement' and in favour of regional autarky.
Throughout the 1930s, the Japanese military expanded rapidly in mainland Asia, until conflicts between Chinese Nationalist and Japanese
regional forces transformed into a devastating eight-year total war in
1937.[24] This war was conducted in the back garden of historic British
interests based in cities like Shanghai. The rapid expansion of Japanese
power in the 1930s put the country on a collision course with the British
Empire (and their American ally) in Asia, and the United States retali-
ated by organising lend-lease programs aiding China and oil and steel
embargoes to Japan. Japanese authorities, and many members of the
public, viewed American and British soldiers stationed in East and
Southeast Asia as defenders of Western imperialism – which, it must be
said, they were. Consequently, the attack on Pearl Harbor was followed
immediately by the ouster of American forces in their 1898 colony, the
Philippine Commonwealth. By 1942, Japanese armed forces inflicted
upon Great Britain its worst military defeat in modern history during
the fall of Singapore. Japanese leaders and ideologues justified these wars
of aggression by describing them as wars of defence, and pointed to the
inexcusable history of imperial violence and exploitation inflicted on Asia
and the Pacific by global superpowers like Great Britain and the United
States. The division between Britain and Japan, thus, predated Pearl
Harbor, but was still something rather new.

Despite the growing conflict, wartime urban life in Britain and Japan
revealed some important similarities, including the role of finance, industrial production, modern culture, and the endurance of imperialism.
Unlike America's division of New York and Washington, DC, or China's
split between Beijing (or wartime Nanjing) and Shanghai, London and
Tokyo combined the financial and political power of two capitalist
empires in one centralised space. These metropoles were also the show-
cases of imperial wealth and conquest, which created an understandable
hostility toward these over-privileged and excessively powerful urban
spaces. Dorothy Hughes noted that, in Liverpool, early responses to
rationing and evacuation orders from London were sceptical: 'Don't
believe it's necessary', one man in his sixties was heard to say in a shop,
'It's only to find work for some of these people up in London'.[25]
Regional hostility was exacerbated by the capital cities' insistence on
their privilege as cultural, economic, and political leaders, even if they

were not representative of broader trends. As Louise Young put it, 'Japanese modernity was not simply made in Tokyo and exported to the provinces'; instead, we should see cities such as Tokyo and London as the 'outliers and exceptions' of modern life, and the regional cities as 'standard-bearers'.[26] Modern Japan and Britain were not defined by Tokyo and London: they had historically important 'second cities', such as Manchester and Osaka; powerful and influential urban areas such as Birmingham, Nagoya, Liverpool, and Kobe; and cultural centres such as Kyoto and Oxford. The modern era also saw the emergence of major cities whose growth was driven by new industries, such as Kawasaki, Hull, Okayama, and Sheffield; as a direct consequence of industrialisation, Manchester's population quadrupled from 1801 to 1851, which was one of the fastest rates of urbanisation in world history – even when excluding the explosive growth of nearby cities like Oldham and Rochdale.[27] Similarly, Osaka's population trebled from the end of the nineteenth century to the 1920s, excluding the rapid growth of the Kansai region as a whole. Both Osaka and Manchester, to take just two examples, required inputs from abroad, including the empire, to feed the factories and workers that drove British and Japanese industrialisation. These regional cities boasted not only world-class architecture, but also the many signs of modern civilisation, including museums, public parks, cinemas, electric lighting, mass transit, dance halls, and reinforced concrete towers. As Virginia Woolf ended her story of traditional England in *Orlando* (1928) with the confusion of the London's department stores, so Kawabata Yasunari began his story of modern Japan in *Asakusa kurenaidan* (The Red Gang of Asakusa, 1930) with the perplexing pastiche of Tokyo's urban environment. The modern city in Britain and Japan was a tangled web of deeply interdependent systems, including rail lines, traffic lanes, pavements, shops, sewers and water supply ducts, telephone and telegraph lines, radio towers, airstrips, hospitals, gas pipes, schools, postal services, and food depots – and this urban machine was deeply imbricated with the global system of imperialism. Bombers targeted these cities as a matter of necessity, as they were correctly seen as the war machine's workshops.

Citizens sometimes recognised the peril of how closely modernity, war, industrialisation, and imperialism were linked. In Liverpool, H. B. Monck often reflected in his war diary on how modernisation, which created the major cities of Britain and Japan, made life worse: 'We pay a big price for our industrialisation', he wrote, 'It may mean a big empire but whether it makes for real happiness and contentment I am doubtful. I never heard of a Norwegian or Finlander crying in a corner because he was the citizen of a small country'. Unfortunately, the Second World

War's devastation demonstrated quickly just how febrile the net of city life was. Urban space, perhaps due to its concrete, stone, and metal, appears to be quite resilient, but when it can be brought low by a single night's air raid, that illusion is quickly dispelled. For ordinary people like Matsubara Kijirō, a paediatrician in Takamatsu, aerial bombardment almost instantly transformed the seemingly eternal city into a much more sinister space. 'This was the final image of my hometown', Kijirō wrote during the firebombing of the city, 'Who could foresee that this quiet city, almost as if in slumber, would in just a few seconds become like the depths of hell itself?'[28] One of the most important similarities between Japan and Britain, then, was the civilian population's confidence in urban power and permanence, followed by dramatic displays of their weakness and vulnerability.

Rather than allow this book to be mired in a tendentious over-statement of their similarities, suffice it to say that Britain and Japan, up to the Second World War, operated as mirrors of each other on opposite sides of the globe – even if those mirrors were not perfect reflections. Of course, Japanese and British political systems, culture, and society were not exactly alike, but was the United Kingdom really more similar to, say, the United States, their paramount ally, which had no monarchy, was a secular federal system, had rapid class mobility, severe domestic racial conflicts, significant immigration from around the world, and a continental economy that bridged the Pacific and Atlantic Oceans since the 1850s? Both Britain and Japan were maritime empires that were facing down enemies with greater industrial might and larger, stronger armies. Both would have their national destinies completely transformed by the emergence of American global power (and, to a lesser extent, Soviet power). Put bluntly, the main difference in the Japanese and British war experience was the fact that Britain was the future superpower's ally, and Japan its enemy. Germany, meanwhile, was a continental country with no significant history of overseas empire, torn between two superpowers, and utterly dedicated to the extermination of an ethnic minority within its own borders. Comparing and contrasting island empires like Britain and Japan, rather than including outliers like Germany and the United States, is a far more effective way to reveal the transnational aspects of the civilian experience of the Second World War.

The Commanding Heights: Air Power and the Morality of Killing Non-Combatants in the Second World War

Despite their historical similarities, it may be unfair to compare Japan and Britain's war experience when the former suffered so much more than the latter. First, Japan's urban residences were predominantly constructed with wood, whereas British homes were brick and mortar, making firebombing more effective against Japan, and firestorms killed more people than explosives. Second, the German Air Force (GAF) failed to produce long-range heavy bombers for the air war that could have wreaked havoc across Britain, especially in lightly defended regional cities. Wartime British Royal Air Force (RAF) aircraft production eventually rivalled that of the GAF, whereas the Japanese Air Force (JAF, including Army and Navy) never had any chance of matching United States (Army) Air Force's (USAF) industrial might. The Army JAF tasked to defend the home islands was trained primarily to fight Soviet forces on land in Asia, not defend against USAF bombers on the sea, and by that stage the more sophisticated Naval JAF had been nearly wiped out defending the empire in the Pacific – by the time the JAF had functioning interceptor command centres for home defence, like the RAF, the war was over.[29] The GAF dropped roughly 75,000 tonnes of explosives on Britain, and launched 12,000 'flying bomb' (V1) and rocket (V2) attacks, mostly aimed at London.[30] The United States, a much more powerful country than Germany, dropped roughly 160,800 tonnes on Japan (excluding the atomic bombings of Hiroshima and Nagasaki), but to much greater effect due to the nature of firebombing. Third, British defences vis-à-vis the GAF in 1940 were better, and steadily improving, when compared to Japan's capabilities vis-à-vis the emerging superpower in 1945, and the situation in Japan was steadily worsening as the country was starved of steel, oil, and even food. Still, statistics can mask the social experience of the war: the bombing of British cities was certainly a serious matter if you were in a city that was under attack. The fact that Leeds was only lightly bombed makes no difference to you if you are living in hollowed out Hull.

The 'rise of air power' was an uncertain process that was, from the military's perspective, only partly linked to the experience of civilians being bombed by a foreign adversary. The RAF's aggressive use of bombing against civilians was in part a product of the German attacks on British cities, but air power had its advocates beforehand as well. Historians of air power have already detailed the early history of bombing theory, including well-known figures such as Hugh Trenchard, Giulio Douhet, and William Mitchell.[31] Initially, however, most leaders, even in Nazi Germany, were dovish about attacking cities simply to slaughter non-combatants, mainly because they feared being seen as immoral aggressors and thereby aiding enemy propaganda. The scars of the First World War and the ongoing pain of the Great Depression also contributed to the suppression of air power in the inter-war era. Anglo-American pre-war budgets were tight and the lack of preparedness among the air forces and defences in the late 1930s, when Germany advanced into Austria and Czechoslovakia, was alarming. Even at maximum output levels, in 1939 the British could not produce enough pilots and fighter planes to defend the home islands, much less support an invasion to aid France. In the spring of 1939, British air strategy was still purely defensive, resorting to retrofitting old bombers to serve as makeshift fighter aircraft. In the United States, as well, Congress saw bombers as 'aggressive' weapons, and was stubbornly cutting budgets for new purchases as late as April, 1940.[32] Effective use of air power did not translate into an awareness of, or concern for, domestic vulnerability. The Imperial Japanese Army (IJA) and Imperial Japanese Navy (IJN) had advantageously used air assaults against the Chinese Nationalist regime in 1931 and 1937, and were planning a greater demonstration of such power in Pearl Harbor. Strikingly, however, the Japanese government had few concrete plans for urban evacuations, even for children, going into the end of the war; worse still, Japanese anti-aircraft guns were slow in tracking low-flying B-29s, especially at night, and were inadequately supplied to defend the home islands – despite the fact that Americans were testing firebombing techniques over Japanese occupied areas in China, such as the attacks on Hankow on 18 December 1944.[33] Thus, despite decades of warnings in military and civilian circles about the future of air power, most countries were found wanting when bombers threatened their territory.

The attraction to aggressive bombing of civilians, by contrast, was too difficult to resist. There was an inherently transnational aspect to the transmission of bombing knowledge and, arguably, bombing ethics, as militaries in each country studied the air power efforts of others.[34] Even before Pearl Harbor, the use of air power in the Spanish Civil War, the German invasions of the Netherlands and Poland, and the Japanese invasions of China in 1931 and 1937 supported the expansion of aircraft production. Indeed, Richard Overy reminded us that it was the RAF (in 1939), not the GAF, that attacked civilians in the early exchanges between Britain and Germany. Consequently, the first massive GAF air raid on British soil was a 'revenge bombing' for the RAF raids which the German public demanded.[35] By the summer of 1939, British factories, including those in (later) heavily bombed cities like Coventry and Bristol, were turning out as many aircraft and plane parts as they could.[36] The Americans were late to embrace air power, but they caught up with a vengeance: after the capitulation of France in June 1940, Henry Arnold, Chief of the USAF, was given over eleven billion US dollars to 'get an air force'.[37] By 1942, Avro Lancaster bombers allowed British forces to strike deep into German territory, and B-17s flown by their US allies similarly were able to inflict heavy damage to industrial, military, and civilian targets. By 1943 the United States was producing more aircraft than Britain, Germany, and Japan combined, and their long-range B-29s would change air power forever.

Beyond strategic reasoning, the 'Blitz' of British cities in late 1940 and early 1941 was also influential in changing the military and public mind-set about attacking civilians. GAF raids strengthened the position of those in Britain who favoured the mass bombing of civilians, which was already part of a longstanding debate on the ethics and efficacy of bombing. Early on, Prime Minister Stanley Baldwin had articulated the view that many strategists later embraced: namely, that air attacks had to 'kill more women and children quicker than the enemy if you want to save yourselves'.[38] As the Allies began attacking German cities, the British drew explicit comparisons between the Blitz and later area bombing of German civilians: for example, Arthur Harris, Air Officer Commanding-in-Chief of the RAF Bomber Command, argued that if 'the Germans had gone on using the same force for several nights against London ... the fire tornado they would have raised would have been worse than anything that happened in Hamburg', and insisted on destroying the German towns of Lübeck and Rostock simply to demonstrate the power of such attacks.[39] US bombing strategy for Japan was influenced by their interaction with the British, who already accepted attacks on non-combatants as the war's new modus operandi. It is not necessary to accept Nicholson Baker's view that Britain and the United States were antagonising the Axis in order to see that killing innocent civilians in pursuit of victory was embraced by Allies and Axis alike.[40]

Wartime documents show us that the normalisation of civilian bombing was not limited to high-level officers like 'Butcher' Harris – ordinary people thought enemy action made area bombing morally acceptable, and this view persists up to the present in our collective war memory. Approaching the topic of civilian bombing, one is beset by moral contradictions: critical analyses of the Allied bombing of German and Japanese civilians must also confront the immorality of the policies supported by the Nazi regime and the Japanese Empire. Still, attacks on sympathetic views of Axis non-combatants are often riddled with logical fallacies such as guilt-by-association. Although the West's cultural revulsion for Nazism is not relevant for the memory of the war against Japan, some historians have borrowed from that moral certainty to insist that the harsh tactics used against the Japanese people were justified by the social, political, and/or military culture of that country. Barrett Tillman, for example, asserted that the bombing of Japanese civilians was required because against 'an enemy who seemed bent upon extinction, there was precious little middle ground for the Allies', attributing this to a 'cultural chasm' between West and East. The debate over the atomic bombing of Hiroshima and Nagasaki has revealed even more divisions between historians' opinions on the morality of attacking non-combatants. Citing Max Hastings, Tillman further argued that the 'myth that the Japanese were ready to surrender anyway has been so completely discredited by modern research that it is astonishing some writers continue to give it credence'.[41] Richard B. Frank, in his study of the use of mass bombing against Japan, pointed to the Japanese military's use of such tactics in China and against Western colonial forces in Southeast Asia and the Pacific; according to this view, Japanese people, including Christian socialists, pacifists, children, and the infirm, were the victims of a benighted leadership that had brought to Japan a war of their own creation.[42] On a basic level, this argument has merit: the people most responsible for the losses suffered in Germany and Japan were the leaders who started such wars, and this is why war crimes tribunals executed them for 'crimes against peace' – Japanese writers like Nagai Kafū articulated this view during the war.[43] The lack of commitment in prosecuting war criminals in the Far East, including those who executed Allied prisoners of war and conducted human experimentation, however, makes this argument for the moral purpose of the war tenuous at best.[44] Even if area bombing was strategically necessary, the genocidal and racist iconography that suffused US wartime propaganda should also encourage us to question the 'justice' of it.[45]

Apart from historians' personal views of the air war, they have also struggled to understand how Allied leaders justified their use of brutal attacks on non-combatants. The motives behind strategists such as Curtis LeMay and Arthur Harris have been ably studied by historians like Tami Biddle, Barrett Tillman, and Thomas Coffey, and this reveals our abiding interest in the morality of their actions – particularly if we believe that their advocacy of indiscriminate bombing of civilians facilitated the end of the war.[46] These examinations of government policy and military strategy necessarily rely on textual representations of participants' justifications, so in fact we shall never know what they 'really thought' about the bombing of civilians; in recording his views of using the atomic bomb, for example, Harry Truman would have certainly considered his historical legacy. Furthermore, Western observers who maintain that bombing ended the war are also inadvertently supporting those in Japan who would use the Allied assault on civilians as a foundation for victim narratives, which disrupts meaningful discussions of the responsibility of ordinary people for supporting wars of aggression.[47] Not all wartime strategists agreed that the massacre of non-combatants was justifiable or even useful. On the atomic bombing, Gar Alperovitz has mobilised many quotes from contemporary US military officials who condemned the use of such a weapon on moral grounds, and Tsuyoshi Hasegawa, after examining Japanese language military documents, demonstrated that the emperor's argument against the continuance of the war for belligerent officers in the IJA was the Soviet invasion of Manchuria, not the bombing campaigns.[48] More importantly, if we accept that German and Japanese support for bombing civilians in Britain and China justified similar mass bombardment of ordinary people in reprisal, because these societies were somehow afflicted with a desire for mass violence, does that mean that there is a similar moral deficiency in Anglo-American culture that encourages us to massacre the elderly, the handicapped, and children? Wherever one's sympathies may be, the pro-bombing view has a problem in its central principle: either bombing and terrorising innocent people was necessary to crush their war effort, or it was useless because the 'enemy' supported the war fanatically anyway; both of these assertions cannot be true, and in both cases we lose the moral high ground by killing non-combatants.

The Nazi regime and the Japanese Empire committed terrible atrocities in their attempts to create a new world order. If one only examines the commanding heights of both history and historiography, the use of any and all means to stop this threat will seem justified. Nevertheless, as Kenneth P. Werrell put it: 'Certainly the cause was just, but were the tactics?'[49] The simple categorisation of Japan and Britain into 'evil' and 'good' powers may be satisfying, but it is dangerous in part because it provides justification for future mass violence. US President Donald Trump advocated targeting civilians in the suppression of ISIS, despite the fact that these tactics have failed in the suppression of terrorism elsewhere,[50] and he later used the chemical weapon attacks against civilians in Syria to justify a military intervention. Many Americans have been troubled by his comments, but elected and supported him anyway. Beyond the incoherence and inconsistency of pandering politicians, this position suffuses the Second World War scholarship on, and memory of, the bombing war against the Axis powers, dripping into contemporary discussions in a truly alarming way. The extent to which the brutality of the Second World War was enabled by popular support, and thereby brought suffering to everyone involved, is thus subject to thorough scrutiny in this book. In order to address these issues without indulging in 'good vs. evil' tropes, it is necessary to examine the experiences and views of ordinary civilians in both Axis and Allied countries side by side.

City People Speak: Sources for the Urban Experience of the Second World War

This diary is suffering. [If only I had] the time to set down all the things that are happening, and they certainly seem to be getting under way, but I, in common with the rest of the world, don't seem to be able to work up any enthusiasm . . . Is it that we are so accustomed to setbacks that we are incapable of rejoicing? Or is it the depressing time of the year, dark days, blackouts, a Christmas that isn't, rising prices, rationing, and air raids?   – Dorothy Hughes, Liverpool, 18 December 1940

On 2 October 1940, Swansea's *South Wales Evening Post* ran an article entitled 'War Diary Craze'. The author noted that the period of aerial bombardment 'has moved thousands of civilians to keep a day-to-day diary, notes of experiences, meetings with people, siren times and indeed escapes from injury', indicating an explosion of life-writing that was spreading across Britain. In Japan, too, diary writing and other forms of record keeping were actively encouraged by schools, relatives, and the military. Tied to the Confucian notion of self-cultivation (*shūyō*), Japanese recruits were encouraged to think of diary writing as a 'mirror of truth' to reflect on their faults and improve.[51] Inoue Tamiko, a 14-year-old schoolgirl during the May 1945 firebombing of Tokyo, recalled that, even though her diary was reviewed (*ken'etsu*)* by a teacher, it 'really did [reflect] my true feelings, and I believe in it even now. I wrote that diary by candlelight in air raid shelters'.[52] We have come to have so many accounts of the war because, fortunately, those who lived through the war considered their experiences to be historically important, and post-war society felt these records were worth preserving, especially at the local level. Unfortunately, we have failed to seriously engage with many of these testimonies, focusing on areas of post-war political interest (and conflict) such as London, Tokyo, Hiroshima, and, to a much lesser degree, Nagasaki. Ordinary people across both countries have left us a treasure trove of personal accounts depicting aerial bombardment; consequently, if we want to truly understand the civilian experience of the Second World War, we have to move beyond myopic post-war preoccupations with capital cities and nuclear weapons.

Britain and Japan both had a long history of bureaucracy that enabled the widespread embrace of official and personal record-keeping. Some citizens of bombed cities kept exceedingly simple accounts, such as

---

* While students knew their diaries could be read by teachers, for the most part teachers did not censor them or change the content; for most teaching staff, it was primarily a composition exercise.

W. Craddock's diary of the destruction of Coventry – which simply had 'raids' recorded for each day – and D. H. Kent's descriptions of air raids over London, which only list attacks occurring during specific 'blitz' periods (e.g. late 1940 and early 1941).[53] Other diary writers, like Edith Christabel Peirse, were invested in personal emotional vicissitudes; following a nasty row with her father, she noted that 'Father in a fit of temper has taken one of my diaries, for spite'. For a dedicated diary writer like Edith, this was a serious violation, but it shows how some writers saw the document as a formal war record, while others embraced it as a confessional.[54] Schoolgirls in Japan, such as Yoshida Fusako, participated in 'self-criticism groups' (hanseikai), wherein girls who had been drafted into war labour pointed out faults to each other and suggested ways to overcome them – Fusako used her diary to record this progress.[55] In Japan, as I have argued elsewhere, diaries were a site in which the author's desires 'negotiated' with the demands of others in order to delineate the boundaries of what was possible for the individual; this was also the case in Britain, where schools assigned students to write diaries to be reviewed by teachers and parents, and soldiers kept diaries to be scrutinised by superior officers. Nevertheless, viewing their rather formulaic diaries in retrospect, the texts could trigger more passionate responses in the post-war, as Narita Shigeru wrote: 'As you can see in my diary from the time [of the Nagoya raids], I kept it every single day. I wonder [now] how the bereaved family members ever managed to carry on after those events. I am emotionally overwhelmed (kan muryō) thinking about it'.[56] Like many diarists, Narita rather dispassionately recorded the deaths of friends and acquaintances during the war itself; were it not for his post-war commentary, the wartime diary would tell us little about how he felt at the time.

Further, one should never make assumptions about who would keep a diary, and what kind of diary, based on the class, gender, or age of the author. William 'Bill' Bernard Regan, who was a bricklayer and wartime rescue worker in the Isle of Dogs, London, kept a diary that alternately read as a strict record of his missions and a personal account of his antics with neighbourhood friends. 'These writings were going to be a diary written at home after each shift', he sheepishly explained during the height of the air raids, 'but it hasn't worked out like that. (Silly me.)' Nevertheless, Bill kept writing day by day, even if it did not conform to his expectations of what a 'diary' should be.[57] Some of the texts used in this volume were produced by participants in the Mass Observation project launched by the anthropologist Tom Harrisson and his colleagues in 1937. Participants could craft the diaries to satisfy the needs of the project organisers, as H. B. Monck described: 'Sent off an instalment of my diary. Was glad to get a letter from M.O. that it has proved useful, was very dissatisfied with it myself'.[58] Nevertheless, like soldiers who were asked to keep official diaries in wartime, personal sentiments appeared regularly in M.O. diaries, and the authors accepted them as accurate reflections of what they thought and felt. In her M.O. diary, Dorothy Hughes wrote about how the experience of being bombed in Liverpool was reflected in her account, and used the diary to encourage herself to be a better member of British wartime society:

> Reading the previous entries, seems that the latest raids must have got me down, and I am ashamed. I find that one gets depressed in spasms, but we must keep up. I'm afraid I think too deeply, state everything too seriously. I am sad, not for myself, although heaven knows my life is no picnic, but for civilisation and the world in general. I feel I am growing too damned sensible! I haven't, I hope, lost me sense of humour, but don't laugh half so much as I used to.

Dorothy was not unusual among M.O. diarists for including personal information in her diary, including 'loss' of her boyfriend, writing 'I shall never love anyone else, as long as I live'.[59] Ordinary people outside of M.O. also believed that their experiences were important, and thus kept surprisingly meticulous records of the war that, today, we value highly as historical documents. Some writers, of course, 'started [a] diary just to pass the time'.[60] The *South Wales* article's author speculated that, while civilians during the war 'were making extensive notes about war experiences with a view to writing reminiscences ... there is not likely to be a market for them'.[61] This was, obviously, a bad prediction, considering war memoirs are among some of the most widely read history genres in the Anglophone world.

The profundity of war narratives around the world begs for more comparative history. How can we truly 'know' the Second World War if we only examine it from the European or Asian perspective? What is 'true' about the Second World War must be so in both Britain and Japan, not just Britain and Germany, or Japan and China. While this book will not examine all fronts of the war, it embraces the comparative approach in the simplest way possible – by looking at two countries that, until the 1930s, established enduring maritime empires in the East and the West. They embraced monarchy, institutionalised a state religion, respected social hierarchy, rejected communism, adored their empires, and placed high cultural value on arts, engineering, efficiency, and, some would argue, racial superiority. One of the tragedies of the Second World War is that this convergence of civilisations did not produce a greater peace, but arguably the most brutal conflict in human history. As this book makes clear, popular support for total war was crucial for this outcome.

1   Give unto Moloch
Family and Nation in the Second World War

> This, then, would be the message of these days: walk into the future
> along whatever path may open up before you. Wherever it will lead is no
> longer in your own hands. Individual and national destinies have ceased
> to be separate, as once they were. What is important, therefore, is to
> have the strength not to look backwards.
>
> – Rom Landau, *Of No Importance* (1940)

Dora Mockett used a dull pencil to scribble this section of Landau's
published wartime diary into her own personal diary account. Landau,
who was a Polish émigré to the United Kingdom during the war years,
urged British citizens to unite against foreign aggression; Dora found
his work inspiring while her neighbours in Hull endured one sacrifice
after another. In both Britain and Japan, diarists were influenced by
mass-media accounts and government propaganda, which they sometimes dutifully copied into private accounts as if these were part of a
personal history. Kojima Yoshitaka, for example, wrote down news
items, such as Japan's bombing of Darwin, Australia, 'with no losses
for our side', and once composed a poem about the joys of sacrifice:
'The dark water [*kokusui*] that you toss away all the time / is so sweet
when you drink it after a hard day's work'.[1] Despite such platitudes,
family matters were a great concern among our six wartime diarists –
even those who proactively served the war effort – and it was clear that
the first institution to tear the family apart was not the enemy, but one's
own government.

The war against the family – whether conducted by the state or by the
enemy in the air – began immediately. Dorothy Hughes overheard conversations against evacuation that expressed scepticism regarding the
state's abilities to take care of children or preserve families, and in
December 1939 the *Protestant Times* in Liverpool put out placards that
read 'The Schools Must Be Re-Opened!'[2] Takahashi Aiko noted the
removal of children from Tokyo, and despaired at how the war aged
the young prematurely. Her elder daughter was forced by the state to
oversee a student evacuation from the Catholic Sacred Heart School

for Girls. Watching her shout orders and organise the primary school students, Aiko was stunned by her daughter's sudden maturity: 'Emi, at what point did you become a grown-up? Be strong, survive, and go with God ... I looked to the moon and wiped away the tears that were welling up from inside me'.[3] Nevertheless, the burden of mobilisation was not shared – the British people were not 'all in it together'. Dorothy Hughes noted that the war had already forced families into difficult positions, as well as exacerbating existing class and generation tensions:

Have heard of lots of young married people whose husbands have been called up, who are banding together and living in one house, in order to pool expenses. Herbert was saying what a large number of men he has seen walking in the mornings, obviously businessmen who have nothing better to do. I don't think it is generally realised what a lot of unemployment there is, particularly among the so-called 'upper' classes, people with their own businesses.[4]

As the war progressed and socio-economic mobilisation intensified, the state intervened in our diarists' lives, tearing their families apart. In January 1945, Inohara Mitsuko was drafted to work in Itami's aircraft manufacturing plant, near her home town, Osaka. She struggled to put a brave face on leaving her home, but she did not appear ready to join society as a working adult:

I woke up early and had the last hot, home-cooked meal by mom, took my heavy luggage and left. Mom carried it for me a while, but she said nothing on the way and seemed very sad. I suddenly felt like my eyes were hot, and I was overwhelmed with emotion. We finally got to the gate to say goodbye, but I left without looking back. And then tears came to my eyes, but I suppressed them. I was thinking, how can I do such a girlish thing when answering the honourable call for student mobilisation?

Sometimes she would find herself virtually alone in a spacious dormitory, which she would only describe as 'so, so lonely'; in addition to air raids, she suffered periodic attacks from fleas, bedbugs, and mosquitoes, after which she would merely write, 'I want to go home badly'.[5] For Mitsuko, the suffering of separation that labour mobilisation would inflict on her was only the beginning; she, like many other teenagers, would have to watch her family being firebombed in Osaka's city centre. Diarists picked up on the generalised feelings of anxiety and fear parents had for their children as well. In Liverpool, Dorothy saw working-class women clutch their children close leading up to Christmas in December 1939, 'as if they are afraid to leave them at home on account of the air raids'.[6] Our diarists gradually understood that war did not simply ask for the purchase of bonds or the donation of metals, but the deconstruction of the family itself.

Japanese and British people alike enjoyed close-knit family ties, often in three-generation households, and were largely reliant on relations to help them navigate a dangerous and confusing modern world. As the wartime state disassembled these systems in order to squeeze every last ounce of strength out of the people, being abandoned by trusted family members was as terrifying as the enemy's bombs.

The Ultimate Sacrifice: Family and Nation in the Second World War

Home is not home anymore.
– Anonymous middle-aged man, Hertfordshire, 27 October 1939[7]

City people instinctively knew that the enemy bomber was coming to destroy their loved ones. During a terrible barrage over Bristol, Mrs M. Coleman, an air raid warden's wife, described how her husband dashed out into danger as soon as the bombing began. Left behind, she crawled under the stairs of their block of flats, and was joined by an elderly woman from the unit above. Although she inscribed her patriotic bona fides ('we are all in this fight – even the kids!'), she was terrified throughout; as the women and children heard a plane diving over them, she thought, 'Ye gods ... this is ours!' The women grabbed pillows and covered the children, 'who must come first'. She heard heavy explosions and thought, 'My husband ... Something's hit him. He has fallen. Oh, dear Lord, keep him safe!' When her youngest child jumped to greet 'Dada' on his return, she wrote,

How I thanked my lucky stars ... What a wonderful sound [the all-clear] is! And yet for the poor folk who were now wounded or had lost dear ones, it was a terrible sound. Every time they hear it they can see themselves standing by ruins, just saying, 'I've lost him, or her, or them' ... I went outside and saw the fires. They looked wicked, somehow.[8]

Meanwhile in Himeji, an iconic castle town in Japan's Kansai region, housewife Shiba Isa had allowed herself to become complacent following air raid warnings that always resulted in no attacks; in 1945, however, the Allies decided to destroy the city, and she was caught off guard. 'The roar of aircraft engines came at night', she wrote, 'and I scrambled to wake my children, grab whatever was around me, including some rice, and run away'. She was alarmed to see soldiers from the nearby 39th Regiment mount their horses and flee in terror with the civilians, into a 'maelstrom of people' on the road. She had three children to manage, including a toddler, when she realised that her middle child was gone. 'I screamed with all my might, searching, and finally was able to find him but, for a moment, I was sure he was dead'.[9] During sudden, intensive bombings, such as the one that largely destroyed Coventry on 14 November 1940, many had to grab their most precious possessions and watch their home towns burn from the outside; citizens of the city reflected that 'we would never see [our] families again . . .'[10] Simultaneously, British and Japanese citizens proclaimed their dedication to supporting the war, giving their sons and daughters to the armed forces and military industries.

At the time, few families interrogated whether the Second World War was worth winning at the cost of a child, parent, or sibling, and this may be one of the reasons why the war was so brutal. The importance of family over nation and state emerged after 1945 as a direct product of war losses.[11] This was in spite of the fact that, compared to today, family was arguably more important for Britons and Japanese during the Second World War era, for finding housing, sustenance, employment, and marriage prospects. Despite Second World War rhetoric that insisted on the difference between East and West, both countries shared very similar values when it came to family. Young men and women still asked for family elders' approval of potential marriage partners, employment was often tied to blood relations, and most people still lived close to extended family, meaning leisure time was frequently spent with relatives, including grandparents, cousins, aunts, and uncles. Before the age of social welfare, critical aspects of health and happiness – including medical care, education, elder care, nutrition, and diet – were heavily dependent on family resources. Consequently, the loss of family members was even more catastrophic for wartime people than it is today, and still they largely trusted the state with their most important assets: their blood relations. The Second World War assaulted some of the most fundamental social relations, making the British and Japanese war experience, in this case, more similar than they were different.

With Friends Like These: The First Strike against the Family

The mass evacuation of schoolchildren from the cities was one of the first and most memorable wounds suffered by families in Britain and Japan. Hundreds of thousands of children, both accompanied by adults and on their own, were removed from urban areas in both countries. Early responses to the call for evacuation were ambivalent or even hostile: Japanese authorities saw such demands as defeatist and, in Liverpool, for example, Dorothy Hughes wrote that locals opposed urban refugees. She had heard 'immorality was rife' among undesirable evacuees from

Birmingham, and Dorothy reflected on the value of the mass evacuation scheme in 1939, revealing the classism that would plague British efforts:

I really think that the best plan would have been to leave everyone alone – let those who really want to be evacuated go on their own account, and let the others take their chance. The whole thing has been a wasteful expenditure of public money, although there is no doubt that it is a first rate experiment in social conditions, etc.[12]

Many British and Japanese parents, especially in so-called slums, held on to their children right up until the bombs started falling – some even refused to evacuate them during the height of enemy attacks. In Britain and Japan, evacuation itself was a disintegration of the family orchestrated by a state preparing for total war.

Evacuated children in Britain felt themselves to be treated rather poorly by the state employees who had promised their parents that little ones would be looked after. The first round of evacuations in Britain came during the 'Phony War' of 1939, when an expected massive air attack (the supposed 'knockout blow') by the GAF never materialised. Teachers and 'helpers of school parties' were instructed to attach labels to their children and to their possessions, with the child's name, school number, and address; the adults who travelled with the schoolchildren were expected to wear such identifying tags as well. Upon their arrival in the countryside, local authorities asked adults from the cities to report

a) children who are likely to prove 'difficult' from the point of view of behaviour or character
b) children who are especially nervous and who might suffer without the company of a fellow pupil, or to walk any distance alone in the dark evenings in the country
c) children for whom waterproof sheets in bed may be thought necessary
d) children whose personal hygiene was known to need attention.[13]

In subsequent evacuations, locals sometimes treated children poorly, reflecting deep-seated class, gender, and regional biases. Children who arrived in the countryside complained of being picked over like cattle at market, being verbally abused, and even put to labour (instead of schooling) by their 'hosts'. To make matters worse, the local governments across Britain frequently made errors in the billeting of unaccompanied children, who constituted the majority of people leaving the cities. Albert Shaw, an 11-year-old from Salford, was even left abandoned in a Lancaster school because he failed to appear on the evacuation roster. Trapped alone in the dark, he screamed and cried until a passer-by called the police.[14] Furthermore, wartime education was tenuous at best. A schoolteacher in Hull, Olive Metcalfe, described how instructions for opening and closing schools during air raids were not promising for those who might wish to enjoy a normal instruction:

If the [air raid] warning goes after school hours i.e. 4pm and the all-clear before 10pm, they have to go to school at a quarter to ten next morning. If the all-clear goes between 10pm and 7am, no morning school at all. If after 7am for the all-clear there is no school at all, morning or afternoon. Very nice too. Strikes me there won't be much education.[15]

Eyed suspiciously for their putative hygienic failings, passed along like unwanted parcels, put to labour, and left uneducated, many British urban evacuees harboured resentments well into the post-war era.

Japanese authorities left evacuation plans to the very last minute, but Ministry of Education officials seemed more dedicated to the welfare of children than their British counterparts. The Ministry insisted that the personal security and belongings of the children 'must, of course, be vouchsafed', and the authorities exhorted teaching staff who travelled with children to fulfil their duties as protectors, educators, and moral exemplars. Teachers 'must earnestly apply their energies to the education of these children, and fulfil this duty with the same honourable resolution as a man who has been called into military service, or the education of evacuated children will be a failure'. In another official document, national authorities even delineated examples of what sort of objects an evacuated child should bring, assuring parents that they would be well taken care of. However, 'weak and infirm children' (*kyojaku jidō*) were to be sent to relatives, deemed to be too difficult for the evacuation system to handle. Similar to Britain, Japanese authorities treated children from suspect social classes harshly. From third grade to sixth, primary school children from the slums of Tokyo were doused with anti-louse powders, fed meagre school dinners, and shipped off to dormitories in the countryside without their parents. In any case, like their counterparts in Britain, Japanese children were tagged and sent along with a rucksack of 'necessary items' that were severely restricted by weight limits. As soon as Japanese children were dropped off in rural areas, they became the problem of local authorities and families, from which the government expected 'full cooperation and assistance'.[16] As in Britain, Japanese city kids who were tossed into the countryside found themselves thrust into an utterly alien world without the benefit of family support – only a state apparatus that had many other priorities to worry about. Nevertheless, while British children were billeted almost at random in private houses, Japanese children were often housed together, with friends and other familiar faces, in temples and other large rural structures; anecdotal accounts suggest that the Japanese system was slightly less traumatic for the children. Despite this important difference, however, their experience was highly dependent on the competency and receptivity of local people in rural areas.

For ordinary people in Britain and Japan, being separated from their families was often worse than the mortal threat of the bomber. Shinonori Mansaku recalled the long, excruciating goodbyes that parents were forced to say to their children as they were moved into rural areas.

In the bustle of all the luggage and farewells, time went by gradually and soon enough it was time to depart. Weaving through all of the people seeing off [their children], our leader cut through the crowd with a flag in hand that read 'Jōbanmatsu Primary School'. When we departed to the right, there were people on both sides of the street, tears streaming down their faces ... and so that was our emotional evacuation by train, putting the city behind us, making a line ever northward to [the country].[17]

Others refused to leave their homes because, in an age before government-subsidised lending and easy mortgages, homes were acquired with great difficulty or literally built by hand. As attacks on London intensified, elderly Gwladys Cox rejected an offer of evacuation to a friend's shelter, writing, 'Delightful of him, of course, but we feel obliged to decline. We cannot abandon our home! If it were bombed in our absence, there would be no one to salvage what remained, if anything'.[18] Adults had to balance the pain of separation with the need to preserve the family during a period of mass bombing; in an age in which single buildings housed three generations, one bad attack could wipe out an entire family line, root and stem. As one Londoner put it at the beginning of the air raids, '[t]hings are getting more lively cannot take risks with children'.[19] Still, in both countries, many families resisted impersonal state-organised evacuations, preferring to rely on country relatives or remain together, even if it meant losing the entire family to enemy attacks. In Bristol, one woman embraced her daughter during a terrible air raid that lasted eleven consecutive hours, telling her, '[i]f we have to go, we'll go together'.[20] Perhaps most important was the feeling among working people that their husbands and wives were their companions, and they refused to be apart: 'I had 16 years in digs, and believe me, I've had enough', one man in Liverpool was overheard to say, 'My wife goes with me wherever I go – if I was to be moved tomorrow'.[21] In Japan, too, this was a common refrain. Nagaoka resident Matsuda Haruko recalled her father announce: 'I'd rather us all die together, as a family, in our house than flee and die one by one alone'.[22] This sort of sentiment could enrage some family members: during some of Hull's worst bombing, Edith Peirse quarrelled bitterly with her father and wrote in her diary that 'he has no thought for me at all, says he is going to live in his home till he dies and not go away'.[23] Even when families fled together into the countryside during air raids, adults forced their children to scatter across fields in order to avoid the possibility of the family being wiped out in one blow, as Kobayashi Takako remembered during the destruction of Himeji.[24] Children who stayed behind in urban areas like Manchester recalled a much more convivial and supportive environment, despite interrupted sleeps during night raids:

Our particular house was overcrowded and in a street congested with families. Some twenty-four children between three and sixteen years of age. There seemed a certain camaraderie between all of us, literally like one very large family. Neighbour helped neighbour and clothes were handed down between families with no sense of stigma . . . To us children, there was a deliciously fearful sense of danger, in this nocturnal adventure. Parents, although they must have been deeply worried and anxious during air raids, did their best to keep their fears in check and to allay any childish alarm.[25]

For families who had experienced the callousness of urban life, the loss of breadwinners and caring parents might as well have been a death sentence for their children. For others, the loss of their children was more painful than death itself.

Still, thousands of adults chose to send their young ones away from the violence, and this could be traumatising for both children and parents, with one London mother writing: 'feeling desolate but not quite so worried for their safety'.[26] Children often reacted with remarkable fortitude and cheer, as long as supervising adults did not spoil their fun. For some children evacuation was fun and exciting, or the retreat to the countryside represented an escape from cramped, unhygienic, and ugly urban food deserts that were in the midst of being bombed. Iris Miller reflected fondly on her time away from Westminster:

Mrs. Henry was very kind to us. In her beautiful garden she had a large comfortable summerhouse known as 'the dugout', and there she would accommodate our family when they needed a respite from the war . . . We had a wonderful holiday with marvellous weather; it is a memory I treasure because I didn't see my father again as he died the following April.[27]

When the bombs fell, initial terror could still give way to childlike merriment among evacuated students. In Kōfu, Mibu Akiko was tasked with overseeing evacuated children as a 'dormitory mother' (ryōbo), and so she had to lead them into the hills when a surprise night-time air raid began near the school. Akiko cursed herself for not bringing the children to the ancient burial mounds (kōfun) nearby for cover:

I couldn't keep the kids together in the dark, and I prayed for the planes to withdraw, even for a moment. But the B-29s just stubbornly – it seemed like they insisted – flew over us again and again. I felt like I had to resolve to die this time but, at some point, they simply pulled away. At that moment, when I had given up all hope, we were fine, and it was like even the energy to rejoice was gone from me. But the kids were surprisingly happy, babbling on like 'Oh wasn't that scary?' or 'Wow!' putting their rucksacks and futons up on their backs or pulling them along, gathering together.[28]

Sometimes the security of travelling with a parent helped defuse the anxiety of separation from home. Eva Merrill's mother was also adamant that the family not be separated, even temporarily, and travelled with them to their evacuation destination. For her, as a child, trekking into the country was exhilarating, like going on a school holiday:

Fleets of coaches, or charabancs as we called them in those days, were lined up outside the school to transport us to we knew not where . . . Parents were virtually sending their children off into the unknown, and there were many demands to 'write and tell us where you are' passed around . . . The coaches all took off in a convoy; it was all very exciting with everybody waving to each other. The mothers left behind looked rather forlorn as the coaches increased speed and some of the children on them became tearful. I thought I ought to be singing my head off . . . but none of the Mums on our coach looked like breaking into song . . .[29]

Thus, children who might initially approach the evacuation experience as exciting were soon influenced by the dour attitudes of the adults around them. Schoolteacher Ōyama Hidenori noted in his diary that evacuated Japanese children 'were numb [bonyari] to these rapid changes in their lives, and it was as if they were being pulled along by the teachers in this case'. Looking over his young wards from urban Osaka, who fell asleep quickly as night stole across the countryside, Ōyama wrote that he was 'overcome by tears'. Indeed, the sight of so many homesick and forlorn-looking children struck the adults around them as one of the first losses of the war: 'When I think of these children', Ōyama wrote, 'separated from their parents, I always wonder, just what can be done [for them]?'[30] Similarly, Class Leader Marguerite Coles accompanied children removed from Hull, and recorded the vicissitudes of their views in a long letter home. 'I shall never forget that memorable Friday', she wrote, when 'the Hull Central Station closed to the public; the endless processions of children with teachers and helpers, all in perfect order, all heavily laden, and most of them silent'. Once the train started towards Scarborough, she noticed that the children cheered up slightly and began to chat.

'I didn't eat much breakfast this morning', 'Me mother says she wishes she could get hold of Hitler, she'd give him sommet', 'Me mum was crying this morning when I left home', 'Me mother came in school to see us off', 'Mine didn't because she didn't want to upset me little sister', 'How long do you think we'll be away?' 'Do you think there'll be a war?' 'Me father says it will all be over and we'll be back again in a fortnight', 'I had me shoes mended', 'Me mother is going to try to send me a new pair, but she can't afford it this week' … 'Me father says Scarborough wouldn't be safe', 'Yes it would, I hope it's Scarborough because there'll be sea and sands'.

After the children erupted in excited talk when arriving in Scarborough, they became quickly quiet and nervous. Billeting among the stern, comparatively well-off population was troublesome considering many of the Hull children were considered 'slum kids'.[31] Whether the children were on an exciting adventure or a perilous exile depended largely on how the locals treated them in the countryside.

In the post-war period, many who had lived through the conflict as children and adolescents bemoaned the 'loss of youth' or a 'childhood without toys' that characterised the war years. As the Hull experience, and others, show, however, living conditions could improve with evacuation. Contrary to precious modern visions of 'childlike children' and 'vulnerable innocents', young people displayed as much, if not more, fortitude than their adult supervisors. Nevertheless, no matter how amusing a trip to the country could be, nothing could compensate for the feelings of anxiety and loss that both children and their parents experienced when being separated. Whether the separation was voluntary or not, the first strike on the home was invariably launched by one's own government.

Sibling Rivalry: Supporting the City, Preserving the Family

The war turned cities into deadly places, and this tore apart the family networks that Japanese and British citizens had built up over many generations. Because British and Japanese families tended to congregate within urban spaces, mass bombings had the effect of simultaneously destroying mothers, babies, grandfathers, and aunts. Urban residents sometimes seemed aware that the bombed city was trying to destroy their families: Eleanor Humphries wrote in her diary about the circumstances that led to the departure of her relatives:

Sister and husband, who live near L's … would not build shelter or have ceilings shored. Were terribly shaken and upset when bomb fell in road. They had … to bring beds down to drawing room and have shutters made for French doors. But they all undressed at night. They did not hear the bomb fall but the house seemed as if squeezed. Walls came in on them, then bulged out and the ceiling sagged and crashed but did not fall. After that terrible experience, their windows being out and doors all mended, they quickly all packed and departed to the country . . . All hotels full. Were told they could sleep on floor of Town Hall until they found billets. Believe they spent the first night in car.[32]

Despite the havoc bombers unleashed on their personal lives, most individuals during the war nevertheless accepted the conflation of individual and family interests with national ones, and stuck with the city even as it killed their loved ones; in other words, they believed, by and large, that what was good for the nation would be good for them individually and for their families. The interests of the city and those of the family, during the bombing war, were mutually exclusive, but too many residents realised this far too late.

One reason for the dedication to the city was that, before the war with Germany officially began, citizens across the United Kingdom felt personally invested in foreign conflicts. Women were especially committed, perhaps because they were not expected to fight on the front lines. Mary Bloomfield (Coventry), Bessie Skea (Orkney), Dorothy Hughes (Liverpool), Dora Mockett (Hull), Violet Maund (Bristol), and Gladys Hollingsworth (Coventry) all wrote about their personal relationship with the war effort. 'Will we keep our pledge to Poland?' wrote Mary, 'Everyone seems to hope so, all wishing to see Hitler and the Nazis wiped off the face of the earth'. Although their attention was usually focused on Germany, after 1941 some looked to the empire's fate in the East: 'Our troops have left Rangoon – defeat after defeat – when will it end?' The world indeed seemed to be falling apart: Dorothy looked to the Russo-Finnish Winter War and wrote '[t]he way things are going everyone will be fighting everyone else'.[33] In the Manichean world view that dominated Britain at this time, those who resisted invasion, like the Finns, became heroes, but those who collaborated were reprehensible villains. Gladys went so far as to paste a photograph portrait of Belgium's King Leopold in her diary and write 'TRAITOR' on his forehead. Total resistance was critical to the prosecution of total war, and Bessie Skea emphasised that this included the rehabilitation of the pre-war order: 'Germany has made a peace-offer to Britain – an insult – but Britain is not looking for peace on her terms. We will fight until Poland is restored'.[34] Nefarious Russians quickly became good friends whenever international events shifted, as Dorothy Kahn described, in her diary, far-off events like personal victories:

Many important events have taken place since the last time I wrote. Russia has now come into the war on our side and although Germany thought it would only be a matter of a few weeks before Russia would have to give in, they are holding their own very well and giving the Germans more than they bargained for.[35]

The linkage of foreign battlefields with personal struggle was not totally irrational: the achievements of a far-off army could, in the age of air power, translate into greater safety at home as it destroyed the enemy's ability to launch air raids. Gladys had a sense that German control of continental Europe would bring disaster to Britain: 'FRANCE CAPITULATES. The whole world stirs ... Hitler and Mussolini to Meet. DARK DAYS AHEAD'.[36] Even with the enemy knocking at the door, however, ordinary people felt the need to stay positive and support their country's efforts. In Hull, Olive Metcalfe engaged in argument with an older man over the course of the war in Europe:

Mr. Rathbone very loud-mouthed saying we were losing the war, which I hotly contested, because even if we were, saying so and getting people down doesn't help. And what's the good, these days, of doing anything that doesn't help. I always try to be full of spirits when I am round home.[37]

Like so many ordinary citizens in the Second World War, Olive felt strongly that one had to be 'full of spirits' and supportive of the war effort, even if the country was losing. This of course included Axis citizens; the commitment of ordinary people on both sides meant that they sent their loved ones increasingly into harm's way.

Indeed, Japanese citizens were making the same grand statements about 'total commitment' which were often exacerbated by a perception of personal connection to the war effort. Ishikawa Chieko, a teenage student drafted into the labour corps of Chiba military factory, embraced the view that her forced labour was actually part of a battle against the US bombers that were laying waste to her home town:

At last our mobilisation orders have arrived. We were inducted at Soga's Hitachi aircraft plant Chiba home office. They have great expectations for us. We got off at Soga station at 9:05am at the main entrance. The women workers all lined up to greet us. Incidentally, the other day a group of B-29s flew over just as we were setting off on parade. We're going to build planes to nail those bastard B-29s.

When news arrived of the total annihilation of Japanese forces on Iwo Jima, Chieko wrote an angry passage in her diary, tying her forced labour to the memory of the troops: 'We must work. We must show those soldiers who sacrificed themselves for Japan's final victory'.[38] Unless individuals were already sceptical of the war effort, brutal air raids did not suppress ordinary people's enthusiasm for it in Japan, just as GAF 'terror bombing' failed to suppress war fever in Britain. Seeing corpses, losing loved ones, and watching one's home nearly destroyed made some

Japanese citizens, like their counterparts in Britain, pull more closely together. After the firebombing of Shizuoka, Tanaka Osamu wrote:

[F]ortunately, our family was unharmed by the raid, but what could one say to console the multitudes who had endured sacrifices? There were no words for it. We invited them into our home – those who lost their own houses and had nowhere to sleep. At a time of deprivation and shortage, we said we had to 'endure until victory' (*katsu made wa to mo ni kurushimō*), and handed out futons and tea.[39]

Japanese communities had mobilised to support their members since the 1904–1905 Russo-Japanese War, and were well practised in using such platitudes and ritualised support activities to paper over the terrible demands that a wartime government made.

Enemy attacks on the family expose the fundamental conflict between the interests of the political and economic leaders who can benefit from war, on the one hand, and the ordinary people who overwhelmingly profit from peace, on the other. At first, family members tried to put on a brave face and support the war effort, often with fatal consequences. On 24 November 1940, a Bristol baker named James Osborne ignored his son's desperate pleas to stay away from the bakery during the vicious German bombing of the city. Osborne said, 'People will want their bread tomorrow, whatever happens tonight', went bravely into the city centre, and was killed before he even reached the bakery.[40] The talk of war was first misconstrued by young people as some exciting new event; one survivor recalled that, during the destruction of Coventry, 'as I walked home my eyes scanned the sky for THE ENEMY. After all I was still at school and the war represented excitement, something different from the everyday run of things!'[41] This exhilaration gave way to fear, particularly as young and old realised that leaders, foreign and domestic, were inflicting violent deaths on them. Yoshida Fusako watched her father take her younger brother to relatives in the countryside, and she confessed in her diary that at night 'I am so, so afraid. I can't sleep'.[42] One British mother recorded her little boy was awakened by air raid sirens at 2am, whereupon he was 'very nervous and sick in the tummy'.[43] Young people had to confront violence on a regular basis. Schoolgirl Patricia Donald wrote in her diary of witnessing a female relative trying to save a foreigner: 'A Canadian got a bit of glass in his chest, and she tried to help him and gave him some water, but it was in a fatal spot'.[44] As the violence increased, it included friends as well, which sometimes triggered hysterical responses. Hosokawa Kikue's school was in Kure, near Hiroshima, which was a port town full of military industries; her schoolmates were drafted into factories, where they died during heavy bombing raids, and she remembers students crying in despair, 'If we're going to die, we should just all die together in a shelter!'[45] Adults, too, had to accept the fact that the war they supported was killing babies. In Wallasey, near Liverpool, a rescue party was fortunately able to hear the cries of an infant buried under the rubble; wiping dust out of the little girl's eyes and mouth, they ascertained that she had been trapped there for days after her parents had been instantly killed.[46] Government exhortations to fight were acceptable in the abstract, but when the air war came home, the prospect of actual violence terrified people to the point that they were physically ill.

The air war targeted civilians, and in so doing purposefully destroyed the family networks that sustained urban life. Dora Mockett, who normally was supportive of the war effort, was very disturbed when she ran into a friend who had been devastated by the loss of three of her four children in the severe November 1940 air raids.[47] First aid responders witnessed, and dutifully recorded, how the assault on the city necessarily meant the destruction of the family:

One of [the First Aid post volunteers] came upon a huge mound of earth blocking his path, the sign of a land mine having exploded. Hearing a woman shouting he climbed over the soil and debris and went to her. She took him to the rear of a badly damaged house and pointed to the body of her dead son ... First Aiders found an air raid shelter had been struck by a blast and there were four injured people inside. One had serious head injuries and when her daughter saw her she was so shocked she also had to go to hospital ... Screams were heard from a very badly damaged house and two First Aiders went into the ruins and found a man trapped in burning debris. The man died but his daughter, badly injured, lived ... A woman's voice could be heard saying she was under the stairs with three children and they were unhurt. Rescue workers were lowered down from the top of the house into the ruins but they started vomiting because gas was escaping ... All was in vain, the mother and children had died before being released.[48]

During the 1945 firebombing of Himeji, Ichikawa Shōjirō, who was only a pre-schooler, ran out as fast as his legs would take him while carrying little boots full of uncooked rice: 'The reason my mother had me carry rice', he recalled, 'was so that, even if [our neighbourhood] was incinerated and we were separated, "You find one of our relatives and they can at least fix you a bowl of rice"'. Who would cook the rice for Shōjirō, however, if the entire city was burned? The experience would haunt him for years after the war: 'I'm nearly fifty now [in 1988], but the red blaze of [Himeji] on fire – I cannot forget it. Even if I die it cannot be forgotten'.[49] For those who were too young to remember the murder of their families clearly, the reluctance of others to discuss it left a gaping hole in their personal history. Patricia Bovill, who was only six years old during the November 1940 'Hull Blitz', only vaguely remembers being buried alive, rescued, and then vomiting over her pyjamas in the hospital; her parents were killed instantly. Even more painful, however, was her grandparents' refusal to help her know her parents. 'I would like my children to know more about their grandparents', she wrote after the war, 'but my grandparents were devastated by it and couldn't bring themselves to talk about it'. The personal history was most important, but Patricia also added, 'I feel that our children and grandchildren should know more about dear old Hull and perhaps have more respect and love for it'.[50] The loss of the city and the loss of the family were difficult to disentangle: parents instructed their children according to the personal networks that had evolved within urban spaces, but the attack on the city targeted the kith and kin who composed its most important human connections.

For the wartime generation, enemy attacks reinforced the paramount importance of family. By 1945, eight-year-old Sakazume Hiromi had become accustomed to the sounds of B-29 air raids over Tokyo's Sumida Ward; she fled into the shelters at a moment's notice, experiencing the contradictions of singing patriotic war songs while the Americans were systematically destroying Japan's imperial capital and its citizens. She and her loved ones had been fortunate for many months to escape injury, but on 9 March 1945, a particularly terrible raid over Tokyo finally reached them. When the siren began ringing, her mother packed all of the family's valuables, insurance policies, family seal, cash, and about a litre of white rice into two cloth sitting mats and took Hiromi to the shelter. Her father, 'because it was considered a man's [job], remained behind to the very end in the house'. Mother and daughter blanketed their heads with futon covers and fire hoods, weaving through the burning neighbourhood to arrive at their appointed shelter when:

... from the entrance, a powerful wind blew the door out. This is when things got really bad. Through the hole where the door once was, like snow falling through, smouldering embers came in the shelter. At the entrance, three or four Neighbourhood Association members struggled to extinguish them. Inside there were people chanting Buddhist prayers, children crying, and there was even one middle-aged man saying, 'This strong blast is surely the *kamikaze* – the Divine Wind of Japan [that expels invaders] – so we will be saved!' At that point, a man came to the shelter with a rucksack, which was on fire, shouting, 'Help me!' The Association members were confused and afraid, and told him to take off his rucksack first, but he wouldn't. That's when I thought: 'My father is dead.'

Inside the shelter, panicked women and children were ordered to urinate on their futons and blankets; these were packed into ventilation chambers in order to prevent the shelter from burning down on top of them. Hiromi was able to briefly look through one of these flaming channels outside at Tokyo, which she described as 'like the inside of a boiler chamber. When I remember it now, I can't help but wonder how I survived it'. Pulled out of the shelter by soldiers the next morning, 8-year-old Hiromi saw widespread devastation. In and out of the shelter all day, she walked by an army horse that had been burned alive, and human corpses were scorched so badly that one could not distinguish men from women. Then her mother said, 'Your daddy might be dead'.

I saw the body of a man, burned to death, curled up outside of our shelter, and I thought he looked like my dad. When I looked more closely, he was the man who had come the other night with a rucksack on fire, asking for help. I froze, paralysed by the thought, 'That could be me'. Then I heard a man shouting loudly: 'Are there any Sakazumes here?' It was my father's voice. Without thinking, I blurted out, 'Banzai!' My father was alive! He had nothing on him, and was soaking wet. The family was saved. He had endured until the last moment, when the house caught on fire, and he knew it was finished. He ran to Oshikami station and jumped into the river, waiting there until morning.

Hiromi and her family went on to a military rations depot, which had also been largely destroyed, but was dispensing what little food remained to whomever wanted it. 'We felt lucky to get anything', she recalled, but was deeply haunted by seeing families that had been burned alive, their corpses still locked in embrace.[51] Bearing in mind that, in the early twentieth century, families were much more likely to concentrate in the same city, or even the same neighbourhood, bombing that aimed at massacring civilians was far more devastating than it would be today. It was clear to young people, if not always adults, that the war on the city was inevitably a war on the family.

Circling the Wagons: Families Respond to Bombing

When the enemy attacked residential areas, most urban citizens abandoned their jobs, homes, and material possessions in order to hold on a bit more tightly to their loved ones. Bertram Elwood recorded a radiographer from Coventry recalling scenes from hospitals during air raids, writing about 'a woman who insisted on being wheeled to her little son, and later to her young daughter, to soothe them to sleep although she herself was suffering with a fractured humerus and thigh'.[52] Rescue workers in Britain and Japan regularly recovered the bodies of parents and children, locked in embrace at the moment of death. Witnessing death and severe injury all around them, it was only natural for children to imagine the same fate befalling their family, and for parents to cling to their children even more fiercely than normal.

As air attacks began, citizens instinctively reached for their loved ones, even though they knew that their arms were no defence against an explosion. Mothers ran into their children's rooms first, husbands looked for their wives, siblings held hands, and children worried for their slower, more vulnerable grandparents. When the bombers reached Bristol and explosions rocked family shelters, one man recalled his wife turning to him and saying, 'Put your arms around me, dear'.[53] During the fire-bombing of Takamatsu, a regional city on the island of Shikoku, school-girl Akiyama Shigeko and her siblings held on first and foremost to one another:

When I saw the flames, I began to shiver and shake uncontrollably. Everyone said the children should flee quickly, so my elder sister took my younger sister on her back, and I grabbed my little brother's hand as we fled. We ran to the fields, ever further south – the darkness is where the fields will be! – fleeing as if in a dream . . . My mother wrapped my 6 month old baby sister in a futon and ran toward where she thought we had gone . . . A baby's neck isn't very strong at that age, so she had to be carried in that way, and I remember my mom sometimes saying how heavy she was. Grandfather, dad, and my eldest sister stayed in the house, and then took whatever they could into the fields.

Unfortunately, Shigeko's grandmother was hard of hearing, so she was too late to escape the conflagration while the Akiyama family divided the tasks necessary for abandoning their home. In Japan, co-habiting grand-parents often did the lion's share of childcare, so young people like Shigeko formed powerful attachments to them. The night of the air raid was the last time she saw her grandmother, prompting Shigeko to write that her grandmother 'died in fear, and if there had been no air raid, she would have lived much longer'. After enduring years of food shortage and deprivation, she eventually married after the war, noting that her husband also lost his mother, elder brother, and three sisters in the destruction of Toyama by Allied forces. 'Any future war', she wrote despondently, 'would be awful for me'.[54] Husbands, whether by cultural conditioning or instinct, were protective of their wives. On the Isle of Dogs, Bill Regan was escorting his wife Vi home when a massive bombing campaign on the working class area of East London began. He held onto her hand tightly, to keep her from being dazzled by the flares but also so that he knew where she was in the dark. When he heard bombs coming their way, Bill dragged Vi to cover with him.

The first one exploded somewhere close, hours later the next one, closer, the third one was whistling straight for us, and I was pushing Vi back against the wall, and it was taking a long time, and this thing was still coming at us, and I wondered if it was going to take very long to die, then the whistling stopped, then a terrific thump as it hit the ground, and everything seemed to expand, then contract with deliberation, and stillness seemed to be all around.

When they finally arrived home, Vi prepared for dinner and spoke to their friends. 'Everyone thinks Vi is wonderful', he wrote half-jokingly, 'no one even thinks about me'. Vi had once told him that she did not fear dying; nevertheless, Bill had a tight grip on Vi's hand all the way home.[55] Family structures, gender roles, and notions of romantic love have changed radically throughout history, but the bonds of familial attachment produced instantaneous responses.

Whereas before the war individuals might, as they do today, put career ahead of family life, the war pushed the importance of wealth and advancement into a very low tier of consideration. Consequently, Gladys Hollingsworth described the scene following the infamous bombing of Coventry on 14 November 1940:

It was terrific, [but] we escaped with shattered windows and leaking roof. Ambulances from Birmingham, London, and USA. Fire engines and rescue workers from every corner of British Isles. Went to get wages, then to Simms at night. The memory of this will last forever in every citizen's mind. Places still burning. Soldiers digging for bodies. Hundreds crowding round Council House, which is still standing, to get news of missing relatives.[56]

The wartime generation was taught a terrible lesson in how warfare would not spare their loved ones, which made other considerations seem petty by contrast. After a terrible raid on Chiba, near Tokyo, Inaba Fuku and her family fled to Kikuma, a short distance away. Her father went missing for an entire day, only to arrive on a bicycle with Fuku's little sister, Kazuko. 'As soon as I saw her', she wrote, 'I was overcome with anguish from the war. She was cold ... Coming all the way to Kikuma on a stretcher, she had suffered terribly. We took her to the doctor, but it was too late'.[57] Seeing non-combatants, including children, die from enemy air raids triggered attacks of fear and anger in those who associated these losses with their own loved ones' vulnerability. One woman in Coventry wrote that her husband, who retrieved dead bodies from the ruins, saw that 'one of the victims was a baby, almost the same age as our youngest daughter. This upset [him] very much'.[58] Not all losses were directly attributable to enemy action, however: one's own government was also a threat to family integrity in the form of compulsory labour and military service. As the state demanded more and more people from the family, the stress could be cumulative and subtle, as Frederick Goodridge noted during a long air raid in Southampton:

There wasn't much said in our shelter, what could be said? But our mother suffered so, and around 11[pm] she couldn't help crying out almost in disbelief 'When is it going to stop, is there to be no end to this?' It hurt me in knowing how it affected my mother, she had enough to bear as it was with three sons in the Army and a daughter in the WAAF.[59]

In addition to blood relations, the war robbed many of their closest friends, who could be considered as dear as family. On V. E. Day, Coventry policeman Ted Bloomfield took his wife Mary up to the top of the battered Coventry Cathedral tower and told her of his loss:

Remembering the bomb that threw him against the Council House walls, killing his best friend Ken Rallings who was going to help get people out of the debris in Much Park Street, and flinging his large body over the wall of the Miss Patricks shop, where his colleagues were forced to stand by helpless and watch him burn. Can we ever forget? Should we ever forget?[60]

Whether by evacuation or by direct bombing, the war was an attack on the structure of human communities, including families, just as bombers aimed at deconstructing electric, water, gas, and transport networks. These assaults were not just the result of enemy action, but the demands of one's own wartime government.

One of the social structures that was tested by the war was Britain and Japan's persistent patriarchy. Many older men in Britain and Japan adopted the role of patriarch in their homes, which conferred authority over others in the household (including other men), but also nerve-wracking responsibility at a time when uncontrollable disasters were striking regularly. After the war, Matsui Ryūichirō discovered a diary by his father, who worked for the newspaper *Yomiuri* when Shizuoka was firebombed. From 7 April to 11 August 1945, the elder Matsui recorded the ruthless attacks on civilians in the city and surrounding areas. When he left his family behind to go to work, he was assailed by fears of losing them; he regularly saw or heard about people he knew perishing, or losing their entire family. 19 June was a particularly terrible aerial attack, in which Matsui had to balance his life at the office with the threat to his home:

Tonight, at 11:30pm, the enemy arrived. The alarm was comparatively [illegible] and so I was at ease, but by 12:30am things quickly worsened. . . . I left the family in charge of the house and went to the office. Then the air attack came [in earnest]. The whole city turned into a sea of fire. We protected the roof of the company [from fire] until morning. By dawn, the inferno was still raging, and the city was glowing red. Fifteen of us worked to save the company building. At dawn you couldn't spot a single shadow, just a burnt plain as far as the eye could see. The old town centre was completely lost. Twenty thousand homes, three thousand lives, all lost. It is the most horrible and devastating experience of our age. Worse comes to worst, [illegible] our home is totally destroyed, [but I hope] at least the family is alright. Tonight onwards, we've nowhere to sleep, and this thought breaks my heart.

Matsui wandered back home through the ruined city, living out the next few days with his family, struggling to find food to eat. 'It's a pathetic existence', he recorded in disgust.[61] Women held up slightly better, perhaps because they were inured to hardship in a patriarchal system. Marjorie Brodie, who had fled into the countryside with her baby, returned to Coventry to find her parents' house the only one standing in a block otherwise flattened by the German assault. The bombers had blasted a hole in the roof of the kitchen, where she found 'my mother . . . cooking something on the cooker with her umbrella up. Nothing was going to stop her from getting something for dinner – bombs, rain, or anything else'.[62] Still, not every victim of the bombing war focused on the family. For those male bourgeois types who lived a charmed life in the city, the destruction of urban consumption produced privileged resentment. In Coventry, one man was heard to complain:

Coventry is a hole – there's nothing to do [after the raids] – I can't even get a drink I like. The pubs are always crowded . . . I know what I'd like, a nice chicken and some champagne, what about it? . . . Damn this war, nothing will ever be the same again.[63]

While urban professional men complained about the finer things, others kept their focus on the family. Remembering her father on the day of his death, Mitsuko wrote in her diary: 'the fact that my sisters and I, always far apart, were able to meet today is some sort of divine miracle. Just being able to meet your sister, whom you may never see again, is a source of joy'.[64] While single male urban professionals could see the decline of their lifestyle as a legitimate casualty of war, patriarchs, married men, and women largely focused their grief on the losses in their family.

The Second World War, like the First World War, also disrupted intimacy, which men and women of that generation recorded only fleetingly; nevertheless, writing about such matters sometimes provided one of the very few safe outlets for sexual feelings and frustrations.[65] For example, many women wrote subtly about their feelings for departing partners. Recalling the moment she said goodbye to her husband as he shipped off from Takamatsu to war in China, Iriye Hisae wrote, 'I was pregnant at the time, and I suppressed all kinds of emotions to send him off with a smile. I watched his large frame from behind, so dependable, kind, and sad . . . I can still hear the sound of his boots as he walked away'.[66] As the war accelerated, Japanese women of all ages were expected to lose even more of their husbands and lovers 'for the nation'. In Hachiōji, 43-year-old Takizawa Toki made sure that, during her husband's departure to the Pacific, she 'did not cry, and sent him off with a smiling face'. Striving to respect her partner's wish that she 'take care of things for him' (*ato o tanomu*), this kind of dutiful separation unintentionally served state interests in mobilising the general public for war:

At that moment, all the emotions I'd been suppressing exploded, and I just cried and cried. But that was pointless. Everyone thought it was 'for the nation', so I just found strength, found my resolve, and thought, *I'm going to overcome everything for my children and parents* ... My husband put his life on the line for the nation, so I have to as well. Even though we're a thousand miles apart, our hearts were one – or so I thought, getting by day by day. Then, on 5 April 1944, my husband arrived unexpectedly. He just appeared at my bed, so I was shocked, woke my parents, and spent the evening as if in a dream. The next day, I went with five children to the station to see him off. I didn't know that this was our final moment on this earth. We waved at him, furiously, until the train could no longer be seen ... Going home, I was returning to my life of solitude and the children saying, 'Mum, I'm hungry!'[67]

Sacrificing as much as possible, Toki took care of the children and her husband's parents while, unbeknownst to her at the time, he was killed by US troops in Guam. Despite bombing and evacuation, her husband's departure remained the defining moment for Toki. Similarly separated by the war, Olive Metcalfe wrote to her husband Christopher about some of the more acute aspects of being away from an intimate partner:

I always relate sex questions in books to the only study of sex I know, and that is you ... I realize too that the marvel of sex in you, that controlled, wonderful thing, that I always took for granted as the usual and the ordinary, is by no means so, but unusual and extraordinary in its cleanliness, fineness, and its approach to the ideal ... Life has been very kind to me in giving me you and not some other man for I cannot imagine any man who could approach your standard.

While sex remained important to their marriage, when she became pregnant, Olive, like Takizawa Toki and Iriye Hisae, felt her husband's absence even more keenly. 'You cannot know how I long for your presence sometimes – just you to take over and shoulder things', she wrote to him while listening to German bombers attack Hull, 'Often I feel like a climbing plant that has lost its wall and is trying to stand alone'.[68] Hisae's longing for her husband Harumi came to her strongly when she gave birth to their child; she named the baby girl Harue, taking characters from both parents' names: 'I just wanted him to know [his heritage] as soon as possible'. Little did she know, her husband Harumi had been killed in China during the brutal fighting with the Chinese

Nationalists. In her post-delivery delirium, she saw his figure in the house, asking 'Where's my baby? Where's my baby?' She pointed to the next room, where the baby was sleeping, and he gazed into Hisae's face, disappearing slowly into the darkness. 'I don't know if it was real or a dream', Hisae wrote, recalling how she was later notified of his 'heroic' death in battle, 'but when you are truly sad, you do not cry'.[69] Despite popular foreign beliefs about Japanese women happily serving the wartime state, they missed their partners just as desperately as their British counter-parts, and both sides were equally committed to continuing the war effort.

The destruction of the city was thus not limited to the eradication of unknown, impersonal concrete structures and other people's homes. Bricklayer and rescue worker Bill Regan found a chunk of stone in the ruins of his east London neighbourhood that still bore the initials of local girls, which had been carved by a boy he knew in 1916. Encountering the stone amid a pile of rubble gave Bill pause to think of the girls, and he later wrote, 'I wonder where they are now. This became a depressing journey . . .'[70] This devastation linked city, neighbourhood, and family loss, creating a sense of shared sadness in both Britain and Japan. Mizutani Shin'ichi pondered in his diary the end of the city he knew, and how the destruction of urban space was an attack on his family:

The last month [March 1945] was chaotic. My life and, indeed, the life of this great city Nagoya, has been completely transformed. Following the air raid on the 12th, 19th, and 25th, a quick succession of attacks has reduced the city centre to ashes, my father's house [in which the family lived] was destroyed, and my wife and daughter have both been seriously injured.[71]

The destruction of the city was the end of a space that citizens had built over centuries, and recognised as home. Fifteen-year-old Ono Kazuo was completely disorientated by the annihilation of his neighbourhood in Takamatsu, trying to navigate heretofore familiar streets that were suddenly covered in destroyed houses, downed power lines, and ruined institutions such as schools, hospitals, train stations, and shops.

No place to rest. In the middle of a thin veil of smoke, the blackened figure of the Mitsukoshi [department store] appeared. I went from Memorial Road to the Tourist Path, where I saw blackened and swollen bodies, and I felt like I was instantly transported to some far-off battlefield . . . It didn't matter how long I searched, our home was no more. I stood atop the scorched earth and fallen tiles when, suddenly, tears poured down my face. My mother and father had worked and worked without rest, always putting their wants and needs last, to build this one bit of wealth; how many tears of rage must they have shed at this, how it was stolen from them through no fault of their own.[72]

The shock and full meaning of the loss of 'home', then, did not fully grab hold of the city's residents until they touched the corpses of their houses, belongings, and old neighbourhoods with their own hands. 'I don't remember anyone crying', wrote Bill Walsh, recalling the destruction of his home in Hull, 'this came later when we went down the terrace and stood on the still warm mound of bricks and plaster which seemed to be so small for what had been quite a large house'.[73] The destruction of city and family inspired resentment as well. Even after the destruction of Shizuoka, Matsui was awakened by American planes flying over them, on their way to attack Kōfu, Hirono, and Kiyomizu; he could hear the rumbling of explosions and see the light of far-off fires as others met the same fate, or worse, as he had. Matsui became frustrated and depressed as the war situation worsened:

In May we lost Mieko, in June the house burned down, in July my mother passed away, the Numazu [relatives] family home was destroyed, and in August Terao has become seriously ill. I just want to die myself. I [just] cry. I wish I could break through this ring of misery, even for one hour.

As head of his household, Matsui felt strongly that he had to see his family through the war safely. By the end of it all, Matsui's frustration with this situation had evolved into wrath; he poured out his feelings into the diary when he heard of the war's end: 'Why didn't they at least tell the citizens how weak Japan is? When I think about that, it's just excruciating. Those military thugs and their impulsive, barbaric ways dropped Japan right into the nadir of this suffering. Who is going to take responsibility for this?'[74] The Onos, Regans, Mizutanis, Walshes, and Matsuis made urban life possible by their collective efforts, so the enemy attacked these families in order to bring the urban cores to their knees. In Britain and Japan, families could not exist without the city, even if they did not always see that the reverse was also true.

While most urban residents 'circled the wagons' of family and friend networks in order to survive, enemy bombers' destruction of the city sometimes removed the restraints of law and common decency. Despite calls for national unity, when a family was bombed out of their home, they frequently encountered the 'hospitality' of urban residents: H. B. Monck described how an acquaintance arrived in Liverpool speaking of 'the selfishness of people', including the cynical price-gouging of desperate refugees for temporary accommodation. It 'gave you an idea', he wrote in his diary, of 'how some people's sense of public duty and citizenship was practically non-existent'.[75] Takeuchi Toshitoyo discovered that, following a bad raid, some citizens of Nagoya were robbing the corpses of cash and pocket watches.[76] In response to exploitation and lawlessness, some citizens felt compelled to take matters into their own hands. The situation in London air raid shelters quickly deteriorated, with locals claiming 'pitches' with bedclothes, fighting with one another over space. C. A. Piper noted how the conditions in Liverpool air raid shelters exposed rampant callousness and brutality in British society:

The more respectable people or, if you will, the less assertive and the more timid, had little chance of accommodation in the public shelters. This selfish monopolising of shelters was, partly at least, broken up by a group of young men, composed of Catholics and Unitarians; armed with short staves not unlike policemen's batons, they visited shelters which had the reputation of refusing admission to the stranger; they appeared to do this with the connivance of the police; I am bound to say that I did not feel a very urgent call to withhold my blessing. Many a bully received a cracked head; some of the crusaders did not escape injury; but this selfish monopolising of shelters by small gangs came to an end.[77]

Attacks on the city thus undermined networks that enforced certain values in daily life, begging a response from vigilantes and self-appointed local authorities. The state was hardly better, however, in its treatment of families. When Kobayashi Takako's mother learned that her son, who had been drafted into the army, died in the Pacific, she cried out, 'Even though our home was burned, if your elder brother came home alive, we could have rebuilt it somehow. The house can burn, but I just want my son returned to me!' Takako's mother cried and mourned for the young man for two years like this, finally demanding the boy's remains to be interred; unfortunately, there were few bodies coming back to Japan directly after the war, and Takako's younger brother had to bury an empty box. Only much later, one of her elder brother's war comrades returned from a prisoner of war camp with a braid of the young man's hair and a broken watch. 'I am deeply struck', she wrote, 'that he had been trained three years ago, and called up three times. But then we finally had his remains [years later], we were able to lay him to rest at home'.[78] In the war against the family, the enemy and the government seemed to be partners in crime, and this made many citizens callous and bitter about the fates that their loved ones met.

In the end, however, personal grief over the loss of family was not enough to stop the madness of total war. In Bristol, a woman described how an incendiary bomb struck her husband while he was helping his neighbours put out the flames. Her son ran out to his father immediately, but a nearby ambulance was already filled with casualties, all of whom shortly died. 'The bombs were dropping and the guns were firing', she wrote, 'but my boy would not leave his dad. A sailor helped to lift him in a small car, and my boy and I held him, terribly injured, all the way to the hospital'. A few days later, the man died of his wounds. Instead of inspiring the boy to flee, he 'joined up' two years later: 'His last word[s] to me before he went [were]: "I'm taking up where dad left off."' Mrs. Weston considered her boy 'a hero'.[79] Similarly, when Yoshida Fusako lost her younger brother Toshio, she was initially distraught. At the time she was an ordinary 15-year-old girl living in Tokyo, afraid of air raids and the dislocations of the war. Toshio's death briefly eclipsed the chaos of bombing as a subject of importance in her personal story.

Oh, my little boy, I couldn't have, in my worst nightmares, imagined what would happen to you. Why did this happen? You were so happy and healthy only yesterday, it's so horrible. Today I saw a dead person for the first time. Oh, you poor little boy. Mom and dad are also grief-stricken.

Her diary was suffused with sad and angry passages about the passing of her brother, such as when she 'spoke rudely' to his doctor on the phone because 'I was not myself'. Her mother stopped tidying the house, a gloom settled over the family, and she felt constantly distracted by her sense of loss. Struggling to finish school and prepare for work placement, Fusako wrote:

When I see things like Toshio's friends, I immediately feel like Toshio is playing with them. I have a ton of studying to do, but even when doing my schoolwork, I just remember playing with my little brother, I get distracted, and I can't focus. No matter how much I grieve, my little brother won't come home to me.

Fusako's depression over her little brother's death persisted for about a month, but soon she was pulled into the state's mobilisation campaigns. Air raid drills, exams, and work training all consumed her adolescent self. While participating in a service for the war dead at Yasukuni Shrine, she wrote, 'Even though I'm only fifteen, I may have to graduate [a year early] with the final year students. I can't really say that's going to be a bore. It's for our nation'. She threw herself into the war effort, working even while she was ill. These declarations can be misleading, however, in light of the enduring power of the family. At the end of the Second World War, when the Soviet invasion of Manchuria made Japan's surrender inevitable, Fusako reflected on the early nationalist philosopher Sakura Azumao: 'Sakura once said that "One should offer oneself up to the Emperor out of respect for the parents who brought you into the world", and I had strengthened my resolve. But, deep in my heart, I am secretly wishing to hurry up and be with my mother and father again'. At the very end of the war, on 15 August, she walked over four miles back to her home, woozy from illness and malnutrition, later writing: 'I came back dizzy with exhaustion. It was extremely hot and

I bore a heavy rucksack, so I really struggled walking, [but] I thought: there's really no place like home'.[80]

Conclusion: 'Family Values' under Aerial Bombardment

Despite the incessant propaganda, families usually put their survival ahead of national victory. Consequently, after seeing how the enemy and the state took away their loved ones, families focused on and celebrated survival whenever they could. Having lived through the worst of Coventry's bombings, Mary Bloomfield felt fortunate to have her relatives with her.

We were in very good spirits, in spite of the terrible sights that we had seen. Our homes were intact, our husbands and family were safe. We were so thankful to be still alive, unhurt. The relief was so tremendous, we couldn't be downcast. We were more awe-struck than anything. We were practical women.[81]

For John and Elizabeth, who were separated only by the sprawl of greater London and Kent, the fires following the air raids of September 1940 inspired fear and longing. John referred to the fires' 'lurid glow', which made him worried for Elizabeth. Elizabeth, in turn, found herself worried for John:

On Monday night I was quite sleepless and terrified, with the result that last night, after feeding Charlotte, I fell into bed and slept like a log until 6, waking momentarily when the all-clear went at 4:45. I hope I shall be able to again tonight. I often think of you, my darling, out in a cold trench when I am warm in bed. Please try to sleep there, if it is humanly possible ... I pray that all or none of us may survive this war; but not one or two ...[82]

To rub salt in the wound, some rejected the importance of family over the state to the dismay of their loved ones. Hirai Kiyoshi, a student from Sendai who was attending Tokyo Imperial University, was constantly harangued by his mother to switch from humanities to an applied science programme – particularly one like medicine or agriculture, which would keep him out of the army. 'She's getting increasingly insistent', he wrote in his 1944 diary, 'because I'm her only son whom she raised up and she doesn't want my life thrown away on the battlefield ...' He resisted her entreaties, due to the investment he had put in his education thus far, but 'it was like a madness for her'. Anticipating severe air raids over Sendai, he added:

... she is just earnestly crying and begging me. She argued with me back and forth, looking at the issue from every possible angle, in her effort to persuade. At first she invited me to consider my future after university, and her ideas only concerned the benefits [of such a degree], but now her instincts are telling her that the war is after her son's blood. Surely, she's foreseeing 'death' in my future ... In her heart she's crying and praying, but on the surface she just smiles patiently, and I have to face my mother's sad face and plaintive cries ... Mother, I know how you feel. But this era and what we have been taught cannot permit me to heed your words. Please forgive me, I am a bad son.[83]

Unfortunately, Kiyoshi was killed in an air raid shortly thereafter, confirming his mother's worst fears. The loss of family was so devastating that it permanently changed lives and outlook at the same time. In Hull, Rita Daniel, then 12 years old, recounted how her family had allowed their vigilance to lapse as repeated air raid warnings were followed by no attacks. Then, when the bombing began, they ran to the shelter with pillows over their heads, wearing only nightclothes and carrying no provisions.

The screaming noise of the bombs as they fell, the noise becoming deafening as they got nearer, suddenly one was covered in rubble with dust choking you. Gerald [brother, aged 16] had been blown clear and began recusing us; he got Margaret [sister, aged 6] out first and then me. I stood on the pavement and a flash lit up where he had put Margaret on the other side of the road, got her to our side (where the shelter was) and then he managed to get the rest of the family out ... The building nearby was a brewery and we huddled in there, kneeling among the hops with Mum's head on my knee.

Her mother complained of having no feelings in her legs. All around them, rats ran among the hops and Rita worried about someone trampling her now disabled mother. She began to sing the hymn 'Abide with Me' to calm her mother, changing the lyrics to 'Abide with Us', when she heard her father, normally a calm and polite man, growl, 'You German bastards'. After the ambulance came and collected them, her mother died in the hospital and the family was separated. 'We had a houseboat on Hessle foreshore where we went to live', she wrote, 'vowing never to sleep in a building with bricks and mortar again'.[84] The war and its demands broke apart, reconstructed, and reinforced the family, leaving a legacy that is difficult to comprehend.

For the most part, the war reoriented the values of that generation in ways that are alien to us today. The citizens of the city in the Second World War watched the enemy massacre entire families, and those that emerged were much less likely to put career or politics above relations; in both Britain and Japan, the families that survived the war built welfare states and social democracies that were the envy of the world. For those of us who had grandparents from that generation, their (sometimes parsimonious) personal practicality, on the one hand, and unstinting generosity for family members, on the other, is much easier to grasp when we understand what total war had done to them. Olive Metcalfe, who had to endure the destruction of Hull while separated from her husband and pregnant with her first baby, was so poor that she spent her rent money on timber to make shelves for children's clothes and 'necessities'. Complaining that nappies were 'dear items', she made her own cot and pram and even used her husband's waterproof cloak as floor cover when bathing the baby. She went for days without bathing, due to a lack of money for coal in the winter of 1940–1941, and was dangerously underfed at the start of her pregnancy, causing her to feel faint and ill. Ruefully considering her options, and rapidly declining cash reserves, Olive then wrote to her husband: 'It has just occurred to me how much we shall love this youngster when it is finally ours. The greater one's struggle, the more personal one's affection, no less yours than mine'.[85]

★

Our diarists often felt the pang of family loss. Sometimes, the story of wartime families has a happy ending such as Fusako's, but often the people of the city had to accept that their loved ones were sacrificed for 'victory'. In the long aftermath of the war, many children would live without their fathers and mothers, sometimes starving or suffering abuse in the early post-war period due to a lack of adult protection. Sisters lost brothers, sons lost mothers, wives lost husbands, and mothers lost daughters in the total war against non-combatants. When students were pulled out of university to serve on the front, Takahashi Aiko overheard one young man on a train remark bitterly, 'So, they used to say a man's life numbers fifty years, but it looks like ours will be just twenty-five'.[86]

For our diarists, the annihilation of family often went hand in hand with the systematic destruction of the city piece by piece. Young people, such as teenagers Kenneth Holmes and Inohara Mitsuko, were still fledglings from their parents' nests, either living at home or alternating between staying with family and striking out on their own. Kenneth sought his family immediately following the horrifying attacks of German V2 rockets on Kensington.

Today I witnessed the nearest escape I have so far had, once again I thanked God that my family and myself were untouched though a little shaken ... It was about 5:15pm and I was slowly strolling down the road, passing a street shelter when I saw a vivid flash just above me. Thinking it was lightning, as it was raining, I took no notice, but immediately after there was a tremendous explosion, followed by the sound of breaking glass. I at once threw myself against the shelter (or was I blown?) and covered my neck and face the best I could with my hands. At the moment I thought the end of the world had come. The earth trembled, the very air seemed to vibrate, my ears seemed to be deafened, and a buzzing sound was passing through them. I cannot adequately describe my feelings, I thought I was accustomed to hearing 'bangs' and 'explosions', but never have I heard such a deafening sound, and it is surprising what one's ears can receive and remain normal ... I was only a few yards from my home but I covered the distance in record time to see if my family were safe. I found my Mother and Father quite safe, and Dad busy inspecting the damage and though no words were said to the effect, I sensed by the look on my Mother's face her relief that at least I too was safe.[87]

A short time later, but thousands of miles away, Mitsuko was seized by the same fears. She was safe in a dormitory for young conscript labourers in Itami, but Osaka was visible from the factory. As the Allied bombing campaign systematically burned large portions of her home city to the ground (with civilians trapped inside), she was filled with fear and dread:

At half past eleven, the sirens rang low over Osaka. Then, I could hear a loud rumbling noise, and our neighbourhood sirens gave the warning as well. I thought, 'here it comes'. After two or three warning sirens, they signalled the arrival of a huge squadron of bombers. We were already hiding in our assigned bunker. We couldn't help but shake and shiver all over. We were slowly freezing, going numb, but trying to shake life back into our legs.

Anti-aircraft guns started blasting non-stop. Occasionally the sky would light up suddenly from what were obviously incendiary bombs. The enemy planes came in droves. I was so, so tired, but I couldn't sleep. When I could, I would just nod off for a moment, and then snap awake. Everyone kept saying, 'The sky is red! The sky is red!' At two thirty in the morning, I went to relieve myself. I was shocked. The entire sky was red. I bet Osaka is in a sea of flame. I began to worry about my parents at home. Then, it started to rain. Was it a blessing from heaven, coming to suppress these fires? ... The next day we learned that Osaka's Ten'ōji and Nishinari Wards were utterly destroyed. After breakfast, I went back to bed, but I couldn't sleep. I have no energy, not until I know my family is safe.[88]

For those who remained at home in the cities, however, the end result was hardly much of an improvement. As fires, rockets, and bombs tore Britain and Japan's urban spaces apart, there was nothing left to call 'home'. Aiko recorded in her diary the bitter moment when her family barely saved their house, only to watch others be utterly destroyed.

The incendiary bombs break apart before your eyes, spewing forth fire. We soaked everything in the house with water. In spite of pouring water on our clothes, at some point they dried out. While carrying more water, my husband said in a high-pitched voice, 'It's no use. Go on, just look at the house'. The neighbourhood association alarm bell was ringing wildly. Suddenly, someone was running around shouting that someone's house in the neighbourhood was on fire, and everyone should all get our buckets in hand ... That our own house was saved was truly like a dream. Just a few houses away, countless incendiary bombs had fallen and through the fire-fighting efforts they were just barely saved. When it was all over, I looked around the neighbourhood and our house was at the centre of a block that, as if drawn straight on a map with a compass, had been [the only one] spared by the flames.[89]

The assault on the city was therefore not just a crude, impersonal destruction of property, like a child kicking down a sand castle. The war pulled our diarists away from their loved ones, destroyed their homes, and tore apart the bonds and conduits that linked a human community together. The sense of isolation and anxiety that suffuses many of the diary accounts demands a closer look at the emotions that the diarists tried to put into words. Even the most level-headed narrator surrendered to strong feelings under such conditions. It should come as no surprise, then, that being targeted by the enemy led directly to irrationality, and extreme behaviour that would have rarely occurred during peacetime.

2   The Muses of War: Terror, Anger, and Faith

War inspires strong emotions, even before a single shot is fired or a bomb is dropped. The psychological problem of mass fear troubled government planners, and it is easy to see why when we look at how our diarists responded to the beginning of the Second World War. In Liverpool, news of war made Dorothy Hughes' entire neighbourhood turn dark, both figuratively and literally:

Heard rumours of outbreak of hostilities. Everyone in the office is stunned, even people who have been very cheerful up until now. Several look as if they are ready to collapse at any moment. Trains interfered with owing to evacuation ... Tried to reassure my mother, although feeling very downhearted. Ashamed at my miserable face, but everyone is the same. No work done at the office. Everyone talking to everyone else. Black out at night ... Dog had a fit. Seems to know things not as they should be ... Someone walking up and down the road all night. Dog barked and had to go down to him.[1]

In September of 1939, Dorothy recorded multiple conversations, into which she engaged or eavesdropped; city residents seemed unsure whether evacuation was necessary, how seriously to take German radio broadcasts, or even how long the war would last. Meanwhile, the state continued to stir confusion and fear by demanding mobilisation at the largest possible level without commenting on future actions: citizens were asked to black out windows and carry out air raid drills, but should the citizens of Liverpool expect to be bombed or not? Some citizens were putting up brown paper in their windows and wearing gas masks while others went about their business nonchalantly. Everything was confusing and unknown.

When air attacks began on British and Japanese cities, panic preceded every other response. The first attack on Japan was the (largely symbolic) 18 April 1942 Doolittle Raid over Tokyo, which Takahashi Aiko experienced directly. She heard anti-aircraft guns blasting away, sending civilians running and shouting into the streets of the capital – 'What's happening? What was that?' The loud blasts and lack of warning were shocking and, with a sense of foreboding, she realised that 'from the sky [the enemy] could fire on you easily, and those on the ground would have nowhere to run or hide'.[2] As the bombings continued unabated, consternation was exacerbated by physical duress, including sleep deprivation and exposure to the elements. Sitting in a chair all night and freezing in her shelter, Dora Mockett complained in her diary about Hull's relentless air raids:

Had a very tiring time last night. Planes kept coming over and the guns had a shot at them. Were in our shelter quite a while on and off . . . Went in our chairs about 2am but could not rest much as they were knocking about. There was a lull between 3 or 4 so risked it and went to bed – we were so very cold. All-clear went 4:50am and we were able to turn over and go to sleep for an hour or so. Mary and I had lunch at the Co-op but were too tired to enjoy it . . .[3]

Following fear came exhaustion, hunger, and cold, becoming a two-front assault on mind and body; for civilians who had no experience of warfare, it became impossible to remain cool and collected under fire.

While diarists like Dora and Aiko captured the sense of despondency and fear that aerial bombardment usually created, teenage schoolboy Kojima Yoshitaka reacted with rage. Yoshitaka was incensed that Allied bombers were able to strike his home city of Nagoya so easily:

13 December 1944: today a terrible thing happened: air raid, Nagoya was bombed by a huge sortie of B-29s. We saw it from the air raid shelter. Those bastards fly around, leaving trails of engine exhaust behind them, completely carefree. The anti-aircraft really fired on them, but they were already too far away . . . Our home was directly under attack.[4]

Calling them 'bastards' and 'American demons', Yoshitaka could hardly contain his anger as he witnessed one air raid after another, feeling increasingly powerless. Caught in the catastrophic firebombing of Tokyo in 1945, Aiko also used her writing talents to explain how helplessness, fear, and fury could come closely packed together. 'I thought that the next raid would destroy our home', she wrote, 'but during this one, which [continued] from midnight to dawn, I was completely shocked'. It is probably impossible for us to imagine, today, the horror we would experience if enemy aircraft ceaselessly firebombed our homes for several hours, facing little or no resistance. Aiko was nevertheless lucky: her home was on a hillside opposite of the area that had been targeted by Allied bombers. The Meguro River stopped the spread of flames near her home when they reached the adjacent valley – which was transformed, in her words, into a 'sea of fire'.

Refugees were coming up the hill, one by one, in front of our house. I could hear a 'shush, shush, shush' sound, which I thought to be incendiary bombs, and then I could see fire pluming up from the ground in a large, wide area. Should I say it was tragic (*seisō*)? Should I say it was a fierce battle (*shōzetsu*)? Even in this world, wherein men struggle with one another, it is not the sort of thing that should be done. It terrified me to the point of revulsion.[5]

The immediate threat of death inspired our diarists to keep records of their emotions, which in turn affected the way they composed their personal stories. Many became episodic, focusing on fleeting sights, sounds, and smells, eschewing coherent narratives for flash portraits of chaos. This chaos caused their previously calm diary accounts to be disrupted, and subsequently they embraced more emotional responses. Some also turned to faith, begging the heavens for guidance and hoping that some supernatural force might intercede on their behalf. When Mitsuko heard that Itami, where her workmates were living, had been bombed, she simply turned her face upwards and began pleading: 'How is the dormitory? Is everyone safe? Oh, I'm so worried! Please, I beg you, let everyone be safe'.[6] Helplessness drove many to prayer or simple pleading, as if they were trying to cast spells against fate, or gamblers begging fecklessly with a slot machine.

Yoshitaka moved through dark city streets of Nagoya while the air raid sirens rang out, complaining bitterly about blackouts and poor city services. Thinking of all of his school friends who had graduated, moved away, or been mobilised, Yoshitaka wrote how his 'heart [was] wild with emotion'. The war created an extreme environment, wherein the rationally-planned course of one's life could be wiped out unexpectedly from above like a deadly bolt of lightning from a wrathful deity. In such conditions, ordinary people like Yoshitaka turned to the sky and begged for guidance, justice, and deliverance:

What will the New Year [1945] bring? Death by air raid, Japan's victory? The end of the twisting path ahead was unclear. What sort of future will next year bring? So many trials ahead of us … oh god, please save us.[7]

Terror, Anger, and Faith: Feeling the City under Attack

A. E. Randall, an Auxiliary Fire Serviceman in Liverpool, composed one of the most detailed contemporary accounts of an air raid available. From 1.45pm to 1.45am, 3–4 May 1941, he kept minute records of everything he saw and felt during the attack on the Merseyside docks. At first, he was paralysed by the sight of the planes, staring up with his mouth agape, 'wondering if there's a heavy one on the way'. He ran upstairs to warn his wife, writing in his logbook that the sky 'seemed full of throbbing planes now with occasional rushing about or our questing night-fighters'. He lit a cigarette 'to steady my nerves', and then: 'There it is! The distant detonation of heavy bombs. On my left too – docks! I wonder? One, two, three, four, five, six distinct explosions and – yes – a blinding flash – no mistaking that – a land mine!' He watched anxiously, scribbling down details whenever he could, comparing the colour of incendiaries to that of a bluish-white welding flame. His mind then raced through all of the people he worried about – his wife, his brother – but the sound of the approaching bombers was sending him into a panic.

It's this damn, insistent, menacing, rhythmic drone of the Nazi bombers coming nearer and nearer (for all the world, as if they were looking for you) that gets me. Rather unnerving ... seems to be an unbelievable time reaching you, its engines throbbing out that (there's no other words for it) one-for-you; one-for-you, one-for-you – It can be heard even about the loudest barrages, above the roar of huge fires too, when we're working on them.

Although he was a teetotaller, Randall admitted he now carried a flask of rum, which he swigged as the bombers came to his home in Liverpool. A blast from a mine then shattered all the windows in his neighbourhood and he hit the floor. 'I got up off my knees and ran out unsteadily', he wrote, 'an awful fear gripping me, till I saw my house still standing though doors and window frames gone. ... Once "stuff" starts falling in your own locality it makes you jumpy, and once jumpy, you stay jumpy'.[8] Randall's account is not a coherent tale with a recognisable beginning, middle, and end, but a disorganised record of the vicissitudes of a citizen's experiences at the mercy of enemy bombers. Drinking his rum, running on shaky legs, and worrying about his wife, Randall's record is a snapshot of the emotional rollercoaster that the citizens in urban Britain and Japan had to endure.

The bombing war was an attack on urban citizens that was largely new to human history, producing many strange effects and experiences; even though Hull had been briefly bombed in the First World War and there were dramatic depictions of bombing in Shanghai (1932, 1937), Guernica (1937), and Poland (1939), very few citizens in Britain or Japan had any real notion of what systematic targeting of civilians would be like. The battlefield was still in foreign territory, but in an age of total war the enemy's targets would henceforth include non-combatants at home; in both Japan and Britain, this could be baffling to ordinary people, who were more accustomed to the idea of adult male soldiers facing the threat of death in some far-flung 'no man's land'. Consequently, they were unprepared for the sudden onslaught that transformed their hometowns overnight. In East London, rescue worker Bill Regan watched his friend Eddie move to enter a house when a bomb blast blew the front door completely away, leaving him holding only the latch. Eddie stood in shock and remarked, 'It blew out of me hand', and Bill recorded that 'he sounded offended'. Wandering around the remains of their working-class neighbourhood, Regan and his friends saw corpse-like survivors sleeping on piles of brick, people hiding in shelters buried under rubble, and 'colonies of cats' running feral in the ruins.[9] Japanese civilians were also disorientated by strange sights and sounds, scrambling through the city in fear and horror. Describing the firebombing of Hachiōji, house-wife Miyada Katsuyo vividly recalled voices calling out names, 'the horrible "boom, boom" noises throughout the night', and, when the fires took over the sky, her 1-year-old daughter opened her eyes, looked at the sky, and suddenly shouted 'It's all red!'[10] Those who survived one air attack could still be vulnerable to shock from another as planes could appear without warning and attack quickly. Gwendoline Matthews, who recorded the November 1940 destruction of Coventry, described how more bombs in April 1941 took residents completely by surprise: 'Sud-denly, very close to us, a large bomb exploded. No one knew it was there and it killed four people. We turned and ran and were very fortunate as I was only hit in the back by flying rubble'.[11] In place of familiar city landscapes and daily rhythms, the bombing war created a surreal envir-onment, replete with alien sensory experiences that were in turn mes-merising and terrifying.

Citizens of the city described their first experience of air attacks in simple terms, often pairing records of physical sensations with surprising psychological and emotional responses. I. S. Haslewood, a London rescue driver, noted that her squad leader sometimes broke down and began muttering that he would not go out into the inferno. Refugees were at first cheerful and chatty, but 'of course reaction sets in later, and it was piteous to see these poor brave creatures break down and cry and shiver'. Rescue workers were soaked to the bone due to assisting firemen with hoses in the streets, and thus began running around the depot in heavy underwear. Haslewood noted that she was assaulted by her own terrors, to the extent that 'my hands were shaking so much I was fumbling wildly with the ignition key, while I could barely keep my foot on the acceler-ator'.[12] A taxi driver caught in the May 1941 attacks on Hull also described the melange of extreme emotions that ran through his mind:

The sounds of bombers throbbing overhead, the glare of flares, the banging of anti-aircraft guns, and the whine and detonations of bombs as they struck and shook the earth, followed by the clatter of falling masonry and slates, whizzing bits of shrapnel and the shattering of glass filled the night for hours. It was very nerve-wracking and frightening. But there was also a sense, at least for me, of frustration and impotence at not being able to do anything about it, but just to hope to keep clear of injury.[13]

British and Japanese citizens also struggled with the fact that the techniques and technologies of war had changed, turning cities into nightmarish landscapes. As a sixth-grade schoolboy, Yoshida Takeshi witnessed the eerie new effects of mass aerial bombing:

The bodies I saw [in one neighbourhood] were not burned. The clothes had been blown off by wind from the bombs, but their skin had not been burned. I thought they looked like dolls. In [another neighbourhood], the corpses were totally black. They didn't look like people – more like figures sculpted from ash. The internal organs, however, came bursting from inside the ash raw and bloody.[14]

Strange and macabre scenes left deep impressions on residents, whose urban habitat was being gutted before their eyes. In east London, Bill Regan responded to a call to the Saundersness School, where a high explosive or parachute mine had annihilated the building and its residents:

What a bloody mess, the whole guts blown away, only the two end flanks standing. There were more than forty people stationed here. I only saw one survivor, the gate-keeper, a man who lived in Pier St. and had lost a leg in the [19]14–18 war. He said he saw this parachute coming down, and thought it was a [British] barrage balloon. It was a [German] parachute mine, and he was lucky to be on the opposite side to where it landed, with the building between him and it. He was blasted into the road, but miraculously none of the debris had hit him.[15]

Aerial bombings could be so bad that civilian victims had no idea who was mourning, who was dead, and who had survived. Waiting at a 'safe point' near a bridge leading to Shizuoka, Kogawa Kōtarō described a typically panicked scene:

There were terrible cries coming from two or three places. Were they young girls and boys who had been burned? They sounded like adults, so perhaps they were mothers holding the bodies of their children who had been burned to death. I was absolutely terrified. I searched for the crying voices through a wall of people, in order to ensure that they were not my family members …[16]

Under such conditions, governments in Japan and Britain wanted to avoid discussion of the effects of bombing in the media, but this act of suppression was useless. One Mass Observer in Bristol noted that 'psychologically this town is dominated by Air Raid. About 75% of conversations overheard in the last few days have been concerned either with local air-raids or with the news connected with raids ...'[17] The emotions that seized the people were not only a by-product of the extraordinary circumstances created by the bombs, but also a creature of clumsy government censorship and unbelievable disinformation.

As a consequence of poor knowledge, then, irrational and emotional responses quickly proliferated in response to attacks from the sky. Some city residents responded by trying to control their emotions through the act of writing itself:

Read this when in fear. Planes overhead will not hurt you; a bomb dropped when at the height they usually fly will pitch from 1 to 3 miles away. The effect of such a bomb even at the highest calibre will do no serious damage outside a distance of 100 yards from the spot on which it pitches.[18]

As bombing intensified, urban citizens coached themselves on how best to confront their helpless situation, which included recording reported 'facts', personally-experienced events, baseless rumours, and ineffective prayers. Usually, these efforts had no impact on their ability to survive the war, which was largely controlled by political and military leaders. Nevertheless, ordinary people wrote down the powerful feelings that the war unleashed, and the turn to magical and wishful thinking that they produced.

Bad News Travels Fast: Anxiety and the Illusion of Preparation

Before the attacks came, news of dire international developments created widespread anxiety in Britain and Japan. In wartime the mass media frequently cooperated with the government to assure the public that the war was going their way, and this was true in both 'free' Britain and 'fascist' Japan. Civilians quickly learned, however, that lived experience of area bombing would be radically different. A teenage labourer in a Hull confectionary, Hilda Ward remembered how, on her way home from work, she and her friend were suddenly caught in a raid, dove into a nearby hedgerow, and shielded themselves with rubbish bin lids.[19] If the enemy was hitting us in our back garden, citizens asked, why should anyone believe the government's rose-tinted view of the war effort? This kind of thinking resulted in citizens' reliance on their 'common sense', baseless rumours, and a kind of survivalist mentality.

While the state preached calm, there were plenty of reasons for ordinary people to believe that things were actually going to deteriorate quickly. First, British and Japanese citizens knew about mass bombing campaigns from news reports of prior conflicts in Spain (1937), China

(1937), and Poland (1939). This did not require access to any form of privileged information; in fact, when the raids began to level the cities, working-class citizens like Bill Regan noted that the cityscape was 're-arranged, and beginning to look like Spain and Poland', showing just how deep the image of total war had penetrated the popular consciousness.[20] Second, air raid patrols, fire watch brigades, and various pamphlets about bombing had been organised before the war began in both countries, so citizens had some inkling of how bad things might get. Third, urban residents were able to connect news reports of battles abroad with consequences back home. For the British, the 1939 Non-Aggression Pact between the Soviet Union and Germany was an ominous development, as Coventry resident Mary Bloomfield recalled, because the government launched civilian mobilisation immediately afterward: 'The first intimation that I had of the seriousness of it was on the evening of Aug 24 [1939] when a van from Hansons with a loudspeaker attached, drove slowly up the street calling up all Anti-Aircraft Reservists'. In the same way, many Japanese citizens suspected that the bombings would intensify as Allied forces came closer to the home islands. In 1944, after the fall of Saipan, Aiko described how 'as [the Allies] occupy one point after another, like a stone skipping over a pond, step by step it triggers an inescapable feeling of unease . . .'[21] Less proximal international events translated into threat at home, as well: in 1945, after hearing of Germany's surrender, even a schoolboy like Kojima Yoshitaka had enough awareness of political information and rumour to be fearful: 'After Hitler's suicide, [Germany] was a mess. They're talking about producing 80,000 kamikazes. We're seeing a lot more B-29s and the counter-attacks are growing in number. Things are about to get a lot worse'.[22] Londoners felt invasion to be imminent, as well, spreading rumours that 'thousands upon thousands of dead German bodies have glutted our South and East Coasts. That in Yarmouth alone they made one public grave for 400 Germans. That our Navy rammed and sank all the heavily laden invasion barges on one occasion, and so on'.[23] In hindsight these fears seem baseless, but the situation in wartime arguably warranted the concern that foreign enemies were at one's doorstep, and the government had already discredited itself, especially in regional cities. The situation in Japan deteriorated so badly that the wartime state monitored public sentiments about the course of the war, and the British Ministry of Information even organised an 'Anti-Lie' office to combat errors in public discourse.[24] Regardless of what authorities might say, ordinary people were intelligent enough to understand that, as the enemy grew closer, the 'home front' was quickly to become the 'battlefront'.

Indeed, the state's attempts to quiet fear through dissimulation only heightened civilian anxiety, and so citizens responded by indulging in irresponsible talk. In Britain and Japan, unsubstantiated rumours ran wild, including potential invasion, traitors behind the lines, and imminent bombings – some of which were stirred up by foreign press, both in allied and enemy nations.[25] In Hull, a friend of Olive Metcalfe claimed to have had a run-in with a 'Fifth Columnist' in Sutton; riding a new bicycle with a black box mounted on it, her husband was convinced the old man was carrying flares to guide enemy bombers.[26] One evacuated schoolboy in Yorkshire was alarmed to discover that, in their attempt to smoke out a rabbit from an oak hollow, he and his mates had inadvertently set fire to the tree, which was subsequently mistaken by the Fire Brigade to be a 'beacon to guide planes to [the] East Moor Bomber Station'.[27] In Japan, information seemed to pass from defence forces through relatives into the neighbourhood associations, at which point 'word got out' (*fure ga tonarigumi kara atta*) that an enemy air raid was coming. Ordinary people were sometimes incredulous: housewife Senuma Yukiko could only 'half-believe' these sorts of rumours, and simply went to bed without making preparations.[28] Still, the atmosphere was worsening. Racially and nationally-charged beliefs about rape and war circulated vigorously around the rumour mill, with many convinced, like Sakai Jun's father, that should the nation lose the war, 'the ones who will suffer the most will be women'.[29] Mary Bloomfield wrote in her diary of 'quislings' drafted in Norway, who were supposedly disguised as clergymen and air-dropped into Britain: 'Those who opposed them were gunned down', she wrote, 'even little children'. Working as a hairdresser in Coventry, Mary heard all sorts of irresponsible claims that local women passed around:

I had to walk round and see my friend Vinnie Higgett who had had an internal operation and was unable to get out of bed. We wondered what would happen to her and others in the same state. Women were particularly afraid as we heard that if you were young, healthy, and able to conceive you might be shipped to Germany to a 'Baby farm' to be mated with Germans … We all decided we ought to have a pile of hand grenades in the bedroom near the windows in case the Germans and their tanks came up our street. I didn't want to be machine gunned so I thought out the idea of putting perchlorate of sulphur – we used it to kill clubroot – into my water softener and offer any Germans who came near a cup of tea. Luckily I was never driven to this.

The rumour-mongering that British and Japanese citizens embraced was a reflection of their loss of faith in the information provided by the state and its allies in the mass media, but also the general terror that mass bombings created. No government could hope to control this phenomenon, even with nearly unlimited resources. Mary concluded, 'Fear and horror began to take a grip on us'.[30] To add to the terror of bombing from the air, in Britain and Japan, the possibility of invasion also felt real. On 8 October 1939, the British government called for a 'Home Guard' to be formed by those ineligible for the draft (usually due to age). 'Dad's Army' ex-servicemen were 'mostly battle-hardened and of course they had beaten the Germans 20 years before', but they did not fully inspire confidence in a populace that was feeling increasingly vulnerable.[31] Rumours and mobilisation campaigns were followed by false alarms of air raids that heightened the sense of anxiety and danger in the city.

The atmosphere in the city was already odd due to the rumours, reported developments abroad, and government misinformation, but this strange mood was exacerbated by skirmishes at the edges of the city as invading and defending air forces attempted to achieve superiority – particularly when citizens witnessed these exchanges first-hand. Gwladys Cox heard the sirens and, from her top-floor flat, gazed on the empty streets in the north London neighbourhood Hampstead, near Camden Town. Her diary entry captured the strange calm that preceded the raids on Britain's capital city:

A single white butterfly is fluttering down West End Lane, alone in his glory. It is amusing to see, and hear, the lady shelter warden, now more important than ever, in rig-out of trousers, etc., plus a tin hat. She is ... blowing her whistle hell-for-leather, adding terror to the scuttle-for-safety. To the East, we see puffs of grey smoke hanging about the balloons; then six planes, presumably British, sprinting across the sky, right over us, to the East. Mr. B.S., who seems to be sheltering in a first-floor flat opposite, waves cheerily up to us.[32]

In 1942, urban citizens in Japan were only just beginning to realise that the home islands were going to be directly attacked. Tsuyuki Isao described the odd scene he witnessed in Tokyo, where residents were still unable to distinguish Japanese and enemy aircraft; while at the beach, he even waved cheerfully up at what later turned out to be an American fighter plane during the Doolittle raid. 'It was a mad time', he wrote, 'and it felt like things were going to a whole new level'.[33] Worse still, residents in places like Coventry had to hear about or even directly witness nearby cities, such as Birmingham, get bombed first, and residents in Hull had to suffer repeated false alarms as bombers repeatedly flew over them from and to other targets in Britain. Random bomb and mine explosions following minor air raids heightened fears across these cities.[34] Because bombers initially attacked production centres, factory workers sometimes found themselves suddenly thrust into chaotic scenes where co-workers were covered in blood, windows were shattered, and they found themselves semi-conscious after being thrown across the work floor. Civilians outside the factories might still be in denial; as Sugaya Sumi put it, 'People on the street looked at the medics carrying me, covered in blood, thought *What the hell?* and stared in shock and terror'.[35] Tension was rising, particularly as children were evacuated; arguments erupted between family members and fights broke out in public areas.[36]

Urban citizens began preparing for the worst, regardless of what the government and the mass media happened to be saying. Furthermore, the survivors of air raids had very few reasons to thank their government's armed forces – once the bombers got through, they were largely on their own. Homeowners were ordered to reinforce roofs, tape up glass windows, store drinking water, and strictly observe blackouts, as even 'the slightest chink could give some clues to enemy planes'.[37] In Britain, many built 'Anderson Shelters', which were little more than thin pieces of concave metal half-buried in back gardens; others converted cellars into shelters, complete with bedding, china, books, food, and games.[38] Messages from the state were contradictory: the war would be won, but prepare for the worst. In Kure, Japan, housewife Andō Toyoko knew that inadequate preparation was tantamount to suicide, precisely because the state had been saying so for some time:

We were told that, when the firebombs came, 'You must protect your own home!' We had all studied how to set and bind broken limbs, as well as gathering the neighbourhood watch (*rinbohan*) in the courtyard and running [fire] drills by throwing water on pine trees. Once we decided to dig out a shelter, it was only the women who got down and dug out all the granite soil (*masado*) in the mountain with pick-axes. We had no physical strength – it was all spirit (*ki*) – so we couldn't dig very well.[39]

Olive Metcalfe assuaged her husband's fears that they were unprepared for aerial attacks in a letter written after the air raids began, but just before the bombing of Hull: 'Bucket of water at front, bucket of earth inside, long-handled shovel (brush shank in the fire shovel) and hose ready (mended again this time with old typewriter ribbon) to fix on tap'.[40] Like his British counterparts, rail worker Kaneyama Misao read the bad news of enemy advances in the Pacific and 'had a really bad feeling about it' (*iya na yokan ga suru*). Writing, 'Right! I must get ready then', Misao rolled up a futon so that he could take it with him at a moment's notice. He also packed his travel essentials and some food into a rucksack. He then readied his boots, overcoat, railway employee uniform, pocket watch, and iron helmet, and put water in a fire-fighting bucket.[41] Other families thoroughly drilled themselves to be ready for the worst. Laurie Latchford described how a well-prepared family got ready for a potential air raid in Swansea:

We had tea, then Essie prepared the shelter. The table was pushed into the corner of the internal walls of the kitchen, a mattress was slid on top, rugs, cushions, a First Aid Kit, water, toys and paper and pencil for Sylvia, and asthma powder for Essie, and finally the gas boiler was pushed against one exposed side, and blankets were hung over the other.[42]

As part of the effort to build the 'Greater East Asia Co-Prosperity Sphere' against the 'West', Filipino constabulary trainee Leocadio de Asis was surprised by Japanese residents' organisation of bombing and fire prevention activities, noting in his diary that he 'was impressed by the seriousness and interest with which the members [of the local Neighbourhood Association] performed the drill (unlike our neighbourhood associations in the [Philippines] whose members do not seem to take it seriously)'.[43] Still, many individuals were not prepared for air raids, grabbing only the most important items: their handbags (with purses and cash), ration books, ID cards, insurance policies, and gas masks.[44] Having moved from Kobe to Aomori to avoid air raids, Ikebe Toshiaki's parents were dismayed to learn that they were in danger in the Northeast as well, but pulled together what they could:

My auntie had heard that leaflets were dropped by Allied planes warning of cities to be bombed, and they included Aomori and Hakodate, so we prepared rucksacks for rapid flight, including enough rice one could carry, miso paste, salt, etc., clothing, air raid caps, baskets instead of metal helmets, and an iron cooking pot.[45]

No matter what preparations individuals may have made, the bombing would affect them all. In any case, urban citizens' scramble to assemble pots, pans, hats, clothes, money, paperwork, food, and other essential items demonstrates just how little stock they put in government assurances that the armed forces would protect them.

As German and US forces drew closer and closer to the islands of Britain and Japan, the psychological atmosphere of the city became increasingly strained, and citizens feared for the fate of their beloved cities. Yoshitake Teruyoshi was working in Nagasaki when he heard of a raid over his home town, Hakata: 'Suddenly, the radio broadcast cut with a "pfft" sound', he wrote, 'and fear began spreading: what happened to Hakata?'[46] While citizens had mixed feelings about their government, they certainly embraced the city as an object of attachment and affection. At the end of 1940, a volunteer driver for rescue squads (part of Civil Defence) reflected on the beginning of the attacks on London:

At night, the searchlights are a blazing design of white streaks in the dark blue sky. In the daytime there are constant warnings, but no one takes much notice of them; certainly no one attempts to take cover ... The wonders of London at night under these conditions are fantastic. There is hardly a car on the roads, and the whole place is lit up with myriads of searchlights crossing and re-crossing in ghostly silence. ... A slight chill crept over me, as I realized how very much I loved my London. An apprehension of what was to come ... The atmosphere was tense with expectation.[47]

Love for the capital city was matched by those who embraced urban spaces elsewhere. Watching fires burn over her home town, Dorothy Hughes wrote, 'Everyone saying: where will it all end? Poor old Liverpool'.[48] The amorous relationship with urban space was also an abusive one, however: the more the wartime city drew the citizens toward it, the more they would experience devastating violence.

Because enemy aircraft targeted civilians who contributed the most to the war effort, it should be unsurprising that the working class in Britain and Japan was the first to suffer enemy bombardment. Perhaps because the city was their natural habitat, labourers responded to being bombed with both frustration and heroics. In Takamatsu, station manager Nōso Masaichi described how workers had to endure a constant condition of uncertainty and fear:

In the station I was speaking with the area's fire wardens, and we were saying there might be a raid by 'Yatsuko-san', which is what we called B-29s, but by dusk nothing had happened. At 10pm an air raid warning went off but ... that was hardly unusual at that time ... I don't know, maybe it was just intuition [*mushi ga shirasu*], but I had a premonition [*yokan*] that something was definitely going to happen this time. After 11pm still nothing, so I strolled around the neighbourhood and then went to lie down under the mosquito net. My dreams were shattered by that horrible siren. When I got out the planes were already in the sky over Takamatsu ... It was like getting caught with my trousers down (*kyo o tsukareta*).[49]

The working class had no holiday homes or foreign connections to save them from the bombing, so they were totally committed to survival of their community. These dangerous situations affected men, women, and children indiscriminately, prompting ordinary people to attempt heroics. Citizens like R. W. Cleaver, a lathe operator in Coventry, dove directly into dangerous situations during enemy bombardment:

Shortly after getting home, incendiaries were dropped in the lane, one dropping in the front garden where children were looking out of the window. This caused the children to panic. As I had done before on previous raids, I took an already-prepared bucket of earth to douse it out, but when I got to the incendiary it suddenly exploded, causing singed eyebrows and burns to my leg, shrapnel pierced my trousers.[50]

Sometimes spurious rumour-mongering and local heroics combined with tragic consequences. As one man recalled in Hull, a group chased a German parachute trooper into the city centre when one of the party shouted, 'Bloody run for cover', as it was actually a landmine.[51] Workers wished to be heroic, or at least prepared, in such conditions, but there were limits on what they could do when subjected to bombing from the sky. All of their drilling, preparation, and heroic commitment to their communities could not protect the working class from being a primary target of enemy assault.

City people still looked to the state for guidance on how to best respond to the initial enemy attacks, but bombers quickly rendered the officials' efforts ineffective – particularly in specially-targeted (and weakly-defended) cities such as Coventry and Aomori, where intensive bombing could wipe out an urban core overnight. In Coventry, for example, Joseph Beale and a group of fellow enterprising citizens built their own shelter at the government's insistence, which was complete with sandbags, reinforced timber, a gallon of tar, and six foot, six inch doors made of solid steel cut from a truck bottom. It seemed quite safe but, on the day of the German raids, Beale opened the door to the shelter 'when a landmine went off across the road. It blew the door in and I was hit on the head by the top bolt. ... I got up and felt the blood trickling down. All the doors were blown in'. Suffering a fractured skull, Beale became 'the first casualty from the Blitz' at a hospital in Leamington Spa.[52] Even the febrile shielding that shelters offered, however, could be quite costly, and not all families could afford them. Some had to flee under stairwells inside terraced houses, where 'we always had chairs, candle, torch, a travelling rug ready so we made ourselves as comfortable as possible'.[53] For all of their efforts, the city's residents had a sense that they would not really be able to defend themselves once the bombing began; as a consequence, sound preparation gave way to a kind of unbridled consternation as individuals feared a bomb 'fated for them' was on its way:

I had been driving for about 48 hours really. I was very tired. Other memories of that night. There are too many. I remember thinking, 'Is it my turn', but when it didn't happen, you tended to feel safe. It was an awful feeling really. You never knew whether the next bomb was for you ... I don't remember what I ate that day. I can't remember eating anything.[54]

Similarly, in the remote city of Aomori, on the northernmost tip of Honshū, the main Japanese island, citizens suspected that the fall of

Iwo Jima and the bombing of the northern city of Sendai might portend an imminent attack, so they made some preparations to evacuate family members and locate shelters. Some citizens, like Kōtō Yasuo, were evacuated as schoolchildren with their parents, but then were forced back into the city by officials who threatened to withhold rice rations if the family did not return to work. The 1945 Allied bombing of Aomori wiped the town off the map in a firestorm, creating panic and confusion even among those who felt prepared. The roads leading south, through the suburb of Namidate and towards nearby rural towns such as Nami-kata, were choked with panicked refugees:

The fires started up all over the city centre and everyone knew it was dangerous, so we ran for our lives towards Namidate – it was like being carried by waves of water. On the road, people were screaming and women carrying babies fell down, apparently having injured their legs or feet. No one could help them or speak to them, we all just ran driven mad by fear of death. To this day the image is burned in my brain of people, one after another, running for their lives into the fields.[55]

Despite months, or even years, of drilling and propaganda, preparation proved almost worthless when the air war began in Coventry and Aomori. The relentless bombing emptied the cities of people, animals, and things: one London rescue worker described the aftermath of the bombing as being a stream of desperate people who were 'carrying babies, dogs, cats, and an odd assortment of shapeless bundles'.[56] It did not take long for the residents of Britain and Japan's cities to realise that, despite many proclamations and promises, their safety was not assured and preparation was a weak defence at best.

The Beautiful Hell: Helplessness, Flares, and Sudden Conflagrations

The social history of area bombing is full of stories that express the extraordinary shock people felt when facing this new form of warfare. In Hachiōji, a city just west of Tokyo, Sekiya Tsuneo remembered how his mother was rendered immobile with terror when the bombing began; he had to carry her on his back as the city burned behind them.[57] D. M. Compton's mother decided, in the middle of a Coventry bombing raid, to go home and make tea, but:

... the bombing was too heavy and [she] came back in shock. We lay her on a wooden bench with upturned tin hat for a pillow. Then coming down the stairs of the shelter was Father Thompson from All Saints Church. He was old and white-haired, and carried a lantern. My mother still dazed thought she had gone to heaven.[58]

Besides shock from bomb blasts, the air war brought to Britain and Japan an enthralling spectacle of bright light, heat, trembling, and booming. One of the first sensations citizens recorded at this time was a feeling of helplessness, because the scene was unfolding before their eyes without consultation or consent. Then, the bright lights of flares and bursting fires enthralled people trapped in the cities; as horrifying as the destruction of their homes was, the spectacle was also beautiful.

British and Japanese civilians were severely disorientated because, prior to the Second World War, they had very little or no direct experience of armed conflict at home; the war sometimes resembled a carnival performance, or a holiday fireworks display. First, the air raid sirens warned citizens to take cover, and the streets would empty, creating an atmosphere of theatrical silence. Next, raiders penetrated the silence in order to drive off or draw away defending planes already in the sky; sometimes citizens recorded excitedly watching dogfights. What was happening? Civilians in the city usually knew nothing and were consequently left to speculate. Describing an attack on a train near Hachiōji, Miyazawa Keikichi wrote in his diary:

When my train got to Hino there was a raid and I was shocked for a moment. I was really uneasy because there was no clear information. I thought, if we can make it to the iron bridge across the Tama River we'll be fine. Just when I got to the bridge, I saw five planes out the window that looked like carrier-based fighters flying wildly about in the sky. I thought, is this a dogfight? Are they enemy aircraft, or are they ours? I saw one belching black smoke as it fell over [the nearby airbase at] Tachikawa. I prayed it was an enemy plane.[59]

After the scouting, small-scale raids, and dogfights to establish air superiority, other planes dropped flares to illuminate targets, which cast a strange, unsettling, beautiful, and almost carnivalesque glow over cities that were observing blackouts. Watching a major attack, Dorothy Hughes described a 'terrific fire over Liverpool ... Flares dropping. Red & Green – all colours. Just like day. Grand firework display!'[60] Shopkeeper's wife Iketani Toyoko referred to the visions of fires over Tokyo as a 'beautiful hell' (*utsukushii jigoku*).[61] In London's East End, dock worker Vi Regan asked the bus driver to stop so that she could see the flares falling down near her home on the Isle of Dogs. Her husband, Bill Regan, held her hand tightly, not allowing her off the bus. She looked at the flare burning out on the street and said, to no one in particular, 'Doesn't it look so beautiful, I'd love to have it'.[62] Flares were dropped by Allied raiders over Japanese cities to light up the bombers' targets, just as the Germans had done to Britain. In addition to the initial ignition of incendiary bombs, these devices made the vision of the blacked-out city under attack briefly dazzling. Kure housewife Itoi Sayoko described how the air assaults surprised civilians there:

There was a [general] warning siren, and then an explosion. I was thinking, 'It's not a Japanese plane, but there's no air raid siren', and then the [air raid siren] started wailing. The thought 'air raid!' popped into my head, and then 'BOOM' – a huge, loud noise and everything turned bright. It was a flare. When I looked out from the house, the flares had illuminated the city streets from the shadows, and incendiary bombs were beginning to fall ... all around the street it looked like lamps held up during a lantern parade, with little lights suddenly erupting into big fires.

The danger of the situation quickly alarmed citizens like Sayoko: suddenly panicked, she grabbed whatever she could and fled into the hills, carrying her 80-year-old grandmother on her back.[63] Although it is hard to imagine today, the lights, sounds, and general spectacle of mass bombing were morbidly fascinating to city people: in her diary, I. S. Haslewood described the eerie glows that illuminated London's skies as the Surrey docks burned:

It was dark when we started to go home, and the dull red glow had flared to a flaming orange smeared with black smoke ... Yes, it made one pause to think. To think very deeply – very solemnly. Planes were droning overhead, and we could see the red, green and white lights. We could see the [anti-aircraft] gun shells bursting near their tails – always near, but never quite near enough. The buses were crowded with excited speculating people ... The noise increased to a deafening bombardment. For the first time I heard bombs whistling down in the distance, and roaring down nearer to, while the guns barked out their defiance. My room was lit up by the hideous orange glare and the ever-ghostly searchlights. I was immensely thrilled and interested – not at all frightened, and spent most of my time hanging out of my window.[64]

In both Britain and Japan, then, mass bombing began as an almost preternaturally beautiful experience. The lights, colours, and sounds of the first stage of attack commanded the attention of the people, who certainly suspected it preceded violent assault, but were momentarily seduced by its deceptively festive pyrotechnics.

After the flares and initial bursts of incendiaries, the sights, sounds, and smells of the mass bombing of the city became quickly menacing, and fascination transformed into fear. When the attack on London began during the second week of September 1940, Gwladys Cox, a housewife in her sixties, was overwhelmed by sensory experiences triggered by this new form of modern warfare:

When the sirens wailed, almost immediately, we heard the nearest and most intense gunfire yet. From the windows, we saw, again to the East, large fires and as we gazed, holding our breath, swift stabs of flame shot down from the sky in quick succession. Every stab sent up a vivid flash of flame, while, already, a high wall of pure, lightening-coloured fire glowed for miles along the Eastern horizon. The rest of London was aflame with searchlights, bursting shells, floating flares and the snaking radiance of Molotov bread baskets [incendiaries] – and the noise! Booms, bangs, pops, crashes, screams, warden's whistles ... while below, in the inky street, the traffic crawled, dim-lit, ghost-like ... I gasped, shut the window and suddenly felt we should no longer remain in the flat.[65]

During the bombardment, enemy fighter aircraft would suddenly appear in the skies, machine-gunning citizens running on the roads, crouched in streetcars, and trapped in moving trains. The screams of locals echoed through the streets, mixing with the din of panicked shouts from air raid patrolmen and fire wardens. Citizens in populous areas like Tokyo's Shibuya Ward, including young people such as 16-year-old student Koide Keiko, emerged into streets filled with fearful neighbours and consternated refugees.

Burning embers mixed with a powerful wind from the south, and there was a funnel-like cloud of black smoke. This was different than the 'fire' of 10 March [1945]; this time, when we got to a [neighbourhood] Shintō shrine there was a huge flame ... There were old people with kids on push carts, and the desperate faces of the mothers on the road who screamed at their children were terrifying ...[66]

Watching fire spread from one area of the city to another, urban residents scrambled to find some sort of protection from the attack. Close behind, fire devoured the city like a hungry serpent weaving through the streets. Within her air raid shelter, Gladys Hollingsworth described the beginning of the bombing that destroyed Coventry:

It was a marvellous night, brilliant moonlight and cloudless sky. The next thing we saw through a small crack to our shelter soon were scores of flares dropped by the raiders. They were like huge stars hanging to the sky to light the city. [The next thing we] heard was the loud whistling and explosions as bombs together with flashes and reports from our ground defences. We crushed down to the bottom of our shelter, straining our ears to make certain no small firebombs dropped on our house. Thousands of fire bombs showered all over our beautiful city.[67]

In diaries, memoirs, and paintings of enemy bombers over the cities of Britain and Japan, authors and artists depicted residents alternately marvelling and screaming at the planes, lights, and fires as the systematic destruction of the city began in earnest. Takahashi Yoshiji recalled staring at the flares illuminating the sky – 'brighter than the day', so bright 'you could see a pin dropping in the night' – and then suddenly called out in a loud voice, 'We're going to die tonight'. When the bombs hit, he wrote that 'this was the first time I noticed how beautiful the incendiaries were – so much so that it overcame the horror, as they showered down like rain on Chiba. I can never forget this scene'.[68] The fires and explosions combined spectacle and terror like nothing city residents had ever seen before. The annihilation of the city was so far beyond ordinary citizens' comprehension, they could only watch, flee, and then watch again.

The spectacle gave way, of course, to extreme physical violence. The fires were so intense that they burned on bricks and concrete, overwhelming people trapped in shelters and buildings; red-hot shrapnel from anti-aircraft guns and bomb casings fell from the sky like scorching rain, searing through roofing and setting fire to buildings.[69] Those who worked in power stations such as J. W. Dorrinton were right in the middle of the bombers' sights; like others who experienced the air war first-hand, he emphasised the sounds of the bombing attacks while fighting to save Bristol:

The bombing had ceased, and the only sounds to be heard were the throbbing of fire pumps, the crash of falling buildings, and the roar of the many fires still blazing. A quiet hour or so passed, but the lull ended at 1am when the 'Raiders Overhead' buzzer in the station sounded again, and 'the muck' started to fall.[70]

High explosive bomb blasts sucked the breath right out of people's bodies in dance halls and cinemas, leaving them dead by suffocation. Citizens fled their homes and went into shelters, as instructed by police and air raid wardens in both Britain and Japan. In heavily bombed cities like Tsuchizaki, these crude civilian shelters were easily pulverised by high explosives. Satō Fujie described one shelter taking two direct hits, instantly killing nearly twenty neighbourhood residents, including a mother and her two children. Her husband, Makoto, went back to identify the dead, but they had been blasted apart so badly that 'you couldn't tell one from another'.[71] In addition to the brilliant sights, citizens recorded sounds, smells, and other sensations in order to capture 'what it was like' when the city was being destroyed. Fifteen-year-old Okamura Toshiyasu narrowly missed a direct hit from a bomb that split a modern concrete bridge right in half. He ran with his mother into the fields near their home in Shizuoka, where they hoped to survive the growing conflagration in the city:

... before long, we were assaulted by burning embers in the air. I couldn't bear to open my eyes, and it was even painful to breathe. It was like being caught in a fierce blizzard of flame. I suddenly realised that the fires were whipping up the wind, and if I remained here I would burn to death, so we all fled to the shelter built by the fields' owner. In the middle of running, my father fell to the ground and my elder brother screamed at him, 'What the hell are you doing?' I was the only one who went in that shelter ... It was clear in the morning, and it was like everything was wiped clean. Here and there were the scorched remains of buildings, standing forlornly, and blackened trees occasionally popped out ... When I thought my father had fallen during the 'blizzard of fire', he had actually been blasted by [a bomb]. His ears were packed full of earth from the hit.[72]

Citizens were watching their city being torn apart, and the urban environment could do little to preserve their lives. Authors wrote as much as they could recall about the experience of being attacked, such as this account of the bombing of Coventry:

The overriding memories will always be of brilliant light. The strong moonlight and the orange of the burning city. I remember too the whoosh of the descending bombs, the hiss of the incendiaries, and the rumbling of falling buildings. The fear as the whine of the bomb started and the almost cessation of breathing until you heard it land. The night seemed never-ending. It seemed as though the noise from the continuous waves of planes would never stop. Occasionally there would be an almost unearthly quiet as though everything in the world has stopped, but then the drone began again ... we walked to Spencer Park and could see the Cathedral burning – I suppose the City but it was the flames coming from the Cathedral I shall always remember and still this intense orange glow. It was an incredible sight neither understood nor believed, as the day before we had had our [students'] Speech Day there.[73]

The enemy robbed the city of its life, which often included the inhabitants, but also its buildings, transport conduits, energy supply, and familiar landmarks. As the city collapsed, the people died with it; when they saw iconic buildings fall, for many it felt as if they were losing a piece of themselves.

Finally, the destroyed cities then became unhygienic mausoleums, filled with the stench of rotting human bodies. After watching Aomori being totally destroyed in one day, Narita Kazuko remembered the 'horrible smell [of corpses] that came down to Namioka town [15 miles away], and the disgust I can feel even to this day'. Perhaps because Coventry was destroyed so quickly, as well, memories of rotting bodies were powerful. One survivor recalled that the entire city smelled of Corridor lime: 'It was evidently some form of disinfectant', he wrote, 'because of the deaths and the rats'.[74] The first air raids were mesmerising, but the aftermath grew increasingly terrible, particularly as the city that ordinary people had come to love quickly became a tomb.

Fear and Loathing: Emotional Landscapes of the City under Attack

When air attacks arrived in Birmingham, people wandered in dark streets and declared: 'What shall we do? Where shall we go? Will it be safe in the cellar? Oh dear, this wretched war'.[75] As citizens watched their home town reduced to ruins, in psychological and emotion terms, the city became what Amy Bell referred to as a 'landscape of fear'.[76] In response, governments in Britain and Japan attempted to control urban citizens' behaviour by showing a confident face in planning and response, but emotions were not so easily corralled. After the fear, anger quickly followed. Fujimoto Kinuko, a 35-year-old high school teacher, watched the destruction of Hachiōji from her front door. She worried over the safety of her parents, saw fires consume her home town, and recorded casualties from machine-gun attacks by fighter aircraft on civilians. On a particularly bad raid, she wrote in her diary: 'Fires inside and outside the city rise up and fill the sky ... the sun was choked by smoke, and ashes rained down from the sky. It was the work of the despicable Americans'.[77] Miyazawa Seikichi was even more bothered by the firebombing of the area: 'The sky was red, roasting, and those damn B-29s were casually flying about and dropping their incendiaries. I couldn't watch it. It was really infuriating (*jitsu ni shaku ni sawaru*). My body was shaking all over'.[78] Modern cities were rarely thought of as spaces replete with happiness and contentment, but the devastation wrought by impersonal aerial bombardments amplified anxieties and resentments in unprecedented ways.

As bombs and fires gutted and consumed the city, space could be radically transformed by a single air raid, which felt like being transported into a horrible new world. Policemen and fire wardens were often pulled into areas they had no knowledge of, as Ballard Berkeley recalled: 'When we arrived [at the London docks] – it was chaos. We didn't know where we were and there was nothing we could do. The place was in flames – streets were gone'.[79] The very earth seemed to move under one's feet: when fleeing to a seaside air raid shelter, one Japanese worker remembered a bomb landing nearby and suddenly being buried up to his chest in sand, completely immobilised in an instant.[80] Sometimes the chaos and fear were triggered by one's own defence forces. In Wallasey, Burkey recalled how British anti-aircraft gunners would pull large cannons through his residential street and unexpectedly fire at the German planes attacking the Liverpool docks, noting 'we didn't even know if it was the gun, or a bomb landing'[81] – Mary Bloomfield admitted that, in Coventry, 'We are frightened by our own guns. The shrapnel is

red hot and as dangerous as bombs'.[82] Seventeen-year-old Igura Masako
noted how most of Hachiōji was flattened, which made the nearby
Mount Takao clearly visible in all of its natural splendour. The city's
Hachiman Shintō shrine, and its gate, stood alone in a scorched plain of
ruined buildings. In the remains of her school, she 'grasped the white
ashes in my hand, and held them tenderly'.[83] C. Brownbill, a 15-year-old
boy near southeast London in Kent, recorded in his diary the disorientation afflicted upon ordinary civilians by modern warfare:

The sirens are wailing out their warning as I am writing this and the moonlight is
so bright you could read a paper easily. There go the guns. I can hear the Nazis
they are firing at, too. I bet London will cop it tonight. German planes on all sides
travelling toward London. Huns putting up a terrible barrage, raiders overhead
now. Island guns firing fiercely ... I went to sleep and I woke some time in the
night the guns were still going they were going all night.[84]

Whether anti-aircraft fire from friendly guns or bomb fragments from an
enemy bomb, the war filled the sky with red-hot shards of metal, which
periodically rained from the sky 'slic[ing] through the roofs or flesh' and
'rattl[ing] on the tiles all night'.[85] From a civilian's perspective, the air
raids were relentless and opaque; why were they attacking us here? Why
now? When will it end?

In their personal accounts, urban residents in both countries recorded
their feelings in an apparent effort to grasp the 'new normal' of surviving
in the city. Deadly panic struck first: Tanaka Tatsumu recalled the initial
scramble that took place when a raid began on Takamatsu: people were
shouting and screaming, men hurriedly pumped water into fire-fighting
buckets, flustered women gathered essential belongings, and the children
'just wandered around, watching the adults panic, and the city itself burn
before our eyes'.[86] British survivors were caught totally by surprise by
relentless GAF attacks. In Coventry, Joan Thornton wrote:

My God! It was hell. There is no other way of describing it ... 10 ½ hours
continuous bombing. We had the glass blow out of the front door, a few slates off
the roof, John's bedroom window broken and the blast forced the lounge window
open ... A picture house a little way from the Gaumont (where we wed) has a
direct hit and it was full. They were still digging on Friday for survivors.

After the bombing, British Ministry of Information vans circled the
streets that were still open in Coventry, warning residents to abandon
the city as dangerous structures were blasted to the ground, unexploded
bombs detonated, and fires extinguished for good. 'I have never known
anything like it', Joan wrote, reflecting on her impotence before the
enemy, 'Of course we never went to bed all night. We just have to thank
God we're alive'.[87] Indeed, the government was sometimes worse than

useless, even telling citizens to go back into the flames. When the fires engulfed Shizuoka, Sano Tatsuo fled the city in a panic, jumped onto the last train, and watched the city burn behind him. As the train lumbered along, he saw that even gardens and fields were on fire, with defence patrols and policemen shouting orders at residents to stay and put out the flames. Sano was wiser: as soon as the train ground to a halt, he pushed his way through the crowds and fled as quickly as he could.[88] When the sirens warned of an impending attack, Gladys Hollingsworth and her family grabbed rugs, blankets, and pillows, rushing into their cramped shelter. Then they heard the planes over Coventry, and the city was thrown into utter chaos.

It seems as though our shelter flew into the air and dropped back. The worst thing about it is people's homes and churches, hospitals, and theatres have been the most heavily hit. Thousands of people have left the city, and there are people still going every minute. We had three fire bombs dropped in the garden. Dad got out with his tin hat on and he put them out with a shovel and sand. A house not far off was completely burnt out and two houses in our avenue were also wrecked. Never expected to come out of our shelter alive. However we are all safe although very nervous. I was shaking all the next day.[89]

Panic and fear forced city residents to confront the fact that no one was going to help or preserve them. Survivors were willing to drop almost any allegiance or obligation in order to save themselves and their loved ones.

In such sudden, unexpected, and terrifying situations, strong emotions produced strange behaviour. Some, for example, reacted with humour, like the nervous laughter some unfortunate person emits in a theatre during a dramatic scene. In Coventry, Gladys Hollingsworth noted how ordinary people tried to pass off their losses with jokes: 'shops that have had windows blown in: "More open than usual," a lady's dress drop whose windows were smashed had "Smashing bargain."'[90] During the 1940 'Christmas Blitz' over Liverpool, Dorothy Hughes wrote in her diary, 'All still running: buses, trains, hoses, Italians'.[91] In Bristol, W. A. Hares described how a pub landlord 'is ready to joke, and tells customers that drinks are on the house, as he does not think there'll be a pub there in the morning!' His account, however, quickly returned to the confusion and terror of the assault:

See my mates. 'We're in for a pasting to-night!' Both of them seem to think discretion the better part of valour ... WHAT A NIGHT. Jones's warehouse enveloped in flames; firemen say they can do nothing. Everybody seems very calm, though none seem to know just what to do ... More incendiaries, more bombs, more big fires. Hell is released on our city. Many soldiers are doing good work, but we've still no Fire Auxiliaries to deal with the local fires. Frontages now begin to collapse! The din is tremendous. Glass and debris everywhere ... It seems hopeless now, for the water supply has failed ... Horses, terror-stricken, are running wild in the streets.

Watching the bombs whistle past him, Hares wrote, 'Nothing matters anymore now, surely! C. and N. have come into the house to die together'.[92] Suicidal and homicidal impulses were never far apart in the bombers' emotional landscape. When an American B-29 crashed near Shizuoka, a surviving pilot emerged to face an enraged mob of Japanese civilians. The mob stabbed the airman in the face with bamboo spears, and he fell screaming, clutching his head. Women and children rushed forward, pelleting the fallen man with stones until he was dead. Others openly wept while they smashed the heads of the dead pilots with rocks, stabbed their eyes with sticks, and hit their bodies with bamboo poles.[93] When the state and social order collapsed, and emotions were allowed to rule decisions, extreme behaviour was inevitable.

Emotional responses were not simply irrational acts, but adaptations to the failure of the government and the city to preserve civilian life in the name of victory. Working for an office for Chiba's main rail network, Watanabe Masanori was chatting with a colleague about the possibility of being bombed when the air raid siren suddenly blared out its warning. He and his work mates piled into a shelter and turned on the radio, watching the city start to burn as the reports came in. Masanori saw one of the nearby office buildings catch fire ...

... and although [our] management office was some distance away and safe, to the north, south, east, and west every corner was engulfed in flames with no exit. The enemy planes circled around and dive-bombed us. Because of the fire from the incendiaries, the wind became extremely strong around us, like a storm. I said it was going to be alright, but there was nowhere to run so I lost all my confidence ... Then we realised that we were downwind, that it was dangerous here, and we had to flee ... We ran to the next shelter, but the enemy planes were still dive-bombing one after another and so there was nowhere to go ... Looking left and right, everything had become a sea of fire, and the wind was fierce. It was like being in a dream.

Thoroughly in a panic, Masanori jumped into a river and sank up to his chest. As hot embers and dust whirled around him, he found his way into an open sewer and managed to escape the firestorm. After cleaning the sewage off his body, Masanori wrote in his memo book, 'Only a person who experienced it knows this pain'.[94] During the height of the air assaults over Britain, many city residents began taking time away from embattled urban spaces to 'rest' in the countryside and escape from a life of fear and panic, but this respite could be dangerous as well. Mary Bloomfield wrote that trekking to the country 'proved in many instances to be bad for us'. While on a shopping trip in Coventry with her husband Ted, a German fighter aircraft completely surprised them, machine gunning the shop and sending them diving to the floor. 'Our courage through the big raids', she wrote in her diary, 'had keyed us up to endure, but once having unwound, we were unable to be so steadfast in the face of sudden death as before'.[95] The 'war' was not just about achieving victory on a far-flung battlefield, then, but finding strategies for surviving the relentless bombing of civilian areas at home.

The emotional world of the bombing war was not limited to fear and panic as bombers attacked, but also the horror of living among the dead. Survivors had to endure face-to-face encounters with the mangled, burned, and dismembered bodies of the bombers' victims. First Aid volunteers in Hull like Raymond Peat resorted to pinning information on corpses and bagged remains of human bodies; doctors gave terminal cases a lethal dose of morphine and marked a crude 'M' on their heads as they died.[96] In Japanese cities, teenagers were mobilised to clean the streets of debris, including body parts. Capital cities, like London and Tokyo, were relentlessly bombed throughout the war, leaving many citizens to encounter the dead again and again. For London rescue driver I. S. Haslewood and Tokyo housewife Mochizuki Masako, the war was literally like moving to the underworld.

Haslewood was the only female member of her team, and was striving to appear strong before the tough men who served alongside her. Although her native Chelsea was a comparatively affluent area with little industrial development, this did not spare it from aerial bombardment by the enemy. The squad responded to a call in Beauforte Street, where an air raid shelter was apparently destroyed near a burning block of flats; her subsequent diary entry reveals the horror with which city residents faced their dead:

The scene was of death and devastation. Huge slabs of concrete trapped poor mangled bodies beneath their jagged weight. Poor twisted bodies – blackened and begrimed from the blast and dust. Bits of bodies lay in puddles of water, blood, and filth. Dear God! That first glimpse of Hitler's work! I felt my stomach heave for a paralysing second, and I thought I was going to vomit, thereby disgracing myself and my squad forever. But I managed to gulp heavily and then felt more or less all right again. There was little I could do after we had searched the neighbouring flats for possible cases of shock – but stand and hand down blankets to the Rescue men in that terrible pit for them to wrap round bodies as they disintegrated them from the debris.

Suddenly, a 'tearing roar' signalled the approach of another bomb, and the squad members scrambled in all directions for safety. Some leaped into piles of glass on the pavement, others dove into ruined buildings, but all were safe. As much as Tokyo resident Mochizuki Masako would have preferred to avoid such sights herself, they were as inescapable in Japan's capital as they were in Britain's; her sister-in-law's son arrived at the house to announce that 'from the Kikukawa Primary School to the surrounding area, [the ward] is full of people burned black ... and the river is full of corpses'; the massive firebombing of Honjō Ward by the Allies forced her, 'shaking with fear', into a 'sea of fire' that was the northeast side of Tokyo. She aimed to find some of her in-laws in the city, and then flee to relatives in rural Ibaraki, but her progress was impeded at every turn:

The train from Akihabara could not get through, so there was no choice but to walk. As far as I could see, there were smouldering ruins, corpses burned black, and people, people, people – like a mountain of bodies. You couldn't tell where the ruins ended and the roads began ... I was shocked with horror, and at first I could neither speak nor cry. I just stood there in stunned silence.

Arriving at her in-laws' in Tokyo, Masako found nothing but ruins; even the chickens in the back garden were reduced to bones and ashes. 'I had no strength to move', she wrote, 'and simply sat on the scorched remains of a [toppled] tree'. Spurred on by her nephew, Masako wrenched herself away from the scene in order to search for the missing relatives, but she found that:

... everywhere, everywhere the [city] was full of dead bodies. Corpses that were burned black were indistinguishable from each other, and even after a day's search we couldn't find a single one of the missing seven from our family. We of course met others seeking relatives, but we didn't know any of them ... At this point, the Army arrived and loaded the dead onto trucks; they pulled corpses out of the river using a long pole with a hook on the end.

As if giving voice to her concerns, her nephew said, 'If we don't flee [the city], we'll end up like this'. In London, returning to the area blasted by a high explosive bomb, Haslewood and her rescue squad pulled up a slab of concrete to discover the body of an old man, still sitting in his chair.

He was not outwardly very much damaged, except for a scalp wound and half a hand missing. He was just sitting there, with his mutilated hand hanging limply down. His blood-stained dusty old face looked quite peaceful – so surely his death must have been almost instantaneous – I do hope so ... [Rescuers] were so respectful and gentle in their handling of the ghastly bodies. So careful to cover up the indecencies of horrors with blankets as quickly as possible.

Haslewood's team bagged bodies and cleared debris, as well as clambering down into 'water-logged basements' in order to calm 'hysterical women and cantankerous old men'. All the while, Haslewood and the men she worked with choked back their own emotions, and sick, as the city consumed, ground, and spat up more bodies of its former residents. 'We could hardly have had a worse baptism into our grim job', she wrote despondently, 'Up till this morning, I had never seen a dead body'. It could be worse, as Masako discovered, when the piles of bodies became all too familiar:

The army was piling the bodies on top of each other, one by one, in the bed of a truck. I looked at each corpse's face as I walked by and – at the very bottom – there was my sister and [my niece] Noriko ... My sister had put her left hand over Noriko's face, which was turned up to the sky, and had wrapped her right hand around the girl's back, leaving the two locked in an embrace. For some reason, their hair was not burned; their hairstyles, gold fillings, and kimono inside their thighs were all fine ... the flesh inside their thighs was still pink ... We could only hold each other and say, 'Why, why, why did this happen to them?' and then fall silent, crying, unable to leave them.[97]

The city's dead choked rivers, roads, canals, and alleyways, and the armed forces were frequently deployed to dispose of them as if they were garbage. Mass graves littered the cityscape, vermin fed on them, and citizens were forced to see the bodies of neighbours, friends, and relatives tossed onto trucks or into pits.

As terrible as the bombings of London and Tokyo were, the vast majority of national resources were committed to defending the capital cities, where the political, financial, and industrial elite lived. Even Britain's vaunted radar system only detected planes over the sea, meaning once they cleared the south coast and flew north of London, they were nearly invisible to the Royal Observer Corps when conducting night raids.[98] As a consequence, citizens in other industrial and port cities were hit especially hard, and did not have the resources, including extensive underground mass transit, that the capitals enjoyed. In Hull, Dora Mockett captured the instant consternation that German air raids inflicted on the citizens there:

About 10:30am saw a policeman and one or two others running [past] the Guildhall, then just when we were wondering what was happening [we] heard a sound like an explosion, then a second later another loud one and the building shook. With that the men came rushing out of the banqueting hall, 'Get downstairs at once, the roof is falling in!' We didn't know what was happening – whether the building might be collapsing or what and thought the enemy had come unexpectedly and were dropping bombs. Anyway, down we went. Austin Collier and Mr. Winders were cut with flying glass ...[99]

Due to its aircraft manufacturing, Nagoya was ruthlessly pummelled by air raids from the very beginning. Factory section chief Ogawa Takashi recorded the surreal and horrifying experience in his wartime diary:

From about midnight, for an hour and a half, there was an air raid focused on the north-eastern quarter of Nagoya. This raid was different from ones before, because first of all they dropped flares, and it was as if someone had lifted a lamp over the city. Then came the explosive bombs. In the north ward, at Kami-Iida, and the east ward, in Yada-machi, many bodies could be seen. In the area around Yada-machi, the bomb craters were practically on top of each other. At the grounds of Chōbo Temple, there was human flesh scattered about, and several cart horses at Kami-Iida, swarming with flies. A downed B-29 was near a primary school in Gokijo, and the body of an American pilot was strewn on top of it.[100]

Once they realised that the political leaders had not provided for their defence, panic seized many civilians in regional cities, causing spontaneous mass exoduses from Bristol, Osaka, Coventry, Shizuoka, Manchester, and Nagoya – with many caught off-guard, taking shelter in ditches, behind walls, and even in drain pipes.[101] Watanabe Teruko described how American B-29s, with the 'unsettling rumbling of their engines' and the 'eerie hiss' of the incendiary bombs, arrived in her hometown without warning, 'Scattering us like new born spiders fleeing the nest'.[102] Still, a revolution against the leaders in Tokyo and London, who had done so well to use national resources to defend their interests, was not forthcoming. Watching the German Luftwaffe set fire to residential districts in Merseyside, H. B. Monck was despondent; the 1940 'Christmas Blitz' was the worst Liverpudlians had to endure, but Monck was not very sympathetic to those who were openly terrified:

Everyone says Liverpool has been shocked about a lot these last few nights and I believe it. I only hope our people will face it. How I shall react if anything happens to me I don't know but I should feel eternally disgraced if I thought that I should fail in the test. I have seen some visitors at my sister's house go down to the shelter each night as soon as the guns fire just like rabbits and although I feel there is lots of excuse for them I regret that I cannot help feeling contempt for them. I don't justify it but there it is.[103]

Citizens in regional cities felt pride in their ability to endure the worst, but the government's focus on the capital was unmistakeable. For the civilians of regional cities, the attacks filled silent space with terrifying noise, wiped out entire communities, and lit up the sky, often with little official resistance. Outside of the metropole, the sense of 'being in this together' was also under assault as political and economic leaders devoted the lion's share of the nation's resources to defending themselves.

Furthermore, not every raid was the same: the size of a city could mask or enhance the severity of an enemy campaign in the eyes of the citizens who endured it. After the terrible bombing of Coventry, residents complained of 'hating' the city, comparing it to a graveyard. When an aerodrome worker attempted to re-enter the city, he found it was just 'piles and piles of rubble ... the police had asked us if we wanted to join the others underneath the rubble. We thought they were joking'.[104] While large, sprawling metropolises with good public transport allowed many more areas for fleeing residents to take refuge, smaller cities were worse off. Heading west on the train toward Hachiōji, 19-year-old student Yagi Jun'ichi kept a diary describing the annihilation of most of the urban spaces west of Tokyo. Writing of his 'shock' as he looked out the window, he described columns of smoke, rising as if belched out of coal-burning smoke stacks, 'drifting gently' throughout the smaller cities and towns west of the capital. Crossing the Tama River, he got off at Toyota and began walking home to Hachiōji when 'soon the ashes of the city were before my eyes'. Meeting relatives in the remnants of their homes along the way, he grew more and more despondent about his home town:

It had been attacked after all. From Ōwada Bridge westward, nothing was standing; it was just scorched earth. The trees were smouldering desolately. There were still fires here and there, and people moved about busily. Buses flew by ... [My neighbourhood] had been burned at the start. My books were all destroyed. I was devastated ... I thought about our family's bad fortune, and my heart was wild with anger ... Going home – there was no home, I have no home.[105]

Similar to regional cities in Japan, the focus on London has obscured the comparatively harder attacks on smaller British cities in national memory. Although London was hit with more bombs, Hull, a much smaller city, took more damage as a percentage of the city space – in part because GAF planes sometimes dumped remaining bombs there on their way back from other targets in northern Britain. In her diary, Dora Mockett described how a direct hit by a bomb had ironically slain all the residents of an air raid shelter, but left the families in surrounding houses with only scratches and bruises. Scribbling with a pencil into a tiny notepad, Dora tried to capture the sensation of nearby bombings: 'It sounded nearer than [the next street] and the house felt as though it dropped a foot to come back again. We all held our breath wondering if another would drop ...' The assaults on Hull were difficult to endure even if one was not directly under them:

[J]just after 9pm they started coming over in waves. The noise was awful and they sounded so low we could hear the propellers – they sounded too as though they were doing some machine-gunning. Then the [anti-aircraft] guns started and the noise was so great we could not tell whether any bombs were dropped. We sat in our shelter for nearly an hour with our coats on, as it was so cold and our ear plugs in.

Recounting all of the casualties in and around her street, Dora described the shaking of her house and the 'swish' sound of bombs falling, simply writing, 'Feel very weary tonight'.[106] By 1944, after the major air raids in Hull had finished annihilating three quarters of the buildings there, Edith Peirse on her fortieth birthday wrote in her diary that 'I was miserable thinking about our going back to Hull, and dreading it more than anything else in my life'. Happier in the nearby spa town of Ilkley, Edith had some reason to be resentful of being forced back into Hull by her father: 'Gunfire, including the new rocket gun [V2] ... I was terrified'.[107] The GAF dedication to destroying Hull was perplexing for its residents, and the national media blackout of raids on regional cities did not help the situation; meanwhile cities like London, which suffered far less per capita, were lionised in the mass media for their heroism under adversity, and this sometimes made the experience of being bombed outside of the capital even more infuriating.[108] Censorship of enemy attacks on regional cities did not erase the reality of being bombed. As Dorothy Hughes put it:

Why the ridiculous censorship ... Surely the Germans know they are over Liverpool, and yet they put the one line in the *Liverpool Echo*, saying [anti-aircraft] guns have been in action in a N.W. town, when the whole population has been dragged out of bed! It seems that we are all children![109]

The Japanese government and their media allies in Tokyo similarly tried to minimise the enemy's attacks on their regional cities, or keep residents in other urban areas completely in the dark, but this strategy failed. The British government in London referred only vaguely to 'a Northeastern town' (Hull/Newcastle) or a 'Northwestern town' (Liverpool/Manchester) in the press, but it hardly masked the severity of these attacks, and often demoralised the residents in regional cities.

Regardless of the state and mass media's attempts to frame how the war would be discussed, civilians noted how attacks on home front cities resulted in a complete transformation, removing entire streets, blocks, and familiar landscapes. Sections of London were being taken apart piece by piece, leaving curious, gaping holes in the cityscape. In her war diary, Gwladys Cox described how bombs fell through building roofs and exploded on the ground floor, thereby knocking out the bottom of walls and bringing down entire blocks of buildings in London's Kilburn.[110] In Kensington, Kenneth Holmes wrote in his diary a particularly terrible experience:

I saw several people suffering from cuts and bleeding, waiting to be treated (a miniature battlefield), houses I had known well, were just not there, and the debris appeared to be around the surrounding houses (what was left of those). Goodness knows! Where the houses that had been struck had disappeared too, [and] it looked as though a huge 'bulldozer' had lifted them from the earth and there was quite an open space.[111]

In Merseyside, too, Burkey noted how a '1000lb land mine' had exploded with such force that a 'whole block of buildings was lifted up and came crashing down on the opposite side of the road'.[112] Fleeing from an explosion, or a nearby fire, was a temporary form of fear; the deepest impression of terror, whether in Tokyo, London, or any of the regional cities, seemed to be a consequence of observing familiar landmarks being systematically destroyed forever. Whether in diaries or memoirs, those who lived through the war in Britain and Japan remembered how the war transformed their homes and home towns, reducing bakers, chemists, schools, churches, and police stations to smouldering rubble. It transformed neighbourhoods from recognised spaces of belonging into what the Japanese called 'scorched earth' (shōdo) and 'charred plains' (yakeno or yakeno ga hara). The war was an attack on the very foundations of society. Fuchikami Akira, a 24-year-old urban professional, saw his native Hachiōji reduced to such a state. In his neighbourhood association, which consisted of eleven households, only his father's home survived the air raids. Over twenty of his neighbours packed into the house until 'you couldn't set foot anywhere inside'. After Japan's surrender, he looked up at the mountains that surrounded the ruined city and thought of the classical aphorism: 'The kingdom is broken, but the hills and streams remain'.[113] City people saw bombers erase the structure of their neighbourhoods and communities, which was one of the primary ways they experienced national belonging; in their eyes, the nation itself was being eradicated.

Residents reacted to the destruction of their home with strong emotions ranging from rage to sadness, desperation to humour. Watabiki Junji, a rail worker in Hachiōji, was warned that the city would be bombed prior to a major raid, but responded angrily to his co-workers, 'What the hell are you on about? Why would they bomb us?' Unfortunately, he was wrong, and the raid began that evening. 'Even though the B-29s were our enemy', he wrote, expressing the expectation that Japan would be attacked, 'they were still fighting dirty'. After hitting the city centre, Allied aircraft targeted refugees in the surrounding hills with bombs and machine-guns. Junji was hit, and then forced to lean on his mother and sister to walk while they were steadily coated by oil that the aircraft dropped from the sky. They had to abandon their home and go to the country house where Junji's father had been born.

It was excruciating. We had four futons, about five gō [~900ml] of rice, and some undergarments that we had to carry on our back, arriving at about 11 o'clock from Hachiōji. Why do we have to deal with this sort of pain? I felt in my heart: why this war, why do people like us, who didn't do anything wrong, have to be made to suffer? Thinking about this, I lay down on my side and someone, somewhere was shouting 'Air raid warning! Air raid warning!' and I just couldn't sleep.[114]

Colin Perry, an 18-year-old junior clerk, responded to the German bombardment of the city with a range of emotions, even if he rarely afforded himself the luxury of openly admitting fear. He and his office mates amused themselves with humour: during the Battle of Britain, when they 'reported' Hitler stealing Michelangelo's 'Moses' from the Louvre, the office staff imagined the German leader furtively kneeling before the Jewish icon to pray, 'Dear Moses, tell me how you got across that strip of water'. More often than not, however, Perry turned to anger during fifty-seven uninterrupted nights of aerial bombardment in 1940:

I am wondering, not anxiously, just how we intend counteracting these 'Nuisance' raiders, for sleep is imperative and it looks as though we are to have another sleepless night. I am (another German – two came over then and I can still hear their drone dying over London) dark-eyed, have a terrible head, and long for Hell's own blizzard which would keep these damn infernal droning machines away for a night. I may be tired and somewhat depressed, but by God all this only makes me the more determined to smash blasted Hitler once and for all. The whole of Britain is now more fiercely determined than ever. I wonder in view of my recent air-raid experiences just how Helsinki and Madrid, to say nothing of Tientsin [Tianjin], Shanghai, etc. held on for so long.[115]

For Perry, and so many others, the frustrations of being freely attacked by a far-off foe needed to be released. Watanabe Shige also felt a building anger over the relentlessness of enemy planes, and linked it to the elusive goal of a good night's sleep:

I could see that the words and actions of my mother and elder brothers were getting increasingly harsh. Between being malnourished, sleep-deprived, and anxious, people in Tokyo seemed to be getting aggravated. You lost track of night and day, and every day there was no opportunity to rest your nerves. Never mind the daytime, there was nothing more infuriating than the night time sound of air raid sirens. As soon as you got into bed the planes would wake you up, so you just slept in your day clothes.[116]

To add insult to injury, the enemy seemed so comfortable up in the sky, casually lobbing bombs down onto hapless citizens below. During a bad raid over London in September 1940, a bomber hit a group of workers clearing rubble from a prior raid in the working class area of the Isle of Dogs. Bill Regan described how his friend 'Nobby' reacted: 'Nobby Clark has a huge chunk of masonry in his arms, and as he was casting it away, there is an explosion quite near, and Nobby staggers around in a flaming temper, raises a fist to the sky, and shouts, "Come back you German bastards, and I'll screw your bleeding head off."' Like Colin Perry, however, Bill Regan tried to balance the rage with humour, describing other friends shouting 'Try again, mate', and 'You missed, now sod off and let someone else have a go', while GAF planes bombed east London's rubble into finer-grained rubble.[117] The emotional landscape of the city under attack was a big tent, encompassing anger, fear, and humour – whatever the survivors saw fit for the occasion.

Citizens of the city were perplexed by their own inarticulate emotional responses to being bombed. When the Isle of Dogs was levelled by the German air forces, Bill Regan sifted through the remains of the city, principally to collect the remains of its residents. On one occasion, in particular, he and his squad of working-class builders from the East End of London found the bodies of two teenage girls who had been buried alive. The dust of vaporised building materials had packed them airtight, preserving their corpses almost perfectly. Bill observed that they both had 'only their knickers and short petticoats on ... their limbs were not even rigid'. Strangely, this disturbed the rescue men more than the pieces of bodies and mangled torsos that they normally bagged up and sent out as human refuse. Some men vomited, and others stood paralysed by the sight of the dead, barely-clad teenage girls.

They were lifelike; I could not let them be handled like the usual corpses. I know I would have belted the first one who handled them with disrespect, but nobody makes a move to shift them, and are just standing there, gawping. I looked up at George, and I just said, 'Stretcher, blanket'. Then I put my right arm under her shoulders, with her head resting against me, and the left arm under her knees, and so carried her up. I laid her on the stretcher, 'You'll be comfortable now, my dear'. I did exactly the same with the other one. I stood up and waited for some smart Alex to make a snide remark, but nobody did. I cooled down a bit after I had smoked a cigarette. I wonder why I had been so angry?

Bill had collected the severed body parts of dead friends on a previous trip, but seeing the bodies of teenagers and, in holding their bodies so tenderly, he was left confused by powerful feelings. Separated from his two daughters, who were evacuated to rural Oxfordshire, the sight of two dead girls stirred up powerful, inchoate, and half-articulate emotions within him. He received letters from his girls off and on, telling him about their lives in school, such as this one from 'little Vi':

I hope you are alright. Our cold is better and we have started school today. And we have some nice sums and I had them all right today. One of the soldiers fell down in the mud dirted his clean trousers and he had just changed them. One of the soldiers are just like uncle Tom. They said they was going to put the search light on to night. We went to Gypsy Friday with Aunty and bought some cough-sweets home. Well lots of love Vi.

Bill read these in quiet moments, and then recorded his thoughts in his diary: 're-read the children's little letters, and made myself thoroughly miserable, and almost wished for nightfall; at least then, your thoughts are concentrated on the job you are doing'.[118] Ordinary people were terrorised, chased, watched their neighbours brutally murdered, their homes burned, missed their loved ones desperately – and to what end? The emotional landscape of the war, as it was recorded by the urban citizens who endured it, is a record of impotence: ironically, while the support of ordinary people was essential for total war, there was also little they could do to defend themselves from it.

Desperation in the City: the Turn to Faith

Born into poverty in 1872 West Derby, Mrs. Anne Shepperd was a devout Methodist who later moved with her husband into Eltham, south-east London. She was described by her granddaughter some years after the war as being a 'practical lady of strong Christian faith'. The 72-year-old was president for her local chapter of the Sisterhood Movement, which was the women's branch of British Methodism. As soon as the bombing began, she launched her grim record of how the war was destroying the faithful:

Terrible news has just reached us. Our good woman, who also works for Minnie and Mrs. Jones, is now in hospital with concussion, her two children 10 and 12 years are also there seriously injured and her husband blown away and beyond recognition except for a few articles about his clothes. This was from a high explosive bomb quite close to them and also to our Elt[ham] Green Church in same road. Others were killed but we don't know who yet … It is all so very terrible.

The skies of southeast London were red from the fires that consumed believers and non-believers alike. 'God help all who are out in this', Anne Shepperd wrote, even as a nearby Baptist church, already heavily in debt and incapable of recovery, was eradicated by bombs.[119] Despite her devotion, Anne's god did not save her friends, co-parishioners, or even local children. Apart from emotional responses, citizens who endured air attacks tried to understand them through the rubric of spiritual beliefs and religious faith; this was partly due to the fact that the impersonal and total nature of air raids made the war seem other-worldly. As the Japanese writer Sakaguchi Angō put it in his story *The Idiot* (1946): 'It looks as if our destinies were commanded by something supernatural. It is fate.'[120]

At the beginning of the war, eerie premonitions and a vague sense of foreboding, encouraged by the mass media's interest in promoting extraordinary stories, led to the fleeting popularity of fortune-telling and psychics. Bertram Elwood encountered an astrologer conducting trade in Birmingham, and estimated he could 'clear £10 per week by working for an hour a day for five days a week' at a time when the average weekly wage was about £6. Most of the consumers of supernatural stock and trade were women.[121] In Hull, Edith Peirse consoled herself by pasting an April, 1939 article from the *Daily Mail* in her diary declaring, 'Astrologers Say No War'.[122] Unfortunately, the ascendance of Jupiter failed to prevent the German occupation of France, which brought the enemy within striking distance of the British Isles. The war on the city made many of its residents feel utterly powerless – as if great, unseen forces were at work – which provoked all manners of magical thinking.

The combination of attacks from the sky and ineffective domestic defence inspired desperate people to turn to the supernatural with the view that gods, bodhisattvas, and other forces might intervene. During the devastating air raids over Bristol, Miss M. Fagnani recorded in her diary the horrors and losses of the conflict. 'God grant it is going to be all right for us', she wrote, 'above all I must keep my faith in God whatever happens'. Meanwhile, her local church St. Michael's was 'gutted' by the air raids, and her father came down into the cellar with handfuls of tiles and earth blasted away from the building.[123] Of course, the deafening silence from the heavens could be interpreted in as many ways as humans could imagine. Doris Pierce's father attempted to use God as a threat to command respect from his daughter during the air war, to which she replied, 'I shouldn't have to answer to him anyway so shut up!'[124] Middle school student Kobayashi Narimitsu wrote in his diary that, following an air raid on Shizuoka that destroyed his school, the class was berated by a teacher who also called on divine retribution: 'You schoolchildren, your will has become weak [*ki ga yurunda*], so we have been scolded by the gods. Take this as an opportunity to pull yourselves together!'[125] Others rejected divine punishment as an empty threat, such as Joan Rice when she wrote that Hell was 'such a dumb idea', because she didn't 'believe in religion's mumbo jumbo of mystical heaven and life hereafter'.[126]

Pushing through a selection from the Catholic book club, Hull evacuee Olive Metcalfe had to put down Jean du Plessis' *The Human Caravan* after suffering eighty pages because:

... fundamentally I do not incline to the self-glorified, intolerant, Catholic conception of the world ... for [du Plessis] individuals meant nothing, and human feelings were at a premium. Perhaps I could have forgiven his style if I had not found he believed in the Fall of the Angels ... Adam and Eve in a Golden Age, and Noah's Flood destroying all the world.

At a time when food, money, and safe lodgings were in short supply, du Plessis' often metaphysical ruminations on the Church's role in the conflict over the future of mankind must have been tiring to people like Olive. In fact, Olive's mother and grandmother were horrified after being tricked into attending an 'evangelical do' disguised as a simple 'At Home' involving knitting, tea, and biscuits. It also turned out to be a covert effort to raise funds to rebuild St. Peter's in Hull. When the ladies returned, Olive's mother went back, causing Olive to remark that it appeared 'as though Mother, against her will, has become a member of a new church'. While many citizens like Olive's mother could be pressured to swell the ranks of churches in wartime Britain, others were recalcitrant: her grandmother 'put her foot down. She thought an afternoon's knitting a much more Christian thing to do'.[127] Supernatural beings gave no indication of their will, so others could use such metaphysical considerations to reject war, authority, and even organised religion. Teenager Dorothy Kahn's brother Kenneth, after becoming a Captain, decided to leave the Army because he felt he was 'not doing God's work' by fighting, subsequently becoming a peaceable farmer.[128] Ultimately, no one could demonstrate help or harm from above; the course of the war was determined by humbler forces.

In most cases, however, religious and spiritual individuals, whether Allied or Axis, believed that supernatural forces would somehow aid them and not their enemy. One might forgive a vicar like Reverend R. C. Taylor, when he claimed divine intervention saved his beleaguered church following days of bombardment: 'It seemed as if we should not be able to have the services anymore but God's power prevailed and we are allowed to carry them on as before'.[129] Children, as well, were prone to believing in the supernatural powers of prayer.[130] Mass Observers conflated religious superstition with their own class and ethnic prejudices. Eleanor Humphries, as an educated middle-class woman, noted her 'amusement' following an altercation with a working-class woman who refused to evacuate her grandchild – who was also showing early signs of the tuberculosis infection that had killed his grandfather. 'Woman arrived all breathless and pugnacious-looking', Eleanor noted ominously, 'Seemed an Irish type'. A clash of values, rooted in the assumptions of both women's class backgrounds, ensued: in the end, the older woman refused to believe that having her grandchild in London posed any risk to him, understandably looking on Eleanor as a troublesome busybody trying to break up her family. Suddenly, the boy appeared with a young girl, 'Eyes bunged up with matter. Wads of cotton in ears and looking really unwell'. The old woman shoved him back, 'Wot'ed you bring'im out for? 'ow dare you. No one aint going to take 'im away from me. I won't 'ave it'. Sawyer and Humphries sparred over the boy's well-being, until Eleanor forcefully made her case:

I stressed the point of subjecting a sick child to the nervous terrors of the air raids and how awful she and the boy's mother would feel if he were killed by bombing. 'No bombs are going to fall on us, we put our trust in God and pray to 'im every night. We ain't afraid of bombs'.[131]

Eleanor's attitude may have been condescending, but her fears were justified: sadly, there is no evidence that these other-worldly powers took any note at all of the suffering of urban residents – especially working-class residents who were the targets of enemy attacks on industrial centres.

Eleanor was wrong, however, in seeing this behaviour as linked to Sawyer's Irish and working-class background. National days of prayer, which resulted in 'miraculous' acts of salvation, reveal a level of magical thinking that transcended ethnic and class backgrounds. Famously, when British forces were trapped near Dunkirk, facing German annihilation, citizens across Britain prayed for their safe return, and a fog descended on the beaches to aid their escape. Desperate times produced many such instances: in Bristol, a small mission dedicated to St. Chad prayed under their seats during a bad air raid, attributing their survival to the Lay Reader's fervent appeal to their patron saint.[132] Some citizens in Britain found these instantaneous conversions to a life of faith disingenuous and ridiculous. Mass Observers in Liverpool, reading about the church services, remarked disparagingly about superficial expressions of religious devotion. Sometimes the pleading of civilians to supernatural forces was not strictly religious; Okamoto Masao watched passively under a stone bridge as his neighbourhood burned down but, when he saw one house seemingly untouched by the flames, he prayed [*nenjite iru*], 'Please make it, please make it'. He soon saw it hit by an incendiary bomb, however, and 'erupt into flames instantly'.[133] Reverend Taylor, as well, begged his god for deliverance from the evil of enemy bombing: 'Evidently we missed London's worst night air raid last night.

Telephoned but evidently nothing in the parish. Lord and Lady Stamp and their eldest son killed. How can England spare genius like this. O God, stretch out thine hand and cut this tribulation short!'[134] Nevertheless, gods, Buddhas, and angels were silent. Fleeing back to a Buddhist temple during the firebombing of Himeji, Shiba Isa remarked that 'the main hall (hondō) and antechamber (kuri), along with the bell tower ... were totally burned from top to bottom, with the pillars scorched black and the thatching still on fire. It seems that the fire was strong, indeed' – or, at least, stronger than the gods themselves.[135] In the end, the belief that citizens had in their gods mirrored the faith they placed in supporting their cause in the war. Gwladys Cox believed it portentous that the National Day of Prayer at the beginning of the attack on London was decided to be II Kings 6, verses 16 through 17: 'Fear not, for they that be with us are more than they that be with them ...' Despite their prayers, Gwladys reasoned, the Germans would be abandoned by God because of their own sinful hubris: 'In his sermon, the preacher reminded us of Hitler's boastful claims to Divinity. Hitler had been extolled by his followers as God himself and had declared that Germans could not be Germans and Christians at one and the same time'.[136] This sort of thinking was not limited to specific religions, nor to particular classes, cultures, or nations.

Prayer often emerged as a desire to call down supernatural powers to protect, or simply communicate with, family members during air raids. Kanenaka Kimi was a 31-year-old woman who lived in the Arakawa Ward of Tokyo, in a town named Ohisa that was slightly away from the city centre. Her younger sister and brother-in-law, however, lived in Honjō Ward, which was in the middle of Tokyo. She recorded in her diary the 9 March 1945 Allied firebombing, when Shimodani, Asakusa, Fukukawa, Honjō, and Kanda Wards, composing much of the city centre, became 'a ring of fire'. When the bombing began, she dashed out in a panic, concerned for her family, whose home was in the centre of the firestorm. She saw a 'long, thin arm of fire reach into the heavens and become a crimson cloud, spiralling out until the sky above my head became completely red'. The next day, 10 March, she hurried with many others to look for her relatives in the city, arriving in Ueno Park, Tokyo's largest green space, but the city centre in nearby Asakusa was completely hidden by smoke and airborne debris. 'Ignoring orders from the Civil Defence Corps to stop, I ran and ran', she wrote, moving from the east end of the city to its centre, the Ryōgoku Bridge. She saw the corpses of the elderly, who had lost their will to carry on, and were burned alive on the streets; she immediately began praying, first to assuage her own fears, and then in earnest for supernatural intervention:

'Please, Hirasaku, please Fumiko, please be alright', I prayed, rushing along. It was as if my heart was flying up into the heavens [*Kokoro wa ama o tobu ga gotoshi*]. Before long, I was at [their neighbourhood] in Morishita. The scene was terrifying: the homes there were all destroyed by fire and there were piles of bodies burned black. I put my hands together and prayed to the Buddhas, making my way to the Fukukawa Primary School.

Japanese modern school buildings had more robust construction, as opposed to wooden residential structures, and thus they commonly served as makeshift escape centres. There Kimi encountered badly burned refugees who were crying and calling out in loud voices, looking for their relatives. Their faces were black and their eyes were red from extended exposure to smoke. Soon, she was crying as well, calling out, 'Hirasaku ... Fumiko ...' but there was no reply. She asked if anyone was from their neighbourhood, Morishita, but no one answered her. Everywhere, people collapsed, slowly dying. She went back to scarred Morishita, and put up a sign: 'Hirasaku and Fumiko, I am praying for your safety. Please come home quickly to Ohisa. Mom is worried about you'. As ambulance services and soldiers rushed around the ruined city, she read omens and signs all around her, and her 'heart was pierced by a premonition of ill-fortune'. The next day, she learned from her sister's Neighbourhood Association that, of the fifty-eight members, all but five 'had met the sad fate of being completely wiped out'. She and her mother found a teacup belonging to the young couple, and burned it as an offering to the dead in a religious ritual.

Oh trail of smoke spiralling here and there into the sky, won't you please pacify the spirits of the dead here? There were tears on my face ... Meeting with Hirasaku's elder sister, we spoke of him and Fumiko, and wept ... I took off my air raid protective clothing and my white apron [*monpe*], going to bed. How many months has it been?[137]

Because of the impersonal nature of mass bombings, which rained down death from the heavens like spite from a wrathful god, civilians such as Kimi turned to prayer, both overtly religious and personally spiritual, to make a symbolic defence against the ruthlessness of the attack. These prayers were unanswered, and many lost their loved ones in the conflagration.

Indeed, from the perspective of civilians, scientific advancement had created a terrifying new form of warfare, which seemed to trigger a return to faith; if one digs deeper into the sources, however, this was not really a religious revival. Clive D. Field argued that Christianity remained a source of comfort for many in Britain during the war, but he also acknowledged that statistical surveys from the First World War to the

Second World War confirmed a fall, not only in church attendance, but also in faith in the Christian God.[138] Conversely, the drop in church attendance did not reflect an acceptance of atheism or Materialism in Britain or Japan. Watanabe Teruko recalled her grandmother finding a small Buddhist statue during an air raid, stuffing it into Teruko's pocket, and praying that it would protect her like a charm or fetish.[139] In Britain, civilians in wartime wavered between astrology, superstitious acts (salt over one's shoulder), and pleading to supernatural beings as each of these methods in turn failed to grant them control over their destinies during a time of total war. The brief resurgence of spiritualism in 1939 also shows that citizens were grasping for any escape from war, or simply the comforts of knowing what was to come. In these cases, spiritualists could become greater advocates for peace than the representatives of organised religions, and certainly more than secular authorities. As one Mass Observer witnessed during a spiritualist meeting in Lancashire:

'The thought of fighting with weapons was horrible'. She knew what war was (here she spoke very earnestly and shook her head slightly) 'to the full' and she had been mixed up in it and all its horrors. She stressed the Brotherhood of Man and said there were some people who said Hitler should be shot. Gently expostulating: 'But you know it's very wrong to say such things. We should not say that'.

Despite the female spiritualist's praise of peace, she still encouraged her audience to believe that, if their 'prayers had been meant and well directed', then war with Germany 'was impossible'.[140] Unfortunately, this was wrong, and blaming the audience for not praying well enough would not resolve the international crisis that brought German bombers to Britain.

The people called out to various gods to save them, and they did so with different languages, dialects, and regional accents. The ritualised behaviours of ordinary people reveal the widespread and penetrating influence of organised religious traditions; in this sense, we must see these acts of desperation not as organised religion per se, but a wider set of beliefs about the supernatural that influenced individual behaviour. These acts, however ineffective, gave suffering people a fleeting feeling of empowerment. In the northwestern city Akita, one Japanese man recalled fleeing with his family during an air raid, diving into a sandpit, and throwing a futon over their bodies as the American bombardment continued above them:

Shigemitsu, our three year old, cried for four hours straight. Four hours ... and then, the planes came humming over us, and all we could do was pray *nanmaida*,

nanmaida. And then, you'd hear the sounds fade away, and you'd take the futon off to look, but you'd hear them coming again and down you'd go. It just seemed like you never caught a break. It was just like – What's that? What's that? *Nanmaida, nanmaida.*[141]

Meanwhile, in Himeji, Kobayashi Takako, thinking 'this is the end of the world', described Kansai speakers desperately shouting *Nan manda butsu*, and those speaking standard Japanese in Tokyo were crying *Namu amida butsu*.[142] These were all dialectical versions of the same phrase: 'In the name of the Amitābha Buddha, I pray'. If the words of prayer were magic, and invoked the power of gods, then the dialect and pronunciation might be important – or perhaps they had the wrong language and supernatural being altogether. Outside of Swansea, during the firebombing of the port town, Laurie Latchford recalled a Welsh villager staggering through the streets repeatedly saying 'Oh my God, Oh my God, Oh my God'.[143] After the May raids in Liverpool, H. B. Monck noted: 'Everyone is appalled by the devastation in Liverpool. If the Germans are able to drop heavier bombs as we have been able to do on them', and then he prayed: 'God help us'.[144] Monck called on God to save the British people from the punishment inflicted by the Germans, but was his Liverpudlian-accented English correct, or was it the Welsh girl's – or was it the Kansai dialect, or the Akita dialect, of Japanese? Even if it was the Christian God who existed, and not the Japanese Shintō deities, would he listen to the Germans or the British? If it was the British, which denomination had the best access to his ear?

Despite these thorny theological questions, ordinary people saw in religion and ritual practice a means to save the people and restore a moral order: in their eyes, prayer was a suitable answer to the seemingly distant, arbitrary, and merciless modern technological terror that the enemy inflicted upon them. John Kay, a working-class sailor in Plumstead, London, continually returned to his faith during the chaos of the German attacks on the Royal Arsenal. He wrote in his diary: 'I experience an indescribable sensation, I am afraid and yet I am not, I am surprised to see that my hands are quite steady and my heart is not thumping, as I expected it would'. His calmness, perhaps, was rooted in his faith in God. 'During the raids I have said my prayers more than once and that has given me courage. I feel that God will protect us – I know he will'. Whether the faith gave rise to confidence or his confidence enabled his faith is hard to say, but Kay was convinced that a supernatural force had spared him. 'We have been very fortunate that no bombs fell very near', he wrote, 'and we thank God that we are safe'; perhaps his confidence, which helped him keep cool during the raids, was responsible for saving his life.[145] In other cases, religion directly threatened its adherents. Nagi Katsumi, a 36-year-old woman married to a Shintō shrine official in Shizuoka, detailed how the family put their lives – and those of their children – in danger in order to preserve the physical representation of the shrine's god (mi-tamashiro). For devout Shintoists like the Nagi family, allowing this sacred object to be consumed by fire would be a grave injury to the god who they revered. A fortuitous encounter with one of the shrine's faithful, a soba noodle shop owner named Kiyomizu Michitarō, was interpreted by Katsumi to be 'guidance from the god' (kami no michibiki). They reached the main branch of the Shizuoka Bank, which had a robust structure of reinforced concrete, and decided to rest. Then Katsumi, Michitarō, and five others kneeled down before the physical representation of the shrine's god, which they had carried from the inferno, and prayed for their lives:

We were warned that 'the bank will probably be bombed' and, while this was terrifying, we had great strength by being with our god ... Our god, with whom we shared a deep connection, was with us during that night in the Shizuoka Bank. The bank escaped the bombing. I think there was something there, which cannot be denied. There existed some thing there, which you cannot understand unless you've experienced it yourself.[146]

Nevertheless, other citizens, particularly those with a dangerous job to do, adopted an impatient and pragmatic attitude toward those who would call on the heavens for deliverance. A policeman in Bristol caught Methodists praying in a church that was too brightly lit. After ordering them to darken their lights, the meeting leader retorted, 'Hush! We're calling upon God'. This rankled the old cop, who replied, 'If you don't put those [damn] lights out, Hitler will soon be calling on you'.[147]

For both good and ill, prayer was a powerful tool to mobilise ordinary people into action, especially if they were part of a tightly-knit religious community in which ritualised behaviour and speech was part of daily life. Many priests and pastors performed a valuable service for those who found themselves abandoned during the war, particularly the elderly. Clergymen were not always very helpful, however. C. A. Piper, a Unitarian, refused a minister from another faith who demanded to perform services in the Unitarian church's air raid shelter; when asked if he would like to help in the practical work of scrubbing and tidying the shelter, the parson beat a hasty retreat.[148] Furthermore, unbreakable bonds within specific religious communities, strengthened by faith in supernatural powers, could put individuals in greater danger. In Shizuoka, Mizutani Teruko explained her paternal grandfather's difficult situation: 'In addition to being infirm due to age [79], rheumatism was hurting his joints, so he loathed to go into the air raid shelter. Friends and relatives asked him to evacuate [to the countryside], but he resolutely refused'. Upon further reflection, Teruko observed that it was her grandfather's faith that anchored him to Shizuoka's perilous city centre, 'because he didn't want to be away from the temple'. With help from the other adherents, he had spent the better part of his adult life looking after and rebuilding the main hall of this derelict building. 'Of course, he didn't dream of binding his family to this fate', she wrote, 'so when the time came he intended to meet his end alone'. Teruko prayed many times during her harrowing escape from Shizuoka's firebombing; when she returned, she found her family was all but wiped out:

In the house next door, I found my mother and younger brother's bodies. I had expected them to survive. Seeing their spent bodies there, I felt all of the strength and energy pour out of my heart ... [Mother] had put my brother in the bathtub, and apparently died defending him. The [wooden] tub was burned away, and the hoops [that bound the tub] were wrapped around my brother's body. Water had poured over him, so he was not terribly burned, and the insignia from his school uniform cap for Shizuoka Middle, in which he had just enrolled, was lying to one side.

Her mother was so badly burned that Teruko was only able to identify her by the remaining patterns on her rolled-up apron sleeves. Nearby, her father was lying in a heap, dead from asphyxiation. Despite being a highly devout family, prayer had not saved them from this terrible fate. Finally, she found her grandfather, who refused to abandon his temple:

His clothes had all burned away, and in one place the flesh had burned right down to the bone, but he had sat there with his hands clasped in prayer, his meditation posture unbroken. 'What a remarkable act of prayer. What an incredible way to leave this world (ōsei)', I thought, and it moves me when I remember it even to this day. He was able to move, but he did not even attempt to run, and just sat there motionless. ... He resolved to watch the temple that he had rebuilt for thirty years burn while he drew his last breath.

Years after the war, when she herself was older, Teruko wrote that she 'understands this feeling well', but at the time, as a teenager, she recalled thinking, 'Why don't you think more about your family?' Of course, because young people were expected to show deference to their elders, she dared not say this out loud. If she had, perhaps her grandfather would have survived into the peaceful post-war years, which Teruko herself was able to enjoy.[149]

If the gods were listening, they gave no evidence of it that could not be explained by circumstance and so, for some sceptics of the wartime generation, this was a damning indictment of man's reliance on faith.

The losses and humiliations that Endō Naoe had to endure during the bombing of Shizuoka inspired her to write: 'It was terrible. I despised the injustice of the gods'.[150] While prayer seemed to save British soldiers trapped at Dunkirk, it also appeared to aid the German armed forces in their destruction of the Coventry Cathedral soon after; the Japanese people prayed for victory in 1941, and thereafter inflicted on Great Britain its greatest military defeat at Singapore, but the American-led counterattack burned countless shrines and temples across Japan; the will of the gods was pitilessly arbitrary, and useless in defence of even their own sacred spaces. The war could strengthen the faith of believers, as well, or simply inspire the use of religious language and imagery to capture its horror: 'The air raid sirens carried on calling', wrote university student Muramatsu Naka about the bombing of Fukuoka, 'it was a sound that called the people into the ground; there was no mistake, this was a voice from the depths of hell'.[151]

We commonly believe that there are 'no atheists in foxholes', but that is not the case. In the Second World War, the 'foxholes' were in back gardens, neighbourhood parks, and places of employment, and we know that they were, increasingly, replete with people who had lost their faith – sometimes as a direct consequence of the war. Endō Naoe put it well:

My maternal uncle, who used to take me to the movies a lot, disappeared beneath the waves during the war [while in the Navy], and his elder brother was permanently disabled by his wartime injuries. My sister and I waited ever so patiently, but my brother-in-law never came home from his service overseas. My niece will never know her daddy's face. More than any other, I think, my niece is the victim of an unfortunate war. I completely stopped praying to any gods. There's never been any word as to how my loved ones died in the war.[152]

In Britain, the writer Vera Brittain gave poetic voice to this sentiment. Not long before the Second World War, when the 'Great War' taught ordinary people at the front just how terrible human conflict would become, Brittain wrote a poem on the impact that modern warfare would have on faith. In 1940, she republished the writings of those years at the start of yet another devastating global conflict:

> God said: 'Men have forgotten Me;
> The souls that sleep shall wake again,
> And the blinded eyes be taught to see'.
> So, since redemption comes through pain,
> He smote the earth with chastening rod,
> And brought destruction's lurid reign;
> But where His desolation trod,
> The people in their agony
> Despairing cried: 'There is no God!'[153]

★

By targeting civilians who had poor access to information and little in the way of protection, the enemy, whether Allied or Axis, conducted mass campaigns of terror. Our diarists frequently noted how the air raids made them feel, or the powerful emotions they saw unleashed in the frightened, defenceless people around them. These feelings were not just directed at the enemy, however, but also one's own government, which failed to protect the city and its residents. Dorothy Hughes described massive damage to Liverpool's Custom House, which was later demolished, and the municipal rail system. Birkenhead was also hit, with ferry boats attacked from the air, and many were killed. 'People are rather anxious to know what we are doing to stop the Germans', Dorothy wrote, 'Apparently they come over and do just as they like'.[154]

The war put our diarists' bodies under terrible strain due to sleep deprivation and, sometimes, malnutrition; this was followed by devastating attacks that shocked them with displays of extreme technological violence. In Hull, Dora had spent days deprived of sleep, food, and adequate heating. One day during the war, she had settled down after being hard at work but, before long, she was jolted awake at just after midnight by another devastating raid.

All was quiet until nearly 2am, and then the fun started. If anything it is worse than [before] – bombs were whistling down, shaking the house, making the ornaments jump, blowing open the coal-hatch, and moving the kerb. Ginnie came over to us and stayed until all-clear [at] 3:15am. Again most of the bombs seemed to be dropped this side of Hull . . . A huge crater in the allotments and the clay was flown up and made big holes in the roof. To complete the job it poured with rain soon after all-clear and all the bedding got soaked. Poor Dorothy's mother was in hysterics and was screaming and weeping. Sheila's mother and auntie were having heart attacks. It was really terrible and we wonder sometimes how much longer we can go on.[155]

Repeated attacks threatened to destroy all familiar landmarks, and forced our diarists sometimes into deep depressions. In May 1945, Yoshitaka, who had been loaded with other children onto a train, was warned of the impending arrival of Britain's allies in an air raid over his home town of Nagoya. He quickly grabbed his younger brother and ran for an air raid shelter just outside of the city. Turning around, he saw Nagoya's famous landmarks wiped out and its citizens being methodically burned alive.

Nagoya is shrouded in black smoke. They say four hundred enemy planes attacked us. I pray for the safety of my father and sister. The north and east wards, as well as the suburbs of Nagoya, are under heavy bombardment, and the red face of the sun barely peeking out from the plumes of smoke is disturbing to look at. Even when I went to the Shōnai River, I could hear the planes' approach and I was afraid of explosions and firebombs, so I turned back home ... There were many empty canisters of incendiary bombs burning on the streets ... Looking from Tenjin-bashi, I could see smoke coming from the direction of our house, and my heart shivered with fear [*kokoro ga ononoku*]. Fortunately, in the north ward, our neighbourhood was spared. I heard Mitsubishi Aircraft Manufacturing at Kami-Iida, the Mitsubishi plant at Ōzone, and other factories were totally destroyed.[*] Rumours are growing that the prefectural and municipal government buildings, as well as the castle, were all wiped out in Nagoya ... Fires dance in the evening sky; rumbling of the B-29 engines; firing anti-aircraft; between life and death, air raids at night.[156]

These fires could not be easily quenched. Dorothy described how GAF bombers came to Frodsham in 'waves', and wrote that, the following morning, 'the fires were still blazing. The light from the fires lit up my bedroom and kept me awake'.

What Dorothy captured, however, in a letter to a friend, was the disorientation she experienced when the city was suddenly subjected to area bombing. During the 'Christmas Blitz' of 1940, when the entire Northwest was under attack, she was astonished at the level of violence meted out and its technological splendour: lights flashed red and green, electricity flickered in the house, and she could hear bombs whistling down miles away. She looked out the window and witnessed Liverpool in flames for a second time in 1940:

With a fire like that there's no use trying to disguise the place. We could actually see the shell bursting in the sky. Talk about the Western Front – it couldn't have been worse than here ... I can hear machine gunning! Reminds one of the gangster films. There, it's going again – rat-tat-tat ... Went to bed about 2:45 heard six mines explode, then one nearer, and I knew the next one would be just where we are. What a shaking! I think it must have been Stuart Road. I nearly died. I really thought it was the end. Oh those things are the most dastardly human invention ever. I could hear dogs barking and cars (ambulances I suppose).

Dorothy tried to infuse the letter with a light-hearted sense of humour, but her diary reveals a more complex set of emotions. She mentioned the raids during the 'Christmas Blitz' as being 'simply awful' and how they 'depressed' her. She speculated what a potential German invasion would bring, with 'terrible air bombardment, gas, and Hell let loose', writing that the prospect made her feel 'ill'. She rounded off her diary entry for

---

[*] The Shōnai River runs across north Nagoya, and into the sea directly west of the city. Tenjin-bashi, Kami-Iida, and Ōzone, were all parts of northern Nagoya or its suburbs during the war. Kojima is commenting on well-known areas around his home.

this period with reassuring words about what the Germans were 'in for' if they invaded, but the fear and anxiety were evidently affecting her deeply. A month after recording her confidence in British defences, she was having nightmares of a German invasion; church bells were ringing in Liverpool, calling her Phil, who served in the Home Guard, to the front line.[157]

The emotions unleashed by the threat of bodily harm often transformed into belief in supernatural forces, but sometimes it confirmed sceptics' suspicions about organised religion and the wartime state. On the 1941 National Day of Prayer in Liverpool, Dorothy scoffed:

Observed large congregations. Didn't go myself. Felt the whole thing is too 'showy'. What's the point of rushing to church on one particular Sunday, just because the King said so? No, practise your religion on all days, at all times, and not just when you want something, or have got a new hat to show off. Go to church by all means if you feel you need it, but I think I am a good Christian and yet never go near one. I don't need low tones, incense, and flowery phrases to keep my thoughts.[158]

Some diarists, certainly, explicitly credited supernatural beings for saving them from death and injury. Nevertheless, while some quickly prayed when close to death, many more called out to more earthly powers. While on the way to her job in an Itami munitions factory, Mitsuko and her friends began crossing a bridge when they heard an air raid siren.

We ran. When we had finally crossed the bridge and came to a corner, our teacher said, 'Sixteen enemy planes are coming, take cover!' We ran and ran. We forgot about everything and ran, taking cover in an army barracks. At the same time a fighter plane dove down and shot at us – rat-tat-tat. Without thinking, in my heart I spontaneously called out, 'Mother! Mother!' My life was saved.[159]

Famously, Japanese soldiers called out for their mothers before they died, even while on suicidal 'banzai' assaults. Scholars such as Emiko Ohnuki-Tierney argued that this reflected their youth, although it is also true that older Japanese soldiers cried out for their mothers on far-flung battlefields in the Pacific.[160] Certainly, people turned to fortune tellers, angels, and supernatural forces in times of crisis and uncertainty but, it would appear, at the moment of extreme peril, many called out for a more powerful force: mother. The emotional landscape of the air war brought forth a desire for whatever gave the diarists the strongest sense, or memory, of security.

3   Romancing Stone: Human Sacrifice and System Collapse in the City

> Every day, by the unchanging laws of nature, not a few people die in traffic accidents, as well as incidents in factories, assembly plants, and construction sites. The thing is, you see, this city –this contemporary Moloch – requires daily human deaths.
>
> – Alexsander Beliaev, *Golova professora Douella* (1924)

Air raids aimed to kill as many civilians as possible, and did so by attacking the environment built to support their lives; consequently, our diarists were caught in a deadly cage of concrete, wire, and steel with fire sent down by enemy aircraft. They had to flee this terrible urban 'Moloch': Dora Mockett described how, after the severe raids over Hull, even cheap hostels were overflowing with refugees, and the city council was unable to estimate when they could assist citizens in rebuilding their homes. 'I understand they are taking people out in buses at night to sleep in', she wrote despondently, 'there must be hundreds of homeless'.[1] The destruction of cities such as Hull, however, was not simply a loss of housing stock. Whenever our diarists endured sustained air raids, they discovered an unfortunate fact about urban life: unnatural, manufactured environments that they are, modern cities were like parasites; they could not feed themselves, build themselves, or clothe themselves without links to the people who toiled in the countryside. Particularly in Japan, once air defences proved feckless against raids, the machinery by which urban people survived in their artificial environment fell apart and our diarists quickly took note of these dire circumstances.

Nevertheless, most of the diarists recorded a willingness on their part, and those around them, to try to keep the system running and save the city; in a sense, the city called on them to die for its own survival. Ordinary people responded to the call for help, particularly when it came to organising air raid wardens and fire-fighting exercises, and our diarists either recorded this phenomenon in their personal records or signed up themselves. These eager volunteers saw their fellow citizens perish while protecting lifeless buildings, telephone lines, and gas mains. Aiko noted how no one was spared, and how her entire neighbourhood was consumed by Japan's 'Total National Mobilisation' policy (*kokka sōdōin*): while primary school students, important figures, and the elderly left the cities, young men were all 'taken by the draft'; intellectuals and technicians were pressed into service as well, sometimes as infantrymen; and teenagers still living at home were forced into working for wartime industries. By the spring of 1945, even a well-educated woman like Aiko, with a doctor for a husband, could not keep her eldest daughter from the state, as the young teenager was sent off to oversee primary school student evacuations.[2] Dorothy read rumours about how the Maginot Line defending France was 'rigged up below ground, complete with kitchens, power plant, and everything else. The thought struck me, to think that civilisation has gone so far as to compel human beings to live under such conditions, like so many ants'.[3] Indeed, many diarists wondered how, under such conditions, their fellow citizens could carry on living like human beings. As the city faced increasing threats to its systems, it asked for more and more sacrifice in order to save them.

It is perplexing that our diarists gave this 'modern day Moloch' so much of their love and loyalty, when it was incapable of returning such affections. Rumours of attacks on symbolic buildings and neighbourhoods were extremely disturbing to patriotic subjects like Mitsuko, who feared that the Allies 'have dropped incendiary bombs on the palaces of the emperor and the empress-dowager, razing them to the ground. So many terrible things, how despicable these demons are'. Mitsuko's anger and patriotism could not mask the fact, however, that the war was turning against Japan, and attacks on the home islands made her life in a major city like Osaka all the more perilous. Food was short, transport failing, communications spotty, and the streets were eerily emptied of children. Toward the end of the war, P-51 Mustangs zoomed into the greater Osaka area and terrorised civilians. Inside an air-raid shelter, Mitsuko hid under a futon with her mother listening to the 'rat-tat-tat' of machine guns, far-off explosions, and the booming of anti-aircraft guns. 'Then, nearby, there was a massive explosion', she wrote, 'and our hearts skipped a beat'. Finally emerging at 3pm, they discovered that a nearby power substation was engulfed in flames and smoke, and fifty people were killed. Due to a collapsed power grid, the trains were no longer running and she could not even purchase a ticket to escape. 'At a time like this', she wrote, 'it is excruciating to not go to work, but nothing can be done'.[4] Dora also found that the enemy's destruction of Hull created a wasteland that was now robbed of its former allure. She noted how the fires and explosions disrupted transport networks and shut all the shops; in many cases, she simply had to abandon the city buses and walk through the rubble.

Went out to look just after 4:30am and the fire was billowing out in great fiery clouds. Thank goodness there was very little wind ... What a terrible night in the town – it is indescribable. The trolley buses only going to Botanic so had to walk from there ... big crater in front of the government buildings ... From the Central onwards are big fires and all the big stores have gone ... most of them nothing but smoke, rubble, and twisted girders. There was terrible damage all over and all gas is off. The electric was doing queer things all night, going up and down and wavering about. The bus station is hit and buses running from Ferensway. At dinner time came home – there is nowhere much to go ...[5]

Fires ripped through the city, gutting the shops, pubs, restaurants, and cinemas that gave urban spaces their life. Enemy bombers opened great holes in the streets, leaving transport uselessly trapped outside of the heart of heavily bombed towns in both Britain and Japan.

Food quickly became a serious concern for all of our diarists. Dorothy noted that several women were suffering under the rationing system, but this was attributable to the fact that their local greengrocer was not doing his job properly. He had 'not been getting his share of the good things. It's all a question of distribution'.[6] Japanese citizens were far worse off, of course, but few wrote about it as elegantly as Aiko did. As an older, well-educated urbanite, Aiko remarked from the beginning of the war that it would rob her of the finer things, and she began experiencing that fact day by day in 1942.

Once again I went out today to look for food, this time in Shinjuku [in western Tokyo]. In a corner of a department store, they were plunking some non-descript fish into batter and frying it in boiling oil, making tempura. I thought, *I was brought here right on time*, and my heart was dancing with happiness. These days you go out for food and anything will do. When you find something that looks edible, it's like you heroically felled a great dragon (*oni no kubi de mo uchitometa ki*). I can't remember the last time we made tempura at home. I can't recall – it's as if it was ancient history.

Aiko queued for a long time to get just enough fish tempura to bring home. She hoped it would make the family happy to have such a rare treat. As soon as they took a bite, however, the fish released a foul odour, as if it was rotten. Tasting only the bitterness of a world at war, Aiko wrote, 'Our sense of satiating a great hunger was [in fact] only a momentary illusion that could not be savoured'.[7] In this situation, bombing had rendered the city, which had earned the love of its many residents, into something much like the wartime state itself: greedy, deadly, and merciless. Enduring yet another raid over Liverpool in March, 1940, Dorothy finally surrendered to the city's terrible condition:

Well, last week Wednesday, Thursday, and Friday we had a blitz. Pretty awful. Land mines, [high-explosives], and incendiaries. Went to bed at 11:30 each night. Couldn't stand any longer. Actually slept, too. Birkenhead is simply awful. Jolly profitable raid from German point of view. Jolly big casualty list. Personally feel after a lull in raids, it is harder to stand them. If we got raided every night, it would be easier.[8]

Unfortunately for Dorothy, it would not be easier and, for the Japanese who endured seemingly endless air raids, it appeared as if the city itself was coming apart right before their eyes.

Unrequited Love: Sacrifice and System Collapse

The wartime city in both the East and the West was a grid of inorganic materials within which a densely-populated community of human beings chased amusement and ensured survival; when this system broke down, it was inevitable that it took living people with it. As the Christmas holidays came and went in 1940 and 1941, British citizens like Violet Maund felt despondent at what the enemy had left behind for them in heavily bombed cities: 'It does not seem like Christmas Eve', she wrote in 1941, complaining that Bristol's 'shops are empty; very few toys for children, and even these are exceedingly dear. Please God send peace soon'.[9] With the annihilation of shops, cinemas, neon lights, mass transit, and restaurants, air raids greatly diminished the city's seductive powers. Many ordinary people sacrificed their lives to defend what was essentially a lifeless (and dangerous) pile of stone, wire, and wood that neither sustained nor entertained them. Writing of Shanghai in the 1930s, Leo Ou-fan Lee observed how, despite the inhuman working conditions and rampant crime, the neon lights of the 'Paris of the East' still managed to draw vulnerable people into its tempting, deadly grasp, with promises of 'Light, Energy, Power!'[10] Louise Young, in writing about urban Japan, showed how this appeal was not limited to the megapolises of the world like Tokyo, London, and Shanghai – electrification, reinforced concrete towers, dance halls, movie theatres, and other attractions pulled people into regional cities as well.[11] Urban residents came to love the city not only because it was 'home', but also because it was fun and full of opportunity; unfortunately, air raids turned these spaces from centres of love and life into deadly traps, and those who gave their devotion to the city were the most likely to die in it.

The inseparable connection between the people, who were mobilised for total war, and the city, which enabled their support, was what drew enemy bombers to urban population centres like London, Tokyo, Coventry, Shizuoka, Hull, Chiba, Bristol, and Nagoya. Geographers argue that cities 'cannot be fully comprehended as merely a set of special relations, biophysical habitat, and impersonal socioeconomic functions'; while a city is a dead heap of concrete, wood, and glass, those materials are '*shaped* into places by the personal works, exchanges, and intelligent participation of resident communities.'[12] Cities were not only were they centres of production; they were also a complex, inter-dependent system that was easily targeted by aircraft, which wartime writers described in their personal records:

I was lying awake in bed and [the bomb] seemed to be coming straight for us. The explosion made the whole house rock. 30 seconds later another aerial torpedo came and wiped out the United Dairies factory, a shop, and two houses in Hainault Road. A school has been hit and the workhouse in Union Road was struck by another aerial torpedo and several wards demolished.

As the system collapsed, it seized its residents, consumed them, and buried them. The writer above, watching London's East End burn and crumble, noted a day later that rescue services were 'still digging for bodies'.[13] When the bombers attacked the city, citizens fled by the thousands, abandoning their homes and communities; those who remained watched these burned to the ground.[14] Bureaucratic systems were at risk, too. The post office in Japan handled written communication and telegraphs, of course, but it also managed insurance, savings, bonds, and many other services for ordinary Japanese. Working at the local post office in Shizuoka, Aoki Shige fumbled with a water pump as the building began to burn from Allied firebombing. He spied his boss scrambling to gather 'important documents' and then running away. 'Right', Shige wrote, 'I'm off too, then!' Reaching a branch office on his bicycle, where postal insurance claims were filed, Shige realised that this building was blazing as well – a massive network of official documents, personal correspondence, and financial exchange was literally going up in smoke.[15] Bombing tore away the city's skin, revealing tunnels carrying water and human filth, pipes delivering flammable gas, and wires crackling with deadly electricity, but it also gutted and consumed the papers that recorded financial contracts, family links, and personal history. Beyond the pipes, nodes, and papers that greased the wheels of urban life, aerial bombing destroyed human networks that depended on written records and bureaucratic procedures; it also exposed 'so many intimate things ... to the indecent stare of strangers'[16] such as private photographs, medicines, and underwear.

It may seem an exaggeration to suggest that people died as a consequence of the deconstruction of steel and concrete rather than solely as a consequence of enemy fire, but this is how those who lived through the area bombing of Britain and Japan described it. The city of Coventry, a charming market town in the West Midlands near to Birmingham, was almost utterly destroyed by German aircraft in what can be considered as an actual 'terror' bombing of Britain during the war; similarly, Shizuoka, a port town on the east coast of Japan (south of Tokyo), suffered a 70 per cent loss of the city from 19 to 20 June 1945. Coventry resident Marcus Sadler wrote:

The damage in the centre of town is beyond words with everything – except one or two shells of buildings – lying flat in a tangled and burnt out ruin for roughly a radius of anything from a quarter to half a mile ... Roads like Smithford Street (where Woolworths and British Home Stores were) are burnt flat – also you can see right across from Broadgate through what was Boots, the Market, the Co-op Stores and the Rex to St. John's Church ... at an angle it is flat nearly down to the Gaumont, and at another angle practically through the Labour exchange ... They can't get all the trapped people out of the shelters under places like Owen Owen and the Market, and are now simply having to give up hope (it is estimated as a hundred or two in those alone – they must have been burnt alive) and are dynamiting the rest down.[17]

Noda Tsuru, a teacher in Shizuoka, described how he ran with other staff into various shelters during the major raid on the city. American bombers mercilessly pounded the city, and Noda described the 'pan-icked breaths and pounding hearts' with which the teachers fled. The infrastructure of the city itself was collapsing, with military officers screaming at them to move on or 'be burned to death'. They considered casting themselves into ditches in front of the municipal prison walls. Eventually returning to his school, Noda noted that the buildings were burned away, leaving the reinforced concrete husk, like an urban skeleton, behind.[18] While GAF bombers lacked the range of Allied planes, the town described as 'furthest from the sea', Coventry, was neverthe-less within their reach, which shocked residents who had assumed themselves safe from attack. Teenage diarist Gwendoline Matthews kept a diary account of the assault on Coventry, which captured the erasure of its urban systems:

Incendiary bomb fell just outside the back gate. Slates blown off the out-house. French windows burst open. Lock blown off front door. Windows broken ... Pop did not go to work on Friday ... I could not get to school. The 'All-Clear' was never sounded. After this raid we had no water for 4 weeks, no gas for 6 weeks, and no electric light for 7 weeks ... Mother and I went out to buy food ... I went to the Co-op bakery. This building was burned to the ground but the men were just rescuing what bread they could. There was a terrible scramble to get loaves ... It was the worst thing I have ever set eyes on. The fires were still burning and the firemen, I remember especially, were playing water on the [Gulson] Central Library. I was always very fond of this library . . . We went on to look at the ruined Cathedral.

What Gwendoline recorded in her tiny pocket diary were many of the salient elements of urban life that bombers wiped out: fuel, water, electricity, housing, the workplace, modern schools, food networks, religious institutions, and the historic library.[19] Similarly, Sakurai Shizuko watched the firebombing of Shizuoka destroy the rail station; familiar neighbourhoods, shops, her house, temples, and even graveyards were unsafe. She was turned away from hospitals and told, 'The doctors can't help you', despite having injuries all over her face and her entire head of hair burned away. During the worst of the raid, her brother tossed an urn out of an open grave and they both climbed inside the hole; with part of his cheek bloody and dangling from his face, he said to her: 'This is it, let us wait peacefully and meet our end like true Japanese people'. She agreed, but her mind was nevertheless filled with a powerful desire to see her mother and daughter again.[20]

Despite the devastation of the city, which killed its own residents in fiery piles of metal, stone, and wood, the citizens rallied to preserve it. In Coventry, teenage girls gathered around the ruins of the central library and morosely collected bomb-strewn books, putting them into the County Court prison cells in order to save as many as possible.[21] City people treated the death of the inhuman system like they would that of a close friend or family member: Barbara Bosworth saw 'people in Broadgate huddled in groups crying and others digging in the rubble'.[22] The ruins were hardly beautiful or endearing – the city stank of lime, corpses, and fetid water. What followed the bombing, then, was a chilling emptiness, as the city was exposed to be something other than a centre of light and life. As Joan Thornton wrote to a friend:

You see they hit the water main, gas, and electricity. They had to just let them burn away. The town on Friday was like hell. No trains, they hit the stations. No buses, no trams, no telephones, no gas, no electric lighting, and no water . . . Of course you will hardly know the centre of [Coventry] now. It seems to look worse now the rubble is being cleared away.[23]

The devastation was thus both material and psychological. In particular, the destruction of St. Michael's Cathedral, a beautiful late medieval building, crushed the people of the Coventry. Remembering her teenage brother during the bombing, Barbara Bosworth wrote that 'Despite all the horror and death he had witnessed for 9 hours – he slumped against the door frame and said, "There's only 4 walls left in the Cathedral."'[24] Forty-four-year-old Susuki Tetsuo, a teahouse owner, first watched the destruction of Shizuoka from his rooftop, noticed that the 'rail station and the area around the Tōkaiken shop* were already aflame, lighting up the night sky'. Looking above him, he heard more and more loud explosions as Allied bombers took the city apart. An incendiary pierced the roof of the house in front of him, and fire spewed in all directions. As part of Japan's equivalent of the Home Guard, Susuki was already in uniform and ready, but he found the battle for Shizuoka was already lost:

There was no one at the headquarters. Even though we had endured strict training for wartime measures, particularly around the gate to Shizuoka – the rail station – there [was no one] . . . the commander, a man replete with a sense of responsibility, Mr. Shiratori, and his sub-commander Mihashi, joined me in the middle of falling rain and exploding incendiary bombs in order to fulfil our duty. Often called the 'triumvirate of valour' (gōki no sanba garasu), we three got the pump out and attached the hose but, in the middle of this expanding conflagration, the water wouldn't come out . . . The headquarters then caught fire . . . the neighbourhood of the Shizuoka Rail power station was a sea of flame.

An old man who Susuki had tried to save was struck directly in the head by a falling incendiary canister, and pieces of the bomb ricocheted off of Susuki's helmet. After the raid, on his way home, Susuki endured 'unbearable sights', including the 'cries of those who were only waiting for death'. The painstakingly-crafted network of air raid shelters was useless in such a conflagration: 'At the entrance of the shelters', Susuki wrote, 'there were blackened bodies, and I silently prayed to the Buddhas as I went by'.[25]

In Shizuoka as in Coventry, the city may have been alluring in peace, and promised much, but it could not defend human beings during war; rather, as it collapsed, it slew them. When the citizens fled its terrible ruination, some began to reflect on the mixed blessing that urban life bestowed. Watching traumatised residents stream out of the wreckage that was once her hometown, Gladys Hollingsworth wrote in her diary:

Refugees flee from this smouldering pile of ruins, to quiet country lanes, often carrying their sole possessions in one hand. They see pleasure in every living thing. No longer do they long for life, the glory, and splendour of huge buildings and busy streets. Little did they realise the beauty of the fields and trees, the occasional buzz of aircraft overhead gives them a start and takes them back to the night of terror never to be forgotten.[26]

As seen in Chapter 2, terror and fear assaulted the citizens, who felt the deadly grip of the wartime city upon them. Just how far panic might take them was a major concern because urban spaces still needed human

---

* The Tōkaiken is an historic shop that was commissioned in 1890 to produce 'box lunches' (bentō) for rail travellers along one of Japan's earliest long-distance passenger rail services. It was an iconic landmark for the city and is still in operation.

bodies to be dispassionately working, dousing flames, operating power stations, and rebuilding lost structures, in order that this creature might survive. In the midst of such devastation and despair, the city was an insatiable beast, still calling for more people to cast themselves into the fire.

All Together for Moloch: Volunteering for War Services

The collapse of the system that sustained modern cities and their communities was not a consequence of lack of effort by ordinary citizens. To a certain extent, the public's support of the war effort was borne out of a need for survival rather than an abstract love for the city: 'There is no doubt that if any one of us had funked it', wrote one Bristolian of the fire-fighting efforts of his neighbours, 'the whole building would have gone up, as we had no assistance from the outside'.[27] Even as Japanese city centres burned, citizens like Inoue Masako stood outside of their front gardens and shouted at terrified refugees to 'go back and put out the fires!'[28] In Britain, like Japan, diaries and memoirs emphasise the ability of ordinary people to stoically 'get on with' the labours that kept the city going. D. Lord wrote that '[a]lmost every morning, I would come out of Faringdon Station and see fresh evidence of overnight incidents, having to pick my way through heaps of broken glass to Shoe Lane and another day of work under fire'.[29] Nevertheless, buildings were replaceable while individual lives were not; the affection many felt for their cities masked the fact that the death of a person diminished a community more than the loss of a church tower. The citizens sustained the city, although their sentimental attachment to it sometimes gave them the impression that it was the other way around. A person's love for the city was always unrequited.

Sacrifice for the city was first and foremost facilitated by the state. Regardless of being Axis or Allied, fascist or communist, democratic or authoritarian, ordinary people largely contributed everything they could during a time of total war. To begin with, some positions within civilian defence forces brought perks such as decent pay and access to canteens.[30] This is not the full explanation, however, as volunteerism seemed to seize many citizens in Britain and Japan. Teenager Dorothy Kahn was champing at the bit: she wrote in her diary after an air raid that there were now '"fire spotters" to watch out for incendiary bombs. We can be one when we are sixteen and I will be sixteen a week on Thursday. Only men are spotting now, though'.[31] Echoing Kahn's youthful enthusiasm and criticism of gender boundaries, Japanese teenager Sonematsu Kazuko also was eager to offer her contribution:

I'm in a bit of a spot. Should I take home economics or medicine? As a girl, I should be taking home economics, but from here on out Japanese girls cannot just busy themselves with girls' things. No, girls will have to be able to do what boys do as well. Boys must go to the battlefield. We want to go, too, but currently the state won't give us that freedom. But now the time will come when they *must* give it to us.[32]

Across Britain and Japan, young people 'joined up' in whatever way they were able, to support the prosecution of a total war against the enemy; few openly recognised that the enemy was doing the same. In an unusual example of insight, Donald Wheal noted the irony in some of these efforts, recalling, 'I was coming home [in May 1940] from Church Lads' Brigade, proud of a black uniform I now recognise as something Nazi youth leader Baldur von Schirach might have envied'.[33] Educated students in Britain and Japan, who were pulled away from their studies to serve the war effort, still managed to rationalise the loss of personal opportunity as a contribution to a worthy cause. Sumiyoshi Konokichi, a Tokyo Imperial University engineering student, wrote in his diary that . . .

. . . we must be resolved to die honourably. This feeling silently grows stronger and stronger. My suffering up to this point has not been in vain. I have no fear of death. I only expect to meet my fate smiling at the beauty of the end of things. This is because I have expended all my energy in faithfully serving my loved ones and the fatherland.[34]

Such dedication to service for the state – whether directly or indirectly, as work undertaken to protect loved ones such as fire-watching and home guard services – was absolutely essential to keeping the city's war machine going. Unfortunately for residents of the city, these activities also made them desirable targets for enemy bombers.

It must be said, however, that some citizens did not feel the need to embrace national service. Some dragged their feet when asked to take up onerous duties or responded with scepticism when called to sacrifice. Laurie Latchford ruminated over his decision not to sign up for a Swansea air raid patrol:

Now I felt tired, and had had no food since midday. Big 'Tom' was standing there [at the meeting]. He had declared last time that he would go next time. He made no move. I didn't volunteer. I went home for supper. Essie welcomed me almost in tears. Strange, she bore the thought of my going into Swansea during the last big raid without too much distress showing, but the thought of me caught unwittingly in the town during a 'blitz' was too much. During my meal I was preoccupied. I wasn't too pleased with myself.[35]

Neglecting responsibility permeated all areas of wartime Britain and Japan, including non-defence chores. Yoshida Fusako, who awoke at 5:30am to participate in her high school's cleaning day, noted that no one bothered to turn up by 7am, 'even though there are many who lived even closer to the school than I. They just forgot'.[36] In Japan, unrealistic and cruel demands by representatives of the state strained the faith and support of ordinary people. Strapping her infant daughter onto her back and putting her 3- year-old son into a cart, Yamamoto Shigeko latched the flatbed vehicle onto her bicycle and, peddling upright, fled with her children to the outskirts of Hachiōji, which was under heavy bombardment:

Like a column of ants, people were pushing through, whereupon Civil Defence Units (*keibōdan*) shoved us back. 'Go back to your homes and put out the fires', they screamed angrily, even saying to me, 'Hey, you can't bring that cart out here!' But almost no one paid them any heed so, of course, I didn't listen either, watching the enemy planes' direction and peddling away from them as fast as I could.

In fact, Shigeko's husband, who worked in the IJA Air Force base in Tachikawa, had warned her specifically to avoid city centres and their immediate peripheries because of the nature of firestorms and strategic bombing. When the Civil Defence officers told her to defend the city, she knew better than to do so.[37] After experiencing a bombing of his home neighbourhood in Tokyo, Sumiyoshi Konokichi – the engineering student who professed his love for the fatherland – quickly turned against the state less than two weeks later:

Last night there was an air raid, so I came to work late. I dropped off some luggage and went home early. A spring day, so sad. The cherry blossoms are past their prime. I watch a training officer instruct his soldiers. He shouts as loud as possible in a high-pitched voice. It is an utterly empty gesture to pass the day, a complete waste of time. Trying to gain some meaning in a sea of ignorance is impossible. The army is a place where one eats, sleeps, and must spin lies with dishonest enthusiasm.[38]

In addition to the foot-draggers and quiet sceptics, there were certainly conscientious objectors, pacifists, and those who were merely ambivalent, but these voices were drowned out by those of the supporters of the conflict, and sometimes directly silenced by the wartime state. In most cases, the naysayers were dismissed by social pressure alone – when a 'Mrs. Foster' complained that '[t]hese raids are getting too terrible, we cannot go on like this, London will be in ruins', Mass Observer Eleanor Humphries asked her sharply, 'what she was rumbling about'. The woman thereafter kept these opinions to herself.[39] The dedication of urban citizens in the face of the enemy was mirrored by the people who enabled that enemy's war machine, locking non-combatants in both Axis and Allied nations into a devastating conflict. Since these supporters were essential to the war effort, they became 'legitimate' targets in the eyes of the enemy's armed forces.

Social pressure and the state thus conspired to enforce a 'volunteerism' in both Britain and Japan, because both countries' society and state apparatus had reason to fear resistance to mobilisation. Many Japanese felt this burden was being borne unfairly along class lines; consequently, Yoshimi Yoshiaki, in *Grassroots Fascism*, discovered that the Japanese authorities nervously observed the reactions of non-elite actors.[40] Numerous Japanese accounts of wartime society describe widespread surveillance by the state, social organisations, and even neighbours. In 'fascist' Japan, this might not be surprising, but such surveillance and social management was also common in 'free' Britain. In Coventry, the British Ministry of Information also kept a close eye on rumours, gossip, and panicked behaviour among the people. Even before the bombing began, a local committee filed concerned reports to the government, complaining that 'families, spread across the country, are devising all sorts of ways of informing each other about the severity of the raids, etc.', and that for the first time 'a rather defeatist attitude has appeared where previously a degree of confidence was felt'. Following the heavy bombing of Coventry in November 1940, the government observers, after a perfunctory statement about high morale in the face of the enemy, delineated further troubles in the city:

Why are bombed-out people being asked to pay for the costs of removal? . . . The constant sight of men trailing about the city looking for lodgings is doing nobody any good . . . Some bad cases of non-payment for food and accommodation exist and aggravate the situation . . . An invasion this Spring? How shall we act? Must we stay put? Who will ring the church bells? Are there any church bells to ring in Coventry after the blitzing? Are there any troops within immediate call, should the invader appear here? . . . The quest for food – no oat, cheese, golden syrup, biscuits, sauce and tinned milk. Why, when the price of a commodity has been fixed, does it vanish from sight? Fruit, eggs, onions, etc. [41]

Nevertheless, it only took a plurality of support for the war machine to go on, and the bombers that the people produced targeted pro-war non-combatants and pacifists alike. Despite the reservations and small acts of resistance among some citizens, ordinary people in both Britain and Japan rallied behind the state. When attacks did strike at the heart of a major city, no amount of preparation was sufficient, and thus demoralising chaos inevitably followed the destruction of defence systems, hospitals, information networks, and transport. After

volunteering to protect the city, then, ordinary people found themselves trapped and buried within it.

The Insatiable Beast: Bombers Deconstruct the City

Mass bombing of the cities was an effort by the enemy to take apart,
piece by piece, a man-made space in order to destroy the infrastructure
necessary for modern war. This included the workers who fired up the
foundry furnaces, the doctors who kept the hospitals running, and even
the men who collected the rubbish. The city then became less a centre
of modernism and life, and more a creature that consumed the people
who lived within it. One Bristol Air Raid Warden described barely
surviving a direct bombing, and then scrambling along as fallen wires
'wrapped themselves about my legs and body like an angry octopus'.
Before long, he discovered others struggling for survival within the
city's deadly embrace:

The scene was pretty grim. A man and his son were both fatally injured. And here
was I, a warden whose duty it was to inspire and instil confidence, in a badly
shaken state! And then a young girl, a member of the family, suddenly appeared
and said in a voice so steady that I shall always remember it: 'Will you turn off the
gas at the main, warden?' That calm voice steadied me.[42]

The systems that supplied, informed, and protected urban space were
ultimately only as good as the people who manned the fire trucks,
telephones, and anti-aircraft guns. Takahashi Aiko complained about
how civil defence unit members (*bōgodan'in*) arbitrarily held up automo-
bile traffic outside of her house, causing loud fights and confusion, until
her husband came out and shouted, 'Stupid bastards, civil defence
idiots – are you drunk?'[43] Nevertheless, if the service and defence
workers were killed, the city was no better than a heap of lifeless stone
to the people who lived in it. With its tubes, wires, structures, and
conduits, this creature was like a robot made of wood, concrete, and
steel, and the people inside it kept the thing running. In other words, the
bombers were right on target: to truly destroy the city, one also had to kill
its people.

Before the pipes and ducts fell apart, more febrile, but equally important, human systems were already showing signs of strain. In both Britain
and Japan, hierarchies in the social order were challenged like never
before. In the state of consternation and uncertainty that pervaded cities
during mass bombings, some citizens responded in a fairly ham-fisted
appeal to authority. One man threatened to hit Laurie Latchford as he
stood up on a train to watch the bombing of Swansea; the man forced

him down into his seat and shouted, 'Don't look! Sit down! Obey the regulations, and everything will be all right!'[44] During the firebombing of Chiba, Uegusa Shōsaburō saw Military Policemen slapping civilian refugees and shouting, 'Put out the fires!'[45] Yabe Masaaki recalled, with no small amount of bitterness, how local 'authorities' such as policemen, veterans, and air raid wardens were like 'foxes who borrowed the tiger's majesty', and used false authority to 'bully the weak' (*yowai-mono ijime*), including his mother. Masaaki's father had been drafted, leaving his mother poor and alone with four young children and an elderly mother-in-law. During an air raid, when they attempted to go into the community shelter, one man shouted at them, 'we're full already, you lot go somewhere else'. Almost immediately, his little sister Aoi (4) began crying in terror, shouting, 'I'm scared! I'm scared!' As Aoi grew more upset, the man screamed, 'Shut up! Get out! Weaklings! My orders have the authority of the Emperor himself!' Even in the eyes of Masaaki, who was just a boy at the time, the man who attacked his mother was a coward, and was only trying to preserve his own life. Finally, his mother said to Aoi, 'Don't be scared ... If you're afraid, just close your eyes'. The girl immediately buried her face into her mother's shoulder, and the woman led her children into the worst of Shizuoka's air raids. Sometime later, Masaaki noticed blood on his right arm, but he could not feel any pain. Feeling 'strange', he looked up and saw Aoi's bloodied head dangling from his mother's shoulder. She had been hit by an incendiary bomb, but his mother refused to stop running. The memory of this loss poisoned his view of social and political authority throughout the postwar era.[46] In Britain and Japan, abuse of authority by fearful civilians resulted in many needless deaths. Superficially these examples demonstrate the resilience of such power under fire; still, the many panicked policemen, firemen, air raid wardens, and soldiers who shouted at, hit, and threatened the citizens they were charged to protect did as much to undermine their collective authority as enhance it in the eyes of ordinary people. As one Mass Observer in Manchester put it: 'Officials have tended to be somewhat intolerant, and have clung to Red Tape as a means of defence'.[47]

After local authorities either distinguished or embarrassed themselves, bombing campaigns targeted the military and defence infrastructures of their enemies. Despite the historical emphasis on capital cities like London and Tokyo, regional cities were arguably even more important to the nation's war machine; consequently the enemy gave them no quarter. At first, domestic defences could be visually impressive to the uninformed. Violet Maund described RAF pilots blasting German bombers near Bristol, which had an important airplane parts manufacturer, writing that 'watching our men go in again and again was a thrilling, though dreadful, sight'.[48] Citizens of some cities assumed that they would never be targeted by enemy fire, even though they supported defence industries. When the enemy came to these regional centres of production, local forces threw up bright flares, tracers, and perhaps a few planes. In November 1940, Marcus Sadler painted a picture of the multi-faceted defence of Coventry:

The anti-aircraft fire was terrific, with the tracer shells from the smaller guns cutting queer white lines through the sky, and the Bofors guns were shooting up flares, and wire mesh traps to try and catch the diving planes. Machine guns on the ground were shooting at other flares from the planes and also potting at big two ton land mines floating down slowly by thirty foot span parachutes. Shrapnel was landing on all sides, and the whistle and whine of the shells, combined with the Screamers and Whistlers seemed like violins and saxophones in some fantastic orchestra the main theme of which was the big bass thumping of the bombs, and the rolling deep throated drums of the guns. It is impossible to put into words and describe it properly it was so terrific ...[49]

Citizens in Tsuchizaki, like Fujii Hiroshi, who was Head of the Municipal Civil Defence Unit, knew their city would need to be protected; while not one of Japan's major metropolises, it was targeted because of its crucial oil refining industry and military installations.

At the time of the air raids, we put a lot of energy into fire-fighting and had a system in place, because I think Tsuchizaki was, well, while not one of Japan's 'big five cities', a first-class regional city. When it was time to invest everything in the war effort, the whole city was quick off the mark to get its fire-fighters organised. The police cooperated fully and, of course, so did the whole city. Every department and branch of the city cooperated with the [defence] plan I devised, which was comprehensive in scope ... In each neighbourhood, big shops and companies all made reservoirs [for fire-fighting].

At the start of the Allied bombing campaign, then, defence force commanders in Japan felt confident, having enjoyed widespread local support and conducted extensive drilling of the civilian population.[50] In Britain, as well, at the start, the appearance of soldiers, fortifications, and anti-aircraft guns inspired many ordinary people, like Coventry resident Mary Bloomfield, to feel confident:

It seemed impossible that on this lovely afternoon men were killing each other, impossible that out of that summer sky death might come, heralded by sirens, hooters, and rattles, if we were lucky, or just the dull hum of engines, followed by the crashing of bombs; yet that was what we were all steeling ourselves to face, a sudden lightening raid, taking us all by surprise. But it didn't come ... We all agreed that Hitler couldn't win, no matter how long it lasted.[51]

Even when the local defences could not hit enemy raiders, optimism was high in the beginning. 'Wait till we get the four-fives, we'll show them', said one man to Bill Regan in east London, referring to 4.5 anti-aircraft guns, 'We could do with something a bit bigger, if only to give our morale a lift'. Lorries drove around the working class districts of London, firing at German planes, in order 'to cheer us up, or confuse the enemy. Anyhow, it's one of Churchill's better ideas'.[52]

The defence of the home islands was a spectacle, and at times it was inspiring for those who watched it on the ground; this sensation of inevitable victory was, however, short-lived. In Japan, regional cities like Shizuoka were left relatively unaided by formal air forces and, by the end of the war, civilian defence forces were often caught off-guard. Shiba Ei'ichi, a 34-year-old prefectural military provisions officer (*ken gunshu-kain*), recalled how the raid of 19 June, which nearly wiped the city out entirely, arrived in the middle of the night well after the 'all clear' had sounded:

We were startled for one moment . . . and then it just hit me: it's a raid! Without thinking, the other men in the dormitory started screaming and shouting, and one could see the same situation emerging in every corner of Shizuoka. For a moment we did nothing, only stood there in shock.

The headquarters of the prefectural government was slammed by explosives and incendiary bombs, causing the five storey structure to catch fire and sway dangerously. He saw military provisions offices, police stations, and local government buildings, all tasked with defending the people and public order, go up in smoke throughout the city.[53] In Britain, the proximity of German forces, at first, and the nature of V-1 and V-2 rocket technology, in the latter stages of the war, made air defence almost impossible. Conventional air attacks could meet little reprisal: a German raid on 25 September 1941 that hit the Bristolian Aeroplane works saw no action from any British planes there, because there were, unbelievably, neither fighter aircraft nor anti-aircraft guns defending the city until two days after the attack; further bungling enraged local officials for years.[54] The focus on the defence of London drew both men and materiel away from many regional cities, sometimes leaving them almost completely open to enemy attacks, which made locals afraid and angry. In Bradford, George Hutchinson noted the fact that 'no resistance was offered has caused much indignation, that no sirens sounded has caused more. The general attitude is that if the authorities can't defend the city they can at least warn the people to take shelter'.[55] One resident in Bristol dreamed of firemen floating through the cities on air balloons, successfully defending the city from the flames; upon reflection, he admitted, 'I suppose it was wish fulfil-ment'.[56] While historical memory might lionise the 'Battle of Britain', the fact is that GAF bombers frequently found easy civilian targets in British cities.

As the local defence forces failed, the citizens slowly realised that they were on their own, and this could generate powerful resentments. For Imperial Japan, a combination of lack of fuel and US mass production of planes meant that the enemy gradually seized and easily maintained air superiority. Under such conditions, some even refused to fight. Fleeing Tsuchizaki, the main port for the northwest city of Akita, Ōno Asakichi encountered an anti-aircraft position that was fully manned by Japanese troops, but remained silent as the American bombers destroyed Ōno's hometown. '"Oi, you soldiers, why aren't you firing a shot," I said. It was terrible. "If we fire on them," [they replied], "a plane will smash us, and we'll all die."' In fact, the soldiers had visited Ōno's home before the bombing, saying they would flee when the attacks came; ironically, Ōno later encountered these men and their feckless anti-aircraft gun hiding on the grounds of a 'National Defence Shrine' (Hokoku jinja), wherein the gods and spirits of the war dead were meant to defend the nation.[57] The collapse of the air defences in Japan reached levels that ordinary civilians could not ignore, even if state propaganda preached inevitable victory. After a raid on Liverpool, Dorothy Hughes returned to the city to find British soldiers on Lime Street 'singing and carrying on. Disgusting'.[58] When the enemy exposed the inadequacy of local defences, it would confuse and frighten civilians tasked with protecting the city. Kawahata Ichirō, a farmer who had been drafted into a transport corps in Hachiōji, was alarmed at how the Allied bombers knew exactly which rail lines to hit in order to cripple efforts in his area, writing, 'it was like the enemy knew things that even the locals didn't – I was shocked by their preci-sion'.[59] Sometimes the enemy was too incompetent to strike military targets, resulting in the needless victimisation of non-combatants in the city. Dora Mockett observed that 'the Germans claim that this weekend they have successfully (?) bombed military objectives in Hull', but the only target they seemed to have struck successfully was the city's mental hospital.[60] If the enemy was incompetent, however, the defenders could be worse. As GAF bombers laid waste to Coventry, the city's emergency services, including fire engines and ambulances, were withdrawn to the outskirts due to the collapse of the city's infrastructure – just when they were needed most.[61] In regional cities from Hull to Coventry, Tsuchizaki to Himeji, the people were largely at the enemy's mercy because the city's defence forces, particularly outside of capital cities, were simply too weak to keep the bombers away.

When the defence systems failed, state actors ceased to be mere apparatchiks and began fending for their own lives, as well. A policeman in wartime Takamatsu, a regional city on the island Shikoku, 45-year-old Okamoto Masao wrote a war diary that reveals how a public employee quickly became a vulnerable refugee himself. First, although he was aware of the American attack methods in the destruction of Himeji and Tokushima, on this occasion the enemy bombers feigned a withdrawal and dropped their incendiary bombs from a higher altitude, catching the residents by surprise. He scrambled to organise his family so that they could put on their protective clothing, collect their valuables, and prepare to flee for cover. Then, Masao sent them off, one by one, to hide in air raid shelters. He noted in his diary that the 'incendiary bombs were falling like rain', but that the (high altitude) enemy planes were eerily nowhere to be seen or heard. 'The strength of the fire was so intense', he wrote, trying to put his air raid training to use while his house started to burn, 'that there was no way that just a few people could put it out'. Despite being a comparatively well-informed civil servant, Okamoto admitted that 'we were completely fooled [by the Americans]'. As a policeman, Okamoto had trained locals in air raid precautions, so he knew that, after a certain point, he had to flee his home before it began taking direct hits from bombs or strafing. Putting his meagre belongings into a basket on his head, Okamoto fled over a Shintō shrine's grounds, then through pine trees, and finally under a bridge. He sat in the muck, being pushed further and further in by increasing numbers of desperate people. Gradually, strong feelings began to build up inside him:

I had this one desire: to live. It's odd. This was in spite of the fact that I thought I was fully prepared to die [for the war effort]. It was getting really cold in the water. My teeth chattered as I shivered. I yelled, 'Come on, Japan. Hang on until you can get even!' When I shouted this, I felt warmer . . . When the attacks ceased, it got very quiet. People began saying, 'We made it! We survived!' We shouted in happiness. We celebrated with the dawn. A kind of ignorant joy bubbled up from inside my heart. I didn't even give a thought to what life would be like after this.[62]

Masao and the others were momentarily joyful, but their survival did not change the facts: the Japanese military's inability to protect civilians from aerial bombardment had eroded public confidence in their status as defenders. After months of shrinking rations and widespread hunger, these direct assaults on the city further exposed the mendacity of the government's promises to protect its people.

On top of the loss of self-defence, citizens could no longer heal the injured around them; to medical professionals, the destruction of hospitals and clinics was particularly heinous, as if it was an attack on the idea of life itself. Even before they were attacked directly, hospitals were ill-equipped to confront the crisis spreading from one section of the city to another. When the bombing started, Matsubayashi Hana, a nurse in Shizuoka, and her fellow staff members, had to hurriedly evacuate their patients, and she wrote that they 'were moving about with the sounds of bombs ringing in our ears. Fires were starting here and there [in the hospital], and then we saw one start at the front door'. After sending off the patients, staff members were ordered to abandon the building. They ran blindly to the river, embers and cinders from flaming Shizuoka burning their faces and eyes. Fire Wardens turned them away and sent them back into the city, where they hid under a concrete bridge with some Japanese soldiers. Stepping over the dead in the streets, Hana later returned to the Shizuoka hospital to find only one pillar left standing; a note posted there ordered the staff to the municipal government building.

We hurried there, and we could see the patients lining up outside. As soon as we arrived we started working. From the basement someone shouted, 'Patient suffering blood loss. Come quickly!' I ran there. There was no time to rest. Soon it was night. Some nurses still had not returned. We were getting panicked. It grew dark but eight nurses were still nowhere to be found. I couldn't sleep. We waited until morning, and then three nurses and one male staff member went looking for them ... The [missing staff] had been hit directly with incendiaries, their bodies blown apart; looking at their apron lapels and ambulance bags – we couldn't tell from the bodies – when we examined them carefully, we figured out [who they were]. I was made speechless by the horror of it, and a sense of sadness and loss overwhelmed me as I wept uncontrollably.

Two of Hana's colleagues, who had presumably been attempting to put out the fire in the hospital, had tried to take shelter in the water trough used for fire-fighting, but only one could fit; the other burned alive outside it. 'The sadness and loss filled my heart', Hana wrote a second time, 'and I was speechless'.[63] In London, one staff member of St. Thomas' Hospital recalled how the repeated bombings of 1940 were almost totally unexpected; when the building was struck, many working nurses and doctors were buried alive under the rubble. One nurse initially survived the first bombardment, enduring her pain as long as possible while covered in heavy debris, but 'mercifully, because of the extent of her injuries, she had died as she was freed'. Doctors injected her with pain killers, and one of her fellow nurses 'insisted' on crawling into the rubble to comfort her as they tried in vain to save her life. The impact on the psyche of hospital staff was deep and immediate:

We were talking on the terrace after lunch in the warm sun when the stretcher party came past. Until then things still seemed rather unreal. Now, as our eyes followed the grim party bearing the blanked shrouded forms to the mortuary we were shocked to silence. The air seemed chill, the sun gone in. None of us I think had met this sort of finality before. We really wouldn't see or hear them ever again.[64]

In both Britain and Japan, the attack on the city's hospitals was an unrelenting deconstruction of the modern machine upon which doctors relied to perform their art. On 15 September 1940 in London and 3 July 1945 in Takamatsu, doctors D. B. Maling and Matsubara Kijirō watched helplessly as their neighbourhoods were taken apart by enemy aircraft. At first, Maling and Matsubara described their experiences as any ordinary civilian would: namely, by composing episodic descriptions of sensory experiences. Climbing to the roof of his hospital, Maling described 'flashes and shell bursts', 'thunderous explosions', and a 'penetrating, pungent smell of smoke, fumes, and cordite', all interspersed with 'agonizing screams and shrieks', before a friend insisted they take cover. Like Maling, Matsubara ascended to an observation area (kanshijo) in a nearby primary school, and saw a 'red sky', followed by 'the booms of explosions from B-29s' and 'a groaning noise' from aircraft engines, whereupon his friend advised they get away from the top of the building. Leaping down, Matsubara narrowly missed being directly hit by a falling incendiary. Briefly, the cities of London and Takamatsu were eerily quiet; then doctors were confronted by the disaster that the bombers created.

For doctors of modern medicine like Matsubara and Maling, the city provided various machines, tools, and devices instrumental to saving lives; this febrile net of material objects and supply routes was torn apart by the enemy. Matsubara took refuge with several nurses and midwives in the only reinforced concrete structure he could find: the municipal government office. Electricity was cut by the bombing, falling dust made everything black, and Dr. Matsubara, who was accustomed to calmly gazing into human bodies and healing them, was suddenly shrouded in a terrifying, paralysing darkness. After discovering he was the only doctor available, Matsubara heard a voice call out – the section head for municipal education – and he discovered that a city official collapsed on the floor. 'I had tossed away my first aid kit [while fleeing]', he wrote despondently, 'I was completely empty-handed'. After administering CPR, Matsubara brought the man back, who immediately shouted: 'Is the emperor's photo undamaged? Will the city stop burning?' He calmed the man by telling him lies, trying desperately to keep his heart rate down.

Once morning broke, Dr. Matsubara knew he was personally safe, but his work had only just begun:

... the injured came in droves. There was one nurse, and me – the doctor – but fortunately there were two boxes of first aid equipment in the municipal government building, so we used those to administer medicine.[65]

Meanwhile in London, D. B. Maling scrambled and stumbled through the wreckage of St. Thomas', helping wounded staff and patients, while the infrastructure of the city was literally falling down on top of him. Maling's London became an inchoate mass of burst pipes, crumbled walls, and trapped bodies:

The basement seemed deserted now and was about six inches deep with water – mattresses, pillows and blankets floating about amid a twisted mass of bedsteads and debris ... Crawling under pipes and over bedsteads and wreckage in the dark and getting very wet we found a small gap partially blocked by an iron bedstead which once negotiated took us out into the open in the midst of what had been College House. We climbed over the wreckage of a grand-piano and a shout from Arthur was answered by a low voice which seemed to come, and in fact did, from the depths of the wreckage. We thought it was a friend of ours, Harold Walker, and tried to cheer him up with a running commentary as we moved bricks and debris. Morphia seemed a good idea so we made our way back to Casualty and managed to persuade Dr. Norman to return with us with a tray with morphia and syringes. Back into the debris again there was no sense in all of us standing out in the open with shrapnel falling, not to mention bombs and bits of loose masonry ...[66]

To add insult to injury, hospitals across Britain experienced incompetent administration and interference from the armed forces, just as medical professionals in Japan were ordered to prioritise military patients or rush to save important people.[67] In one Bristol hospital, patients and nurses sang to calm the nerves of those panicked by air attacks, until a bomb blasted the nurses off of their feet and blew a patient across the room into another bed; an infirmary near Liverpool was hit with a bomb so large that it annihilated three hospital buildings, buried patients under rubble, and set fire to everything, including the ambulances; in Manchester, one hospital was nearly annihilated, and patients fell through four floors to the basement below – with some survivors reacting to 'the sound of an air raid warning, even if unaccompanied by gunfire, [with] great nervousness and complete inability to concentrate ...'[68] For those watching the destruction from the countryside, the loss of modern medical services had severe consequences: for example, Hull evacuee Olive Metcalfe, who was pregnant with her first child and only barely getting by in rural Yorkshire, heard 'the dread news that staggered me ... there is now no maternity hospital <u>at all</u> in Hull. I had built all my many untold plans on the supposition of its existence but apparently it was evacuated ... to just nowhere – sort of dissolved into thin air'. She was told by a nurse to have her baby at home but, because her husband was serving in London, this meant she would be left entirely on her own after giving birth and 'a nursing home is absolutely out of the question' due to the high costs.[69] In an age before the National Health Service, the medical establishment was incapable of controlling the crisis created by war.

Similarly, Japanese hospitals were so overwhelmed that they began simply offering palliative care to the dying. In Tokyo, which had been set alight by US bombers, Takahashi Aiko watched mournfully as a truck loaded wounded near the city centre: 'The victims were lined up like logs of firewood. To me, they didn't look alive at all. I've never seen anything this horrible, not even in paintings of Hell itself'.[70] Meanwhile, in the nearby city of Chiba, Takahashi Eiko suffered an even worse experience after she was caught in a terrible firestorm and took refuge in the grounds of Chiba Shrine. Burning cinders landed on her clothes and her mother tried to extinguish them, loudly chanting Buddhist prayers (*nenbutsu*), but these proved ineffective and Eiko was badly burned. 'Am I going to burn to death? I don't want to die', she thought, 'it's painful, excruciating – no words for it'. Her mother flagged an ambulance and rushed her to a military hospital, where a gruff triage nurse shouted, 'Soldiers first! Then those with external wounds. Burns last!' Eiko was in excruciating pain, squatting in a crowded hallway littered with sleeping and injured people. Finally, a medic gave her some medicated bandages, but the burns on her hands, legs, and back were still torturing her without respite. She and the other patients, between fifty and one hundred, were then herded into a recreation room, where a khaki sheet had been thrown down with some pillows to 'rest'.

I collapsed onto the floor to sleep, but I didn't really. It was more like I was paralysed with pain. A young nurse or two came by to see me and give me a drink, but there was no running water so they must have carried it in by hand; 'Yes please', you'd say, and they'd let you sip some from a small cup. They wouldn't take your temperature, and certainly didn't try to cool you down. One nurse was heard to say, 'If there's any tetanus vaccine left over, give it to the burn victims'. I was secretly hoping there would be some, and before long they came by and gave me a shot – I was so thankful. Every drop of that is priceless.

Eiko looked over to see a little boy sleeping nearby, who looked 'in rough shape', with a compound fracture on his right arm and blood seeping through the bandages. His mother sat next to him calling out in a strained voice, 'Kuni! Kuni!' but he soon died. Below her, that evening, a pregnant woman went into labour, but she had taken shrapnel in her stomach. There was no maternity ward, so she gave birth in a corner; when the baby did not cry, she called out 'where's my baby?' but the nurse remained silent. When she failed to deliver her afterbirth, they searched desperately for a doctor, only to find a veterinarian. Others were suffering mental breakdowns, screaming and shouting, and some were apparently refugees from a mental asylum. Eiko found herself thinking, 'Damn it, this is stupid, someone just do something!' At the end of her ordeal the next morning, a nurse and medic arrived to say, 'This is a military hospital, but we took in civilians. You all have used three months' of medical supplies in one day. There's nothing more we can do for you, so go on to another hospital'.[71] The failure of the hospital system underlined the feelings of helplessness that struck the hearts of civilians in Britain and Japan. The city, with all of its spectacular modernity, including promises of scientific hygiene and medicine, had failed them.

Another serious consequence of the deconstruction of British and Japanese cities was the loss of housing for their millions of residents. In Britain, citizens in regional cities like Swansea, Hull, Bristol, and Coventry discovered that the loss of housing could be much more devastating than in the capital. After the attack on Swansea, Laurie Latchford described how 'houses had been shattered by [high explosive] bombs; modern villas stripped of their tiles. Others, the roof timbering sliding earthwards to cover shattered walls; bedding, pictures, rugs, chairs and broken debris in one great pile'. Later, he encountered a stunned-looking family of three wandering the streets, watching the searchlights and shell-bursts. Advising them to take shelter, the father simply said they had nowhere to go.[72] A disturbing scene rapidly developed in the countryside nearby urban centres as city residents fled aerial attacks. On a bus near central Hull, Olive Metcalfe saw people pile inside, 'all clutching parcels and looking a bit distressed. Among them were three little girls, very young, with a man. He said their house was down and it was feared their parents dead. All the incomers were folks who had been "bombed out."'[73] In late November 1940, Willy Buchanan described the refugee crisis in Warwickshire following the air assault on Coventry; although she tried to maintain a positive attitude, the fact was that the city had been destroyed and its residents made homeless:

We came through the awful air raid safely but the house suffered. The roof got blown off and the windows blown in, and on top of all that it poured of rain and we got flooded out ... We are all right at nights, we have been going to a farm since the raid and they have made us very comfortable. We cycle backwards-forwards. The house isn't fit to sleep in yet as it's so damp. We stood on our doorstep and watched the raid. A house across the street got a direct hit and a landmine dropped not many yards away and blew the roofs off all our row. It was an awful experience, they are still digging people out yet, and the town is an absolute ruin. The destruction to houses is terrible and there are thousands and thousands of people without homes.[74]

Because of the GAF's destruction of housing stock, even rural and holiday accommodations were mobilised. As early as 1942, Bristolian Violet Maund tried to book a cottage for some time away from the bombed out town, but found that the homeless situation had rendered her completely unable to leave the city because all spare rural housing had been taken over by 'some Ministry or other'.[75] Once driven from their homes, urban citizens took an increasingly hostile view of the government that was supposed to protect them; this was exacerbated by the perception that the central government was mostly concerned with protecting itself. Manchester citizens fled bombing south to the Cheshire plains, camping in fields and becoming, in the view of some Mass Observers, nearly seditious in their antagonistic views of the leadership in London.[76]

The flammable materials used in Japanese homes, however, made them much easier targets of bombers, which meant even more people were rendered homeless by bombing attacks. Unfortunately for Inaba Fuku, her family's home was in Chiba, which was a centre of military and industrial production. While all of her relatives were able to fit safely into a shelter during an air raid, she could hear the bombs falling all around the neighbourhood.

Boom, boom, boom, the earth shook, and sand fell hissing from the ceiling of the shelter. The inside became dark and stifling. 'They're close', I thought. My nine year old brother was at the shelter entrance when the whine of falling bombs could be heard, and then he quickly leaped inside ... Before long it was quiet. Up above, my brother screamed, 'The house is gone!' No way, I thought, and went outside to look. Gone. Our house, the one in front of it, and all around, there wasn't a single building that was sound. About six meters away from the shelter there was a gaping hole in the ground, and just nothing.

Years later Fuku still could not find the right words to describe the sensation of having her entire neighbourhood wiped out in a single attack, writing 'it just disappeared', 'it was blown away', and 'it flew up to Heaven'. She and her family spent the rest of the war living in a 'barracks', which she felt fortunate to have, even if they were only given one 10 × 10 metre room for the whole group.[77] Most citizens felt that they had no choice but to leave their belongings behind and flee for the countryside, often with very little in their rucksacks apart from some food, cash, and insurance policies that were unlikely ever to be honoured.

To make matters worse for homeless refugees, enemy bombers often targeted transport, so these systems were rendered useless when civilians tried to flee the city. In Liverpool, Dorothy Hughes wrote that the trains 'have stopped. The planes haven't though. They're still coming. [There] must have been hundreds without any exaggeration. The hum has <u>never</u> stopped'.[78] Some citizens felt that they had been deliberately abandoned by their government as trains and buses were halted, or that other cities were in fact poaching their means of transportation: in Chorlton, Manchester, one woman heard several citizens complain that 'Our buses seemed to have vanished from the roads ... we had lent so much to other bombed towns that we were disorganised when the "blitz" came. I feel there is some truth in that'.[79] Others feared that transport infrastructure made one particularly vulnerable to arbitrary enemy fire. Marcus Sadler noted that, in Coventry, German planes 'bombed the people on the main roads streaming to get out', and that the city was almost inaccessible due to craters left in the streets.[80] As American aircraft approached the Japanese home islands and established air superiority, Grumman fighter planes attacked the country with near impunity, and one of their preferred targets was trains. Katō Hideo recalled a particularly terrifying experience in Himeji: after hearing about the appearance of a few dozen aircraft in a nearby town, the station manager thought it wise to send the train quickly away from the city:

... so the train crept north slowly, about 40km per hour, I think. Then the enemy planes came overhead. The conductor thought it was too dangerous not to stop, so he braked gently. The passengers were all craning their necks from the windows to see the enemy planes. Then they started firing directly in front of the train. As soon as the train stopped, three of us leaped out and dove down under the cars. This time the enemy machine guns hit the boiler and opened two holes in it. Steam came pouring out and blew away, immobilizing the train. After the raid, we went into the first passenger car and saw that a woman who had been carrying a small child was shot, both of them through the chest, and that there were people killed with blood pouring out of their mouths. The ground was already red with blood, with arms shot off, thighs split open and legs dangling – you just could not bear to look at such a horrible scene.[81]

In southeast London, elderly Anne Shepperd recorded in her diary the flight of her fellow Methodists from their bombed-out homes in Eltham. As they fled into the streets and crowded onto trains out of the capital, enemy planes attacked them mercilessly: 'Machine gunning has been going on in our roads yesterday and this morning. Some of our folk were out and had to get to cover. We know of others who have terrible experiences. Trains to London too are being machine gunned'.[82] The sudden destruction of city transport and communications made urban citizens feel even more vulnerable. *Mainichi News* (Nagoya) reporter Ōi Masao described how information and transit networks were paralyzed in just one night:

> The municipal electricity supply and the commuter rail lines were all cut off, so everyone in the office has to come in on foot. Automobiles can reach neither the Aichi Prefecture Anti-Aircraft HQ nor the East Coast Military Command HQ, so information can only be disseminated in person, and no telephones are working. It's as if your legs and ears have been taken away. Consequently, even filing a news report is more excruciating than I had ever imagined.[83]

The city closed both information and transport networks as a result of the area bombing campaigns, leaving ordinary people with no access to news or travel. The walls of these towns began falling down on the citizens inside.

For those who managed to escape the deadly urban jungle, wrecked food distribution networks meant that further survival would be challenging on multiple fronts. Although Britain and Japan observed rationing measures, food supply was still filtered through a pre-existing for-profit system of shops, which presented some inefficiencies and limitations. Mary Bloomfield wrote in her diary of a Coventry shopkeeper who panicked and 'sold his stock before it was blasted to smithereens'.[84] Dorothy Hughes complained that food items bought in Liverpool's shops were inedible due to shortages – meat pies with little or no meat were hardly appetising.[85] Similarly, Laurie Latchford noted that in Wales, by 1941, the shops were empty: there were 'no sweets, food rationed, merchandise of all descriptions hard to get'. Even American supplies could not compensate for the collapse of the British food economy. Bomb strikes on Swansea crippled the water supply: as Laurie went inspecting bomb damage in the city, loudspeakers mounted on a van proclaimed 'Water must be reserved for drinking and washing only!'[86] Even before the bombs hit Nagoya, Inoue Haruko recalled that the food system provided less than the bare minimum, including soybean products, dried fruit, spring onions, and some wild grains; white rice was insufficient and so it was always mixed with potatoes. The quality of rations was often subpar, so Japanese families went to the market for meat and fish but, even after lining up for ages, 'it was completely inadequate'. Inoue relied on relatives who were fishermen to survive, also resorting to fishing for eel on her own as well as cooking and eating wildflowers such as dandelions and Japanese aster (*yomena*). Fukubu Miyoko added that, under such conditions, the city became a garden:

The food situation [in Nagoya] got worse and worse every year [from 1940], so people began farming brownfield sites near railroads, producing cabbage and white potatoes. Sometimes we'd happily go to collect our food, but the cabbages were gone, with only the roots left and holes where the potatoes had been. We'd cry and cry, taking the potato shoots to eat. At that time, a family of four was rationed one sardine [*iwashi*] per ticket. There was nothing really to flavour things. We went to the park to collect dandelion leaves, which we made into a garden salad [*oshitashi*]. We crushed yams into powder for little cakes [*danko*], wheat was pounded into soup dumplings [*suiton*], and we'd cook buckwheat noodles with yams which smelled great, but just left us starving.[87]

For both Japanese and British citizens, food shortage was so severe it almost became comical. In Southampton, Sylvia Brode remembered her mother buying a leg of mutton with her father's wages right before a terrible air raid evicted them from their home. As they wandered from strangers' homes to reception centres, her father carried the modest hunk of meat with them, trying to keep the family dog from consuming it on the sly. Some days later, 'the leg of mutton was becoming a frightful embarrassment, but it was eventually cooked and eaten ... It tasted wonderful'.[88] For Olive Metcalfe, who was separated from her husband and heavily pregnant, the decline in food availability was dire; as she was afflicted with bouts of self-recrimination, she wrote to her husband Kit about the impact the food situation might be having on their unborn child, whom she had nick-named 'Bud':

I have failed you again Kit and I dread what Bud will be like. I won't be able to be proud of it. I know perfectly well it is not healthy inside me, else it would not have hammered and jolted and twisted so unceasingly for three months. I know it is under-nourished and skin and bone – but that is the fault of the war which can't let us have any proper food. So I don't want you ever to see it before I get it fattened up and looking pink instead of yellow. Oh Kit I am ashamed and worried ... I had been hoping that somehow the mental state of the mother didn't affect the unborn baby but Dorothy today says it does very much. Oh I'll just say my prayers tonight and pray it won't – too much, otherwise the poor little mite hasn't had a ghost of a chance since Christmas.[89]

If the citizens had to suffer together, these deprivations might have been bearable, but the well-off in Britain and Japan largely avoided this level of pain. Food shortages were not shared by all equally: rural people fared better than urban, the wealthy better than the poor, and capital city residents were given preference. Bertram Elwood, who took a day trip from Birmingham to London, remarked in his diary on the 'comparative abundance in London', delineating some imbalances in the finer things in life:

Londoners seem to me to have had the benefit of one or two extras which make all the difference at a time when diet is apt to be monotonous. The most obvious food I have in mind in this respect is cakes. After the empty cake shops of Birmingham it is refreshing (and annoying too) to see the London shop windows crammed to overflowing with cakes and pastries in almost as profuse a variety as before the war. ... I don't think I have seen a Birmingham shop window dressed with cakes for more than a year. Other items [include] breakfast cereals, tinned evaporated milk, sweets. There seems to have been a more generous supply of fruit to London and at a cheaper rate.[90]

Residents of regional cities felt strongly that Londoners did not share their struggles, and that those who lived close to the centres of government and finance enjoyed greater economic benefits simply by virtue of being born in the capital city. Whether in London or Manchester, however, the countryside struggled to support urban residents' food needs, especially as they were expected to billet refugees and deliver food products through a devastated transport infrastructure.

While the main causes of food shortage were wartime disruptions to production and labour shortages, in some cases the distribution system itself was arbitrary, corrupt, or simply dysfunctional. These issues were not mutually exclusive, however, as food crises combined with air raids resulted in looting, hoarding, and other extreme behaviour. In Britain, shortages and shortcomings in the rationing system were infamous, and shopkeepers sometimes played favourites concerning who they would sell goods to such as chocolate, alcohol, and tobacco.[91] Rescue workers rummaged through wardrobes and drawers in bombed homes, and landlords of the buildings decided to look the other way.[92] Panic-buying of tinned food began in Coventry before war was even officially declared and, after air raids, looters freely roamed the streets stealing fuel, food, and even old ladies' clothing. 'Much has been said about the comradeship of the Blitz', one woman observed, 'but it also has its dark side'.[93] H. B. Monck noted that constant air raids on the Merseyside docks forced local post offices to close and shops to shutter their windows three or four times per day. He wrote that, to make things worse, shop workers grabbed any opportunity to close up: 'People stand outside the shops while the staff inside discuss their own affairs'.[94] In the central Japanese town of Kōfu, policemen were forced to take charge of a rationing depot that was being raided by civilians after the city's devastating air raid. Tada Susumu recalled one of Japan's fearsome Military Police (*kenpeitai*) commanders ordering him and his men to stop the looting by actually distributing the food to the people – a rare moment of humanity 'for an MP'.[95] Joining a 'soldier who's got plenty of guts', W.A. Hares jumped through the dangerous blazes consuming Bristol as 'people start salvaging from the apparently doomed shops and houses'. Shocked at the total lack of emergency personnel, Hares felt a kind of carnivalesque atmosphere was seizing the doomed city: 'What a night! And what a party!!'[96] Most did not see the breakdown of order and supply systems in such a light, however. Gladys Hollingsworth and Dora Mockett despaired over the end of gas and fresh water in Coventry and Hull, which led directly to unsanitary conditions. In the midst of the bombing, volunteer services dragged coal and timber from ruined homes to boil water and cook provisions for refugees, and mobile canteens careened through the rubble-strewn streets, usually insufficiently provisioned to feed the refugees fleeing destroyed cities.[97] Officials in Coventry began tearing down what remained of the city centre to fight vermin, disease, and the danger of falling masonry. Days after cities such as Coventry and Takamatsu were destroyed, residents Gladys Hollingsworth and Kirai Fujiko were still complaining of disrupted services and 'horrid smells' arising from corpses and smouldering buildings.[98]

To add to the distribution network's problems, local shopkeepers were either unable or unwilling to stay open during periods of heavy bombardment, and shoppers were certainly put off by the possibility of being caught in a raid. In addition to the loss of shops as a supply network, these spaces had also been invaluable conduits of information for neighbourhood residents. As one Coventry resident tried to track down survivors of the air raids, she claimed that the shopkeepers were the best places to begin: 'In those days corner shops did know everybody'.[99] Doing the weekly shopping under air raids became a source of constant frustration for city residents. In Chelsea, London, I. S. Haslewood noted that:

... all but the smallest privately-owned shops shut during an air-raid. If you are unlucky enough to be caught in a big store when the alert sounds, you can either make a dash for the street entrance, or else you are herded into the basement shelters, and then may not leave again until the all-clear is sounded. If you successfully make the street, you are not much better off, as the shops are shut and you are not too popular with the police and wardens wandering about in the open should the raid be bad. So you can well imagine the monstrous waste of time on a day like this. It is just utterly exasperating. There are moments when I could cry with sheer irritation at the unwarrantable interference on the Germans' part into our harmless private lives.[100]

More seriously, the loss of local shops meant that provisioning would be extremely difficult, as both Britain and Japan cooperated with shopkeepers to distribute food. When shopkeepers fled, or found their businesses destroyed, the state in both Britain and Japan turned to the extensive cooperative system to manage crisis rationing. During the destruction of

Coventry, Levi Fox's diary detailed the vicissitudes of trying to supply a city with needed bread when the entire system of distribution had been destroyed from the air.

Bread Position: In morning thought to be serious. Report late yesterday afternoon of queues at small shops ... If 2 or 3 men available could bake for 24 hours continuously – 1000 or 2000 loaves. Known, however, that all other bakeries with exception of Suttons, out of action. Assumed that Coop-Mutual Aid Scheme was working, but an unconfirmed report was picked to effect that last night only ½ loaf was being allowed per person by Coop.

With thousands of loaves of bread needing to be shipped in by emergency measures from nearby cities such as Birmingham, Coventry was struggling to cope – even when bread was available elsewhere. Queues formed across the ruined city, and angry residents demanded food for their ration cards.[101] Victory gardens, state relief, and eventually even American aid were insufficient for Britain's needs. 'Daddy has become so thin', observed Violet Maund in Bristol, 'his gold ring slipped off and became embedded in the soap'.[102] While Japan's food shortages were certainly far worse than anything the United Kingdom had to face, Britain's wartime generation was alarmed at how their loved ones seemed to be wasting away before their eyes.

For the Japanese, the shuttered shops forced distribution tasks onto the over-taxed state apparatus and its partners such as the food cooperatives, which frequently failed in even the most basic provisioning requirements. In Fukushima, Suzuki Yoshiko wrote that, in her capacity as an employee of a village cooperative, which was controlled by the state rationing system, shortages in critical areas such as milk had become truly lamentable; some mothers were so malnourished, she wrote, that 'their breasts produced nothing'. Working under such conditions, women like Yoshiko could only adopt a 'strong and harsh attitude' toward the 'furious' mothers who came demanding rations that did not, in fact, exist.[103] Those who served the state in Japan saw first-hand how the destruction meted out by enemy bombers crippled the very mechanisms that kept the city residents nourished. Fifty-seven-year-old Aojima Tokuji was in charge of the Shizuoka Prefecture Rationing Division, as well as helping to oversee food rationing and defence in the city of Shizuoka itself; his 1945 description of the impact of enemy bombing on food provisions reveals how fragile the systems for feeding city people were. First, Aojima pointed out that Allied bombing destroyed much of Japan's food processing infrastructure, such as their facilities for polishing and preparing white rice for mass consumption. Distribution centres, staff, and their housing, all suffered 75–90 per cent losses, resulting in a 'state of shock and paralysis'. This was quickly followed by calls to take up 'our holy mission' to feed the people in the city, but the mission failed to reach the city centre where it was needed most.[104] In fact, food shortage was created by the enemy as a means to destroy the city. During the debate surrounding the use of atomic weapons, wartime strategists in the US Navy, including Admiral Chester Nimitz, argued strongly that their blockade against Japan was bringing the nation to its knees. Historians have recently come to agree with the Navy's assessment, suggesting that Japan's food situation was so dire that the Soviet intervention in Manchuria and the proposed American invasion of Kyūshū, to say nothing of the terrible atomic bombings, were all unnecessary to end the war.[105] In Japan, as in Britain, food was a legitimate target.

An unexpectedly devastating casualty of the war against the city's systems was the death of entertainment. Although humans only need food, water, shelter, and medicine to survive, what drew them to the city in the first place was its provision of amusement, and this was represented by a network of cinemas, dance halls, arcades, restaurants, department stores, and drinking establishments. For example, contemporary observers noted that Bristol had a poor level of morale during the war, which was attributable to its shabby air raid shelters, poor response to fires, widespread sickness, slow rebuilding of housing, crushed public transit, and, surprisingly, a nearly complete lack of amusement and luxuries.[106] One of the principle allures of a modern city was its ability to entertain, and before the aerial attacks on British cities, diarists regularly recorded outings for drink, dance, and song.[107] Indeed, evacuated urban youth in Britain often complained bitterly of how 'boring' the countryside was, especially the lack of cinemas, some even planning to return to war-torn urban spaces.[108] Survivors of the air war over Japan, whether in the imperial capital or regional cities like Morioka, also reminisce about an urban culture that the war ended, which included a plethora of popular music venues, radio comedy programmes, a thriving theatre culture, and a rich film industry that suffered incalculable, irreversible damage from incendiary bombs.[109] (In)famously, the British Mass Observation organisation attempted to ascribe differences in civilian morale during air raids to essentialised regional characteristics, such as 'tough and hard' Liverpudlian sailors cheerily enduring the strain of war contrasted with Manchester's 'background of softness' and 'noticeable strain of selfishness and strict utilitarianism'. These prejudices masked a deeper truth about morale: the decisive factor in civilian response to air raids appeared to be the impact on infrastructure and access to city centre amusements.[110] Loss of transport for Manchester was devastating, whereas Liverpool's pubs, dance halls, and public transit remained comparatively safe in its historic urban core. City residents across Britain and Japan lost the ordinary amusements that made urban life bearable, even if the state did not ban such activity as a luxury or suspicious activity. Murata Eizō, who described amusement during his rural Iwate upbringing as 'limited to fishing and gathering chestnuts', organised baseball games while he worked for the railroads in urban Sendai. Dodging conscription, which was a death sentence by the 1940s, Eizō instead applied himself to work only, which kept him away from his beloved sport: 'When the war intensified, baseball wasn't exactly illegal but one or two boys would be conscripted by the army, disappear, and the league would go into a natural state of recess. It got so bad we couldn't even organise a game of catch'.[111] Although historians like Barak Kushner have documented the continuance of amusement during the war, even on the battlefield, the death of fun was symbolic of the fate of the wartime city.[112]

Although it may seem excessive to emphasise the importance of pubs, cinemas, children's plays, and dance halls at a time when people were losing their lives, these were absolutely crucial, particularly to the working classes at a time when radios were still expensive, there was no television, and reading novels for entertainment was a fairly bourgeois past time. In the East London neighbourhood of Plumstead, the baths were a draw for the working people who lived near the old Royal Arsenal. On 8 September 1940, targeting the Arsenal, German bombers shocked John Kay and his friend Ernie after they had gone there for a swim. The bath attendants rushed in and shouted at the men there: 'Hurry up boys and get out, it is not safe with this glass roof overhead!' They scrambled out to witness the air raid assault on East London:

We hear the AA guns go into action and then a terrific explosion which seems to shake the building. We take cover just inside the baths wondering where the next is going to fall and feeling rather shaken. It is quieter now and we have a look out towards the river to see columns of yellow smoke rising. Ernie says 'that's one in the Arsenal'. . . . In the sky we can see wave after wave of enemy bombers, there must be a hundred of them or more. We see the shells bursting all around the planes but they somehow seem to just miss. The Germans stay on their course and are directly overhead. . . . The gunfire is deafening and then planes wheel round in a semi-circle and start unloading. It is like Hell let loose, the bombs are dropping like wild fire. We hear them whistling through the air and the fellow with us says, 'Here they are lads get down'. We crouch down on the floor by the wall and the bombs scream through the air, the explosions appear to come from the Arsenal and the sky is becoming black with smoke. The noise is incredible.

Throughout the ordeal, the two working-class men worried constantly about their young wives back in a rented flat. Dodging and weaving through the raid, they hurried away from the baths to find them. Later, Ellen Searle, who had planned to go to the baths for a birthday commemoration, was shocked when she discovered that hundreds of people had been killed there. The baths, in fact, had been transformed into a working morgue.[113] It was an experience shared across Britain: in Hull, one woman recalled 'seeing people queuing up to identify the dead' outside a waterworks facility – then turned into a mortuary; watching this from her parents' living room, she remembered how 'depressed' and 'frightened' she felt watching them claim friends and family members.[114] The city was no longer the centre of fun and good living; it had become a death trap. Looking back on his wartime childhood games, including 'Sapper and Land Mine', Kaneya Seiichi wrote that they offer 'a reflection of the era ... when the military state suddenly suffused everything'.[115] The destruction of city amusements meant that urban space became little more than a minefield, a hostile ecosystem, and a morgue; in order to survive the bombing, the state not only mobilised man, woman, and child against their will, it also wrecked and ruined the pastimes that gave their lives small doses of pleasure.

Devil Flames: Fire and the City

Loss of defence, medicine, food, housing, and amusement were terrible deprivations to suffer, but the real demon of the war was fire. The uncontrollable flames that erupted after an air raid terrorised and slaughtered residents, as if giving life to the bombed city's malevolence. Consequently, ordinary people gave the fires personalities, sometimes calling them demonic and devilish, other times comparing them to sinister creatures: 'The day after the bombing', wrote Shizuoka resident Endō Naoe, 'smoke was still rising, and you could see remaining flames licking the city like the tongue of a serpent'.[116] The hands and fingers of bombs slinked and jumped into the city's most vulnerable corners, setting alight private spaces and public sanctuaries alike.

After the bombers receded, citizens were forced to watch passively as the city was set ablaze before their eyes. GAF raids exacted a heavy toll on poorly-defended regional cities such as Swansea, but even well-defended dock areas such as Merseyside and Surrey, which had many wooden structures, were quickly consumed by flame. Laurie Latchford captured in his diary the mood during the beginning of the firebombing:

While the [sunlight] still lingered, Jerry came in from the west. Parachute flares were dropped immediately. The night was made as hideous as the night before.

Figure 1: Conservative Party poster celebrating the 1902 Anglo-Japanese Alliance. Courtesy of London School of Economics and Political Science.

Figure 2: Japanese schoolchildren are evacuated to the countryside in 1944. Courtesy of Asahi News.

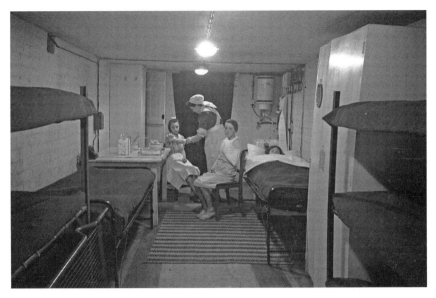

Figure 3: Evacuated British schoolchildren are treated in a Hull air raid shelter. Courtesy of Hull History Centre.

Figure 4: Bristol volunteers remove the wounded and the dead after an air raid. Courtesy of Bristol Records Office.

Figure 5: Citizens trekking out of the ruins of Osaka. Courtesy of Asahi News.

Figure 6: Citizens trekking out of the ruins of Hull. Courtesy of Hull History Centre.

Figure 7: Destruction of iconic buildings in Hull city centre. Courtesy of Hull History Centre.

Figure 8: Firefighters try to save the famous Ginza area in Tokyo. Courtesy of Asahi News.

Figure 9: Two women pose in front of bomb damage in Hull, 1940. Courtesy of Hull History Centre.

Figure 10: Japanese youth directs traffic in firebombed city. Courtesy of US Marine Corps Archives, Quantico.

Searchlights were criss-crossing; tracer bullets went on their uncertain way towards the flares; the ear-dulling noise and sharp flashes from the gunfire hardly paused; the orange points from the sky bursts of shells followed the searchlights; and all along the sky over Swansea, the flicker, flicker, flicker as incendiaries hit the ground ... I heard a fireman during the September raid, at his hose in front of a burning building, speaking to himself, say, 'There she goes!' and exhale noisily.[117]

Then, the 'hand of fire' swept through the streets and 'storms of cinders' blew over rooftops, spreading fire like a virulent disease. The fires snaked through the streets, and the citizens dodged and weaved to avoid them. Japanese authors described their experiences fleeing from incendiary bombing raids with the verb *kuguru*, which means to weave through, dive under, and evade. Thirty-seven-year-old housewife Furuya Hama initially performed her civic duty by being part of a 'bucket relay', but abandoned the city once other participants began disappearing. 'Weaving through' (*kugutte*) the alleyways toward the sea, she and her family members doused their coats in water, put the soaking rags on their heads, held hands, and 'ran as far as our breath could take us'.[118] This evil presence could suddenly appear at any time, feeding on backdrafts and sudden gusts of oxygen-rich air. Sitting inside buildings and shelters, Coventry refugees saw 'huge explosions very close and nearly all our windows and doors were burst open and smashed. Several times we felt the blast like a warm wind go past us and I wondered when we should be hit'.[119] In a cruel irony, the light of the initial fires in Japanese and British cities attracted yet more bombers. Violet Maund observed a bomb gut a street, open up the gas mains, and how the consequent fire 'shot up a flame higher than the house, thus scaring everyone as, in the darkness, it made them an easy target for the enemy "upstairs."'[120] Watching these forceful fires build up from afar could be a surreal experience. Twenty-seven-year-old housewife Kojima Haru saw the red presence emerging in the dark of evening in Hachiōji, and wrote, 'It was a sea of fire beyond my imagination ... It was like watching the mad dance of demon coming from the fiery depths of Hell'.[121]

As uncontrolled fires swept through Britain and Japan's cities, causing night to become day, residents faced an inhuman enemy that could not be defeated or reasoned with, and the image of an evil fire remain etched into personal accounts of the attacks. D. B. Maling, a medical student in London during the war, recalled how the city was consumed by flames: 'There was a whopping big fire across the river by Liverpool Street station burning furiously and lighting up the whole of the city. The dome of St. Paul's was just to the left and looked blood-red in the glow'.[122] In Shizuoka, Endō Naoe not only compared the flames to a serpent's tongue, but also called them 'demon fires' (*oni-bi*) – drawing on early modern Japanese images of other-worldly will-o-wisps that fell suddenly from the sky or erupted unexpectedly from the earth. She was enraged at the injustice inherent in the arbitrary nature by which incendiaries chose their victims; with nothing to defend the city from firebombs, which could fall on the city at any time, Naoe said these weapons made her 'utterly terrified'.[123] Bristolians in particular noted the surreally devastating effects of firebombing in Britain. One woman noted that the fires on the night of 24 November 1940 were so terrible that they illuminated the entire house.[124] As survivors in Britain and Japan sought refuge in nearby hills and forests, they grimly watched explosives and fires consume their homes. Laurie Latchford captured in his diary the feelings of helplessness and despair that ordinary people felt as enemy bombers were able to successfully lay waste to British cities; standing beside three others, 'making no movement, silent', he watched the devil fire dash and jump through the streets, consuming the city:

A most appalling sight hit me. There were leaping flames over the whole stretch of Swansea, from behind Clyne Hill to the dock's entrance. The fires seemed to run to the sea edge and beyond. The gently moving sea was aflame with reflected light. At that distance there seemed no divisions between the fires. The windows of the houses on the hills overlooking the town mirrored the flames so that it seemed that the houses themselves were alight. The Guildhall tower stood as a dark shaft against the burning buildings behind. St. Mary's Church could just be defined, blazing, with fire pouring from the tower. It seemed as though the whole of the centre of the town was being devoured even to the Victorian boarding houses by the sea. Futile had been Swansea's gallant fight of the last two nights.[125]

Flames snaked through the homes of ordinary people, killing without discrimination the elderly, children, and women. The city called on ordinary people to defend it, often at great personal sacrifice, but the devil fire was not easily vanquished.

In fact, these wildfires exposed just how poor the cities' systems were for combating them on a large scale. Auxiliary fireman Cliff Lachem described how badly Bristol was left burning, despite having multiple rivers and canals from which to draw water:

We entered Victoria Street and this was like Dante's Inferno, raging fires in the buildings, belching out of the windows and doors, and the wind was like a tornado. The flames were hundreds of feet high, the heat was terrific, even the shop window glass was melting. I should think we were the last to go up Victoria Street that night. We got through all right and then on to Bristol Bridge ... looking back we could see the Castle Street area was all afire ...[126]

Bristol's fire services, even when volunteers were able to report for duty, were operating at less than half the needed levels to combat the dozens of major fires ravaging the city centre. At the height of the firebombing of Bristol in November 1940, one woman, writing in her diary, described how she touched the sitting room window woodwork and found it was 'so hot you can hardly bear your hand on it'.[127] The fire seemed to spring from the very planks and shingles on which urban space was built, like a spirit of death birthed by the city itself. Shiba Isa recalled how Japanese people talked of a 'sea of fire' (*hi no umi*) in nearby neighbourhoods, and feared how the 'fire ran' (*hi ga hashiru*) from one section of Himeji to the next, completely unstoppable by fire services. Also in Himeji, Nakayama Teruo described how the citizens rallied to establish bucket relays to suppress the fires, 'just as we had drilled countless times before' but the conflagration that engulfed the city pierced their hearts with sheer terror: 'In front of that incredible scene', he wrote, 'we realised that there was absolutely no use in doing it ... Into a sky burned crimson by fire, two of three enemy [B-29s] came over us [again] like enormous, monstrous birds, dropping fire'.[128] From the hellish heat of the fire, urban citizens in England were suddenly plunged into a frigid, glacier-like urban environment. During the record-setting chill of the 1940–1941 winter, firemen in cities across Britain, such as Bristol and Hull, had to fight fire while surrounded by ice, sometimes creating surreal scenes of crystallised trees shining against the red glare of blazing buildings nearby. W. A. Wares wrote in his diary of the 'very nasty work' involved in stumbling across ice-clad roof tiles to put out an incendiary bomb, all while staring at the deadly spiked railing below.[129] Wartime photographs of Hull show streets coated in the iced-over waters from fire hoses while warehouses and office buildings blazed nearby; fire-fighters returned to their station soaked to the bone with ice crystals forming on scorched mitts and coats.

The flames were not only a threat to life and limb, but a demonic force that seemed to target and destroy the very systems on which the city residents relied for their lives. Like a ravenous beast, fire spread through and consumed telephone poles, melted tarmac, ate through electric wiring, and gnawed through the wooden foundations that supported structures. Mary Bloomfield's husband, Ted, used his motorbike to help those in distress during the Coventry bombing of 14 November 1940. He discovered, however, that the city's fires had turned the urban environment into a hellish landscape determined to destroy him:

There were some good fires going already ... The first incendiaries hit the Alvis and it blazed furiously, then the Rialto cinema was hit and on fire ... There were fires all around [Ted] in Much Park street. Two factories near to the police garage were well alight ... The Market Hall, the city centre and the cathedral were burning well. The people were quickly got out of the shelters under the Market Hall ... To get back he had to ride his motorcycle on the pavement outside the Council House as all the shops on the opposite side of the road were ablaze. As it was he was scorched by the intense heat. He turned down little park street, Bushells was blazing fiercely and he had to ride in the centre of the road and blind through it. The heat was intense. It was impossible to reach the top of the street as the flames were meeting across the road and the roadway was blocked by piles of bricks and girders ... in fact, the whole of this area and the city centre was a blazing inferno.[130]

Nevertheless, these conflagrations would pale in comparison to those that consumed Japanese cities, where residential areas were largely composed of wooden buildings. Fukazawa Kōji, a middle-aged Shizuoka prefectural government accountant, described in his diary how civilians attempted to defend themselves against fire. On 19 June 1945, at approximately 12:54am, he was awakened by alarms and saw incendiary bombs littering the city centre. He wrote that the resultant fires in Shizuoka were so bright it was like midday, and even the surrounding hillsides were visible. He soon noticed that his neighbour's first floor roofing had caught fire, so he quickly sent his wife with his two young children to the rice fields for safety. Next, with his eldest three children he planned how to defend their home:

My eldest boy stripped naked and doused himself with water. Climbing onto the roof, if any incendiary bombs landed, he would drop them onto the wet rice fields to the north of the house. I stood naked in the garden [to help], and if the enemy planes came I would hide under a tree. My eldest daughter was to retrieve and organize our household valuables. Each task was thus divided among us.

They managed to extinguish most of the flaming canisters, although they could not rest for a moment and were soon dripping with sweat from the heat of the burning city. Just when it seemed that they would get a reprieve, a US Grumman fighter plane, following directly behind the fire, strafed the city streets, killing civilians who had turned out to fight the flames. Fukazawa fled into the rice fields, with bullets ripping through his home and then splashing in the water around him. The next day, he saw that close to 90 per cent of the city was in ruins. He tried to clean his front stoop, but the grime and mud simply would not wash away.[131]

At the nadir of the urban hell created by enemy bombers, the physics of fire allowed a truly terrifying devil to arise. Thermal columns emerged from extremely hot fires, sucking in oxygen inside and outside of fiery rings, causing what we now call 'firestorms'. Although firestorms are generally associated with the Allied bombing of Japan, they also formed in Coventry, tearing apart much of the historic city centre. Marcus Sadler wrote to his mother about how the German attack created firestorms similar to those that would consume Japanese cities:

In the first quarter of an hour we had counted thirty two planes over, and these followed through until 5:45am without ever one minute going past without at least one coming in. It sounded just like your bees do when they swarm. After the first ten minutes or so the fires got going – the second H.E. [high explosive] dropped had hit the main water supply, and they couldn't get hardly any water to fight the flames – the fires extended over an oblong of about 3×2 miles solid flames with a nice border of smaller fires all dotted around. The glow from the fire lit up the whole place as far back as Kenilworth like a red daylight. The [defensive] balloons could be seen plainly with the bottom half all red, and the top all yellow from the moon, like a lot of berries up in the sky.[132]

After the city was gutted by the fires, some residents tried to come home, only to find it completely transformed. Coventry native Joan Thornton was dismayed to the point of tears at what had become of the city, recording in her diary how the vicious fire had seized the city and remade it.

All the buildings around the Gaumont are down. The Queens Hotel McCarthy's (where I used to work) which adjoins W.H. Smith's, and that furniture shop Holbrooks are burned to the ground. Holbrooks was still burning at 10am Friday morning . . . there is not a shop or office [in Broadgate] still standing. Just heaps of bricks and rubble and red clay. It is heart-breaking. That big store Owen Owen is just a shell. Burned out . . . The Cathedral is a heap of rubble, a front wall and a spire. That really made me cry when I saw it.[133]

The firestorms of Coventry sucked the oxygen out of buildings, suffocating the inhabitants, and burned many others alive. Ted Crosby, who volunteered as an ambulance driver, had the ill-luck of being on duty during the heaviest raids. In Broadgate, where Coventry was literally burning to cinders, he was doused with water and told to go into the flaming ruins of the Owen Owen building – luckily, this was called off. Before long, however, he was called to the Gaumont Theatre, which had taken a direct hit, where he found the unsettling remains of the city's victims: 'We found one lady whose lungs had been exhausted by the blast', he wrote, 'they had collapsed. We found a lot of people had died like that. It was the evacuation of the lungs. It sort of suffocated them. There was nothing you could do'.[134] In Hull, too, Raymond Peat recalled watching a massive explosion take his friend's 'breath away' and send an ambulance flying into the air.[135] The fires that consumed

Hull were so bright that they could be seen dozens of miles away by residents in Hornsea and even Scarborough, striking fear into the hearts of northerners everywhere.[136] News reports of London's valiant resistance under fire were of little comfort there.

The heat of the fires caused strange and disturbing phenomena, such as burning bricks, melting streets, and even pest infestations. Iriye Hisae's grade school daughter told her that, after being taken out of Takamatsu during a raid by a woman she did not know, she looked up at the power lines of the burning city and saw they were covered with fleeing rodents.[137] A former Auxiliary Fire Patrolwoman in Hull, Esther Baker, recalled how 'just as rats flee a sinking ship, so it seemed that insects abandon a burning silo, and over the next few weeks Central [fire station] was inundated with crickets'; the sound of the insects at dusk accentuated the fact that the city of Hull was being destroyed – as if it was being turned into a 'rolling meadow' overnight. Similarly, Amatsu Tsuyako noted that the heat from the smouldering ruins of the city led to a proliferation of fleas, which 'swarmed our trousers until they were black. When I think of it, even now I get shivers down my spine'. Before putting her children to bed every night, she had to remove dozens of the pests from her clothes.[138] After the devil fire, then, came the plague of insects and vermin, swarming both the living and the dead.

With so many casualties piling up in Britain and Japan, the city failed to transport and dispose of its numerous corpses. In Kōfu, Japan, Ueno Kōsaku was a middle-aged section Head of the Municipal Civil Defence Unit (*shikeibōdan kachō*) and, as part of his duties, he had to dispose of dead bodies across the city. He described how they first burned each body and then loaded them into trucks, five to eight bodies per vehicle. 'Because it was summer', he wrote, 'the stench was indescribable and, looking at the corpses, sometimes you'd just pass out'. Ueno recalled how some people simply had to quit the job and others, during a time of food shortage, could not bear to eat their lunches, 'simply retching over and over'. In such cases, even enthusiastic citizens could not do their jobs, and consequently they were put on stretchers and fed alcohol until they could calm down. Ueno personally oversaw the disposal of 833 bodies, of which many could not be positively identified by bereaved family members who visited the mass graves; in many cases, even the sex of the corpse was burned beyond recognition.[139] The cost in materials and property is difficult to estimate, but the loss of human capital – the workers, engineers, doctors, writers, schoolteachers, parents – is incalculable. The war turned cities, with all of their concomitant webs of steel, wire, and wood, from centres of progress and innovation into a tangled, thorny tomb for their residents; in fact, the Second World War transformed vibrant cities into elaborate morgues. For days after the November 1940 air raid on Coventry, the British Army deployed thousands of Irish soldiers to exhume the bodies of those who were buried by bombings, and then re-bury them in a mass grave as the citizens looked on. Gladys Hollingsworth wrote despondently in her diary how Coventry was 'smashed to destruction in one single night ... Can anyone imagine such a prosperous thriving industrial centre, and 10 hours later, a graveyard and a rubbish heap'.[140] Japanese and British people buried thousands in their cities, including children; as the soil collected around the bodies, these 'Molochs' silently consumed the people.

The city was a system designed by humans for their own benefit but, in the heat of war, it trapped their bodies and destroyed them. The loss of the familiar transformed the urban system from an exciting home into a ravenous beast, or a demonic spirit imbued with the power of scorching, hellish flames. As Violet Maund described it, the city was cracked open, and its modernity was, at best, feckless and moribund:

Poor Bristol! Our museum is gone, and many other places are smouldering ruins ... Bristol is certainly broken. No water, gas, or electricity. The windows in our house are blown out, and we have to wear our winter coats all day in the house ... We have no facilities for making a cup of tea, as the 'all electric house', of which I was so proud, is useless with no current.[141]

Burning buildings, ruined water supply, collapsed food stores, and exploding gas mains were just the obvious manifestations of this inorganic creature's deadly grasp; the loss of the city as a recognisable and beloved landscape also assaulted the hearts and minds of the people who called it home. The city was no longer the centre of 'light and power', but a creature to be fought and feared. As one Japanese housewife saw it, the war made the shattered bodies of the dead and the crumbled ruins of the city into a single corpse:

> *Whenever it rains at night*
> *I always see the same dream*
> *The after-effects of the war*
> *Piles of broken bones, scattered about*
> *Surely, these were once parts of human bodies*
> *Now they mix with the broken ruins of the city*
> *Nothing to remember or reflect upon ...*[142]

★

After leaving Liverpool in November, 1940, for the countryside, Dorothy Hughes found that country people were astonished to learn that the city had been reduced to utter ruins. As Dorothy discovered, contrasting rural life against what urban residents had to endure revealed how much abuse the city had to take:

Things don't change here much – the vagueries of nature are all that they worry about. I think it will be the country people who will have to carry on after this business is over – the rest of us will be nervous wrecks. ... Lots of the local lads are of course in the forces. Those who are at home do their bit in the Home Guard. The blackout doesn't worry them at all, naturally. There is more social life than in town! Their chief worry is the gunfire – six miles away!

Meanwhile in Liverpool, citizens endured multiple attacks both on the spaces that they loved and the human beings living in them. Dorothy described a girl who walked about with 'her coat all spattered with blood' when windows were blown in during a raid, and multiple attacks had left the area devastated. Three days before Christmas, 1940, she wrote in her diary that the bus ride home was 'a very depressing experience' due to the relentless attacks on the north-western port city. The state and military had failed the people: Dorothy often commented on how the city officials failed in their task to protect the areas around Liverpool from devastation by firebombing. She sarcastically noted how the radio assured citizens that the fires were 'under control', even as she saw the burning city 'make a red glare in the sky. A nice target'. A war that had seemed distant and abstract quickly became personal: 'The house is shaking. I hear there are big naval vessels in port. Their guns are – my God – three terrible bursts ... The whole foundation, walls, and everything absolutely dithered'. Even though Liverpool's centre was one of the least affected during the war, the next day Dorothy could not get into the city – the docks and main streets were littered with damage, bombs, and land mines.[143]

When our diarists were in urban spaces, by choice or necessity, they took time to describe how the intensification of aerial bombardment brought out the best and the worst in the city's inhabitants. As the system that supplied urban people broke down under explosions and fires, ordinary people struggled to keep the city alive, and our diarists were no different. Dora Mockett captured the collapse of the city succinctly: water supply, transportation, fire control, communications, government, entertainment, shelter, fuel were all broken apart:

I had not got my bottle in bed so had to wait for the water in the sky ... part of the Central Fire Station and the General Post Office just on the yard where the vans etc. go in and out. There is a great hole in the post office, the Food Control section looks knocked about, and a lot of the windows of the Town Clerk's section have gone – one of ours is cracked. East Hull has been hit <u>very</u> badly, [including] houses, cinemas, shops, and shelters ... Rush for the canteen today, queuing up as all gas is off ... Have stopped East Yorkshire travel tickets ... on account of petrol shortage.

She tried to capture how the whole of east Yorkshire was paralysed by the enemy attack, cutting the city off from the supplies it needed to survive. The attacks on urban spaces such as Hull were not just about killing civilians, then, but destroying an entire modern system, which was supported by state institutions such as transport, communications, food distribution, and materials for building and energy. The symbolism of the attack's first target did not escape her: 'The [post office] was the first thing to be hit with the first bomb to be dropped – the clock stopped at 1:28am'. Like a clock frozen in time, the modern city's gears were grinding to a halt.

Not only were the government mechanisms that drove the city being torn apart, but the private market, which depended on a stable government for its health, was dying. Kenneth Holmes noted the rapid decline in services, saying that 'business in all large stores is very slack'. Rationing meant that many shops were simply unable to stock properly so, when doing the shopping, one never knew what to expect. Kenneth also witnessed the extraordinary difficulty with which British hospitals had to operate.

In one hospital 200 patients were in wards at the time and the wards were severely damaged. Every window was shattered, ceilings crashed down on to the patients' beds, and doors were flung off their hinges ... Fire broke out immediately but the flames were soon smothered by the NFS. Children escaped injury from the flying glass and falling plaster because they were sleeping on mattresses <u>underneath</u> their beds and cots, this is a regular procedure.[144]

As mentioned previously, among all our diarists, Takahashi Aiko wrote most eloquently about the problems Tokyo experienced with food provisioning. Throughout most of British and Japanese modern history, the city and its inhabitants treated the countryside with disdain or condescending romanticism. The assault on the city exposed its vulnerability, however, and Aiko was perceptive enough to take note. When a rural person came to her husband for personal medical treatment, she remarked, 'this tells us how well they're doing in the countryside'. Continuing in her diary in January 1944, Aiko showed just how low the normally haughty city residents had fallen:

From time immemorial farmers have not been blessed in life, but in one leap, because now everything is about food provisions, they hold the key to our lives.

They sit in the throne as masters of production and make a killing on the black market. The people of the city, in order to survive, will bring anything to the countryside. We now seek our brides and grooms in rural houses in order to make familial connections, which is a technique of getting by. The things in our city cupboards and dressers are being carried into the countryside. And now the people of the city have started speaking with deference to those in the country, which they had never done before. One cannot say whether these feelings, born out of a reversal of position [and possession], are good or bad, but I daresay that any sense of resentment against the other is déclassé.[145]

The city had reached the bottom of its existence, and it continued to survive only by virtue of its inhabitants' commitment to making it so.

Indeed, the British and Japanese empires were built on the willingness of good people to sacrifice themselves for the national enterprise. Even after her 'depressing' experience on a train from bombed-out Liverpool, Dorothy wrote that 'everyone just goes about their business as if they experienced a terrible nightmare. Personally, I am very calm. I am amazed at myself. I think I should have been a warden. Give me a tin hat and I'll go anywhere'.[146] It would seem that our diarists were ready to throw themselves right on the frontline for saving the city. Inohara Mitsuko recounted how she and her fellow teenage labourers single-handedly saved a nearby town during a firebombing attack. Everything seemed to be going normally at the factory for her when:

... suddenly, the glass in the windows began making a cracking noise. Surprised, we moved away from them and went outside to look at the sky, when we heard a hissing from incendiary bombs falling in great numbers. They fell near the dormitory and a fire began growing quickly. Shouting 'Fire bombs! Fire bombs!' we put them all out.

Their joy was short-lived, however, when more bombs were dropped, 'like rain falling from the sky', and fire spread everywhere in the area. Mitsuko and the other young girls put their backs into combatting the flames with a water pump and a bucket relay. 'The fire sounded like a handkerchief being torn apart', ripping through nearby buildings, and then their pump ran out of water. 'Water, water, water! Ah, is there no way to fight this fire?' she wrote, 'If only we had a minute more time, or a drop more water'. The girls fled the flames and decided to create a bucket relay using water from the roadside. Larger men stood idly by, watching the girls exert themselves, getting in their way and, as Mitsuko put it, 'really aggravating us'. Mitsuko wrote effusively in her diary about the sacrifices she, her former classmates, and their teachers made during the period of student mobilisation. When her teacher left, she berated herself for not doing more to make him happy and adding to his worries.

Thinking on his sacrifices, she wrote, 'This is something I cannot ever forget. No matter what happens, I won't forget it'.[147] Like affection for a long-lost teacher, or the abstract love one feels for a far-off celebrity, the emotions that drove ordinary people to defend the city were unrequited. Our diarists gave all to defend and sustain their neighbourhoods, and all they received in return was loss.

4   Defending Our Way of Life: Gender, Class, Age, and Other Oppressions

---

> I live near to a number of very poor people. Their main aim in life is to get a bare living and some even fail to do that and yet they are as determined to defeat Hitler as people with a good deal more at stake. They are slaves already to our economic system so it looks as if their love of freedom was quite genuine.   – H. B. Monck, 4 November 1940

Area bombing during the Second World War had a tremendous impact on the societies that endured them – and yet our diarists also marked how much things seemed to stay the same. Dorothy Hughes, when visiting the cinema to enjoy a Marx Brothers film, was harassed by a 19-year-old lad with apparently nothing better to do. He was relentlessly 'digging' her and offering her cigarettes, which she indignantly 'threw on the floor, keeping my eyes glued to the screen'. After much abuse, he finally turned his attention to another girl, but Dorothy's experience only demonstrated how, for all of the wartime proclamations about 'being in it together', the war did not instantaneously resolve pre-war problems. Months later, in December, 1940, Dorothy complained that she was 'tired of (house)-working, cooking, buying, washing ... Sometimes it all depresses me ... What is going to happen when it is all over? I cry sometimes thinking about it. In fact I cry often these days'. Later, she reflected, 'There's many a time when I wish mum were home'.[1] Our diarists struggled with issues that were related to the categories that historians consider definitive for the modern period, namely: gender, age, and class.

When enemy bombings increased in severity, the state called on all members of society to contribute equally to the defence of the nation. As usual, however, some were expected to contribute more than others. Even when working-class people were bombed out of their homes and on the run, the upper classes gave them little support. Dorothy described the situation around Liverpool:

I heard over the weekend people have been inquiring in the district what accommodation is available for evacuees from Bootle. This is arousing great indignation in the breasts of the spick and span householders, Bootle people being notoriously dirty and 'slummy'. If they want to put anyone in our house, we should give it up and go into digs. There's quite enough to do without the added trials of evacuees.

To make matters worse, in Dorothy's view, the poor lacked the fortitude that the higher classes inherently possessed. Expressing her fears and doubts about the conditions of a German invasion, she wrote, 'Freedom is worth any sacrifice, but will the poor people appreciate that?'[2]

In addition to class, our diarists noted the importance of age in determining who was suffering most around them. Dora Mockett some-times recorded the imbalances in the duties and vulnerabilities of indi-viduals suffering through the attacks on Hull. When a bomb smashed a block of flats, one woman reported clawing her way out of the debris, but her 'blind mother was killed'.[3] Area bombing could not distinguish legitimate targets, like military installations, from clearly inhumane ones, like schools. In the devastating spring of 1945, Aiko and her husband saw the local Catholic Sacred Heart School 'engulfed in a sea of flames'. Young schoolgirls fled into her neighbourhood screaming and in despair, seeking help; Aiko was deeply upset:

[Two girls] from outside of Tokyo, who were staying in the Sacred Heart dormitory, came running chaotically to us. They didn't know who was where. They were all on their own, separated from their parents, and I held those girls, overcome by a feeling of love for them as if they were my own. One of the girls, shivering and crying, told me that they came with only the shirts on their backs, because they had no time to grab anything.[4]

In Britain, the sudden, arbitrary, and unpredictable nature of V-2 rockets made the very young and the very old even more vulnerable. On Boxing Day, 1944, Kenneth Holmes, who was doing his best to inscribe Lon-don's spirit of resistance into his personal record, was taken aback by the attacks on non-combatants including women, children, and the elderly.

... there was a vivid flash in the sky followed immediately by a deafening explosion which flung my two friends and I to the ground and we were covered from head to feet in dust. Masses of flame and debris seem to shoot through the sky. My eardrums seemed about to burst ... We made our way to the scene guided by the light of burning gas mains. A woman rushed up to us in a state of frenzy in her night attire covered in grime and dust, blood streaming from her face and pleading with us to save her child trapped in the wreckage of her home. We tried to grope our way beneath the wreckage in a vain search for the child, when we heard a groaning sound, and a feeble voice saying 'Oh please somebody help me' was that of an elderly woman, pinned down by the weight of the debris, and ceiling, and after a struggle managed to extricate her, and found that she had been thrown forward in a sitting position with a chair still beneath her, but trapped by her legs with the weight of the debris on her. The dear old lady seemed more concerned about the welfare of her cat which she was missing when the bomb struck and also asking if her legs were alright because she couldn't feel them. So with great difficulty we managed to remove the wreckage and drag her away to the care of a policeman who by this time had come along from the other wrecked property. So what happened to the poor child for whom we began the search[?] I never knew although feel sure it could not have survived the ordeal. The whole scene was horrible – a foggy cold winter's night, busted water mains, fountains of fire from broken gas pipes, muffled groans from beneath the ruined homes, indeed the worst incident I have experienced.[5]

Diarists described in horror the destitute and lonely old women, the orphaned children, and helpless injured people they saw subjected to military assault. Dorothy worried about her elderly neighbour, who insisted on going out under blackouts in Liverpool: 'As she is extremely deaf, I don't see how she manages', Dorothy wrote in her diary, 'One of these nights she will have a nasty accident ... At the moment it is more dangerous in England than it is on the Western Front'. A month later, she heard two elderly residents complain about rumours of tax rises: 'You know, it's people like us who are going to suffer', one older woman remarked, 'We've saved a bit for our old age, and now we are going to be taxed out of existence'.[6] How could this be 'war', our diarists asked, as they stumbled through the rubble of their home cities, bearing witness to the indiscriminate slaughter of ordinary workers, women, and the very young and the very old.

Defending Our Way of Life: The City Divided by Age, Class, and Gender

During a devastating air raid over Himeji, Kobayashi Takako recalled her middle-aged mother angrily shouting, 'How can we run away? All the men have fled, but if we allow our home to burn down, where will we live?'[7] Despite the fact that women had to face being abandoned by the men in their lives throughout the war years, privilege and power were surprisingly resilient. The dispossessed and disenfranchised were desperate to find their place in a society that was fighting for survival, but the war's punishments were not meted out in the same way that power in peacetime society operated. In general, it was easier to survive if one was wealthy, female, adult (but not elderly), and able-bodied. Meanwhile, the stresses and dislocations wrought by the war exacerbated existing conflicts, many of which were the consequence of pre-war social structures such as ageism, gender discrimination, and class hierarchy.[8] This book has frequently referred to urban residents as 'ordinary people', or 'the people', especially in contrast to wartime political, economic, and military leaders. Nevertheless, we must now disaggregate 'the people' because, as Angus Calder, Yoshimi Yoshiaki, Amy Bell, Fujii Tadatoshi, Sonya Rose, and others have shown, there was no 'people's war', nor was there a coherent 'people'. In many cases, the state actually aided these divisions or created new categories of belonging through its efforts to organise wartime society. In other words, defending the British and Japanese 'way of life' involved re-enforcing socio-economic inequality, even if it made the nation weaker during a time of war by undermining unity.

For the most part, the divisions in Japan and Britain mirror each other, but there was one important difference: on the one hand, the Japanese political party system was jettisoned in 1940 pursuant to a call for wartime 'unity' while, on the other hand, partisan debates continued to divide the United Kingdom. Japan's modern history of political protest, suffrage movements, and vigorous inter-party rivalry were gradually worn down by militarism, popular jingoism, and, in the long run, the extraordinary pressures of total war, beginning with the Second Sino-Japanese War in 1937. By the time Matsuoka Yōsuke called for the dissolution of the political parties into a fascist-inspired 'Imperial Rule Assistance Association', Japan had suffered years of right-wing political terrorism against business leaders, liberal politicians, and popular rights activists going back to the early 1930s. While Japanese citizens maintained a variety of ideological and political viewpoints, expressing these openly invited unwanted attention from the Special Higher Police – Japan's 'thought police'. By contrast, British citizens expressed critical partisan opinions even as the nation 'rallied behind' Winston Churchill's Conservative Party. In his diary, Bertram Elwood condescendingly expressed his 'uncanny insight into the working of that Tory mind', disparaging the 'old school tie boys' and their hostility to communism, which he believed poisoned them against the country's Soviet allies. The reference to the patterned ties worn by elite public school graduates was strictly a class antagonism, but Bertram also inveighed against the general views of Conservative Party constituents: 'What a delightful prospect it must be', he wrote acidly of the Eastern front, 'for the Tories to see their two chief enemies slowly annihilating each other'.[9] Nevertheless, total war sustained non-partisan politics under the rubric of unity and the threat of external annihilation so, while Britons continued to voice their opinions about politics, in effect they obeyed the state more or less as reliably as the Japanese did.

While superficially citizens and government embraced unity, wartime society and government policy was rife with contradiction as they tried to sustain pre-war gender, age, and class boundaries. First, historical documents and post-1945 memoirs of life at war tell us that 'we're all in it together', but this was simply untrue – at least in the sense that the wartime government did its utmost to preserve the pre-war order, even if it made the nation weaker in the face of the enemy. Still, although 'the people' were both divided by the state through its laws and by society through its customary rules, the war also introduced some new expressions of age, class, and gender that challenged pre-war boundaries. Katayama Ryūtarō, a 50-year-old shopkeeper near Hakata (in the southwest island Kyūshū), described these contradictions well:

One by one the young men were sent off to war, and those left to guard the home front against air raids dug shelters, organized bucket relays, and undertook training in fire prevention ... People who were fit and healthy were drafted or sent to work in armament factories, steelworks, or coal mines. Also, there was hauling soil for airfields, unloading at the docks, all kinds of things to do. Girls were the same: mobilized for military work, unskilled labour, and looking after the wounded soldiers ... When the sirens rang out at dusk, we would put up curtains over the windows not to let any light out. Men wore military leggings, women wore white work trousers [*monpe*] and practiced with bamboo spears, and we all worked with pride to defend the home front.[10]

As just one example, then, women were not just traditional 'good wives, wise mothers', but also efficient labourers and necessary frontline workers. Thus, the needs of the state did sometimes come into conflict with pre-war assumptions about the proper place of working people, women, and youth; nevertheless, British and Japanese society worked hard to maintain their 'traditional' identities. As Penny Summerfield put it, in Britain, as in Japan, governments were aware that parents appeared 'readier to relinquish control of their sons than their daughters to the state.'[11] Because state and society put forward new demands while trying to enforce the old order, it was perhaps inevitable that age, class, and gender not only affected the ways in which civilians documented the experience of war, but also became more acutely aware of these differences than they would have in peace time.

Eat the Young, Despise the Old: Total War and the Burdens of Age

Although it has rarely been addressed within the historiography of the Second World War, age was one of the most important factors in determining who was exposed to danger during area bombing campaigns. For starters, teenagers were often the most enthusiastic about making personal sacrifices for the war effort. Even after seeing his hometown destroyed, Ono Kazuo thought to himself, 'Japan must win this war!' and redoubled his dedication to war work under fire. As one might expect, teens like Kazuo in Britain and Japan rebelled against their parents' wishes, dodging air raids in order to visit centres of entertainment such as dance halls, pubs, and the cinema. The exigencies of the war could also make obedience difficult:

... in those days you would never have done anything – and I can remember driving down by houses during the raids as the shrapnel used to come, hitting the roof and come sliding down and you'd duck down, and the Air Raid Wardens used to come out and say, 'Come down in the shelter!' and I'd say 'My mother'll kill me if I don't get home!' Those were my conscious thoughts.[12]

The dislocations and destructive possibilities of the war made older people fear for the future of their children. After the bombing of Bristol, Violet Maund wrote in her diary: 'Joyce's birthday – 17 years old. God bless her and see her safely through this terrible war'. Soon enough, however, Joyce was called on by the state to serve: 'The Prime Minister in the House asks for the registration of girls and boys from 16 to 18 years', Maund wrote, 'My God, when will this end? I am far fitter to help in the war than babes of 16'.[13] Unfortunately, the war spared few: bombing took the lives of new-born babies, war industries forced young people to labour, and the infirm elderly found themselves at the front line inside their living rooms.

For the young, the war demanded a particularly heavy burden: as adults were drafted, preoccupied with work, or killed, children were left abandoned, even during air raids. Gladys Hollingsworth watched Coventry children 'running about without not only homes, food, and clothes but mothers and fathers who are never to be seen again'.[14] In C. A. Piper's air raid shelter in Liverpool, this reached a level of genuine crisis: all too often, when adults failed to turn up to clean the shelter, the work was left to unattended children, who enjoyed even less social power than women. In some cases, women sent their children to the shelter all alone, even on Christmas Eve, prompting Piper to tell them angrily that the children could come, but they 'are not in our charge and under our authority'.[15] In Japan as well as Britain, young schoolchildren were often left alone because their parents were dead. Yoshida Takeshi, after the firebombing of Chiba, had to look for his parents in the ruins. His father's body showed that he had been partly burned alive, and then collapsed in front of a police box. Next, Takeshi heard that a body had been found in an air raid shelter, which had sustained a direct hit by an incendiary bomb. His mother had suffocated inside, but was completely unburned, including her Western-style clothing. Removing her gas mask for identification, Takeshi noted, 'Her cheeks flushed, as if she were still alive'.

His parents had fled during the raid, but the shelters and government facilities could not save them. Later, when he returned to his home, Takeshi discovered one reason why they were delayed was that they were busily burying valuables in the back garden. 'Plates, papers, and other things came out of the hole', he recalled, 'but much of it was burned beyond use'.[16] Adults had privileged so many things – money, possessions, position, reputation, and above all national pride – that they left their children vulnerable even in the middle of area bombing campaigns.

Nevertheless, citizens of the city, regardless of age, were uniformly disturbed that the war was causing the deaths of children who could hardly be considered 'combatants'. In Coventry, a woman was heard to say, 'It was the terrible sights you saw. There were four poor little children lying dead'.[17] During the firebombing of Fukuoka, Imamura Hajime was horrified to see 'a toddler who had lost a hand but didn't have the strength to cry, and a mother looking like she had lost her will, staring blankly'.[18] Young people were also shocked and horrified that war meant taking on physical violence and death themselves, as they often had a weak grasp on those concepts. In Wallasey, which was hit along with the Merseyside and Liverpool air raids, local boy William Burkey witnessed a family refusing to bring their young baby into a 'damp and cold' air raid shelter, only to be utterly wiped out by a bomb's direct hit.[19] In Nagaoka, Watanabe Teruko vividly remembered being trapped during a 1945 air raid when she was only 6 years old; she was scared and abandoned with her near-blind grandmother, who announced, 'We're going to die here'. They were eventually saved by a sympathetic policeman, but she recalled 'shaking, looking up at the sky, and feeling my little child's heart filling with fear'.[20] One man in Bristol, holding his infant granddaughter under the stairs during the intense GAF bombing of 16–17 January 1941, even noted that 'What touched me the most was that the baby knew as if by instinct that something was wrong, and clutched my fore-finger each time a bomb fell'.[21] Indeed, adults, who observed this sort of behaviour among children and young adolescents, often recoiled at the horror that war brought on the unsuspecting young. Joan Rice, a 21-year-old WAAF trainee, looked at a baby boy sharing her air raid shelter and wrote in her diary, 'It's so strange to think that we human beings are doing this to each other, which could include this wanton killing and has already included the killing of other people's babies'.[22] For better or for worse, the murder of children did not force citizens in Britain and Japan to abandon the war. In Hachiōji, 29-year-old railway defence worker Kogami Kōichi lamented the victimisation of women and children, but managed to accept their suffering in order to carry out his duties:

At a crossroads near where the sports hall is now, there was a baby crying. There was no one else there for the baby to turn to. Beside the baby was the corpse of its guardian (*okamisan*), a woman of about 32 or 33 years old, who had taken a direct hit to the head [by an incendiary bomb]. The baby was strapped to her back, and screaming. It was so sad, and I wanted to do something, but I was at work and couldn't lend a hand. I notified someone from the civil defence unit ... a few dozen metres away, and then left.[23]

Like the trapped baby, the little bodies of children were not as sturdy as the adults who launched these total wars; they could not flee or protect themselves in the same way, but adults subjected them to war conditions nonetheless. I. S. Haslewood's London rescue squad found 'seven people out more or less alive' on the first day of the raid, but the final one was a small boy. Although he appeared unharmed, he died on the way to the hospital, prompting Haslewood to write that 'his poor young body could not live through the agony of the shock'.[24] Similarly, Mizutani Shin'ichi lamented the frailty of an 8-year-old girl in Nagoya:

Hiroko has, in the end, passed away. I thought she was improving, but this month her throat was hurting, she lost her appetite, and she became extremely weak; the wound on her hand was bleeding again, and so it's because of [the wound]. In any case, she became a victim of the enemy bombing, bearing an unbearable pain in her little 8 year old body, going through twenty days of suffering – when I think of this, it's just too much.[25]

In Bristol, some young people who were killed by enemy bombers had no adult left to claim their bodies; these children were buried in unmarked graves with no relatives to mourn them and no one remembering their names.[26] Children who survived the war into adulthood vividly remember their physical vulnerability and, in some cases, it continued to affect their quality of life years into the post-war. Watanabe Shige, who was the same age as Hiroko, fled with his mother from incendiary bombs when:

I heard a 'whoosh' sound, and I was blown into some shrubs in the hedgerow of a primary school. After spinning a few times, I rolled into the road again. When I stood up, I saw that the bottoms of my trouser legs were on fire. I didn't know how to put out a fire like that, so I just screamed, 'Ow, it's hot! Hot!' all while kicking my legs. The more I kicked, the more the flames spread. Fortunately, schoolteachers and air raid wardens were close by, and they shouted 'That child is burning!' and doused me from head to toe with buckets of water, putting out the flames.

Despite being a non-combatant, the Allied forces had burned young Shige and scarred him for the rest of his life.[27] Urban citizens decried the enemy's inhumanity for killing children, but this did not trigger

serious reflections on the punishments the home army inflicted on
'enemy' civilians. H. B. Monck, a retired policeman in Liverpool, saw
RAF bombers return from Germany fully loaded with their bombs
because they failed to find proper military targets. He mused in his diary,
'Makes me think they are asking too much of human nature. After all,
although we believe that Christ said turn the other cheek to be smitten, as
a matter of practical politics we don't always do it'.[28] Adults knew, on
some level, that the war they were supporting was indiscriminately killing
civilians, including children, but they usually supported area bombing of
foreign cities anyway.

Meanwhile, the older generation ruled over teenagers and young
adults socially, culturally, economically, and legally, and they attempted
to control how these young people should behave. In Britain, this
included those elders who had lived through the First World War and,
in Japan, those who had served in conflicts such as the 1904–1905 Russo-
Japanese War and the 1931–1932 invasion of Nationalist China. Their
efforts to 'guide' teenaged youth revealed the importance that adults
put on defending the pre-war order, and the older folks' lack of preparation for the unprecedented total war to come. Bessie Skea recorded
her frustrations with the older Scots of her local community in her
diary:

Shapinsay is too bad, all the same; they've stopped everything: dances, concerts,
ploughing match, shows: practically everything that can be stopped. Of course we
have a great many Terriers [local male Territorial Army conscripts] away, thirty-
five, I think, and the older people believe it isn't right to have anything enjoyable –
but what on earth is to hinder us having Red Cross concerts in aid of the troops?
All the youngsters are complaining and longing for a dance – myself included –
and I do think it's too bad. They won't even have a Farmer's Union Social! There
is the SWRI, Women's Guild, and Bible Class of course, but nothing else, except
knitting socks! The rest of Orkney is not cutting out everything – but it's no use
grumbling.[29]

Older Britons and Japanese possessed no relevant wisdom or knowledge
of the conditions that the new war would create, including political views
that young people might adopt. Bertram Elwood, who stayed in a hostel
while traveling in Worcestershire, noted that English youth had been
highly politicised by the Second World War. Looking at graffiti, he
thought many would dismiss it as 'irrational' or 'semi-educated' but,
for him, 'it is an indictment of a system, under which the youth is
reduced to scrawling on a lavatory wall as a means of self-expression'.
Noting the lack of obscenity and 'crude drawings' (which one might
otherwise expect from toilet graffiti), Bertram carefully copied the com-
bative politics of wartime youth:

Capitalism is Imperialism, Imperialism means war. Word for the world Utopia ...
Socialism.

Socialism as known today is the rats' socialism. What about practising the
respectable man's socialism, which means conservatism. [Scratched out,
re-written by another as:] British Union. [Arrow pointing to 'conservatism':]
BUNK!

Workers of England Unite and work for a People's Government.

Workers of the World Unite. You have only your chains to lose, you have the
world to gain.

If we do not have Communism in England we are going to have fascism in
some form or another! ... Peace and Prosperity for the working man and woman.

Blow up everything. Nihilism is the only salvation.

Remember 1914–1918? Then take Dr. Blosser's tasteless vitriol now.[30]

Like Britain, Japan had its share of radicalised youth in their late teens
and early twenties. Despite the fact that left-wing thought was widely
suppressed in Imperial Japan by the Special Higher Police, there were
still plenty of young people who despised class divisions and other
privileges in a supposedly 'unified' society. Similar to Bertrand's experience, Japanese views commonly found their expression as graffiti, even
on school blackboards: 'Have faith in communism', 'Down with Japanese imperialism, defend our Soviet', and 'Turn this war into a communist revolution!' One young film technician was arrested for writing on a
lavatory wall the following screed:

Give us freedom / Emancipate the means of production / Abolish capitalism and
establish Republican communism / New society and new culture / Where women
participate in building socialism / And receive the same wage / Without taking
away men's jobs / Men and women side by side / Work to build socialism.[31]

Young people may not have shared the political views of their elders, but
they were nonetheless sucked into the deadly machinations of the
war that adults created. War worker Tamura Yasuko recorded in her
diary the frustration she felt in being pulled away from school to work the
night shift in one of Japan's many war industries. On top of the exhausting labour, by May 1945 she was also growing tired of the wartime
politics and interruptions in her education.

Working all night is really tough. I won't complain about how unfair it is, but it
leaves me exhausted. You get in the bath, go to sleep feeling nice, then work;
I went to bed at 8:30am this morning, and when I woke up it was 4:30. There's
no time to study, and this makes me sad. I wanted to buy a book in German, but
because Germany is now a 'fallen nation', the environment is too hostile.[32]

For the wartime generation, these experiences could lead to significant
post-war resentments and claims of 'stolen' or 'lost' youth. As one

Coventry survivor put it: 'When we were under the stairs we used to chat and sleep really. The best part of our young life went like that. It was such a waste'.[33] The adults controlled many aspects of young people's lives, but they did not determine the ultimate expression of youth's political, cultural, and social values, which were birthed by the war that their elders conceived.

Meanwhile, adults ceaselessly mobilised teenagers and young adults to serve a war that they had had no voice in deciding. Fifty-two-year-old primary school headmaster Kogawa Saburō's diary detailed numerous programmes designed to push young people into some form of service or another, including support for the Youth Corps News (*Shōnendan shinbun*) and direct distribution of their publications to his primary school students. He also received 'Young Women's Volunteer Corps' (*teishintai*) and took up collections for sundry pro-war youth groups.[34] In Britain and Japan, younger and younger people were drafted into the armed forces and war industries as forced labour; consequently they were targeted by adults in enemy forces, and routinely massacred. Young men who were not on the front line, either at home or abroad, could suffer as well. The 'Bevin Boys' in Britain were conscripted teenagers and young adults who were chosen, at random, to be pressed into coal mining, which was very dangerous labour indeed. Since conscientious objectors were also frequently assigned such unpleasant work as alternative service, this work was not recognised as war service until a half-century after the war's end, when most of the 'boys' had already died. One woman, who recalled bringing them scraps of meat being eaten by dogs in bombed out Coventry, wrote that it:

... was very wrong of [the government] to pick out those boys' names because some of them were training ... they were just snatched out and put into the mines. They were told they were being just as much good in the mines as they would be fighting. They probably wouldn't get hurt so much. They didn't have much time off, they had to keep going.[35]

In Kure, which was a port city with a major naval installation, Takatori Minoru, an adult, worked in a factory that produced batteries for submarines, but he also oversaw many teenagers who were forced to work there during the war. Takatori vividly recalled how the Allied attacks on Kure came in waves: the first wave killed workers in the factories, the second caught them fleeing, and the third was even more devastating:

In the third attack, the seaside air raid shelter I'd been hiding in was smashed by a blast wave, and there were fourteen or fifteen people in there. Of that number, maybe three survived, or so I heard later. When the shelter was destroyed, the tide came in and soaked us all. I think it was probably impossible to save those who were buried alive in that situation. The schoolgirls I had led out of the factory were certainly dead by that point. I feel strongly that it was my fault, because I led them there, earnestly thinking I could save them.

While fleeing from the bombs, he encountered a teenage boy (*shōnen*) who was working as a janitor for the company. A terrible barrage drove them away from the other refugees from the factories, and they found themselves alone. Suddenly, a bomb shaped like a massive egg landed some twenty metres away and, mysteriously, did not explode. Watching it, shocked, Takatori saw the boy crouch down and begin crying, 'Mother! Mother!' Takatori then returned to help emergency medics dig the dead schoolgirls out of the collapsed shelter. 'We pulled four or five bodies out', he wrote, 'but even now I cannot forget the image of a chunk of a girl's body hanging from an electric pylon'. Nakajima Eiji, who was part of the crew digging out the corpses, recalled grimly that 'I retrieved between thirty and forty bodies, all schoolgirls. It must have been terrifying, excruciating. They were holding hands tightly when they all died'.[36] Teenagers and young adults had little input when it came to deciding the course of Japanese foreign affairs, but they were among the first on the front line, whether it was on the battlefield or in industries targeted by the enemy at home.

In addition to the young, the very old often suffered the effects of the war in disproportionate ways. Older people who were winding their careers down for retirement found themselves thrust back into highly stressful work, including volunteer services to which they were expected to contribute. 'So many of the younger men have left for the Services that the older men have now more than their work to do', wrote Violet Maund, 'Daddy complains that it has come at the wrong time of his life, and he feels the strain'.[37] In order to help the elderly, younger civilians prepared hot drinks in thermoses and one woman recalled heating 'some house bricks ... in the range over. We used to wrap the bricks in flannelette pieces to give to the old people in the street shelter. Through-out the night, we ensured the warmth of the old folk'.[38] The kindness able-bodied younger people felt for the elderly, however, did not trans-late into effective protections for them during air raids. Miyada Katsuyo echoed many Japanese who lived through the Allied bombing campaign when she noted the higher casualty rates among the elderly: 'When we fled the city, there were many older people who ran with us', she wrote, 'but when we returned afterwards, oh, he didn't make it, she didn't make it – their bodies littered the streets'.[39] The area bombing campaigns created a crude and unforgiving environment wherein the physically fit would survive, and those with stiff joints, or who were easily tired, would be consumed.

Many elderly people in Britain and Japan, who were living either on pensions or depending on the generosity of family, were made homeless and helpless by the air raids; on top of this, their fragile health was deeply affected by the stress of air raids and the rapid decline in their nutrition under rationing. As GAF raids were increasing over Coventry in late 1940, Joan Thornton began to worry about her elderly mother: 'Mother is very nervous. I should like to be able to push her off into the country, for a few weeks. She is getting very thin and so upset at all this and so nervous. Every time the sirens go she can't hold a limb still'.[40] Young adults could adjust to the new extremes of war – reduced caloric intake, dashing through dangerous situations, dealing with high stress – but those who had become accustomed to a more peaceful life were unable to make the transition, particularly if they were already ill. Kawamura Masako recalled her sister crying with her grandmother, who was very sick, in an air raid shelter during the destruction of Hachiōji. Masako's mother reprimanded them both:

'We can't be weak and useless like this. Get your chin up, we have to be stronger! We can't let grandmother die on her own like this. When the time comes, we'll die as a family – all together'. Mother said this, making every effort to comfort grandmother. Tears appeared in her eyes nonetheless.[41]

In Coventry, an older woman named Mrs. Cockerill was trapped with her husband by the raids, and she wrote a long letter revealing many wartime troubles particular to old age. She was unable to contact her son, who was close by but cut off by the enemy attacks on the West Midlands. 'We are not very good in health', she wrote, 'in fact we are both under the doctor at the present time'. Her husband was very ill, and suffered 'nasty heart attacks' as a direct consequence of the raids. Even worse, the aerial bombing took them completely by surprise, so they had neither food nor water in their shelter. The bombing hit their house, and the rain came in to soak their beds and clothes. They had to 'beg so hard' to get someone to fix their roof, and Mrs. Cockerill could not bear to be evacuated away from her husband, who oversaw the repairs on their house. The shops were ruined or closed, the gas was off, the water was off, and the prices of food were growing beyond their means. They never dared undress, even at bedtime, 'for fear we have to rush for shelter'. When they fled the city centre, Mrs. Cockerill discovered that the local woman who took them in would not help them get food, and was even extorting money for their lodging. 'I thought it was very unkind of her', she wrote, 'and they are charging terrible prices for putting us up, but if ever they have a raid like us and, which I hope they never will, it will let them see how unkind they have been and how glad they will be for a little kindness'.[42] Despite admonitions to sacrifice together, British and Japanese citizens still preyed upon vulnerable elderly people as resources became scarce.

Most ordinary people felt compassion for the elderly, but these feelings of kindness did little to alleviate their suffering: aerial bombing campaigns were indiscriminate. M. E. Brodie, the headmaster of Stokes Croft Endowed School in Bristol, found himself responsible for the old residents of a nearby alms house. Donning his Home Guard uniform, he led the poor elderly residents through a shower of incendiary shells into the school basement, brushing the sparks from their clothes as they fled. One old lady insisted that she would be safer in her room, which was shortly flattened by an explosive bomb's direct hit.[43] Older Japanese parents felt that their weakness put their children potentially at risk, and consequently begged their adult children to leave them behind: 'I'm old so it's OK if I die', pleaded Gishibe Ayako's mother, 'but you are young so you must live!' In Ayako's case, however, she was unable to leave her mother behind, and thus carried the old woman on her back while fleeing Allied attacks.[44] During the assault on Coventry, Mary Bloomfield described how her husband Ted dug out two old women still sitting in their evening chairs, buried under a pile of wooden timbers and bricks; when visiting friends, they found an old woman 'crippled with arthritis and had sat all night in her wheel chair between two inside walls. All around them was devastation'.[45] Older citizens who could not see or hear properly also had little idea when air raids were beginning and ending, and where hazards might lie. During a devastating firebombing campaign over Himeji, Kobayashi Takako described how her sister had to shout into the ear of their aged grandmother – 'It's over now!' – who only replied, 'Oh, really?' but could not walk and had to be carried by Takako's siblings.[46] In the end, the primary problem faced by older citizens during an air raid was their decreased mobility, which made them highly vulnerable to fires, bombs, and other threats. By most accounts, the elderly felt this vulnerability keenly, and it terrified them. As C. A. Piper wrote of his Liverpool air raid shelter:

We had a large proportion of elderly and lonely people, and people who, on account of infirmity, could not get into the public shelters. In our premises they found congenial companionship and the sense of security arising from being with other people. Doubtless this sense of security was largely illusory, but certainly on our premises they were more secure and sheltered than in their shattered houses.[47]

Mobility problems certainly compounded the risks of physical injury and death throughout the air raids over Britain and Japan, but memoirists and diarists focused more on the psychological impact of the war on the elderly; when older people begged to be left to the bombers, they were also putting an incredible emotional burden on the survivors, including their children.

The very young and the very old shared a similar fate during the mass bombing of the city: being physically weaker than the able-bodied adults, they were more vulnerable. In fact, the very first war death unearthed by Bill Regan on the Isle of Dogs in London was 'an elderly man, fully dressed, still sitting in his armchair, but totally embedded in fine plaster, and brick rubble. We could not lift him out, until we had freed him entirely, the stuff was packed almost solid around him'.[48] During air raids such as the one over Himeji, Nakayama Hideo noted that 'those who took refuge in shelters were roasted alive' and, among the refugees fleeing the city, 'people ran silently, holding the hands of the elderly, who carried the little children on their backs'.[49] After bombs blasted out windows and Venetian blinds, elderly parents felt even more exposed, as Violet Maund wrote about her mother: 'She is afraid of being murdered in her sleep, poor darling!'[50] Still, physical disability was not always a liability. Despite their relative vulnerability, some elderly residents showed considerable resilience in the face of enemy attack. Dora Mockett wrote in her diary of encountering in Hull's Queen's Square:

... an elderly woman who was living all alone there surrounded by ruins and burned out warehouses. Also talked with a little old lady with a shawl on her head who lived in Wellington St., and she told us how she goes into the shelter at the pier and spends her nights there – two of our brave women.[51]

In Bristol, W. A. Hares enlisted a deaf man to help others take cover during a devastating raid on 4 December 1940, and found that his inability to hear the raid made him fearless. Having lost his hearing at sea when surviving a torpedo attack, the otherwise 'disabled' man was 'Just the right man in a pinch!' Soon after, the man (whom Hares had come to call 'Deaffy') helped him save Hares' own home, putting out fires from incendiary bombs with his boots and hat.[52] Nevertheless, it is safe to say that children and the elderly fared comparatively poorly in the race for survival in the city. The inhumanity of the air war is perhaps best exposed by the fact that its preferred targets were those least likely to offer any resistance.

Conscription often left communities in the hands of adult, able-bodied women, who in any case had to run households and sometimes work as well. From January 1942, British women aged twenty to thirty were also conscripted for a number of services, including Auxiliaries, Civil Defence, and industrial labour, but in far fewer numbers than men; Japanese women and schoolgirls were also forced, either formally or through social pressure, to provide assistance to the war effort. Nevertheless, conscription was mainly a male burden, and to women was left the full responsibility of domestic work and labour outside the home. In Britain and Japan, the women left behind, and the children they tried to protect, reflected on the injustices and difficulties that such a situation presented. 'A neighbour's boy brought in his puppy, for us to admire', Violet Maund wrote in her diary, 'He has now left school and is working two weeks' day work. His hours and night work are far too long for his youth. He should still be at school enjoying boyhood'. By the summer of 1942, Maund understood how gender and age could conspire to create new kinds of victims during air raids.

Another raid on Weston-super-Mare last night. Up at 2am for an hour. It is sad to see these elderly women who, up to this present war, have always known security and peace since their childhood, experiencing these dreadful nights. And many have come from the East and South East coast for what they thought was the comparative security from air-raids in the West Country. The children seem more adaptable and will play and laugh during the raids, but these elderly gentlewomen feel the loss of their strong Victorian papas, and are so frightened that they are meek, obedient, and trustful.[53]

For Takimi Hiroyuki, who was only 5 years old during the bombing of Hachiōji, his childhood memories are pockmarked by events that he could not properly understand at the time. It was a world in which, due to conscription, all the adults around him were women, and his household was 'practically all children'. When the air raids began in the middle of the night, his mother tapped him lightly until he woke up, and the sounds of sirens and shouting voices 'made even a child tumble into the depths of terror'. The elderly and children then turned to the women who had been left behind by conscription to keep them alive. When the bombing began, they were plunged into what Takimi called a 'Hell' (*jigoku*) of fire:

In the air raid shelter ... children were screaming intensely from fear, and the old folks clasped their hands in prayer to the gods and buddhas. My mother and the other adults were exhausting themselves by packing the entrance with cloth and corrugated iron sheets lest even a flicker of fire get in. Nevertheless, a fire started [near the entrance], and I learned [later] that they thought this was the end. Mother wet hand cloths from a bucket [she had brought] and passed them along to the children. The old folks said that, in the middle of this Hell, a buddha had appeared (*jigoku ni butsu-sama ga arawareta*), and the kids all said it was so good, it was even better than candy. All their crying stopped.[54]

For adult women in Britain and Japan, who had hardly foreseen being responsible for house work, labour, fire prevention, finding food, and protecting their children and elderly relatives from bombing, the war was an impossible job. In diaries and memoirs, women described their bodies becoming emaciated from lack of food and rest, their nerves shattered from constant interruptions by air raids, and loneliness and isolation due to the absences of their partners, siblings, and other male relatives – and yet, even in this state, they were the most likely to turn up to fire patrol, shelter duties, and philanthropic events. It is not hyperbole to say that, whether one's country was a 'fascist aggressor' or a 'liberal democracy', wartime state and society were held together for the most part by the efforts of women.

To make matters worse, while the very old were victimised in their homes and the very young bombed in their schools – or forced to work in factories and coal mines – many healthy adults refused service while actively supporting the war. The hypocrisy of adults who, of course, also controlled the majority of the nation's wealth and power, did not always go by unnoticed. While the young threw themselves into the war effort, some older people, mainly men, who had blustered, bragged, and begged the state to go to war, ran away to safer lodgings in the countryside. One rescue worker complained in her diary that:

...all the 'brave' old soldiers are making one excuse or another to leave the depot. Several of them have found themselves to be seriously ill and have under the 'regrettable' circumstances been forced to hand in their resignations, with a bogus doctor's certificate. One of the Rescue men disappeared from Beauforte Street never to be seen or heard of again ... It is a pity that they talked quite so big before the blitz came along. It boiled down to this – they have just accepted £3 a week for doing absolutely nothing for over a year now in their country's hour of need they have just turned pale yellow.[55]

It was not merely the civilian defence forces who were failing when facing the enemy, as regular troops and even battle-hardened soldiers abandoned their duty to defend the people. In Himeji, Kobayashi Takako was taken out of school and forced into providing labour for the wartime state. Takako was resigned to do her duty, but when she arrived at the bombed-out remains of her girls' school, she only saw IJA troops fleeing the scene: 'Ah, we're present [for work] but the soldiers refuse to protect us and just run away'.[56] In Japan, some of the worst tasks, including cleaning the streets of corpses, fell to teenagers who were conscripted out of school. It is little wonder, then, that many young people who survived the war in both Britain and Japan would go on to demand, post-war, a radical restructuring of the political, social, and economic order. The middle-aged people who supported war, and profited by the old system, abandoned the young whenever the situation became too difficult, leaving that generation to literally clean up the mess.

Able-bodied adults frequently accepted that victimisation was a necessary consequence of winning a total war. Nevertheless, while adults, whether working class or bourgeoisie, female or male, teenager or pensioner, could be expected to think about their responsibilities for supporting such a merciless conflict, the same cannot be said for little children who had no economic, social, or political power. Thirty-five-year-old housewife Yamada Kikue was fleeing the bombing of Hachiōji when her 6-year-old son Masao cried out, 'Mama, look!' He thrust his hands at her, and she saw his right hand was gushing blood at the wrist – a direct hit from an incendiary bomb fragment. The boy's grandfather thought the wound insignificant, but it continued to bleed, ruining two futons, so Kikue took Masao to the Tama Mental Hospital, the Civil Defence Corps, and a factory to find some sort of medical aid – all in vain:

Two or three days passed, and it was the middle of the summer, so his wound started to get infected. It was a mess ... We had to amputate the hand ... It probably saved him, but in the winter it stung like freezing ice to him. He kept rubbing and waving the stump around, saying, 'Fix my hand, fix my hand!' He'd ask me, 'Mama, when will a hand come out? When will I grow fingers?' ... It was excruciating for me.

As soon as he enrolled in school, her son was relentlessly taunted for having a missing hand. She wanted to make him long sleeves in order to hide his stump, but was told that the cloth rationing system 'wouldn't permit it'.[57] The collapse of the hospital system in Britain and Japan even affected babies about to be born, who could hardly be considered 'combatants' or 'supporters'. At St. Thomas' in London, D. B. Maling, a final-year medical student from New Zealand, described how the German bombing ruined the infrastructure of the hospital and caused complete chaos. As large wooden beams and glass fell about them, they shuffled heavily pregnant women into more fortified areas of the building, even carrying out an 'impromptu' delivery on the ground floor.[58] In Shizuoka, panicked deliveries kept midwives and doctors running throughout the city. Babies were delivered to malnourished mothers suffering from scabies, onto dirty futons, without adequate sanitary towels, and during air raids in almost total darkness due to blackout restrictions. One midwife, Harima Toki, described how she was seeing to a pregnant woman in the middle of labour when an Allied air raid began. 'What are you messing about for', someone shouted at her from the front gate, 'If you don't get out, you're in trouble!' The baby was very close, however, so Toki told the mother: 'Listen, if we're going to die here together, there's not much we can do about it, so let's just stay here. In any case, I'll stay with you until this baby is born. You've got to hang in there, too!' Despite incendiaries and bombs falling around them, Toki remained alone with the mother, and safely delivered the baby.[59] Regardless of the machinations of the state and the 'justice' sought by urban citizens in wartime Britain and Japan, women continued to give birth and babies were subjected to bombing and privation.

The deaths of children have weighed heavily on the conscience of adults of the wartime era, and rightly so. Hoshi Tomoki, a resident of Fukushima, had always assumed that the war would take his life along with his baby daughter's, writing: 'Toyoko, go before me; your father will follow you through the fire of Anglo-American rifles'. It would not be so easy for Tomoki, however, as his little girl languished:

Even though the war ended, I had no sweets to give to my girl, and we lived a life of malnutrition and nothing, nothing. Before long, she was assailed by illness. She was abandoned by doctors without necessary medicines. Even if no milk came out, we could only give her a breast from a loving parent, covered in our tears and the cries of parents trying to take everything back. Our pleas were in vain, and our child crossed over into a new life in the next world.

Tomoki was devastated by this loss – a cruel consequence of the conflict that the people had largely supported or refused to openly oppose – and it haunted him for the rest of his life. The child, who was blameless, was taken by the war but he, the adult, had to live on. While his daughter was dying, he was still able to play 'hide and seek' with her, writing, 'I cannot forget the warmth of her tiny hands on my back, laughing and cooing'.[60] There are many conceivable justifications one might offer in defence of area bombing in the Second World War, but the slow, painful death of Tomoki's child – as well as many other children in Britain and Japan – should force us to reconsider calling it a 'good war'. It was certainly no good for the very old and the very young, who are among society's most vulnerable.

Regressive Burden: Class Divides Britain and Japan in the Second World War

This war's going to be the worst possible. I think it will last for years – maybe ten years. Some of us will never live to see the end of it. Then again, look at finance. Lots of people who have been able to live comfortably will find it very hard to get along. Up to now we've had to look at our money once or twice before we spent it, but from now on we won't even be able to look at our money. We'll be hard up all the time. The war has got to be paid for. And afterwards? What sort of world will it be after all this? – Middle-aged woman, overheard by Dorothy Hughes in Liverpool, 7 December 1939

The German Air Force, at the beginning of the major bombing campaign over London during September 1940, targeted working-class neighbourhoods essential to wartime production, including the Isle of Dogs in east London. Serving as a rescue squad volunteer, bricklayer (and Samuel Pepys enthusiast) William Regan recorded how Britain's working people endured the devastation there. His diary included jokes, sad anecdotes, and astute observations about the role of labourers in the war effort. After a particularly bad raid on his blue-collar neighbourhood, Bill went looking for one of his friends, but found the man's house had been flattened by enemy bombs. 'I knew him very well', Bill wrote in his diary, 'so I had a look around, but only found the remains of the shelter torn out of the ground. No trace of him and his two sisters, I felt depressed'. Presuming his friend was killed during the raid, Bill began to write about the relationship they shared: 'We both belonged to the Dockland Settlement, and in 1930 we had all gone on a camping holiday to Oar Point, near Beaulieu, he and I had spent several late nights with a wireless set, listening to foreign stations, it was like travelling abroad'. Returning to the rescue depot, he insisted that the squad find the corpses of his friend and family members, even though it was clear that they had been killed. Before long, working beside his neighbours, they found the bodies.

We gathered three bushel baskets of remains, I picked up two left feet. One of the men saw a body perched on the rooftop. Nobby Clark climbed up and recovered it. It was badly mutilated, it was some time before we were able to identify it as female. I had picked up two left feet, and with a right foot, Major Brown thought the three feet accounted for three people. I said that 2 left and 1 right, meant two people. Some of the men were feeling queezy, so rum was dished out. I was [teetotal] so I gave mine away, and eventually we found enough evidence to account for 3 people[61]

Even when encountering the brutalised corpses of his friend and the family's daughters, Bill refused to relent in his quest to collect them. As upper-class citizens of Britain and Japan largely fled the bombs to the countryside, working-class people largely remained to clean the streets, keep the factory fires burning, and bury the dead. In order to understand the civilian's experience of the Second World War, we must first understand how class structures influenced perceptions of war effort 'contribution', genres of life writing, and exposure to risk.

As historians have shown particularly well in the British case, class had a major impact on how individuals thought about contributions to 'total war'.[62] Infamously, Sir Hugh Elles damned some of Bristol's underclasses by clearing them out of the Portway tunnel, which they had been using as a makeshift air raid shelter; writing to a fellow official, he noted that the 'redundant population together with their goods and chattels has been winkled out. ... The remaining malcontents can accommodate themselves where they can'.[63] Additionally, Mass Observers recorded multiple expressions of class hatred, directed both up and down the socio-economic ladder. Scoffing at the evacuation of London, one 60-year-old railway worker was heard to say: 'Let the scum get wiped out. Only the scum came out of the rowes. ... Talk about slum clearance: this evacuation has been the best there's ever been'.[64] Meanwhile, workers knew the ownership class was not sharing the risk while raking in the profits. Angry about the proposed forcible conscription of local women into the watch, one man wrote to a local paper to complain, 'Would the "C.O'.s" [commanding officers] leave the women to fight [German paratroopers]? I should like to know, so that I can explain to the wife if she is compelled to watch business premises while the businessmen are in their caravans or country cottages'.[65] Anxieties and hopes about the instability of class boundaries dominated British literature on the 'Blitz';[66] by exposing class boundaries more vividly, the war effort sometimes encouraged individuals to push strongly against them. Joan Rice recorded in her diary how some Londoners scoffed at her WAAF uniform, saying aloud on the tube, 'They only take those society and titled people'. Perhaps as a consequence of her involvement in the war effort, however, Rice came to despise the country's enduring class system:

Obviously, England is a declining power; obviously, Communism has come to stay; obviously, the breaking of British class barriers is a long overdue necessity if the country's ever to survive. Do you realise only 3 per cent of our populace, the lucky percentage with a public school education, can ever hope to receive any of the really first-rate jobs? Oh, the colossal conceit of a country, to limit its selection of brain ability from a future 3 per cent.[67]

Despite some effective public relations campaigns by the peerage, British class antagonisms defined the war experience, with workers having to man their stations while owners took cover. Class privilege expressed itself in access to services, food, and transport, and the wartime state's claim to facilitate necessary areas of the economy first was only true if it did not violate the interests of property owners, titled nobility, and political elites.

Japanese society had a long history of rigid class division as well, including a hereditary peerage, but mention of social class during the war could be taken as a sign of sympathy for communism, which would have been quickly reported by the local neighbourhood association to the Special Higher Police.[68] Nevertheless, Japanese people constantly referenced class when evaluating individual contributions to the war effort. During air raids, some managers recalled workers ignoring their orders to take cover, even when they 'screamed until our voices were hoarse ... because it was our responsibility to keep the employees safe'.[69] It is debatable, however, how concerned Japanese managers and owners were with the welfare of labour, especially since the wartime state gave neither carrot nor stick to ensure worker safety. In any case, while managerial staff in Japan occasionally adopted paternalistic attitudes toward their workers, the private property system inevitably created imbalances in exposure to risk. Yoshida Yoshio recalled how his father had to 'protect the house of the landlord' instead of his own during an air raid; presumably he did this in exchange for access to the rich family's shelter because 'there wasn't enough room on our property for a personal shelter, due to it being too cramped'.[70] In post-war Japan, as in post-war Britain, resentment over class privilege often erupted in the national press, leading to Labour victories in the UK and even a brief Japanese Socialist Party government under Katayama Tetsu from 1947 to 1948; it is perhaps no accident that national health care emerged in both Britain and Japan as a consequence of the state's wartime demands for working class sacrifice. Still, class was expressed more subtly in Japanese documents, so some 'reading between the lines' is necessary. For example, workers always emphasised how integral they were to maintaining the systems of urban production, and how this required both toughness and sacrifice. Railway signalman Yaba Masayuki proudly recalled how 'even during air raids, the trains always ran'. Masayuki told stories of how rail workers always had to keep their eyes open for 'flashes' (*pika*), at which point they would drop whatever they were doing, including cups of tea, and 'hit the floor'. Workers nevertheless manned their posts, even at the worst of times. Once an older employee came and shoved the men out of the office and into a shelter: 'Those who were at the signal station', Masayuki recalled, 'they all got done in. One of them, his head was taken off – just one, his head ... Anyway, two more were blown apart by the blast. What did I feel like? I dunno. It was like I was dreaming'. The workers' families had to collect the bodies from the rail station that night, 'bawling and crying all the way'. They took the bodies gently, Masayuki recalled, 'and the sound of their voices, I can still hear them. I'll never forget it'. During the war the working class was suffused with young women, even in traditionally male industries like rail. Murai Kasako, who started working the rails when she was 16 years old, also expressed pride in labour's ability to rise to the occasion as a class. While she witnessed terrible carnage as Chiba's trains were subjected to sustained attack, she noted that Japanese workers had a strong sense of shared identity. 'Apart from getting married', she wrote, 'working on the rails was my happiest time. It's not like now, where you go in the mornings and come home at night. You'd sleep alongside your co-workers in a single futon ... we'd sleep shoulder to shoulder'.[71] Nevertheless, working-class pride very rarely ran against the interests of the wartime political and industrial elite. Workers' strong sense of solidarity was corralled by the state and business owners into supporting mobilisation efforts, which was a major success of defining 'worthy' work as labour useful for total war.

Because class determined educational opportunities, it also shaped the way in which people in Britain and Japan composed their descriptions of war; class and life-writing, as a series of genres, were therefore strongly linked in both countries. For example, those who were educated in elite institutions employed more literary artifice to describe the war experience; this was largely a consequence of how they were trained to write, and what they chose to read as part of their self-styled identity. Upper-class individuals who lived outside of elite writing circles still embraced their style, including a contempt for their perceived inferiors. Edith Peirse, who had previously complained bitterly of her need to return to Hull, made her class antagonisms clear in a diary entry composed in Altrincham, Cheshire: 'I am living a nightmare life in a filthy, insanitary hovel amongst ignorant, low-bred people, and notice Aunt L. is a horrible example'.[72] Upper-class descriptions of wartime life as a rural retreat have some basis in fact. Tom Harrisson, who headed the Mass Observation project, accused Southampton's local politicos and high families of abandoning the city every night, which was returned with accusations of 'defeatist bias'. While Mass Observation writers were frequently the object of criticism for inaccurate reporting, one anonymous writer in Southampton's *Echo* did admit 'I believe it was true that a large percentage of the town's business and civic heads left each evening ... at about 5pm to rest in the country around'. Further accusations, usually anonymous, surfaced: 'It's obvious that the Mayor wasn't the only one missing when things got warm: ordinary folk detailed as firewatchers looked after property while owners, usually those who did the ordering, were away in the New Forest or somewhere safe'.[73] Meanwhile, the managerial class did not seek to write compelling war literature, but positioned themselves as factual reporters of the war's progress. White-collar workers in the professional economy often used their personal accounts to record what they considered to be salient details relevant to keeping an 'accurate' account of the war. Keeping a strict record of the food situation in Coventry, Levi Fox's diary hardly diverged from a day-by-day analysis of 'facts' and events. Adopting a distinctly bureaucratic tone, Levi decided that such a genre was more useful in documenting the war experience than a personal account of his emotional tribulations.[74] Thus, class and education were not perfectly determinative, but strongly influenced the way in which British citizens recorded their war experience.

In Japan, upper-class, elite writers drew on the country's rich literary traditions to write highly self-reflexive prose about their individual experiences. Akutagawa Ryūnosuke, a successful and celebrated fiction author, reacted nostalgically to the firebombing of Asakusa in Tokyo, pining for a neighbourhood that had so inspired his literary pursuits. In the memory narratives of the Second World War in Japan, post-war leftists emphasised the ease with which the ownership class evaded area bombing. In popular representation, such as the film *Grave of the Fireflies* (Hotaru no haka), children born into privilege returned post-war to enjoy the beautiful scenery ('I missed this lovely view!') while ordinary citizens' children literally starved below them. For the most part, 'we're in it together' did not include those who benefited most from position and possession in Great Britain or Imperial Japan. In their memoirs, politicians and intellectuals mourned the death of a ribald, multi-faceted, and globalised pastiche that characterised early twentieth century Tokyo, later calling for the revival of a putative 'Taishō democracy'. Still, these much-celebrated authors, liberal politicians, and public intellectuals cannot represent how ordinary people expressed themselves, and this included those outside of the working class. For example, educated middle-class Japanese could keep quite detailed records of the Allied bombing campaign's assault on their native cities; as in the British case, this seemed to be an expression of their educational backgrounds and professional identities. Kaneda Kyūgorō was a white-collar worker in Tokyo's affluent Shibuya Ward, and his diary was a meticulous account of the city's destruction:

24 May [1945], wind speed 15 knots, clear skies
    Air raid siren at around 10pm. A squadron of about 100 B-29s pass Kawasaki [City] and Setagaya [Ward] in the west, and then carried out waves of attacks. Incendiary bombs are dropped in the vicinity of Setagaya 4-chōme and Taishōyū.

Kyūgorō dispassionately documented, in his personal diary, the primary schools that he estimated were 'burned to the ground' during this attack. He also made sure to keep a disciplined record, as best he could, of the areas of Tokyo that were being laid waste by the enemy. Even though he was literally witnessing the destruction of his home, he did not record any emotions, even when an American plane 'fell to the ground near the Setagaya No. 1 High School, landing near the campus and turning the area into a sea of fire'.[75] Hachiōji municipal government bureaucrat Iguma Junjirō kept a very similar diary, initially recording his meetings with other managerial officials, doctors, and section heads. At the end of the war, without any apparent emotion, he recorded the losses as they flowed under his watch:

7 August [1945], Tuesday
    1000 yen borrowed from the Agricultural Labour Association (Nōgyōkai) to compensate unaccounted expenses relating to municipal work for disaster victims, assisting the wounded, and collecting the dead ... 100 bodies collected. Burned. Two bottles of sake. 20 bottles of whiskey.[76]

Whatever Kyūgorō and Junjirō may have been feeling, the genres that they used to record their war experience revealed very little about their inner lives. For the managerial class – particularly older males – it was more important to record the 'facts' than it was to document the vicissitudes of their hearts.

Regardless of one's political or class sympathies, the popular view that the owners took shelter while the workers died, is largely accurate. To begin with, enemy air forces deliberately targeted where the working class lived and laboured.[77] During the war, working-class people, even when not serving directly on the front lines, knew that they would be targeted by enemy bombers more than their 'betters'. Before air raids began, they were able to see the consequences of modern battle as sons, brothers, and uncles returned with wounds and stories. A lathe operator in Coventry recalled how, at 5am in June 1940, with 'sunlight streaming through' the machine shop, he was emotionally struck by a passenger train 'filled with tired, worn soldiers who had been evacuated from Dunkirk'.[78] For others, the consequences of total war were not obvious until the bombing came to the home islands. A train conductor in Fukuoka, Naga Yohei, had to pull the train away from the bombing of his hometown and watch it from afar. 'What I can never forget', he wrote, 'is seeing how the lead plane was dropping incendiaries over the Torikai 3-chōmei [neighbourhood in Fukuoka], which was where my house was. So, the spark that lit the fire over Fukuoka started with my home'.[79] Working-class people, even if they were still in school, had a unique view on how the bombing campaigns aimed to disintegrate the interconnected system that sustained the city. In east London, blue-collar girl Joan Elliott wrote a diary describing how labourers, who lived within centres of production and literally kept the city running, would be attacked first:

They left us alone until 5[pm] and then it was indescribable. West Ham Hospital was bombed and set alight. Electricity failed and all the sky was ablaze with fires. Bombs on Keogh Road and a slat off No. 2 roof, Warwick Road believed bombed. They bombed us from 8:40–5 at night and we thought it was our lot. From Oxford Street (West End) to East Ham was afire. The docks caught fire and simply blazed.[80]

Whether an arms factory or a civilian industry, enemy aircraft made a beeline for the places where Britain and Japan's labourers earned their wages, and quickly turned these man-made spaces into death traps. Akagi Ryōzō, who was a technician in one of Kure's hydroelectric plants, was shocked to see how, after an air raid, buildings were blown apart and 'scattered like leaves' by Allied air raids. 'A chunk of concrete was blasted from the wall', wrote Nakajima Eiji, who was also there, 'and crushed twenty people, including technical officers and workers'.[81] Regional cities, which suffered from much weaker defence systems, were sometimes left completely vulnerable. Toshima Mitsuharu, a married railroad worker with two children in Takamatsu, Shikoku, was deeply angered by the American planes' apparent ability to bomb the city with impunity, referring to the aircraft as 'the despicable enemy'. He continued to go to work for the salary upon which his family depended, put his children to bed every night, and even adopted a 'relaxed' attitude toward the air raid sirens when:

... at 3am, there was this 'shush, shush' sound, like falling rain, and so I quickly took one child on my back, my wife to the other, and I led [my daughter] Nobumi by the hand ... There was a terrible smell everywhere. The kids were saying, 'I'm afraid!' The 'shush' sound continued; then, the incendiary bombs started falling with a 'plunk, plunk' sound; my belt started slipping, so I was afraid I'd drop my child [from the sling]; I couldn't run; we made it by the skin of our teeth to Shioda [in the country]. We rested for a moment. When I looked back I saw a fire piercing the heavens. Takamatsu was engulfed in flames.[82]

In the eyes of owners, managers, and the enemy, workers were mainly resources, like rolling stock or iron ingots, whose survival was important to the war effort, but nothing particularly worthy of nostalgia. For the working class, however, the destruction of the factories and rail lines, apart from the deaths of their colleagues, was the annihilation of their home.

While it is tempting to portray workers purely as victims of area bombing, this is too simplistic, even if they suffered more than other classes in both countries. One worker in Coventry's extensive aircraft manufacturing facilities recalled how it could 'make you very proud to know you had done your part even though you wasn't actually in the fighting'. Nevertheless, his factory was destroyed in the November air raids, which he and his workmates 'worked to clear . . . for several weeks'. Once the machines were serviced and production resumed, 'we all arrive for work to find it [razed] to the ground again'.[83] Had workers united politically in Britain, Germany, Japan, and the United States against any sort of international aggression, the war effort would have collapsed overnight, and indeed many wartime radicals, like Tom Wintringham, were urging this. Instead, while working class people knew that they were on the front line they largely supported the war effort anyway (as long as they were adequately paid). In doing so, they made themselves attractive targets for enemy raids while business owners continued to reap profits from their labour – often at a safe distance from area bombing centres. Some workers refused to lay down their lives when so many owners felt free to retreat to the countryside with the lion's share of the wealth. H. B. Monck, who lived in a working-class area, was alarmed to learn that some workers had taken to staying in the air raid shelters permanently rather than return to the factories during air raids.[84] In Japan, there were panicked reports of teenage conscript workers walking off the factory floor in protest. While few bothered to record their reasons for abandoning the urban workplace, owners, middle-class observers, and government officials despaired to see so many flee, even if they were not sharing the risk themselves.

The situation was still worse for those workers who served the military-industrial complex that formed the backbone of the entire war machine. Enemy attacks scattered the workers, who were barely protected by the armed forces. A. Owen recalled how raids on Hull had devastated industry there, which led to the government moving the surviving workers away from home to locations such as Manchester to compensate for 'shortages' in labour there.[85] Worse still, the owners of factories and big businesses made little provisions for protecting their workers. Ronald Coles, a draughtsman, recalled how the working man was often left to his own devices:

At Bristol Aeroplane works, after the first daylight raid in September, every time the alarm went, there was a mass exodus from the factory, on foot and on bikes, off to the nearest open country, as fast as you could go. The workers didn't trust the shelters at the factory, which were only two or three feet under the surface, so hundreds of us took to our heels and fled out of the nearest works gate. We went to the Filton golf course, or to a railway tunnel with alcoves in the wall where you could shelter when the trains went through: we felt anywhere was safer than the works. The Company did try to stop it, they locked the gates, but the workers just burst through them. It wasn't an organised flight, it was spontaneous, and probably about a thousand of us did it.[86]

The country's use of labour for war-making could leave workers with bitter memories, especially in Japan, where the state was forced to accept an unconditional surrender. Air raids reduced factories to rubble, wrecked machines, and destroyed raw materials, leaving production paralysed. At the end of the war, Akagi Ryōzō reflected that 'on that day, of course, my honourable offerings to the Japanese Imperial Navy came right to an end. After the Kure military works were destroyed, I'm ashamed to say I can't even remember clearly what it was we were making there'. One of his co-workers agreed, saying that they 'threw everything we had into production. We gathered two tons of civilian metal materials for making *kamikaze* plane parts … and when they arrived on the docks the war just ended'.[87] In Japan, the state's call for sacrifice did not produce victory, which in turn birthed a much more radicalised workers' movement in the post-war era.[88]

Working-class people had other reasons to stay in the city besides higher wages; some were tightly intertwined with social roles set out by the wartime state, such as serving in air raid patrols, heading veterans' groups, filling in as voluntary firemen, or directing the local women's group. Bill Regan wrote frequently in his war diary of how the working class pulled together in a time of crisis. When his depot was bombed, he dashed back to help restore order. He found 'old Trice the gatekeeper', who was disabled from the First World War, 'wandering round. He seems to be suffering from shock, and is wet through, and except for that he seems to be whole, so I lead him to the boiler-house shelter, get his wet coat and shirt off, wrap a blanket round him and sat him on a bunk'. Women and children from the nearby workers' cottages filtered into the depot, which the men on staff scrambled to attend to: 'Charley Crawley was dabbing at a woman's forehead, which was gouged and bleeding, and she is holding hands with a girl about seven years old'. Most importantly for these men, however, was looking after each other. Like soldiers on the battlefield, working-class men depended on one another for survival during periods of heavy bombing. During a bad raid in September 1940, Bill's friend Eddie found their co-worker Kirby, who had been crushed by a water tank. They cradled him, and Eddie, who was normally prone to pranks and ribald humour, gently comforted him by saying, 'Here's your arm, it's alright, you must have fell on it, and you've trapped a nerve, that's why you can't feel it'.[89] The city was dependent on working men to weather the dangers of war with good humour, stick together for the good of production, and not abandon the government's mobilisation efforts. Yamashita Toshitsugu was a 40-year-old factory foreman in the southwest city Fukuoka, but also served as an assistant director of his local Neighbourhood Association. He was considerably less educated than affluent Tokyoites, but he still adopted many of the critical roles that the wartime emergency called for, such as overseeing the evacuation of the elderly during a raid and ensuring the safety of women and children – all while keeping his own family together. Yamashita recalled the 'extraordinary system' (*hijiō taisei*) that gripped Japanese society at that time, wherein everyone was organised and had a role. Working-class Japanese like Yamashita, who filled the gaps left by a state apparatus crippled by communication and transport failures, were the backbone of the war effort. 'Often', he recalled, 'when the air raids came, I kept strict self-discipline, moving about in silence. At that time, with the incendiary bombs dropping all around me, I could be unexpectedly cool under pressure'.[90] Not only were working-class people necessary (and targeted) because they actually produced things for the war, they were also essential (and targeted) for the services upon which urban life was based.

Civilian accounts in both Britain and Japan occasionally note heroics from the armed forces, but almost every writer acknowledged the ordinary civilians who stepped forward to defend their own communities as best they could. In this sense, the working person's war was like a microcosm of the civilians' experience altogether: the state, military, and government leaders were focused on defeating the enemy so, in the meantime, the people would have to look after themselves – even if the decisions of their leaders made them targets in the first place. The burden of civilian suffering in war was regressive in terms of class: the workers bore the brunt of area bombing attacks, were asked to survive on less, had fewer opportunities to flee, and had to keep the city operating as well. It should be unsurprising, then, that the working class emerged from the ashes of Second World War area bombing prepared to recreate the socio-economic order in Britain and Japan.

Defending Borders: Men, Women, and the Burdens of Gender

Saw a lot of young fellows on Seaforth Station, apparently having been to be medically examined for the Army. There looked a pretty rotten lot, to my mind. Still, as the woman sitting behind me in the train said, they're some mothers' sons.   – Dorothy Hughes, Liverpool, 15 January 1940

On 7 December 1940, Violet Maund struggled to get a fire burning in her kitchen, because the 'all electric house' she was so proud of had shut down during the German air assault on Bristol. In her diary, she complained, 'How did our grandmothers get their menfolks' breakfast ready in time for them to go to their morning work?'[91] Because able-bodied adult men were all potentially expected to serve in the armed forces, or work long hours in key industries like manufacturing and coal mining, women were given particular burdens to bear by wartime states that maintained the culturally-defined boundaries between the genders. 'Weeping was unforgiveable for the wives of Japan (*gunkoku no tsuma*)', wrote new mother Iriye Hisae, who lost her husband on the China front, 'the only time I could cry without reproach was when I was in bed with my child'.[92] One of the most striking similarities between wartime Japan and Britain was the social, economic, and political defence of traditional roles for men and women: each had their respective rights, burdens, and expectations.

Gender divided men and women in obvious ways, including military conscription for men and the mobilisation of women (and some men) as labour, but it also worked in a subtler, less plainly visible manner: while men served in factories or armies, women often had to pick up the pieces (or mess) left behind them. After the November 1940 bombing of Coventry, Willy Buchanan, writing to her relatives in Worcestershire, pointed out that she was still needed at home: 'I should like to come, but Charlie has to work. His place wasn't too badly damaged, and as we have no gas or electricity and have to boil every drop of water and milk, he would never manage by himself'.[93] On top of keeping home industries and normal chores in order, women were expected to 'defend the home' as well, which was an impossible obligation to leave in the hands of ordinary civilians. Takizawa Toki, whose husband was called up in 1943, described the situation in plain terms:

The shops all closed one after another. Hachiōji became a ghost town. Day after day there were air raids. The all clear sounded, and then it'd start again anyway. I would take the kids in and out of the shelter. It was so difficult, while my husband was away, to make sure, all on my own, that our children and elderly parents didn't die ... I thought, I have to do my best. Right, from now on I'm going to make myself be like a man.[94]

Similarly, on top of the stresses and fears that were common to all experiences of the war, Mrs. G. Robins had to look after her husband, the household, and two small children. Constant raids meant moving the children up and down the stairs at all hours from their beds to the makeshift shelter in their cellar. Meanwhile, her husband, Ernest, was working long hours. 'My Ernest says he must get some sleep', she noted after a bad night spent on her deck chair in the cellar, 'If he goes to bed he does sleep but what a responsibility with two children. I wish someone would have them so that I can stay in my own home'. While she was fortunate enough to not be expected to work on top of everything else, the loss of sleep clearly ran her down throughout September 1940. When she awoke in the morning, instead of her comforting middle-class surroundings, she was confronted by images of death and destruction:

Very little sleep, fierce gun barrage, bombing, felt pretty sick and not very confident after seeing the wreckage of the night before ... There is of course the possibility we shall not survive but I think while there is life there is <u>hope</u>. The awful drone of those machines overhead needs fit of sticking with two darling children to think about.[95]

State and society demanded that women defend and sustain the home, but women were kept out of many employment opportunities by expectations of their 'proper role'. On top of this, they were asked to look after men who served at home, as well. After departing the Hull city centre for the countryside, Olive Metcalfe frequently complained about the lack of money in her household while her husband, Kit, was away on a meagre army salary. She pleaded with Kit to come to her and help her get through her first pregnancy. When her friend's wife was planning to return to work after giving birth, Olive wrote that 'no woman should ever work and try to look after a husband too; I knew by experience it is killing'.[96] Neither Japan nor Britain embraced a revolutionary view of gender, as was attempted in the Soviet Union, and both empires continually reinforced gender roles in the areas of economy, society, and politics; they did so even when it put strain on citizens' lives and the war mobilisation effort. It would appear that, for people in Britain and Japan, defending gender boundaries was as, if not more, important than defending national borders from the enemy.

As British and Japanese historians have already noted, definitions of acceptable masculinity were increasingly dominated by military service of some sort, which women demanded of men, and men of themselves.[97] Boys could often be far more politically-minded during the war, which may have been a consequence of the impending threat of conscription – a possibility concretely expressed in mock military exercises overseen by, for example, Youth Corps in Japan (*sei/shōnendan*) and the Junior Training Corps in Britain. D. Lord mobilised himself, and his friends, to serve state goals early on in the war, including putting on a show with tin soldiers to raise funds for the Red Cross. As the 'young masters' were withdrawn due to military induction, boys like Lord assumed many responsibilities, including organising their own Home Guard. Even if this path did not ultimately lead to serving in the armed forces, like Lord, many boys proactively engaged with the state to support the war effort as part of their transition to a socially-recognised form of manhood.[98] In Japan, boys like Satō Ichio were surrounded by a growing military culture (and militarised political system) in the 1930s, wherein the sight of classmates marching away in uniforms and boots was increasingly common. The environment demonstrated the 'terrifying nature of education', which encouraged him to embrace army service and militarism itself. 'Even now', he wrote after the war, 'I can feel how difficult this was – people who were educated by others, teaching other people [like me], who were uneducated and didn't know anything about anything'.[99] In Manchester, the new bride and young mother Ivy Barnes noted the converging burdens of conscription, bombing, and a husband who was sent away:

It was the end of our light-hearted youth ... Alex was finally called up so he was glad I lived near to mother ... A V2 fell at the back of my house and had I been there I would have been killed. Thirteen people plus a new-born baby were killed. Alex went to India and returned in 1947 – a changed man.[100]

In wartime, the state in Britain and Japan reached out to Boy Scouts, Youth Corps, and other forms of organised male socialisation in order to achieve its mobilisation goals, which put young men directly in harm's way.

Indeed, those who embraced socially-acceptable manhood found that it was a deadly call to answer. In Hull, a group of male voluntary first aid workers from the Francis Askew School, including some Boy Scouts, were entirely massacred by a single bomb save one, Raymond Peat. Ambulance parties were organised by school bulletin boards, during which Raymond's elder brother insisted on taking his place when the Hull docks were razed. Oil-based incendiary bombs were so hot that the boys saw brick buildings burn. Watching families perish in fires and schoolmates die, the young men were also asked to report to the mortuary and 'wash some of the casualties to make them more presentable'. Reflecting on the sacrifice young men were expected, by women and older men, to make, Raymond wrote, 'If these men, including my brother, hadn't volunteered to do this work they would still be alive and their families would have lived totally different lives'.[101] Not every man who entered civil defence services suffered or perished, of course; some men knew when to flee, even if it amounted to a dereliction of duty. As Nakajima Shigeya explained, his unit of fire-fighters (shōbōdan) in Hachiōji had enough sense to withdraw to the outskirts of the city when their vehicle was destroyed and they began taking serious burn injuries. In a farmhouse outside the city, Shigeya and the other men watched Hachiōji from afar, only returning once the fires subsided.[102] Some men refused service outright but they could be harshly criticised, even by their own family members. H. B. Monck wrote bitterly of his two sons, who both lived abroad, that 'they are both patriotic but neither of them have mentioned the possibility of coming over to fight for the old country'.[103] The march to conscription and military service was seen by some young men as a death sentence that was cruelly dispensed by elders in positions of authority; these elders were men who, it must be said, did not have to face such dangers.

In both Britain and Japan, then, men commanded other men to face dangers that women were not expected to share. Air Raid Patrols, fire-fighting, police work, and wartime labour including mining, manufacturing, and other sorts of dangerous professions that were targeted by the enemy – these were all male-dominated fields. First, it is important to note that predominantly male risks came with predominantly male privilege; men could be higher earners in an economy in which women were expected to survive on much less. While men took pride in being providers, wartime women had little patience for fragile masculinity – as Olive Metcalfe explained to her husband Kit in a particularly hard letter:

What am I like when I am paying money I owe? You know. I cut down my own food to starvation level; I sit over three cinders; I sell my clothes ... I'll be scraping and saving ha'pennies and pence as I have been doing for so terribly long. You will probably be angry if I do, but unfortunately you have precious little influence in matters of finance which I take as my own responsibility – though it may hurt you to hear it.[104]

Nevertheless, in a time of war, gender roles for men were also full of deadly virtues in a way few women had to experience. Kit, for example, volunteered to be an anti-aircraft gunner during the air raids on London. Gishibe Ayako, a young woman living with her mother, joined the crowds rushing away from a raid on Chiba when she ran into a young medical student. He made a path for her, saying, 'Please, young lady, you go first'. She went ahead of him, and then felt him grasp her kimono tightly.

... he had collapsed. He had taken [shrapnel] from an incendiary bomb right in the stomach. Buckets of bright red blood came gushing out of him and he died there. I thought it pitiless that we, who survived, should run past those dying, so I looked to him to make sure he had died. Then the head of the neighbourhood association came and shouted, 'Run! Run!'[105]

The acceptance among some men of a heroic masculinity made them behave in irrational and dangerous ways. In Coventry one serviceman with a fractured leg had his wound bandaged, returned to his unit, and came back to the hospital dead with a broken neck.[106] Still, men who threw themselves onto the front line of fire-fighting, police work, and anti-aircraft defence relied on support from women both in the work-place and at home. Some men, like A. E. Randall, recognised this, writing, 'I'm a lucky guy, being blessed with a wife of wonderful nerve'. In the end, however, it is unclear if the burdens of gender, in terms of threat to life and limb, were truly shared during the war, and Randall gave this some consideration before setting out into the flames consuming Liverpool: 'I still think she didn't sense the danger as I did – or did she? I could not get her to go into a surface shelter. She didn't like them, so she stayed in the cellar and, for the second time that night, I kissed her goodbye'.[107] Aerial bombing, however, could act as the great leveller: the terrible losses of the war transcended the divisions of gender when men and women had to bury each other. Former teacher trainee Ozaki Aiko recalled:

Even now, it's like a horrible nightmare. On the floor of the boys' art classroom, we found eight bodies of eight of our friends lined up. From the time they died in the morning air raid they had been there for many hours, and there was a strange smell floating around the room. We three, choking, spoke some words to our dead friends, and cleaned them off with alcohol. On the parts where they had been cruelly damaged, we put them back together, fixed their bodies, and wrapped up their bodies in cloth. Then we put clean robes on them, tied the waistbands, and arranged the bodies. Now they could be sent off in clean, new coffins, their faces reflected in the tears from our eyes. They looked peaceful now, so that fear and pain they endured was unseen.[108]

Girls buried boys, men buried women, sons and daughters buried their mothers and fathers – even if the wartime state tried to maintain trad-itional gender roles, the bombs they dropped on their enemies did not make such distinctions.

War also invaded gender boundaries in unexpected ways: as men were in short supply, women were expected to take on various duties on behalf of society, industry, and the state, and this empowered them in ways that were previously very difficult. As historian Fujii Tadatoshi pointed out in the case of Imperial Japan, the wartime state could hardly have carried out mobilisation efforts without the proactive support of women – including reporting pacifists and socialists to the infamous 'thought police'.[109] In Britain, local authorities often found women more reliable than men when it came to completing jobs that kept the city running. C. A. Piper, who kept a wartime diary recording the events of a Liverpool air raid shelter, routinely noted that the tedious, but necessary, tasks of keeping the shelter tidy, clean, and hygienic was almost entirely done by female volunteers – the men rarely lifted a finger.[110] Of course, women who declined active service of any sort, and remained at home, could quickly find themselves trapped alone, feeling terrified, while the enemy dropped fire over residential areas.[111] Nevertheless, it was far more dangerous to 'do one's duty' and take the place of men in defence and industrial work. In Nagoya, Kawano Yoshiko, who worked in the communications department of the Eastern Air Defence Headquarters, mobilised herself in her personal diary as the bombings of eastern Japan intensified:

The importance of performing one's military service is an obvious issue, so one cannot hesitate for a second. As long as one has life, one can make war. There are countless lives resting on the shoulders of those who work for the war, and those lives are sacred, especially during a war to defend national sovereignty.[112]

At first, girls were asked to look after younger children, taking on the roles of mothers and aunts while elder women were pulled, or coerced, into the industrial workforce. Although Japanese and British women's duties, as stipulated by the state, were largely voluntary in the early stages of the war, the government quickly called for drafted 'volunteers' to supplement the losses and lack. In July 1943, 19-year-olds were pulled out of Japanese universities and, in early 1944, 'Young Women's Volunteer Units' (*joshi teishintai*) appeared, which included even younger girls. Women saw it as a point of pride that they could exercise agency, even if it was on behalf of the state: 'In our house we only have daughters', wrote Nagano high school student Kuroyanagi Minako, 'and since we can't offer any soldiers, my mother and I thought we should at least give one person for the country'. Another teenage girl, Arai Takako, recalled how important young women's proactive support for war was:

My dad was too old to join the services and my brother was still in primary school. There was no one in our family who could offer the country anything directly, so when the call came to my school I raised my hand and volunteered without consulting anyone at home first. Relatives recommended that I matriculate into higher education, but that went in one ear and out the other. I was ready to leap into the munitions factory, and *I was happy about it*. Only after the war ended did I understand *the terrible power of* [wartime] *education, and how I was seduced into volunteering for war work*.[113]

With war work, however, came risk of injury and death. Women were finding that the rhetoric that they, and other men, used to send young males into deadly battlefields and dangerous jobs quickly became applicable across the gender line, even if women were still not expected to serve in formal military units abroad.

Consequently, while gender politics were still fairly conservative in Britain and Japan, women saw more opportunities to distinguish themselves in the general war effort – especially young women. Girls were helping with relief services and often putting themselves at great risk. One man in Bristol recalled a 17-year-old girl manning a telephone throughout a long night-time air raid, all by herself, donning a gas mask and a tin helmet.[114] As GAF air raids grew continually more brutal in 1940 and 1941, more and more girls entered critical industry as labourers or joined voluntary forces to defend British cities. Still, British exploitation of teenage women in such dangerous work paled in comparison to what was happening in Japan. Outside of civil defence forces, younger and younger girls were joining (or being drafted into) the labour force related to military and industrial production. Koike Kinu, a 15-year-old enrolled in high school, was forced to work in a munitions factory in Nagaoka. On 20 July 1945, while inspecting some materials the other girls had made, she spotted a B-29 bomber in the sky, trailing smoke behind it.

A friend said, 'Oh no, why is that plane smoking?' Then, there was an extremely loud noise, and the earth was shaking. You could hear the tinkling of glass as all the windows in the factory were shattered. The girls all ran out of the factory screaming, throwing themselves onto the ground. Glass shards had cut into our heads, necks, and backs, so many students were injured ... We later heard it was the same weight and shape as the atomic bomb that was dropped on Hiroshima. According to one explanation, we were a practice run [for Hiroshima].[115]

The adult men who enabled the use of teenage girls as conscripted labour felt some degree of horror that they were now on the front line, targeted as the male workers who preceded them. Ogawa Takashi, a factory section chief, described in his diary how the US bombing campaign increasingly brought gruesome death upon the schoolgirls who had been forced into working for the state. After watching countless B-29s set fire to the Nagoya city centre, he could see that the factory they worked in would be next. Although they tried to evacuate, there were few places to flee, and the city's defence systems were completely feckless.

That's when the students were showered with incendiary bombs, and one of them said, 'Inoue was hit!' I ran, but she was already dead ... I don't know how long it was before we got the all clear. We had to collect the workers and get them back in the factory. One man came running back white as a ghost. One of the girl workers was killed at a trench, hit directly by an incendiary bomb. An ambulance squad rushed out, but there was nothing they could do. Next to her was an unrecognisable corpse ... There was a police investigation. There were some policemen the other day who gave a haughty lecture on our air defence. Someone said, 'There's no way [their techniques] are going to defend anything'. Those policemen were all burned to death.[116]

The deaths of schoolgirls – some as young 13 years old – in state-mandated labour service offended some men's sensibilities, but that hardly stopped the authorities in male-dominated Japan from putting schoolgirls in the most dangerous forms of war labour. Had Britain faced a situation as dire as Japan's in the Second World War, it is likely that young girls in Liverpool, London, Glasgow, Bristol, and other key cities would have been similarly deployed.

The gender divide in Britain and Japan also had to confront many contradictions as a direct consequence of war mobilisation. For upper-class women, the patriarchal system was sometimes simply an annoyance, but it was also ultimately inescapable; Edith Peirse constantly criticised her father, with whom she shared a house in Yorkshire during the war:

How I hate this miserable life with father. He's impossible to live with. Wish I could get away and leave him. He's a damnable rotter, and not fit to live in the same house with a decent woman. LIAR, the utmost HYPOCRITE and SELFISH BOOR utterly without MANNERS.[117]

Meanwhile, young men faced a more severe form of gender discrimination: they were drafted and sent away, often to die, which underlined the cheapness of male life in the eyes of the wartime state. Women, for the most part, proactively supported this form of discrimination while enjoying the privilege of exemption. Some women, however, found that playing such a role on behalf of the state left their hearts deeply conflicted. In Fukuoka, which was a major port for departing Japanese military vessels, Inoue Senri helped to organise Women's Defence Organisation (*Kokubō fujinkai*) groups to see off and encourage conscripts being sent to the Pacific Theatre. Arriving before sunrise, army officers strictly instructed the women to refrain from saying anything inappropriate to the men.

We boiled water in a large pot and then gave the men canisters of it [for tea]. Looking at them, you could say they were champing at the bit, but some were obviously uneasy. They were conscripts, so many had family dependents. We said, 'Be well', let them board the [troop] ships, put out our cooking fires, and then went home.

For Senri, whose son was also in the army, her position was difficult: she smuggled letters back to family members from these conscripts, but she continued to actively support the organisation's efforts, which were indispensable to the seamless delivery of young men to their deaths.[118] Furthermore, particularly during heavy bombardment, women could inflict abuse upon young men and boys, exercising surprising power. In a patriarchal society increasingly deprived of men, women young and old struggled with each other, and young boys could be caught in the crossfire. Patricia Donald recorded such an instance in her diary:

Miss Howitt was very cross and tyrannical with John tonight because he was naughty (which is only natural for 6 yrs. old) she kept on shaking and hitting him, so it was no wonder he cried, as he was in a crying state already. I got him into bed quietly, when she had to go and get him out again and made him cry.[119]

Thus, in considering the importance of gender in British and Japanese war efforts, intersectionality is crucial: gender without consideration of class or age is a weak method for understanding what it was like to be male or female in the Second World War. Class background greatly influenced who was sent to the worst battlefields, and older men rarely found themselves 'under the gun' in the Second World War. Older, upper-class women had very creative ways of avoiding work obligations or civil defence 'volunteer' services that put poorer, younger women in danger. Adult men, by virtue of fulfilling the primary obligation in war (serving as combat soldiers), were still treated as dominant by British and Japanese society, even if they were put in the most dangerous situations. Furthermore, those men who stayed behind, for whatever reason, largely reinforced traditional gender roles, along with female collaborators in every class and region. At the commanding heights of politics, economy, and military service, men ruled at home, and even dominated the military auxiliary service sectors, both in Japan and Britain.[120] Propaganda campaigns in the Allied and Axis camps proclaimed the war was to defend the nation and its way of life, which included patriarchy, but also classism and exploitation of the young.

The fact that so many gave so much in service of political, economic, and military leaders who enforced such unequal systems is truly incredible. As the only woman in her rescue squad, I. S. Haslewood worked hard to be the equal of the men who she drove around the ruins of London during the GAF's worst raids. She often remarked on the surprising kindness with which working-class men treated her, despite her comparative physical weakness on the job. Only once was her competency questioned, and it was by a middle-aged male superintendent for the area, who she referred to in her diary simply as 'X'. He approached her aggressively on a bomb site and asked sharply 'what I was?' The squad was digging desperately to save some women trapped in rubble, so she had little patience for this man.

I stared coldly at him and told him firstly that I was a woman – secondly I was driver to No. 9 Squad of Stretcher Parties of Depot 1, and thirdly I was now dealing with the salvage ... He is one of the worst hated and most inefficient men in Chelsea. ... while the men were digging one of them asked for a blanket with which to screen the small passage that lead to the women – to prevent further dust falling in upon them. X answered in a loud voice, 'Don't be so ridiculous – get on with your work – the women will be dead by the time you get them out anyway'.

Haslewood blamed 'X' for the subsequent deaths of the women trapped in the rubble, whose lives he had casually dismissed. 'I shall never be surprised to learn that X has met with a nasty accident some day when he is out on a job', she wrote bitterly, 'The men are determined to "get him" sooner or later. I trust that it will be sooner'.[121] In Haslewood's case, as with many others, the divisions of gender were overcome by the value of service.

For many women of that era, staying at home and raising one's children was the socially and culturally celebrated ideal to which they aspired. Men largely wished to maintain their privileges within Britain and Japan's male-dominated society and economy, or aspired to obtain such a position vis-à-vis the women in their lives. Nevertheless, the reality of area bombing, military service, rationing, and labour conscription challenged these ideals. One Manchester woman recalled the extraordinary demands put upon women working on their own during the war years:

I remember my mother working in the ammunitions factory at night. She couldn't go in the day time since there were too many kids to take care of. In the day she would do the washing, cooking, and ironing, mending, bed-making and looking after us – then she went out into the frosty night when it was dark and we would not hear her come in ... I remember once when my mum didn't have the rent money and got into debt. She was told to go down to the Town Hall and suffered the 'Means Test'. You were only allowed one bed, one table, and your saucepans, everything else had to be sold before you could get some money. If you were lucky to get something, it would be about half-a-crown.[122]

The wartime state demanded total mobilisation of all people, equally, to defend the nation's way of life, which included the divisive system of patriarchy; this was a contradiction that did not escape the notice of women and men in the Second World War. It is clear, however, that without the proactive support of women, the war effort would have collapsed overnight, and that this was true in both Axis and Allied countries – for countries whose war efforts we laud, and for those we perceive as immoral aggressors.

Social Organisation and the Contradictions of War Mobilisation

Total war claimed to mobilise every citizen of the city to fight against a far-off enemy, regardless of class, gender, and age differences. In a sense, this sort of war was democratic, because it promised to kill everyone without discrimination; strategic bombing was an equal-opportunity murderer. Nevertheless, Britain and Japan were organised along fairly clear lines of age, gender, and class, and both the citizens and leadership believed that this social structure made their country stronger. Calls for 'unity', therefore, were disingenuous; they were in fact calls for discipline, obedience, and order for the sake of the war effort.

In the end, power operated according to social definitions of privilege, which cannot be limited to one category such as class, gender, age, or even geography. Outbursts against privilege and power were common in Japan and Britain but, it must be said, more so in the latter. The war experience made young working women think differently, as one Manchester worker recalled:

Problem was, a lot of women had a lot fun and independence and could never return back to those cossetted days prior to the war. They had received not only independence and true worth, but many perks unseen before-hand and unseen by many families who were experiencing discomforts due to the rationing. A lot of envy and conflict between their elders in the large family were experienced. When the war came to an end, many of the girls had to quit their jobs or give up their uniforms. Suddenly, they had nothing to do in the post-war years, save mostly factory work.[123]

Even stolid middle-class diarists such as Bertram Elwood found himself irritated by the media's insistence on the importance of privileged individuals. When President Roosevelt's mother died, the British press covered it extensively, and Bertram wrote angrily in his diary, 'Why should the world be kept waiting for Roosevelt's mother. The world isn't interested in his mother ... Let the dead bury the dead'.[124] The need for total commitment by all of 'the people' naturally elevated them in their respective countries, but not all in the same way. Historians of Britain and Japan have turned their attention on the injustices of the wartime period, particularly in terms of class, race, and gender. As always, however, the intersection of these categories is more relevant than any one of them alone. When the British government put all women on notice that they might be mobilised for 'war work', Dorothy Hughes remarked that it would 'shake up some of the people in places like Southport'.[125]

Too long, in Dorothy's mind, had gender and class conspired to absolve a large number of women from sacrifice.

War work was often grim and joyless; as the joke used to go, a worker applying to the wartime Ministry of Labour for a post was told, 'No fear. You'll start as a foreman and work your way down'.[126] Nevertheless, full employment during wartime meant that working men – and, increasingly, women – had considerable power when negotiating with employers, particularly in skilled labour. Both Britain and Japan saw the state intervene to protect workers from the abuses of unregulated capitalism; this was not because bureaucrats were far-seeing or compassionate, but because skilled labour was more important than short-term profit for the ownership class. Andrew Gordon demonstrated how in Japan the defeat of labour unions nevertheless was followed by an activist wartime mobilisation state that, while still inimical to organised labour, was also intolerant of profit-making corporations that hurt the war effort; this meant that wages went up, as did worker insurance and pension security.[127] Whether or not there was a 'Spirit of '45' that inspired the establishment of Labour Party dominance in Britain, it is clear that the war gave working people the confidence to reject a return to the pre-war economic system, birthing enduring social welfare systems such as the National Health Service and strong labour unions.

In the early post-war period, public intellectuals pointed to another category of person for whom the war was especially intolerable: the young. Age, as a category of analysis, has been largely lost, except, perhaps, in the study of evacuation. During the war, Morizaki Azuma's elder brother, Minato, once said to him, '14 and 15 year old children are strapping bombs to themselves and attacking ships with their bodies. Can we look on silently while this happens?' Training as a pilot, Minato was fiercely devoted to the younger boys in his academy, and was heard to shout, '[Prime Minister Tōjō Hideki] murders 14- and 15-year old boys' and 'If this was a factory where the management cared more about paying deference to royals than injuries suffered by their workers, we'd smash them with a strike action'. Nevertheless, Minato committed ritual suicide the day after Japan's surrender to the Allies, and he was only 21 years old. Minato's training diary, which he began at age 16, is replete with patriotic promises to offer the nation his 'ultimate sacrifice'. Reflecting on Minato's diary, younger brother Azuma wrote,

Rather than say that Minato's death was that of an obedient warrior offered up to a broken Fatherland, I wonder if his beautiful words were simply window-dressing as an invective against those people who have continued to crush Japanese youth, and so he died because of them. These past 25 years, this question has never left me.[128]

The primary contradiction of the total war state was that it called for unity while reinforcing division; the secondary contradiction was that while it celebrated power, it was heavily dependent on the 'weak' – teenagers to work in factories, retirees to return to work, and grandparents to take up childcare on behalf of working mothers. Had the 'weak' refused to support it, the wartime state may well have collapsed.

support

*

Our diarists often made mention of the inequities of the wartime system, showing at least an awareness of how social, political, and economic structures were able to weather the onslaught of area bombing. Aiko, who certainly occupied a privileged position in Japanese society, nevertheless joined ranks with other women to practice bucket relays in firefighting exercises. During roll call, she noted, 'it was said that some households didn't turn up, some were late, and in some cases [wealthy] housewives only sent their maids'. Once the bombing began in earnest, Aiko noted that the working classes of Japan – and anyone else near the centres of industry – received the most ruthless bombardment. 'It's truly as if the enemy is burning Tokyo one ward at a time', she wrote in her diary, 'Up until now [1945], the disaster areas have largely been near major factories and in busy areas of Shitamachi so, while terrifying, we just watched things from afar'.[129] In 1945 Aiko had to join the working classes in living in fear, but she realised that, for the most part, the wealthy did not bear the same burden as those who built the war machine, maintained it, and lived nearby it.

Few reflected on the divisions within wartime British society with as much vehemence as Dorothy Hughes. After enduring several raids against Liverpool and its surrounding towns, Dorothy found herself feeling increasingly despondent and angry about the situation in Britain.

The whole futility of it depresses me. I don't look at it so much from a personal aspect. I feel so sorry for others not able to stand up to the strain. I'd like to know if the Germans feel the same. I've just been reading [Mass Observation's] report on post-war conditions as visualised by the Observers. I think the 'less class distinction' etc. is all baloney. All this happened last time [in the First World War]. Talk of a new order is futile. It will always be the same. Top dogs and underdogs, 'haves' and 'have nots'.

Her frustration was not a facile critique of inequality, however: for Dorothy, the war exposed working-class putative weakness before the GAF – their lack of 'go-to-it' spirit – and this suggested that Britain's class inequalities might be justified. 'In a way, it is perhaps as well it should be so', she wrote, because the 'old school tie merchants are . . .

doing their bit while the dock workers refuse to work overtime'. Dorothy believed that direct, proactive contributions to the war effort defined the worth of a citizen. She lambasted 'fashionable ladies' in places like Southport, an upmarket Merseyside resort town near Blackpool, which she wrote were 'full of young women doing nothing. It's a case of "all hands to the pump" nowadays'. Nevertheless, she also thought it was 'not fair to subject women and kids to this battle', and supported the evacuation of non-essential women – presuming all adult men, regardless of age, were fair game for dangerous work. For the men left in the bombed-out cities, she envisioned them corralled into hostels and forced into 'communal feeding'.

For those women who she deemed fit, however, the perils of war were acceptable. When a military man complained that female recruitment into home defence forces was 'trying to do the same with women as the men', Dorothy was enraged: 'the government may have to compel women to join the [Auxiliary Territorial Service because of the] prejudicial attitude adopted by the men, who advise their womenfolk not to join'.[130] For Dorothy, the war should have been the great re-organiser, but still along recognisable lines, and service the sole definition of worth and value both in society and the labour market. For better or for worse, the war was not just about defending national sovereignty, but the British and Japanese 'way of life', which included gender, class, and age discrimination.

Conclusion
Victory for the People: Pacifism and the Ashes of the Post-War Era

> There is nothing so bad – that might not be worse. There is nothing that time cannot mend. All troubles, no matter how thick they come, most surely will come to an end. — Gladys Hollingsworth, 1940

During the Pacific War (1941–1945), when Japan launched an apparently suicidal war against the United States, ordinary Japanese people widely expressed support for the government's actions. Nevertheless, some Japanese men, particularly those who had been deployed as soldiers to prior conflicts, already knew that 'just wars' were a farce orchestrated by government propaganda. Hasegawa Tetsuo recalled how his father, a veteran of the 1937 war in China, was reticent during the escalation of hostilities with the United States:

... he never spoke of it, but did one time say this to my mother: 'Once we attacked a house [in China], and the head of the household came out, waving his hands and pleading with us desperately. We didn't understand him, of course, but he was begging us to just spare the lives of his family members. We couldn't disobey our superior officer, though, so we killed all the adults in the house. The children were screaming in loud voices. We thought it impossible to leave them behind, so we killed the children, too'.

When they were alone, Tetsuo's father used to tell his mother, 'I'm never going back to war. It's horrible'. Unfortunately, he was taken by the state again and sent to the Philippines, where his troop ship was sunk by enemy aircraft. After recovering in a military hospital, he wrote a simple letter in pencil, which a comrade brought back home under the nose of the censors. Even this letter, his last statement to his family, was destroyed during the Allied air raids on Shizuoka, erasing some of the final remnants of Tetsuo's father from the earth. Nevertheless, Tetsuo's mother recalled the strong anti-war sentiment the elder Hasegawa had come to embrace, and Tetsuo, who was too young to read the letter during the war, accepted this version of events – namely, that one should 'oppose and resist war with all of one's soul', because war 'treated humans no better than insects'.[1] It is unclear if the Hasegawa family's tale was an accurate recollection of the letter's contents or a construction of post-war memory in Japan, where such sentiments are almost a form of political orthodoxy; nevertheless, those who actually experienced area bombing often tried to communicate a great disgust for armed conflict to post-war generations.

At the same time, we must not forget that most citizens during the war fully embraced the call to arms and did not tolerate merciful attitudes towards the 'enemy'. Japanese historian Yoshimi Yoshiaki, and more recently Samuel Yamashita, have dug deep into Japanese personal records from the war years to show the widespread and earnest support for the invasion of China and the subsequent war against the Allies.[2] The fact that popular support accelerated Japan's imperialist aggression is not, however, a controversial argument; it is only when we criticise the jingoism of the Allies that we encounter resistance. As this book has shown, the people rallied to support the state in both Allied and Axis countries, so we must consider British 'national unity' to be equally important in determining the war's brutality. On 10 February 1940, as battles raged in France and air raids had yet to begin, Hampstead resident Gwladys Cox sat with her family listening to Parliamentary debates concerning the war. This was the end of Neville Chamberlain's political career, and Gwladys noted with some sadness that opposition members were attacking the Prime Minister for 'being too old'. Nevertheless, like most British citizens, Gwladys had already embraced the logic of total war: 'There was only one interruption, at the end of his speech, when someone shouted, "We want peace!" Of course we do, but not at Hitler's price'.[3] Men, women, and children in Britain and Japan waved flags, bought war bonds, and volunteered their sons for service, all of which facilitated the state's ability to carry out a 'total war'. They were able to see the brutality of such a conflict when it directly victimised them, but very rarely extended any sympathy to ordinary people in 'enemy' countries. Nevertheless, the end of the war challenged these simple divisions, because total mobilisation had come abruptly to an end. Working alongside Italian and German prisoners of war near Manchester, Daphne Byrne recorded the exultations on VE Day, which included Axis POWs who could look forward to returning home. She then 'wandered across the fields with the dog to sit on a stile alone', and wrote in her diary of her 'mixed happiness and sadness. All so wonderful and difficult to take in and appreciate.'[4]

Historians have recently questioned each country's unity and social cohesion during the war years, pointing to black market activity, looting, and strike activity as signs that Britain and Japan did not enjoy the sort of unity that the war demanded; as David Ambaras and Saitō Tsutomu demonstrated, youth in particular was a source of anxiety for war governments, and for good reason as they pushed boundaries and formed counter-cultures.[5] Throughout this book, it has been clear that British and Japanese society were not as unified as many have believed; it is more compelling to consider horizontal similarities of war experience between both countries, particularly the shared burdens of British and Japanese working classes, women, and youth. Nevertheless, both Britain and Japan excelled in producing social, political, and economic systems that ensured if not uniform enthusiasm, at the very least grudging compliance. Compliance was often captured through suasion, by convincing the public of the necessity of war. British Labour politicians like Stafford Cripps critiqued the link between unity, collective defence, and the 'inevitability' of war in 1936:

We cannot, by a mere refusal to participate, prevent war, for it is not caused by the desire of individuals to fight, but by the apparent necessity for fighting against our own will and better judgement. Every country will be defending itself against the wickedness of its neighbours in the next war as it was in the last, and the necessities of defence will force millions of our people into the armed forces and factories.[6]

So, while the myth of unity among the people must continue to be deconstructed by historians, the fact of widespread obedience, and its function in promoting never-ending total war, must also be accepted. Much of this had to do with the fact that ideas of national belonging were never successfully challenged, and they continue to be resilient to the present day; but in addition to this, widespread cultural valorisation of war mobilisation and social opprobrium for anti-war sentiments were even more decisive.

One of the most important transitions we have been going through has been the acceptance of the 'people's war' narrative among those who had no experience of the war, but nevertheless choose to personally identify with it, and celebrate it, through mass media.[7] As early as 1980, the famous historian of Britain's working class, E. P. Thompson, bemoaned the dominance of right-wing memories of the war, which contradicted, for example, his own nostalgic recollections of civilian anti-imperialism.[8] In other words, the nationalism that poisoned the world prior to the Second World War has very nearly appropriated the sadness and loss of the war years. The emotional response to cinematic, textual, and pictorial representations of the war will inevitably be different from the sort of personal, individual remorse and reflection that Noda Masaaki felt was so necessary for the war generation. As he suggested, the 'loss' of that sadness, either through the attrition of memory or shifting memorial culture, will undermine our ability to sympathise with our former enemies, generating the very divisions that we hoped the trauma of the Second World War would help us to overcome.[9] The hatred of war that followed the Second World War, which was rooted in the ongoing verbal and textual recapitulation of wartime suffering, is partly a collective narrative told by people post-war (who had mostly never directly experienced bombing). It is also borne out of deeply personal views, however, that were embraced during the war itself, such as the inherent immorality of targeting non-combatants, including children. Disaggregating the two – wartime 'awakenings' about the horror of these conflicts and post-war collective narratives based as much on compelling story-telling as fact – requires critical analysis of the wartime documents and the post-war tales.

Popular Conflict: Pacifism in the Age of Total War

Jan Gotlib Bloch famously tried to warn the British people in 1901 of the 'impossible war' they were unwittingly preparing to fight. A financier and industrialist, Bloch had a front seat for the insatiable creature that emerged out of Western Europe's military-industrial organisation. While facing the possibility of war with Russia, Japanese pacifist Abe Isoo was inspired by Bloch to devote several issues of a journal in 1902 to argue that war was 'banditry' conducted against commoners.

> Historically, war has been designed to profit a minority at the expense of the majority. Those who sought political power did so by arousing the common people and turning their attention abroad, thereby keeping their thoughts off injustices at home ... If the [Japanese] people agree to the opening of hostilities with Russia, they will only succeed in extending by so many decades the life of oligarchic rule in our land. Our military government now stands in a position of unique advantage to themselves. Do we wish to prolong this situation by giving in to their wiles?

Inveighing against the rhetoric of nationalism, Abe also attacked Japan's atavistic gender roles, its neglect of children's rights, and pernicious class discrimination. Like British pacifist G. D. H. Cole and Labour politician Stafford Cripps, Abe saw militarism not as an aberration of normal peacetime life, but as inextricably linked to the ubiquitous reactionary political forces that organised society.[10] Many a Cassandra shouted warnings to the general population in Britain and Japan before the first enemy bomb dropped on their cities, but the people refused to listen, because they were too committed to defending 'our way of life'. After the sacrifices of the Second World War, one might assume that the forces that spawned militarism were politically confronted, or that a simple, apolitical pacifism was embraced by the population of Britain and Japan but, for better or for worse, this was not to be.

First, Japan's costly 1904–1905 Russo-Japanese War and Europe's 'Great War' of 1914–1918, failed to produce a cultural revulsion of conflict sufficient to prevent the Second World War, even as the people had a larger and larger say in government policies. Historians have already demonstrated the hostility with which various actors attacked the purveyors of peace in the inter-war period. During the Second World War, Japanese pacifists were crushed by both society and the state, and sometimes simply silenced through media suppression and political censorship laws; to advocate peace was equated with support for the nations' 'enemies', which undercut the public sympathy pacifists might enjoy. Japan's history of attacks on pacifism is well known, but in Britain peace advocates were also under duress. The British Peace Pledge Union, whose formation enjoyed massive public support from 1934 to 1935, in its publication *Peace News*, frequently criticised the social problems that gave rise to war in almost exactly the same terms as Abe Isoo had some thirty years prior. Its emergence coincided with the 1934 Incitement to Disaffection Act and the 1936 Public Order Law, the language of which would have been familiar to activists facing the Public Security Preservation Law (*Chian iji hō*, 1925) in Japan. The British government used such tools sparingly, however, and primarily against Oswald Mosley's fascist movement – at least until the post-war period.[11] In any case, the British government never felt compelled to protect its military members from anti-war literature, which was the main motivation for the 1934 law. Almost simultaneously, the Spanish Civil War divided the Union, and the Second World War split pacifists again, especially as editors in *Peace News* appeared incapable of criticising military aggression coming from Germany – which appeared to give credence to images peddled by pro-war talking heads, who represented pacifists as Nazis in disguise.[12] By 1944, even John Middleton Murry, an editor of *Peace News*, had to admit that 'a simple movement to prevent war was untenable in the mass society, and inadequate as an answer to Hitlerism'.[13] George Orwell turned against the PPU as well, darkly intimating that British Union fascists had infiltrated them. So, ironically enough, pacifists in Britain were said to be Axis sympathisers, and pacifists in Japan were accused of being pro-Allies.

In order to comprehend why pacifists in Allied and Axis countries were derided and ignored, we must discover why ordinary people supported the state during a time of total war. As demonstrated in this book, city residents defended the urban 'Moloch' with their lives, which inspired admiration and imitation among others; if your neighbour sacrificed his life defending the city and you were unwilling to help in the fight, it truly reflected poorly on you. As Richard Overy put it, ordinary people were essential for the war effort and therefore 'they acted both as agents of authority but also as informal community monitors, reinforcing consensus and broadening the field of participation'.[14] Reading back on his diary account of the 24 November 1940 air raid on Bristol, school headmaster M. E. Brodie wrote in 1943 of the ordinary heroes who 'carry on and stand their ground in spite of the dangers'. He highlighted a fireman who nodded at the growing flames and simply said, 'No water'. Instead of fleeing, he remained, waiting for help that never came, and perished in the flames that gutted much of Bristol's city centre.[15] When thus responding to the call, urban citizens functioned as cogs in a massive war machine that drew on workers, housewives, and even teenagers. Yamashita Toshitsugu, who was a middle-aged factory foreman during the war, summarised well how entire families could organise themselves into units that were convenient for wartime mobilisation:

In our house, I was the assistant director of the Neighbourhood Association (*chōnaikai*), so I was responsible for training in air raids precautions, fire prevention, and evacuation procedures – I was sort of in charge of ensuring the safety of the elderly, women, and children. We evacuated my elderly mother, my eldest son was in the army, my second son was in middle school, my eldest daughter was in the state primary system (*kokumin gakkō*), so it was a system of emergency measures. During air raids I usually maintained a strict, silent discipline when going about my business. At that time, in the middle of terrible incendiary bombardment, I was surprisingly cool and collected.[16]

Confronting war required strict obedience, which in turn aided the continual mobilisation for further war. Ordinary people played a part by hiding their objections, shaming complainers, and even turning a blind eye to the devastation that the war created. London housewife Mrs. G. Robins explained how daily life forced some citizens to endure the demands of the war even as it destroyed their homes:

The time bomb that went off in Highgate Rd. made me feel very bad for a little while. They are sudden and a terrific noise. These night warnings last from about 9 o'clock until 6 o'clock next morning. Last night so much gunfire the whole house go into the cellar for the night with blankets, hot water bottles, and of course we fly about making tea in between the din. ... I was very distressed but that was only natural after Sunday's bombs. The damage is great around but I do not go to see it. It is best to keep one's mind away from undesirable sights if one is live amongst it.[17]

These accounts reveal a powerful, widespread impulse to suppress dissent and complaint in British and Japanese society during the Second World War, and 'get on' with the work of wartime life. War support worked most strongly in the self-restraint individuals felt when tempted to 'whinge' about one's own suffering or express doubts about the whole enterprise of total war. As the GAF, RAF, and USAF all converged on 'virgin targets' (untouched, strategically insignificant civilian areas) to break the will of the enemy, ordinary citizens largely adjusted themselves to the new conditions, in part because their families were already thoroughly woven into the machinery of total war.[18] The self-discipline modern urban citizens exercised in support of the war made possible the state's worst behaviour.

To begin with, despite the Orwellian calls for 'unity' in times of national crisis, citizens of the city knew this was a lie, but they did not significantly challenge it. During the war, the bombs exposed both the structure of the city and its society. After the 14 November 1940 attack on Coventry, Dick Cottrell wrote a letter about the destruction of the city, and the popular response. First, the bombing laid waste to the systems that constituted Coventry as an urban space:

I managed to slip into Coventry this morning on my bicycle ... Of the town itself – well there is no town left. All the shops in the centre are gone. The main streets are hard to find. At least a square mile of the city centre is gutted and when I say gutted I mean gutted. Not an article is left in any of the shops in fact every shop is burnt out. Coventry is without electric light, gas, tap water, radio (the radio is on the services system) like electric light. No papers, no post, no telephone system, and [there] is a legion of the lost, and indeed they are lost.

Second, this in turn exposed several areas of resentful division within the putatively unified front against Germany, which were particularly apparent during the city's most desperate hour. Cottrell echoed what many people in Britain and Japan felt regarding the government's attempt to lead the people to victory: 'The papers say 200 killed 800 injured. No one in Coventry believes these figures', because in fact he had seen much more. 'Wal says that over 2000 have been killed', wrote Cottrell, 'and the injured beyond the ken of man. You will see in the papers that the people of Coventry are not down-hearted and are giving three cheers at all times of the day – don't believe it!!!' Not stopping at the critique of government figures on the severity of the raid, Cottrell continued to lambast the bland pleasantries and condescending benevolence of more comfortable citizens who cheered on the stalwart residents of regional cities from the side-lines.

If [the residents of Coventry] ever did cheer, then believe me they are sick of it and want better and more practical things than fine word speeches and promises and charity from well-meaning out-of-work well-to-dos ... This morning I saw in Coventry army brass hats standing on the steps of the ruins of the Midland Bank directing operations. What is wanted was some Navy bummels with these gangs and plenty of Hi up Hi up, and a bit of cussing thrown in. There are some of these tea vans going about giving cups of tea away, but what is wanted are plenty of the travelling shops because people do not want charity and while they have money in their pockets. Also what is wanted is a local news sheet printed in a motor van if necessary giving information to the homeless and bereaved. Not bellow at the poor devils through a megaphone, nobody ever knew what a microphone said anyway.[19]

The bombs not only exposed the manufactured divisions within one's home country, but between one's nation and 'enemy people' as well. Iketani Toyoko, a shopkeeper's wife in Tokyo, described seeing a white person, speaking English, being held and interrogated at a police station in Japan during the war.

My son had been drafted and sent to the Pacific for a few years. I heard nothing from him, and I thought, 'Is this what he's going through? Or is he dead?' When I thought of this, it seemed that, despite the conflict between nations, this young white man had a mother somewhere, and so I had a strange sort of pity for him. In a small voice I said, 'Poor lad', but I was not the only one to whisper so. Even though he was the enemy, he was a lovely young man (*utsukushii shōnen*). The air raid warden chief scolded me: 'You traitor!' (*hikokumin*), so tears started down my cheeks. What on earth was I crying about?[20]

The chill that fell over criticism of war had important consequences for the 'mass society', which did not just exist in Nazi Germany, but also in Britain, Japan, America, the Soviet Union, and indeed any country with adequate literacy and mass media. Those who spoke out, even unintentionally, were publicly shamed and thereby silenced.

In fact, many citizens in both Britain and Japan secretly despised the war from the outset. In a diary by an elderly man in Kyoto Prefecture, Samuel Yamashita revealed the contempt with which some Japanese viewed the ill-considered constant conflict that the armed forces so adamantly supported. 'They tried to mollify us with moving war stories', wrote Tamura Tsunejirō, 'So it's come to this. At this rate our country will be destroyed'.[21] In some cases, the opposition to wartime rhetoric seemed to stem from an individual's scepticism of its facile claims. In this sense, the reduction of the 'enemy' to a monolithic Other insulted the intelligence of ordinary people. J. L. Pratt, a devoted socialist, enjoyed reading *I Had a Row with a German* until the author proclaimed, 'My last chance would be gone to send some loathsome murderer to his end'.

Pratt reacted strongly: 'Exactly what in the minds of the RAF exempts them from being "loathsome murderers" too?'[22] In Japan, farming families attempted to avoid conscription, which was echoed by post-war rural cultural societies in northern Japan – in other words, the motivations of poor farmers were not uniformly patriotic. Some soldiers, like former schoolteacher Kimura Genzaemon, disparaged the superficial jingoism of civilians:

The only person who welcomes the call to war is one without education, such as children, ladies, and the (uneducated) elderly. The intellectuals, as whole, are bystanders. Does the Japanese Spirit (*Nippon seishin*) find culture so intolerable? There were certain ladies who prayed for our troops. Something about it struck chords of anger in my heart.[23]

British citizens like Dorothy Hughes did not see the Germans as implacably evil foes, but acknowledged their achievements in art and music; she acknowledged that the British were 'hostile to the enemy for bombing our towns', but that she could not 'work up any enthusiasm for this. They are only carrying out their instructions, in the same way as our RAF'.[24] Furthermore, disgust for war in general and a desire for peace were ubiquitous. Even in far-off Orkney, Scotland, 15-year-old Bessie Skea possessed enough critical acumen to look at the madness of total war objectively:

I don't believe that the German people in general want to fight; they are only doing it because they have to, judging from what a German pilot, who came down somewhere in Scotland, said. He came down in a parachute, landed badly and broke both his legs. When found he looked up and said in excellent English, 'Well, damn this war!' That is the opinion of most of us, too.[25]

British citizens did not believe that they 'started the war' with Germany, but many in Japan strongly believed that they did not 'start the war' with the West, either – it was the culmination of nearly a century of imperialist aggression, going back to the unequal treaties and Perry's 'Black Ships', that needed to be resolutely opposed by the 'yellow people' of the world. In the end, regardless of who 'started the war', it was the people's support for total war that made it possible, and brought upon themselves the devastation that affected both countries for decades.

Recording the 'truth' of the good war in one's personal records, however, could overcome the tribalism and 'stiff upper lip' that often afflicted the war years, only to become even more common in post-war memory. Despite post-war celebrations of bravery, for those on the front line of the war at home, the experience did not always warrant simply putting on a brave face. After missing several trains to see her sister in Bristol, I. S. Haslewood felt that irrational, emotional responses were forgivable sins for those that had to endure bombing at home: 'I record these shameful happenings, because above all things I do not wish to pose as the ever-smiling little heroine who can take it unceasingly'.[26] Citizens in Britain and Japan also felt that the conflict was needlessly killing many innocents, and that it provoked many troubling questions, including the worth of life versus the worth of victory in war. In Swansea, Laurie Latchford watched the Royal Sussex Regiment march off, and wondered in his diary: 'A quiet, orderly lot of men, and physically good to look at – what is their future?'[27] Takahashi Aiko was never very keen on the war, even when the Japanese empire was at its zenith after the fall of Singapore in 1942. In the summer of 1943, she began complaining bitterly of the food situation and the dangerous situation Japan's political leadership had put them in. Soon, her son was being called out to participate in patriotic youth parades, which caused her great unease given her scepticism regarding the morality of the conflict. On 10 June 1943, she encountered a line of soldiers being sent off to war, and she noted that the feelings of Japanese civilians had changed:

When the war began, entertainment brigades followed the soldiers, the streets were just a sea of waving flags and people went out from one block to the next. Now, however, the fighting is getting fiercer and fiercer, and daily life is getting increasingly difficult and painful, so there are fewer people there. Some are waving flags, others are not, and no one has the strength to shout out military ballads. Among those seeing off the soldiers, it's just relatives and some people from the neighbourhood association presenting them with rice balls – it's very lonely and miserable.

Aiko's house was near a rail station, so she noted the change quickly as more and more soldiers went by. Looking on them going out day after day, she wrote, 'Oh, here's another group of people on their own funeral procession'.[28] Olivia Smith, a middle-class British housewife much like Aiko, viewed her country's apparent national rage with a similar revulsion: she believed the desire to vilify an entire people was attributable to class and education. After trading barbs with a Francophile friend, she reflected on her own support for Germans:

We also had a fierce argument over the question whether or not the inflammation of anti-German feeling is a good thing. Whether, in fact, it is desirable or necessary to hate one's enemies. I personally feel most strongly that national hate is terribly and completely wrong. Of course it is natural for ignorant, uneducated and unintelligent people to feel it, but I believe that educated people who let themselves go, and foment hate in others, are acting criminally ... It is a reversion to savagery. Such emotions are the antithesis of civilisation.[29]

The death of so many people, whether they were 'innocent' or not, was troubling to civilians, who were hardly inured to the experience of warfare, and this bred a deep resentment for war among many citizens who lived through it.

Survivors of Second World War attacks on the city continued to steer their countries away from further conflicts, even during the tumultuous Cold War, but nuclear weapons and globalisation changed pacifism irrevocably. In Japan, the repudiation of the wartime leadership was total, even if many civilian bureaucrats who had supported the war remained in post in order to build America's 'unsinkable battleship' against communism in East Asia. Still, many who supported the war effort accomplished an about-face when it came to aggressive foreign policies after 1945. Tada Susumu was formerly an investigator for Japan's Special Higher Police, responsible for suppressing communism and anti-war protests. Thinking back to the disastrous end of Japan's total war, he wrote:

When we heard the emperor's broadcast in the old prefectural government building, we knew we'd lost the war and we all shed bitter tears. If only it had ended earlier, Kōfu would not have been bombed, Hiroshima and Nagasaki would have avoided atomic weapons, and hundreds of thousands of people's lives, as well as their wealth, would have been saved. It makes me burn with rage over the utter incompetence of the wartime authorities, who made me lose a 30-room manor house, my own home, and even reduced me to beggary for a short time ... When I finished nineteen years of service in 1951, my heart ached, thinking that there is nothing as horrible and empty as war. I believe we must eradicate war from the earth in the future, and that is the greatest good that humanity can hope to achieve.[30]

As Susumu pointed out, Hiroshima and Nagasaki seemed to change the tenor and focus of pacifism after 1945. Since it seemed unlikely that a future total war – a 'Third World War' – would include field armies or even conventional area bombing, pacifist movements focused on the new threat from nuclear weapons and adopted a transnational outlook.[31] In Japan, the 'peace movement' (*heiwa undō*) was inextricably linked to Hiroshima, but it also drew energy from the cities devastated by area bombing, like Himeji and Osaka, and linked itself to global pacifist organisations. In Britain, the old Peace Pledge Union members became part of a broader movement that culminated in the Campaign for Nuclear Disarmament, the Committee of 100, and the publication of *The Journal of Peace Research*. In the 1950s and 1960s, British citizens protested military installations such as Aldermaston, where nuclear tests were conducted, just as Japanese protestors focused on US bases where they suspected nuclear weapons were being transported, such as those in Okinawa. The possibility of a nuclear total war conjured a new kind of pacifism, which had a much stronger emphasis on transnational solidarity that endures today. The first editorial in *The Journal of Peace Research* began with such visions, and demonstrates how these were linked with late twentieth-century globalisation:

Imagine a world which we can call GCW, 'general and complete war' ... [where] there is no restraint on the choice of means of destruction ... Hobbes had the vision, nuclear physics has perfected the means ... Peace research should also be peace *search,* an audacious application of science in order to generate visions of new worlds ... That peace research is international and interdisciplinary hardly needs repetition. It is concerned with the human condition all over the world, and this should be reflected in a geographical and disciplinary distribution of topics, authors, and research teams.[32]

Meanwhile, conventional, local conflicts such as Vietnam also drew anti-war ire from activists in Japan and Britain against domestic government policies.[33] Local violence also proved enduring: the worst clashes between Japanese pacifists and the state took place during the 1960 ratification of the US-Japan Security Treaty. Similarly, although the British government ultimately felt no need to use the 1934 Incitement to Disaffection Act from 1934 to 1945, remarkably, they deployed such extraordinary powers against peace activists protesting violence in Northern Ireland in the 1960s and 1970s.[34] As pacifists shifted their focus to a globalised, anti-nuclear movement, they lost touch with locally-rooted experiences of war devastation that gave them so much power directly after the Second World War. This left the memory of the Second World War largely in the hands of those who would solely celebrate it as either a national victory or pure victimisation, requiring a renewal of national unity and strength.

   In the twenty-first century these heroic and patriotic narratives, as well as the media preoccupation with the horrors of the Holocaust, has obfuscated the suffering ordinary people in Britain and Japan had to endure while they supported a total war, or relegated it to the background. Such ignorance truly is bliss. On 11 November 1941, Bristol bombing survivor Violet Maund went to the cinema to see a film called 'One Night in Lisbon', which was a pro-British US film starring Fred MacMurray. Bristol had already been largely burned by German firebombing, which included the destruction of her local library and other landmarks. 'An American idea of a London air raid', she wrote in her diary, 'is funny to those who have experienced the real thing. May they always be able to keep their illusions'.[35] During the Second World War, the Americans who remained at home knew little about what it meant to be the target of enemy air raids, which may very well have made possible public support for further conflict in Korea, Vietnam, and many other theatres. War is still waged around the world, but those of us who live in countries such as the United States, Britain, and Japan need never experience it first-hand – with the exception, of course, of terrorist attacks. We therefore now all live in the 'illusion' that most Americans enjoyed in wartime, where we learn about bombing, loss, and fear through films, radio, television, and history books. It is a fortunate position to enjoy, but it obligates us to confront how terrible armed conflict was for ordinary people – in other words, how bad it is for 'us'. Contrary to the heroic images we often see of the Second World War, for the British and Japanese living in the city, at least, it was a time of death, privation, anger, horror, and destruction. How could we possibly have come to see such a devastating conflict as a 'good war' to celebrate?

Opening a Great Divide: Remembering the Good War in Britain and Japan

6 August 2013 was the 68th anniversary of the atomic bombing of Hiroshima, when many pacifist groups in Japan hold exhibits and events. At the same time, the Japanese government launched its largest warship since the ill-fated dreadnaught, the *Yamato*. Prime Minister Abe Shinzō of the conservative Liberal Democratic Party, in what could be con-sidered a belligerent speech act aimed at Asian neighbours, dubbed the new vessel the *Izumo*, which was the name of an infamous vessel that bombarded Chinese troops defending Shanghai in 1932 and 1937. The 1937 clash triggered a total war between Japan and the Nationalist Party of Chiang Kai-shek that devolved into a 'China Quagmire'. This war, while rarely examined by historians, eventually caused the United States to begin economic sanctions against Japan and resulted in the 1941 attack on Pearl Harbor. Was the timing and naming of this vessel a coincidence? Prime Minister Abe suffered no electoral consequences for this act.

Contrast the consequences of Prime Minister Abe's behaviour with those of Winston Churchill's immediately after the Second World War. Leading up to the 1945 general election, Churchill gave strident anti-communist speeches and made calls to take the fight to the 'socialist camp'. The Tories were subsequently dumped by a war-weary popula-tion, leaving Conservatives baffled for years afterward, blaming wartime 'socialist propaganda' for their loss at the polls.[36] After years of rationing, bombing, and homelessness, the people had had enough. Pacifists in Japan have sustained incessant attacks by right-wing forces, and LDP leaders such as Abe have insisted on the necessity of revoking Article 9 of Japan's constitution, which forbids the use of force beyond the country's borders. Neoconservatives in the United States, who want to deploy Japanese military power in service of American interests, applaud the re-armament of Japan. Although the Japanese government insists that the *Izumo* is a non-aggressive ship that will only be used to carry helicopters for rescue missions and self-defence, it can easily be converted to launch F-35 stealth fighter jets, which can carry tactical nuclear payloads into Chinese airspace. Meanwhile, Abe's government refused to sign a multi-national agreement which foreswore the development of nuclear weapons. On 9 August 2013, Tomihisa Taue, the mayor of Nagasaki, wrote a vituperative open letter of complaint, stating that the Abe government had 'betray[ed] the expectations of global society'.[37] As Mayor Tomihisa indicated in his letter, we are quickly approaching an era in which there will be no living memories of the Second World War.

The destruction of the city during the Second World War showed its citizens, for a brief moment, that it was no object to be loved, but only a collection of man-made contraptions that could easily turn deadly; nevertheless, city residents returned, because they had invested so much of their hopes and dreams in a lifeless thing that could not love them back. Bertram Elwood, when traveling from Birmingham to London in September 1940, was appalled at the devastation wrought by the GAF, but he also reflected on the opportunities this presented. 'In future', he wrote in his diary, 'towns should be planned as a whole instead of piecemeal ... Is the English climate so execrable that it precludes our imitating the French and having pavement cafes[?]' He hoped that the congested, dirty corners of the city, many of which had been destroyed, would not simply be rebuilt, but 'transformed into a place worth living in as well as working in'.[38] In Coventry, Gladys Hollingsworth noted the horrible suffering its residents endured due to fires, bombs, poor sanitation, and homelessness, but immediately began thinking of rebuilding the city just months after the city was levelled by enemy bombers:

Shall we ever see our city anything like it was before, or are we to be thrilled with a modern, new, clean, well planned city, we wonder. Our first thoughts are for water, gas, light, and heat. It makes one wonder if all this has been sent to show us exactly what luxury and happiness we have lived in with never a thought of thanks or appreciation.[39]

In post-war Japan, the reconstruction of cities eventually followed a similar logic, as programmes such as the 'income doubling plan' focused on economic growth as a form of national pride. Like Britain, regional cities appealed to the central government to fund their reconstruction, insisting that the war was the central government's responsibility, not that of local city governors. Because Japan lost the war, this added another layer of outrage to the criticism of Tokyo: why should the prefectures outside of the capital foot the cost of repairing the cities destroyed in a war launched by elites in the capital city?[40] Britain and Japan, which had suffered terribly from civilian bombings, also were sites of vigorous anti-nuclear and pacifist demonstrations – although it must be said that Article 9 of Japan's post-war constitution made it much more fertile ground for such political activism. Nevertheless, despite being on opposite sides of the conflict, the terrible attacks on British and Japanese urban citizens established an enduring scepticism regarding the worth of armed conflict.

As a consequence, we must decide how to remember this event, including whether we should maintain our story of the Second World War as a 'good war'. The lesson that citizens in victorious countries such as Britain, Russia, and the United States learn in school is not entirely wrong: the appalling atrocities committed by Axis powers in the East and West had to be stopped, and the war was fundamentally won through the sacrifices of ordinary men and women. For Axis 'losers' of the war, like Japan, the death of unrestrained militarism and the birth of post-war economic growth, which catapulted the nation into a position of wealth, were some of the most satisfying victories they have enjoyed. Such a (re)turn to economic prosperity as the benchmark of national pride was evident in civilian writings early on. Kobayashi Takako, writing of the aftermath of the 1945 aerial bombardment of Himeji, noted how a man half-blinded by the raids collected empty firebomb canisters into a massive pile, and then was able to sell them at a good price due to a widespread metal shortage. Takako wrote that he proudly claimed those spent husks 'were turned into pots and pans after the war'.[41] In Britain, the terrible losses of the Second World War inspired demands to create a better post-war society – even while bombers were still striking the British Isles. On 12 November 1941, hearing of labour troubles in a friend's company, G. F. Glover had discovered just how callously employers in Britain were willing to sack people they did not like, and then expect workers to miraculously appear – and remain loyal – during times of low labour supply (as in during the war). Stating that British employers had no concept of 'real democracy', Glover continued 'and still they go on as if conditions were 1896, very peeved that men are so "independent." (What are we fighting for?)'[42] Documentary film director Ken Loach may have deliberately overlooked the existence of conservative citizens in his 2013 film *The Spirit of '45*, but the personal records of ordinary people who lived through the war indicate that the establishment of Britain's welfare state was strongly influenced by the brutal shortages and sacrifices endured by the war generation. This was the era in which Sir

William Beveridge argued for a system of security by attacking the 'five giant evils' of want, disease, ignorance, squalor, and idleness.[43] At the 1962 consecration of the new Coventry Cathedral, the famous pacifist Benjamin Britten composed his 'War Requiem', which decried the inhumanity of the 'Good War'. With so many Britons, especially citizens of heavily-bombed Coventry, present for this event, the disgust for the unnecessary sacrifices of the Second World War could have hardly fallen on deaf ears. The first and foremost victory of the Second World War, then, was creating a citizenry who harboured a deep-seated hatred of war.

Memories of the bombing have been conflicted in both Britain and Japan, but they share similar problems – particularly, the emphasis on the experience of elites and citizens in capital cities. Most Japanese cities that were bombed have local 'Societies for the Record of Air Raids' (*Kūshū o kiroku suru kai*) which compile and publish diary excerpts, memoirs, and oral histories. Some of the regional cities' editions reach one or two paperback volumes that can prove difficult to obtain; Tokyo's Society, however, published a lavish five volume hardback edition that is still widely available today.[44] In Japan, the national media and government's focus on Tokyo memories of firebombing are driven as much by the large market of the capital city as they are by the fact that most of the country's major publishers are based there. Japan differs from Britain significantly, however, due to the atomic bombings of Hiroshima and Nagasaki, which have also taken up a large share of the media interest in the bombing experience. Novels such as *Black Rain* (Kuroi ame) and *Bells of Nagasaki* (Nagasaki no kane), films including *Barefoot Gen* (Hadaashi no gen, also a manga) and *Spare This Child* (Kono ko o nokoshite), and oral history collections such as *Children of Hiroshima* (*Hiroshima no kodomotachi*, 1977) have all contributed to a national fascination with the horror of atomic bombing in Nagasaki and, chiefly, Hiroshima. The experience of citizens in Hiroshima and Nagasaki, however, could hardly be represen-tative of urban mass-bombing; in fact, it is probably the uniqueness of the atomic bomb that has managed to attract such attention from the public – even capturing foreign attention away from the deadlier attacks on the capital city. Such a situation is arguably unique to Japan, but the relative ignorance people today have about the situation in heavily-bombed regional cities such as Kawasaki and Kōbe, bears a strong resemblance to the British case.

British narratives of the 'Blitz' have been dominated by London, even though other cities suffered more per capita, such as Coventry and Hull. Like Hiroshima, perhaps, Coventry is comparatively well remembered for the loss of its iconic cathedral during the 1940 air raid. In the post-war era, Coventry and Hiroshima, in fact, became sister cities in pacifism. To commemorate the fifty-year anniversary of the war's end in 1995, Richard Branson commissioned identical sculptures by Josefina de Vasconcellos to be placed in the ruins of the Coventry cathedral and the Hiroshima Peace Garden. The plaque on the objects reads, 'Both sculptures remind us that, in the face of destructive forces, human dignity and love will triumph over disaster and bring nations together in respect and peace'. Hull's experience, by contrast, was suppressed during wartime, and largely ignored until the 1990s due to the post-war preoccupation with London. Hull residents have resented the London-centric view of the bombing war for a long time, and in their eyes even Coventry seems to have attracted too much attention. A. Owen, who was attempting infrastructural repairs in both Hull and Coventry, expressed the irritation many Hull residents felt at being passed over for endless narratives about others' lives in the air war:

I would be inclined to agree with your assessment as to Hull suffering more serious damage than Coventry ... When you take in all the other areas which received the same treatment during the blitz and add up the [Hull] total it is tremendous. I then, with two more from Hull, travelled to Coventry ... and although the damage in Coventry was heavy I believe that in comparison to the size of both cities we in Hull received the greater losses in life and damage per square mile.[45]

In addition to Hull and Coventry, Plymouth and Southampton were heavily damaged during the years of heavy bombing, 1940–1941, whereas much of London, including iconic landscapes that escaped relatively unharmed. In fact, Dietmar Süss argued that the London-centric approach to the war experience was, at least in part, a consequence of the wartime normalisation of resistance behaviour:

Morale in the British capital was regarded by propaganda experts as the essence of 'good' behaviour, a narrative that New York's mayor, Rudi Giuliani, made use of shortly after the 9/11 attacks on the city, when he compared the resilience and heroism of its citizens with the historical example of London. 'London can take it' was by no means only the title of a successful propaganda film but an incentive for other cities to keep to the normative pattern of 'good spirits' and desist from criticism of the war.[46]

Indeed, only if the architecture, society, and infrastructure of regional cities are seen as expendable is it possible to say that the bombing experience of greater London can be taken, in any way, as representative of Britain altogether; otherwise, the relative exclusion of regional cities from the war experience is difficult to accept – especially considering how terrible the war was for people outside of the capital. Hull bombing survivor Ann Naylor recounted a darkly humorous tale concerning a time when her neighbours, who were blind, hosted relatives from the South during the war. When her father checked on the couple, he met the visitors as well, and asked, 'Have you enjoyed your stay, and are you sorry to be going back?' The visitors responded, 'We enjoyed being with the family very much, BUT WE CAN'T WAIT to get home to London and have a good night's sleep and bit of peace and quiet!'[47] Focusing on London not only does disservice to the 'British' history of the war, it also runs the risk of reifying wartime propaganda that enforced a kind of heroic normativity that was inaccurate both for the nation and even London itself.

Nevertheless, these regional problems with historical memory should not encourage a relentless balkanisation of the war's history and a retreat to 'civic pride'; such an approach would undermine the importance of showing the commonality between people in places like Hull, Takamatsu, Osaka, and Manchester. The individuals who perished in the Second World War were not less or more important depending on which city they called home, and the people who suffered area bombing knew this. For Dora Mockett, the death of non-combatants in Hull and the destruction of a beloved city could not be separated; as anti-aircraft guns fired, the Prudential building, which used to be a city landmark, was utterly destroyed, and she wrote, 'Hundreds of soldiers have come into Hull and are working like Trojans on demolition work. Had a mass burial yesterday of the raid victims. I don't suppose we shall ever get to know how many there were ...'[48] The 'civic pride' approach, then, when it ignores the loss of individual lives, only mimics the narrow-minded nationalism that drove the war in the first place. The phrase 'for our country' (*kuni no tame*) haunted Yamagoe Yone in post-war Chiba. Her friend's father had uttered this phrase when he sent his daughter – Yone's close friend – to a girls' school, 'and settled her affairs, in case she [died] for the nation'. Yone's anger over the wartime state's demand for sacrifice is palpable:

In that environment of widespread militarism, there were so many people who died, smiling, 'for the country'. I don't think I would have. But, how many precious lives were lost under this phrase, 'for the country'? I can't stop thinking about it. ... We can't let this phrase, 'for the country', carry on. We have to start placing value on individual lives.[49]

The war cannot be understood through studies that focus on London, Tokyo, and Hiroshima, but resorting to facile localism only creates other, albeit similar, distortions. The war must be seen not only through British eyes, or in sole comparison with Germany, but also through the writings of people in places like Japan, China, and the former European and Japanese colonies.

The age of total war may well be behind those privileged enough to live in the prosperous 'first world', which is now characterised by professional armies that often employ lower classes – the odd helicopter-flying royal family member notwithstanding. This is, in many respects, good news for politically conservative forces, because the experience of being targeted by a distant enemy radicalised the civilian populations of Japan and Britain, however briefly, to eschew foreign conflicts and demand greater services from the state at home. If we allow the memory of the war to slip into facile triumphalism or localism, however, we will forget the very lesson that the wartime generation felt they had to learn the hard way.

The Worm's Eye View: Ordinary People and Total War

The arguments for and against bombing typically focus on the men who made such decisions and, especially in the post-war era, defended them; but, whether their views were right or wrong, by and large they were not the ones being bombed. More problematic is the widespread support for the war effort that many ordinary people embraced, even while they were targets of enemy violence. In private documents, Japanese and British citizens felt no compunction in advocating the wholesale slaughter of the enemy, and even cheered young men as they departed to die in foreign lands. Yamaki Mikiko, as a young woman, saw off pilots from the Haramachi Army Air Force base to almost certain demise in the Philippines and Okinawa. Reflecting on her participation in the farewell ceremonies, she wrote:

Because I was the recipient of militaristic education, I thought, even in the midst of crying for them, that these young men had to throw away their lives. I was incapable of critically re-evaluating the concept that these were 'valuable deaths' ... We women thought that we should die before the Americans came and had their way with us. I just thought, *why do I have to die?* It was a terrible thought, in the middle of a nightmare. War is death. There is no such thing as a 'valuable death', a 'pointless death', an enemy's death, or an ally's death. War is simply murder, for some reason or another.[50]

Here, Mikiko revealed an important dynamic in the process toward pacifism: when she sent young men off to pointless deaths, she was able to compartmentalise the horror of war and her complicity; once her own death was a possibility, the promise of peace became more alluring. Now that the wartime generation is quickly passing into history, it is doubly important to look backwards and continue our frank assessment of the moral quandaries of the Second World War, including the troubling fact that civilians were both victims of bombing campaigns and instrumental to their success.

'Total war' in the twentieth century required civilian support whether the state was directed by elected officials or not; it mobilised man and woman, elderly and youth, and thereby made them targets of enemy violence. Ordinary citizens noticed this fairly quickly: watching waves of incendiary bombs falling over south Wales, Laurie Latchford observed, 'There seemed to be one target only: Swansea. There was no attempt to find a specific [military] target'.[51] As Coventry resident Howard Dodman pointed out, sloppy technique and inaccurate bombing technology meant that any sort of 'targeting' was futile:

The damage to military objectives in the city was surprisingly low when things were cleared up and the roll call made. A large number of factories were hit and a few were written off, considering the colossal extent of loss suffered by civilians one is absolutely amazed to find the factories nearly all back to normal. It seems to be a case of 'you can't help hitting factories occasionally if you aim at houses!'[52]

Before the war – in fact, as late as 1938 – the RAF considered attacking civilian populations to be immoral, and the United States, under the Roosevelt administration, harshly criticised the 1937 Japanese firebombing of Shanghai as 'barbaric', promising not to bomb 'unfortified cities'.[53] How quickly these morals were abandoned. The German military dropped the pretence of avoiding civilian casualties, engaging in terror bombing, and the Allies acknowledged attacks on civilians as necessary to the war effort, taking the mass assault on non-combatants to a level undreamed of among the Axis. Wartime debates did not necessarily challenge the assumption that civilians should be killed, but rather how openly the government should announce this in front of their own civilian population.[54] Recent reassessment of those debates has triggered passionate arguments. A. C. Grayling insisted strongly that:

... deliberately bombing cities and towns to kill and terrorise civilians, not all of whom were engaged in manufacturing arms or aiding their country's military, and many of whom were children and elderly folk – and at the same time, destroying much that belongs to the culture and necessities of those people, including schools and hospitals – contravenes every moral and humanitarian principle debated in connection with the just conduct of the war.[55]

Was the bombing of civilians, under any circumstances, a 'war crime' and, if so, what does that mean for our collective memory of 'the good war'? In the context of the bombing of Dresden, David Bloxham argued that there is an important distinction between a 'war crime' such as killing a POW, and a 'crime against humanity' such as the carefully-planned genocide of

the European Jews.[56] Given the strong racial views that circulated in the
US media about Japanese people, however, this line is not always clear.[57]
The methodical, even 'scientific', destruction of population centres in
order to destroy the enemy's productivity – or merely to terrorise him –
is certainly not the same thing as the Holocaust, because the government
policy is not, strictly speaking, 'genocidal', but it is not merely an isolated
'war crime' such as killing a POW, either. Whether or not the planned,
technologically-sophisticated mass murder of non-combatants is a 'war
crime' according to contemporary or wartime definitions may not be a
terribly valuable exercise to endure. That does not mean, however, that we
can indulge in casually dismissing this aspect of the Second World War as
'necessary for victory' or 'brought on by the enemy' in order to justify
wartime governments' past actions. Area bombing 'enemy' civilians may
not have been a war crime, but it was certainly, in the terminology of
wartime discourse, an atrocity. A more difficult question, however, is who
bears the responsibility for these acts.

The support ordinary people had for murdering non-combatants in
other countries is troublesome and perplexing. Japanese citizens, who
had cheered the progress of the brutal Imperial Army in China, were
often shocked by the Americans' willingness to use air power against
urban centres, but also curiously accepting of the fact that new forms of
warfare should kill innocent people en masse. Even Japanese schoolboys,
like Hamabe Mitsuru, drew pictures of air balloons and futuristic
weapons that would target American cities with mass bombing.[58] In part,
the extraordinary vigour with which countries bombed their enemies'
citizens during the Second World War was a product of the experience of
being attacked. Lawrence L. McReavy reflected at the end of the war
that, in Britain, 'exasperated people were clamouring for reprisals as the
only effective deterrent against such attacks (which, admittedly, they are
not), and our government had promised that reprisals would be taken.'[59]
Rather than see themselves as the victims of an enemy military leadership, civilians often hypocritically called for the mass murder of non-
combatants, which by necessity would have included individuals for
whom support for war was impossible, such as children. British citizen
Bertram Elwood summed up this sentiment well: after he deduced the
German air raids ineffective due to their inability to keep sustained
pressure on cities such as his native Birmingham, he reflected in his diary
that British leaders 'should have learned a valuable lesson from this'. He
thought giving German civilians time to recuperate would be a mistake:
'I cannot understand why we should distinguish between civilians and
military targets. I should have thought that the people were the greatest
military target of all . . .'[60] It would seem that, in the age of Imperial Japan

and the British Empire, the targeting of non-combatants was not solely the strategy of a far-off and nefarious military and political leadership, but a policy embraced by the very people whom it would strike first.

Perhaps area bombing was not simply the by-product of nationalistic rage and crude tribalism, but a sound strategy that would end the war early and actually save lives. If we step away from the carefully-worded public justifications articulated by generals and presidents, however, the boundary between anger and strategy is not very distinct. American soldiers, when defending their decision to kill Japanese people, whether enemy troops or women and children, often mixed rage with sound tactics. US Army Chaplain Charles V. Trent, in his explanation of the process by which American forces achieved victory in 'Island Hopping' campaigns, shows as much pathos as planning:

The stage was set; the actors, impatient, fidgety, were pacing the wings. And, on the morning of February 29th the curtain was rent asunder by a devastating naval and aerial bombardment. The troops, startled by this clanging of the shield of Mars, hastened to their task. ... Thus the 1st Cavalry Division received its baptism of fire in what the Associated Press calls 'one of the most brilliant manoeuvres of the war'. ... The severance of the only remaining line of supply to Rabaul and Kavieng left in these two much-heralded, impenetrable bastions of the enemy's defensive system, 50,000 Sons of Heaven to starve, die and rot.[61]

British civilians shared these views, especially after being bombed at home. One Bristol woman who survived the 24 November 1940 fire-bombing of the city wrote that:

... the city looked bruised and battered. Its heart was plucked out, almost. Our back yard is littered with grey ashes and burnt bits of paper. The streets are grey and the people seem stunned. But we shall get over it. Jerry is not going to get away with it, never fear. Our turn will come.[62]

The Japanese, of course, believed that their use of violence against the 'Western powers' was also ethically sound – in this case, by the horrors and injustices of 'white' colonialism and imperialism. Upset at the level of oppression he witnessed in Dutch Indonesia, where the 'white imperialists' lived well while the Indonesians suffered, one Japanese soldier exclaimed in his diary that the colony featured 'a situation where extravagance has no limit, and it has been squeezed from the blood of the natives'.[63] Whether justice or strategy, Allied or Axis, both passionately defended their attacks on civilians to be morally acceptable, and it still literally enrages some scholars to hear otherwise today. It is therefore naïve to think that military strategy in area bombing was divorced from emotional inputs during a time when populism was driving foreign policy – both in the democratic 'West' and the authoritarian 'East' – and the people were clamouring for 'justice' and 'revenge'. Nevertheless, Bertram Elwood dismissed his enthusiastic acceptance of killing non-combatants as a product of wartime radicalisation:

I make the above remarks with a full knowledge of what bombing means. I know what a terrible, filthy weapon it is. I have known fear. I have felt literally sick with that impotent rage of having such a terrifying weapon used against me, just sitting and having to take it, and not able to fight back. I have picked up bodies and bits of bodies whilst the bombs are still falling. I have seen little children laid out in a row, their faces dumbly turned to the cold light of the moon; or cuddling each other, mute in death. I have seen all these things and I still say – bomb the Germans; bomb them hard; bomb them indiscriminately. I say this not out of hatred of revenge but because I think it will help shorten the war.[64]

For Elwood – who was neither a military man nor a political leader – good strategy should be bought at any cost, and the continuance of older forms of wartime fair play, such as sparing the elderly and children from violent death, were at best an annoyance, and at worst a potential barrier to victory. It necessitated the abandonment of the very definition of pre-war morality, including the protection of non-combatants, and this new brutality was supposed to hasten the end of the conflict.

Assessing the impact of aerial bombardment of non-combatants on the progress of a war is a venture with mixed results at best, and a morally dubious exercise in self-exculpatory wishful thinking at worst. It is clear that US leaders, such as President Harry Truman, believed that using the atomic bomb on Hiroshima might end the war more quickly and save American lives – despite advice against using the weapon on non-combatants from senior military officials.[65] But Harry Truman's opinion on what might force Japanese leaders to surrender is completely irrelevant when considering why they actually surrendered. If historians familiar with Japanese language materials are correct, the area bombing campaign was not the reason the Empire collapsed. Social historians of Japan are increasingly convinced that it was the starvation of the Japanese home islands that brought the country to its knees.[66] Hasegawa Tsuyoshi, while acknowledging the role of the bombing in pressuring the Japanese state, still held that the 1945 Soviet invasion of Manchuria was ultimately decisive, and Koshiro Yukiko, in a critical review of Hasegawa's *Racing the Enemy* and in her own *Imperial Eclipse*, insisted that all factors were insignificant when compared to the Soviet threat.[67] Japanese historians debate why the country surrendered, but very few scholars, today, think that the mass murder of civilians convinced the military leadership, who had already demonstrated a callous indifference to such massacres, to give up the ghost. Meanwhile, fittingly, few historians view GAF area bombing as a factor in convincing the British people to surrender. Although citizens in Britain did not overcome class and gender differences during the war years, we know now that aerial bombardment either had little or no impact on resistance – or, worse, strengthened it. Diarist Gladys Hollingsworth of Coventry suggested that the news of British military losses in mainland Europe were more devastating for morale than direct bombing of civilian centres.[68] Consequently, defending the efficacy of mass bombing non-combatants as the only, or even most important, means of winning the war is probably wrong; furthermore, it is an ethically perilous position to embrace. Meanwhile, ordinary people in the Second World War had no contact with strategists like Curtis LeMay and Arthur Harris, and were often left under a veil of ignorance effected by state censorship when it came to the rationale behind mass bombings. In any case, while counterfactual approaches to the use of various strategies against Britain and Japan may be interesting intellectual exercises, they do not tell us much about the experience of *being bombed* as a civilian.

Urban citizens were the target of bombers because their support, in the age of modern warfare and mass politics, was absolutely essential for victory – much more important, indeed, than the views of wealthy industrialists, political leaders, or military strategists. Citizens in Britain and Japan, even if they had personal experiences of being bombed, nevertheless largely supported the bombing of the enemy, including when 'innocents' like children died as a result. In regional cities across Japan, like Morioka, young people called up for service usually embraced their fate. After being conscripted, Satō Keiji, who was only a high school student at the time, dressed himself in his uniform complete with pistol and sword and reported for duty. Everywhere around him, in one rail station after another, he wrote:

... the grounds were filled with young men participating in [the rally for student soldiers]. I remembered being overwhelmed by the feeling that 'finally, the time has come'. At the time, information came primarily by radio ... and there was considerable trust in the 'Reports from the Imperial Headquarters' (*Daihon'ei happyō*). From 1943, the news changed from the earlier despatches of battlefield victories to darker reports, and we felt that the tide of the war was turning against us, but I nevertheless felt that *we must win*.[69]

Satō's insistence on national victory is not meaningfully different from the 'stiff upper lip' attitude that British citizens putatively embraced during the war. Meanwhile, class, gender, and age divided urban populations in their experience and exposure to risk. Was a British worker more similar to his fellow labourer in Japan, or did he share more interests with the royal family at home? Did Japanese housewives share more concerns with British middle-class women, or were they better off throwing their lot in with the generals and political leaders? The mass media of both countries whipped their people into a 'war fever', convincing the general population of Britain and Japan that they were as different as man and machine, human and animal. As both countries arced quickly toward total mobilisation of their civilian population, which in turn made them targets of enemy assaults, they appeared to be both compellingly close to one another and yet irreconcilably in conflict. What the 'worm's eye view' teaches us, then, is that calls for unity against another population is the quickest path to bringing unnecessary and unconscionable violence against non-combatants both abroad and at home.

Nevertheless, the shared narratives of the war, in both Japan and Britain, created the impression of a shared national experience. British and Japanese people now look back on the war period as a unique, and sometimes positive, time of unity, usually in an unfavourable comparison with the complications concomitant with current multiculturalism. In Britain, the memory of unity can dangerously approach the valorisation of a people coming together to prosecute a righteous conflict, the violent consequences of which this book has repeatedly demonstrated. For the side that lost the war, like Japan, the collective memory of a wartime unity is run through with troubling contradictions: on the one hand, the memory of 'being one' can be positively contrasted against 'selfishness' in the same way that it has in Britain; on the other hand, the terror of total war is vividly and mercilessly recapitulated in public spaces, thereby becoming a foundation of Japan's post-war pacifism. Koide Toshio described the legacy of the war thus:

When I think back [on the war] now, at a time of then unimaginable prosperity, I sometimes hear a voice saying, 'We're all compatriots, aren't we?' This may be the feelings of an ignorant man without education or cultivation but, didn't we all suffer together? On this crowded island nation we did not lock horns with each other like mortal enemies, but rather made Japan go forward in a good direction because we are all, at the very least, Japanese people. So, if we take this one step further, aren't we all human beings? If so, then we should hope that we will make sure that the world won't engage in war again – or perhaps that's a naïve wish.[70]

Certainly many readers of this book will see such a wish as tragically naïve, even though most of us have no desire to see our countries at war. The dismissal of peace as 'naïve' and war as 'realist', however, may be the first step towards new conflicts. Perhaps war is inevitable and sometimes necessary. Nevertheless, we should always begin with a frank examination of what wars do to ordinary people like ourselves. From this perspective – the 'worm's eye view' at the bottom of the ladder of social, economic, and political power – the Second World War was never a 'good war'. Rather, it was the worst war, and ordinary people like us helped make it so.

Notes

Introduction

1 Bloomfield, 'War Stories', 25 August 1939.
2 On the British side, see the work on Dresden in particular: Taylor, *Dresden* and Addison and Addison and Crang, *Firestorm*. On the American firebombing strategy, which sought to maximise civilian casualties, see Tillman, *Whirlwind*.
3 Süss, *Death from the Skies*, 99–100.
4 Iriye Hisae, 'Sensō: 35-nen no kūhaku no onna toshite', *TNK*, p. 184. Some Japanese liberal intellectuals, like journalist Kiyosawa Kiyoshi, were outraged by the targeting of Japanese civilians by US forces. Sugawara Katsuya, 'Great Bearer', p. 456.
5 Strachan, 'On Total War and Modern War', pp. 341–370.
6 Neiman, *Evil in Modern Thought*, p. 303.
7 Ōmura Seitarō, 'Hi no umi', untitled memoir, *FD*, pp. 78–81.
8 Hughes, diary, 22 December 1939.
9 See the 2006 Human Rights Watch report on Hezbollah and the IDF: www.hrw.org/reports/2006/lebanon0806/2.htm [accessed 25 June 2013].
10 Fogel, *Nanjing Massacre*, introduction.
11 George Orwell, 'Looking Back on the Spanish Civil War' (1943).
12 Yoshimi Yoshiaki, *Grassroots Fascism*.
13 Hughes, diary, 3 March 1941.
14 Dower, *War without Mercy*.
15 Monck, diary, 13 September, 7 December 1940.
16 Yokouchi Tomi, 'Jigoku no soko de bōzen jishitsu', in *KK*, p. 98.
17 Mark Metzler, *Lever of Empire*, p. 5.
18 Ian Nish, *The Anglo-Japanese Alliance*.
19 Duus, *Abacus and the Sword*.
20 Nish, *Alliance in Decline*; Shimazu, *Japan, Race and Equality*; Smethurst, *From Foot Soldier to Finance Minister*; Schencking, *Making Waves*; Garon, *Beyond Our Means*, Chapter 5.
21 For more on the Japanese visits to Tyneside shipyards during the Tokugawa shogunate, see Conte-Helm, *Japan and the North East of England*.

22 See the classic analysis of Japanese attempts at autarky: Crowley, *Japan's Quest for Autonomy*. For more recent interpretations, see Nakamura Takafusa, 'The Yen Bloc, 1931–1941', and Myers, 'Creating a Modern Enclave Economy'; Barnhart, *Japan Prepares for Total War*.

23 Byas, *Government by Assassination*.

24 Lary, *The Chinese People at War*; Mitter, *China's War with Japan*.

25 Hughes, diary, 29 December 1939. Hughes also noted with some alarm that there was a 'large increase in number of people smoking – also women smoking in the street, which has never been seen in Liverpool before, although I dare say it has in London'. 21 October 1939.

26 Young, *Beyond the Metropolis*, pp. 11, 10.

27 Kidd, *Manchester: A History*, pp. 21–27.

28 Matsubara Kijirō, 'Shizuka na machi ga', in *TNK*, p. 99.

29 Tagaya, 'The Imperial Japanese Air Forces', pp. 179, 187, 191.

30 Collier, *Defence of the United Kingdom*, pp. 494–528.

31 See the summary in Lowe, *Inferno*, and Werrel, *Blankets of Fire*, pp. 7–18.

32 Werrel, *Blankets of Fire*, p. 22.

33 Werrel, *Blankets of Fire*, pp. 152–159.

34 Sheldon M. Garon, PC.

35 Overy, *The Bombing War*, pp. 83–89.

36 Collier, *The Defence of the United Kingdom*, pp. 63–75. As Collier's 1957 classic military history showed, the initial phase of mobilisation in Britain greatly favoured fighters over bombers, as a 'knock out blow' was expected. Thus, the British bombing campaign had the benefit of learning by experience, from the German attack, what strengths and weaknesses aerial bombardment of civilians might offer.

37 Werrel, *Blankets of Fire*, p. 22.

38 Quoted in Kenneth Werrel, *Blankets of Fire*, p. 9.

39 Lowe, *Inferno*, pp. 62–63.

40 Baker, *Human Smoke*.

41 Tillman, *Whirlwind*, pp. 257, 261. Max Hastings' *Nemesis* includes no new research using Japanese materials.

42 Frank, *Downfall*.

43 Totani, *Tokyo War Crimes Trial*; Minear, *Victors' Justice*. Nagai wrote that the 'damage that the inhabitants of Tokyo suffer has more to do with the misrule of the Japanese military government than with American aircraft.' Quoted in Sugawara Katsuya, 'Great Bearer', p. 457.

44 Kushner, *Men to Devils*.

45 Dower, *War without Mercy*.

46 Coffey, *Iron Eagle*; Biddle, *Rhetoric and Reality*; Tillman, *LeMay*.

47 Hogan, *Hiroshima in History and Memory*.

48 Alperovitz, *Making of the Atomic Bomb*; Tsuyoshi Hasegawa, *Racing the Enemy*; Yukiko Koshiro, *Imperial Eclipse*, pp. 223–254. Also see the summary in Pape, *Bombing to Win*, pp. 87–136, in which 'military vulnerability', or an inability to defend the home islands from either US or Soviet forces, was decisive, not the civilian casualty rate.

49 Werrell, *Blankets of Fire*, p. xiii.

50 Kramer, 'Russia Shows What Happens When Terrorists' Families Are Targeted', *The New York Times*, 29 March 2016.

51 See my examination in *Writing War*, Chapter 1.

52 Inoue Tamiko, '1-jo gakusei no nikki yori', p. 633. For more on student diary writing, see the special issue of *Japanese Studies* edited by Peter Cave and myself, 'Historical Interrogations of Japanese Children amid Disaster and War, 1920–1945'.

53 Craddock, 'St. Stephen's Boy's School, Diary 1940', and see Kent, 'Collins Diamond Diary 1941'.

54 Peirse, diary, 28 May 1944.

55 Yoshida Fusako, diary, p. 126 [14 October 1943].

56 Narita Shigeru, untitled memoir, pp. 195–196.

57 Regan, untitled diary, 17 September 1940.

58 Monck, diary, 6 August 1941.

59 Hughes, diary, 21 March and 23 November 1941. Also see Last, *Nella Last's War*.

60 Bloomfield, *Wartime Memoirs*, 5 September 1939.

61 Quoted in 'Introduction', Latchford, *The Swansea Wartime Diary of Laurie Latchford*, p. 20.

Chapter 1

1 Kojima Yoshitaka, 15 November 1943.

2 Dorothy Hughes, 4 December 1939.

3 Takahashi Aiko, 17 June 1945.

4 Dorothy Hughes, 22 October 1939.

5 Inohara Mitsuko, 8 January and 14 June 1945.

6 Dorothy Hughes, 13 December 1939.

7 Anonymous, Notes on evacuation of children (M-O).

8 Coleman, 'A Warden's Wife', pp. 31–32.

9 Shiba Isa, 'Yakedasarete', pp. 38–39.

10 Brackets indicate grammatical errors that I have corrected. Anonymous, 'The Bad Days of the War'.

11 Gregor, 'A Schicksalsgemeinschaft?', pp. 1051–1070.

12 Dorothy Hughes, 8 November 1939.

13 Anonymous, 'Further instruction for teachers and helpers of school parties', 31 August 1939 (M-O). As the children and young teens left the city, sometimes the schools were filled with soldiers and, later, foreign troops. For example, Bristol's Clifton College was emptied in February 1941, after the destruction of the city centre, to host US troops. Stranack, *Schools at War*, pp. 12–13.

14 See the descriptions in Welshman, *Churchill's Children*, and pp. 55–56 for Albert Shaw.

15 Metcalfe, letter, 24 June 1940.

16 *SGS*, pp. 19–27.

17 Shinonori Mansaku, *Gakudō sokai no kiroku*, p. 36.

18 Cox, 'London War Diary', 16 September 1940.

19 Robins, diary, 6 September 1940. The Robins family had already moved from Godalming back to London, only to anticipate yet another evacuation.

20 Allen, 'The Beetroot', p. 46. Other Bristolians felt the same: a friend of Violet Maund's refused to take cover in the city during a raid, 'being frantic to be back in her own home'. Maund, *Diary of a Bristol Woman*, 10 January 1941. In Liverpool, C. A. Piper wrote 'my people were mostly of the kind who said, and meant what they said, "we are going to stay at home and take whatever is coming to us."' Piper, *A Century of Service*, p. 66. As Theresa Fuller remembered, her working-class father refused to let his children leave Salford, even during the bombing of the docks; he felt strongly that the family should face annihilation together, rather than the possibility of his children growing up as penniless orphans. PC: Stretford, Manchester, 24 December 2012.

21 Dorothy Hughes, 2 December 1939.

22 Matsuda Haruko, 'Fuhatsu no shōidan', p. 91. Yoshida Yoshio's father, who worked in a paper mill in Nagaoka, also refused to evacuate his family in order to keep his job, which often included working long hours into the night. Yoshida Yoshio, 'Chichi wa jibun no ie yori jinushi no ie o mamotta', *NK*, p. 333.

23 Edith Peirse, 9 July 1944.

24 Kobayashi Takako, 'Onna bakari', *HK*, p. 42.

25 Heather Bryan, 'War Memories', *MW*.

26 Robins, diary, late September or early October 1940.

27 Quoted in Brown, *Evacuees*, p. 41.

28 Nibu Akiko, 'Sokai jidō o tsurete', *KK*, p. 102.

29 Merrill, *Looking Back*, pp. 12–13.

30 Ōyama Hidenori, diary, p. 627.

31 Coles, 'Personal evacuation (with school children)', 22 September and 1 October 1939.

32 Eleanor Humphries, 3 October 1940. Apparently, sleeping in cars was common in South Wales as well: Latchford, *The Wartime Swansea Diary*, p. 239 [20 February 1941].

33 Dorothy Hughes, 29 November 1939; also see 4 January 1940, and many other entries around this date.

34 Bloomfield, *Wartime Memoirs*, 1 September 1939. Although the Soviet Union was later an ally, British citizens deeply supported Finland's efforts to protect its independence. Maund, *Diary of a Bristol Woman*, 9 March 1942; Hollingsworth, 6–10 January and 28 May 1940; Skea, 22 March 1938 and 2 October 1939.

35 Kahn, 'Exercise Book', July 1941.

36 Hollingsworth, 17–19 June 1940.

37 Metcalfe, letter, 19 June 1940.

38 Ishikawa Chieko, 'Gakuto kinrō dōin nikki yori', *CK*, p. 66 [21 March 1945].

39 Tanaka Osamu, 'Maruta no yō na shōshitai', *SK*, p. 21.

40 Osborne (Mrs.). 'A Baker-Hero', *BSN*, p. 46.

41 CHC, 1656/3/1: Anonymous, 'Memories of the Blitz'.

42 Yoshida Fusako, diary, p. 120 [6 August 1943].

43 Robins, diary, 27 July 1941.

44 Donald, diary, 21 August 1940.
45 Nakajima Kikue, untitled memoir, *KuK*, p. 37.
46 S. C. Leslie, 'This Was Your Victory', no pagination.
47 Mockett, 19 March 1941.
48 Peat, undated news interview, probably 1991.
49 Ichikawa Shōjirō, 'Wasurerarenai makka na hi', *HK*, p. 46.
50 Bovill, letter, 8 May 1991.
51 Sakazume Hiromi, 'Tōchan wa ikite ita', *TDK* v. 1, pp. 67–69.
52 Elwood, 11 September 1941.
53 A. E. Davies, memoir, p. 57.
54 Akiyama Shigeko, 'Mada mitsukaranai sobo', *TNK*, p. 98.
55 Regan, diary, p. 39 [Christmastime 1940].
56 Hollingsworth, diary, 15 November 1940.
57 Inaba Fuku, 'Shuki: isshun ni kita jigoku' [Notebook: Hell came in one second], *CK*, pp. 107–108.
58 Bonham, untitled memoir.
59 Goodridge, 'When Is It Going to Stop?', *SB*, p. 73.
60 Bloomfield, *Wartime Memoirs*, 8 May 1945.
61 Matsui Ryūichirō, 'Chichi no nikki ni tōji o shinobu', *SK*, pp. 312–315.
62 Brodie, untitled memoir, pp. 2–3.
63 Anonymous. 'Grumbles', 20 June 1942.
64 Inohara Mitsuko, 20 June 1945.
65 On the First World War, see Hunter, 'More than an Archive of War', pp. 339–354.
66 Iriye Hisae, 'Sensō: 35-nen no kūhaku no onna toshite', p. 182.
67 Takizawa Toki, 'Otto no rusu o mamoritsuzukete', pp. 25–26.
68 Metcalfe, letter, 6 January and 23 February 1941.
69 Iriya Hisae, 'Sensō: 35-nen no kūhaku no onna toshite', op. cit.
70 William Bernard Regan, diary, p. 28 [September 1940].
71 Mizutani Shin'ichi, diary, p. 88.
72 Ono Kazuo, 'Machi ga moete masse', *TNK*, pp. 78–79.
73 Bill Walsh, letter, 8 May 1990.
74 Matsui Ryūichirō, 'Chichi no nikki', pp. 315–317.
75 H. B. Monck, 18 December 1940.
76 Takeuchi Toshitoyo, untitled memoir, *NK*, p. 194.
77 Piper, 'Liverpool Unitarian Mission'; Piper, *A Century of Service*, p. 65. On the situation in London, see, for example, Cox, 'London War Diary', 12 September 1940.
78 Kobayashi Takako, 'Onna bakari no hito-ya', p. 45.
79 Weston, 'Laughter and Tears', *BSN*, p. 50.
80 Yoshida Fusako, diary, p. 123–129 [30 August to 8 November 1943], p. 131 [9 August 1945].
81 Bloomfield, *Wartime Memoirs*, 16 September 1941.
82 Belsey, correspondence, 8–11 September 1940, in Harris, *Blitz Diary*, pp. 67–68.
83 Hirai Kiyoshi, diary, *WK*, p. 25 [30 November 1944].
84 Daniel (nee Harper), letter, 15 May 1991.

85 Metcalfe, letters dated 7 and 11 January 1941. See letter of 24 February 1941 for the detailed explanation of how she constructed her own cot, pram, and other items for the baby.

86 Takahashi Aiko, 29 August 1944.

87 Kenneth Holmes, 5 November 1944.

88 Inohara Mitsuko, 14 March 1945. From the middle of the day on March 13 to the early morning of the next day, most of Osaka's city centre was destroyed in this attack.

89 Takahashi Aiko, 26 May 1945.

Chapter 2

1 Dorothy Hughes, 31 August 1939.

2 Takahashi Aiko, 18 April 1942.

3 Dora Mockett, 8 April 1941.

4 Kojima Yoshitaka, 13 December 1944.

5 Takahashi Aiko, 3 May 1945.

6 Inohara Mitsuko, 22 June 1945.

7 Kojima Yoshitaka, 29 December 1944.

8 Randall, 'One Night of Hell', 3–4 May 1941, 1:45, 12, 12:30pm, 1am.

9 Regan, diary, pp. 22, 23, 35 [September, 1940].

10 Miyada Katsuyo, 'Taga-jinja e nigeru', *HaK*, p. 12.

11 Matthews, 'Memo' ['War Diary, 1939–'], 8 April 1941.

12 Haslewood, 'The Blitz on London', 10 September 1940.

13 Murphy, letter, 6 May 1991.

14 Yoshida Takeshi, 'Ikite iru yō na haha no kao', *CK*, p. 326.

15 Regan, diary, 18 September 1940.

16 Kogawa Kōtarō, 'Yami kara mo kuroi shōshitai', *SK*, p. 122.

17 Anonymous, Air Raids, Bristol (M-O).

18 Robins, pages from a diary notebook, entry from early September 1940.

19 Ward, correspondence, 10 May 1991.

20 Regan, diary, p. 4 [September 1940].

21 Takahashi Aiko, 18 July 1944.

22 Kojima Yoshitaka, 11 May 1945.

23 Haslewood, 'The Blitz on London', 1 October 1940. Nevertheless, Haslewood was extremely sceptical of these murmurings: 'The rumours of attempted invasion have been legion. Really it is as bad as the rumour about the Russians passing through England in the last war. Everyone knew someone who knew someone else who had seen the Russians. So in this war I have met many people who have friends who know for a certain fact that invasion has been attempted several times'. Dorothy Hughes also felt frustrated about the rumours that circulated Liverpool, including talk of the destruction of the docks. Hughes, 22 August 1940.

24 Yoshimi Yoshiaki, *Grassroots Fascism*, and Dietmar Süss, *Death from the Skies*, p. 53.

25 Gwladys Cox mentioned news of invasion from German presses, as well as mass bombing that would clog the transport network with refugees

and make work impossible in London. Cox, 'London War Diary', 12–13 September 1940.

26 Metcalfe, correspondence, 24 June 1940.
27 Dent, correspondence, undated post-war memoir [probably 1991].
28 Senuma Yukiko, 'Hachiōji kūshū to haha no shi', *HaK*, p. 23.
29 Sakai Jun, '"Sensō wa makeru" to iu uwasa', *SF*, pp. 42–43. Also see John Dower, *War without Mercy*.
30 Bloomfield, *Wartime Memoirs*, May 1940. Violet Maund also feared answering basic questions from a uniformed police officer, for fear that she may have inadvertently 'helped the wrong side'. Maund, *Diary of a Bristol Woman*, 16 May 1942.
31 Anonymous, unsigned letter, probably 1991.
32 Cox, 'London War Diary', 2 September 1940.
33 Tsuyuki Isao. 'Tekiki ni te o furu', *TDK*, p. 42.
34 Thornton, correspondence, 28 October 1940.
35 Sugaya Sumi, 'Chi no naka no shi', *TDK*, p. 34.
36 Bloomfield, *Wartime Memoirs*, 24 August and October 1939.
37 Harvey, 'War Years', *MW*.
38 Cox, 'London War Diary', 3 September 1940.
39 Andō Toyoko, 'B-29 80-ki ga raishū', *KuK*, p. 42.
40 Metcalfe, letter, 19 June 1940.
41 Kaneyama Misao, 'Jitensha de nigete', *TDK*, p. 478.
42 Latchford, *Swansea Wartime Diary*, p. 238 [20 February 1941].
43 De Asis, *From Bataan to Tokyo*, p. 18.
44 Compton, memoir. Some citizens, like Violet Maund, had to experience an air raid before investing in IDs: 'These will serve to identify us should we be buried under debris, or receive a direct hit'. Maund, *Diary of a Bristol Woman*, 8 April 1941.
45 Ikebe Toshiaki, 'Kūshū ni matowaru omoide', *AK* v. 21.
46 Yoshitake Teruyoshi, memoir, *FD*, p. 77.
47 Haslewood, 'The Blitz on London', 3 September 1940.
48 Dorothy Hughes, 24 December 1940.
49 Nōso Masaichi, 'Ekichō toshite', *TNK*, p. 82. Also on 'mushi ga shirasu', see Ikeda Kikue, 'Asa no bakufū', *TNK*, p. 86.
50 Cleaver, 'Blitz Memories', p. 2.
51 Johnson, correspondence, 10 April 1991.
52 Beale, 'Memories of the First Coventry Blitz'.
53 Anonymous, 'Memories of the War'.
54 Crosby, 'Memories of the First Coventry Blitz', 6 June 1990, p. 2.
55 Ikebe Toshiaki, 'Kūshū ni matowaru omoide'; Kōtō Yasuo, 'Wasurerarenai Aomori no kūshū'; Ichikawa Tomoaki, 'Aomori kūshū no kioku', *AK* v. 21, p. 20, 12, and 17.
56 Haslewood, 'The Blitz on London', 28 September 1940.
57 Sekiya Tsuneo, 'Haha o seotte', *HaK* v. 3, p. 6.
58 Compton, memoir, p. 1.
59 Miyazawa Keikichi, diary, *HaK* v. 3, p. 264 [19 April 1945].
60 Dorothy Hughes, 23 December 1940.

61 Iketani Toyoko, 'Teki nagara utsukushii shōnen' *TDK* v. 2, p. 642.

62 Regan, diary, p. 39 [Christmastime, 1940].

63 Itoi Sayoko, 'B-29 80-ki ga raishū', *KuK*, p. 44.

64 Haslewood, 'The Blitz on London', 7 September 1940. Bill Regan also noted the extreme noise of aerial bombardment, writing in his diary that 'You would have to be stone deaf to rest in any kind of centre'. Regan, diary, p. 4.

65 Cox, 'London War Diary', 9 September 1940.

66 Koide Keiko, 'Tachikirareta kokoro' *TDK* v. 2, p. 465.

67 Hollingsworth, undated letter copied into back of diary, late 1940 or early 1941.

68 Takahashi Yoshiji, 'Shuki: Hizan o koete utsukushikatta hi no ame', *CK*, pp. 302–303.

69 Robins, diary, 22 September 1940, listening to 'the shrapnel falling like rain'.

70 Dorrinton, memoir, *BB*, p. 77. This describes the 'Good Friday' raid of 1941.

71 Satō Fujie and Satō Makoto, 'Senaka ni bakudan no kizu o se-otte', *TK*, p. 20.

72 Okamura Toshiyasu, 'Akai mōfubuki', *SK*, 117–118.

73 Anonymous, 'Memories of the Blitz'. Ted Crosby also noted, 'I had been associated with the Cathedral all my life. It was an awful feeling to think it was burning . . . It was awful the next day when I found it had been destroyed'. Crosby, 'Memories of the First Coventry Blitz'.

74 Narita Kazuko, 'Aomori no kūshū no kioku', *AK* v. 21, p. 13; Ault, 'Memories of the Blitz'.

75 Anonymous, Air Raids, Birmingham (M-O).

76 Amy Bell, 'Landscapes of Fear', pp. 153–175.

77 Fujimoto Kinuko, diary, *HaK*, p. 258 [1 August 1945].

78 Miyazawa Keikichi, diary, *HaK*, p. 262 [10 March 1945].

79 Berkeley, Special Constable in London, p. 281.

80 Hiraoka Tsutomu, 'Hayase chiku (Ondo) ni bakugeki', *KuK*, p. 37.

81 Burkey, *Boyhood Blitz*, p. 21.

82 Bloomfield, *Wartime Memoirs*, 16 September 1941.

83 Watanabe Masako, 'Honoo no machi', *HaK* v. 3, p. 27.

84 Brownbill, diary, 13 September 1940, 9pm.

85 Bloomfield, *Wartime Memoirs*, 13 October 1940.

86 Tanaka Tatsumu, '300-hon no shōidan', *TK*, p. 207.

87 Thornton, correspondence, 17 November 1940.

88 Sano Tatsuo, 'Shizuoka ni hajimete kūshū ga atta hi', *SG65*, pp. 72–73.

89 Hollingsworth, undated letter copied into back of diary, late 1940 or early 1941.

90 Hollingsworth, undated entry at the end of her 1940 diary.

91 Dorothy Hughes, 27 December 1940.

92 Hares, 'A Broadmead Diary', *BSN*, pp. 11–12.

93 Yokono Kōichi and Asahina Masanori, 'Tsuiraku shita Amerika-hei, I & II', *SG65*, p. 63 and 65.

94 Watanabe Masanori, 'Gesuikan no naka dde inochi hiroi', *CK*, pp. 312–315.

95 Bloomfield, *Wartime Memoirs*, 12 January 1942.

96 Peat, correspondence, 7 May 1991. Also see Haslewood, 'The Blitz on London', 28 September 1940, wherein she described how rescue workers opened tunnels to trapped (and often dying) victims in order to give them morphine.

97 Haslewood, 'The Blitz on London', 8 September 1940; Mochizuki Masako, 'Dōkoku no hibi', *TNK* v. 2, pp. 160–164.

98 Shields, 'The Battle of Britain', 186.

99 Mockett, diary, 22 March 1941.

100 Ogawa Takashi, diary, in *NKS* v. 6, pp. 20–21.

101 Mockett, diary, 14 March 1941.

102 Watanabe Teruko, 'Shi o kakugo shita toki', p. 302.

103 Monck, diary, 21 and 23 December 1940.

104 Albrighton, memoir of Coventry blitz, 20 March 1990, p. 2.

105 Yagi Jun'ichi, diary, *HaK*, pp. 335–337 [26 July 1945].

106 Mockett, diary, 5 February, 1 September, and 16 February 1941.

107 Peirse, diary, 4 January and 20 April 1944. On Hull's war damage, see Gillett and MacMahon, *A History of Hull*.

108 Post-war the feeling that 'Hull has been left behind in the assessment of the bombings' was especially strong. Turner, correspondence, 14 May 1991. E. K. Allison also voiced his irritation with the post-war narrative: 'I've worked away from Hull, much to my regret now, and have felt most frustrated being unable to convince strangers of the hiding Hull took'. Allison, correspondence, 16 May 1991.

109 Hughes, diary, 23 July 1941.

110 Cox, 'London War Diary', 1 September 1940.

111 Holmes, diary, 5 November 1944, 3pm.

112 Burkey, p. 23.

113 Fuchikami Akira, 'Yakenokori no ki', *HaK*, p. 56.

114 Nunobiki Junji, 'Shōidan no osoroshisa', *HaK*, pp. 62–63.

115 Perry, *Boy in the Blitz*, p. 94. For the office joke about Hitler and Moses, see p. 52.

116 Watanbe Shige, '26-nenme no akuma no odori', *TDK*, p. 628.

117 Regan, diary, p. 26 [September 1940].

118 Regan, diary, p. 30 [Christmastime, 1940] and p. 25 [September 1940].

119 Shepperd, 'A Diary of the Blitz', 6–20 September 1940.

120 Quoted in Sugawara, 'Great Bearer', p. 460. I have slightly edited the translation.

121 Elwood, diary, 26 September 1941.

122 Peirse, diary, 8 April 1939.

123 Fagnani, 'On Christmas Steps', *BSN*, 24 November 1940, 3 January 1941, pp. 24–25.

124 Cited in Bell, *London Was Ours*, p. 119.

125 Kobayashi Narimitsu, 'Nikki', *SK*, p. 8.

126 Rice, *Sand in My Shoes*, p. 7, 78.

127 Metcalfe, correspondence, probably 5 July 1940. Olive does not name the author, but given the description it is almost certainly Jean du Plessis' *The*

Human Caravan: The Direction and Meaning of Human History, published in 1939 by Sheen & Ward.

128 Kahn, 'Exercise Book', 23 May 1944.
129 Taylor, 'Diary', 18 February 1941.
130 A boy told his grandmother that they were spared during a terrible raid on account of his prayer to see his mother and father again. It is unclear if this prayer was ultimately answered. His father was 'in France during the capitulation'. Melkins, 'A Child's Prayer', *BSN*, p. 48.
131 Humphries, diary, 21 December 1940.
132 Wookey, 'A Vision of St. Chad', *BSN*, p. 40.
133 Okamoto Masao, 'Senshōdō nisshi', p. 24.
134 Taylor, 'Diary', 17 April 1941.
135 Shiba Isa, 'Yakedasarete', p. 39.
136 Cox, 'London War Diary', 8 September 1940.
137 Kanenaka Kimi, 'Dannen ni sagasedo' *TNK*, pp. 170–172.
138 Field, 'Puzzled People'. The trend toward secularisation, while peaking in the 1960s, had deep roots in the early twentieth century: McLeod, *Religion and Society*.
139 Watanabe Teruko, 'Shi o kakugo shita toki', p. 302.
140 Anonymous, 'WRL Report 19', page 4 [27 August 1939].
141 Various interviewees, 'Futon kabutte nenbutsu tonae', p. 128. *Nanmaida* is a colloquial form of *namu Amida butsu*, or the *nenbutsu*, which in this case is a Pure Land Buddhist prayer for salvation.
142 Kobayashi Takako, 'Onna bakari no hito-ya', p. 40.
143 Latchford, *Swansea Wartime Diary*, p. 234 [19 February 1941].
144 Monck, diary, 8 May 1941.
145 John Kay, 8 September 1940.
146 Nagi Katsumi, 'Go-shintai to tomo ni', *SK*, pp. 69–72.
147 S.P.S., 'Hitler's Coming', *BSN*, p. 39.
148 Piper, *A Century of Service*, p. 68.
149 Mizutani Teruko, 'Kōka no naka ni nao seimei arite', *SG65*, pp. 27–31. N.B., 'kōka' (also read 'gōka') is, in Buddhist eschatology, a world-ending holocaust; the title, and her memoir, thus contrasts the eschatology of her Buddhism with the peaceful life she enjoyed after the war.
150 Endō Naoe, 'Joshi teishintai', *SK*, p. 178.
151 Muramatsu Naka, untitled memoir, *FD*, p. 75.
152 Endō Naoe, 'Joshi teishintai', p. 180.
153 Brittain, *Testament of Youth*, p. 94.
154 Hughes, diary, 2 September 1940.
155 Mockett, diary, 15 July 1941.
156 Kojima Yoshitaka, diary, 14, 17 May 1945.
157 Hughes, diary, 22, 27, 31 December 1940, 28 January 1941.
158 Hughes, diary, 23 March 1941.
159 Inohara Mitsuko, diary, 30 July 1945.
160 Ohnuki-Tierney, *Kamikaze*.

Chapter 3

1 Mockett, diary, 20 July 1941.
2 Takahashi Aiko, diary, 15 May 1945.
3 Hughes, diary, 12 December 1939.
4 Inohara Mitsuko, diary, 28 May and 28 July 1945.
5 Mockett, diary, 8 May 1941.
6 Hughes, diary, 23 November 1941.
7 Takahashi Aiko, 21 February 1942.
8 Hughes, diary, 17 March 1941.
9 Maund, *Diary of a Bristol Woman*, 24 December 1941. Even before the bombing, however, citizens engaged in panic-buying: in September 1939, Dorothy Hughes noted that Liverpool's shops were 'full of people at lunch time – buying shoes, stockings, and woollens. Where do they get the money from?' Hughes, diary, 13 September 1939.
10 Leo Ou-fan Lee, *Shanghai Modern*.
11 Young, *Beyond the Metropolis*.
12 Hewitt, 'Place Annihilation', p. 258. The annihilation of these systems would later lead to the integration of that memory within urban space: Karacas, 'Place, Public Memory, and the Tokyo Air Raids'.
13 Letter by 'Will', in Harris, *Blitz Diary*, p. 62.
14 Typically, those who abandoned the city left their house keys with the local fire wardens or air raid patrol members. For example, see Maund, *Diary of a Bristol Woman*, 19 October 1941.
15 Aoki Shige, 'Shizuoka yūbinkyoku enjō', *SK*, pp. 354–355.
16 Haslewood, 'The Blitz on London', 28 September 1940. Haslewood subsequently resolved to clear her drawers of embarrassing personal items.
17 Sadler, correspondence (letter to parents), 19 November 1940.
18 Noda Tsuru, 'Go-shin'ei o mamoru', *SK*, pp. 361–365.
19 Matthews, diary, 14 November 1940.
20 Sakurai Shizuko, 'Haka no naka no shōnetsu jigoku', *SK*, pp. 93–95.
21 As many noted in their memoirs, the Gulson Free Library was founded by a former mayor of Coventry in 1873, and was apparently well-loved by city residents. Similarly, Violet Maund noted the destruction of Bristol's Cheltenham Road Library as a significant event. Maund, *A Bristol Woman's Diary*, 12 April 1941.
22 Bosworth, untitled memoir, p. 2.
23 Thornton, correspondence, 17 November 1940, and 6 February 1941. On gas, also see Robins, diary, 9 September 1940, wherein she was forced to use kettles to wash clothes after the mains were cut.
24 Bosworth, untitled memoir, p. 3.
25 Susuki Tetsuo, 'Shōidan ga rōjin no atama ni', *SK*, pp. 57–59.
26 Hollingsworth, final undated entry in 1940 diary.
27 Hares, 'A Broadmead Diary', 16–17 March 1941, p. 19.
28 Inoue Masako, 'Kōshūkaidō wa hi no kawa', *HaK*, p. 18.
29 Lord, memoir, p. 47.

30 Dorothy Hughes spoke to a British soldier in Liverpool who complained that Air Raid Patrolmen earned more than conscripts for the army, but she also noted that the soldiers were eating well enough to put on weight. Hughes, diary, 11 December 1939.
31 Kahn, 'Exercise Book', January 1941.
32 Sonematsu, diary, p. 807 [6 January 1945].
33 Wheal, *World's End*, p. 109.
34 Sumiyoshi Konokichi, diary, *WK*, p. 24 [2 April 1945].
35 Latchford, *Swansea Wartime Diary*, p. 235 [19 February 1941].
36 Yoshida Fusako, diary, pp. 122–123 [26 August 1943].
37 Yamamoto Shigeko, 'Bōgeki no kakoi no soto he', *HaK*, p. 5.
38 Sumiyoshi Konokichi, diary, *WK*, p. 24 [2 April 1945].
39 Humphries, diary, 11 October 1940.
40 Yoshimi Yoshiaki, *Kusa no ne no fashizumu*, p. 34.
41 Castle, *We're All in the Battle*, pp. 1, 17.
42 Rich, 'From a Bedminster Warden', *BSN*, p. 29.
43 Takahashi Aiko, diary, 27 March 1943.
44 Latchford, *Swansea Wartime Diary*, p. 234 [19 February 1941].
45 Uekusa Shōsaburō, 'Shuki', *CK*, p. 296.
46 Yabe Masaaki, 'Shōidan chokugeki, muzan ni mo korosareta imoto', *SG65*, pp. 31–34.
47 Manchester: Anonymous, Air Raids, Manchester, 'Notes on the Effects of Air Raids on People in Manchester', p. 2 [10 January 1941].
48 Maund, *Diary of a Bristol Woman*, 27 September 1940.
49 Sadler, correspondence (letter to parents), 19 November 1940.
50 Fujii Hiroshi et al., 'Keibōdan no hibaku shori kara', *TK*, pp. 168–184.
51 Bloomfield, *Wartime Memoirs*, 3 September 1939.
52 Regan, diary, 17 September 1940.
53 Shiba Ei'ichi, 'Chokugeki o uketa kenchō', *SK*, pp. 339–341.
54 Reid, *Bristol Blitz*, pp. 10–11.
55 Anonymous, Air Raids, Bradford (M-O).
56 Anonymous, Air Raids, Bristol: 'Christopher's Dream', 26 September 1940.
57 Various interviewees, 'Futon kabutte nenbutsu tonae', pp. 125–126.
58 Dorothy Hughes, 1 December 1940.
59 Kawahata Ichirō, 'Kūshū zengo no Katakura kaiwai no kurashi', *HaK*, pp. 156–157.
60 Dora Mockett, diary, 25 February 1941.
61 Bonham, untitled memoir.
62 Okamoto Masao, 'Senshōdō nisshi', *TNK*, pp. 22–24.
63 Matsubayashi Hana, 'Junshoku shita 8-mei no shiritsu byōin kangofu', *SG65*, pp. 34–35.
64 Anonymous, St. Thomas' Hospital memoir, page 2.
65 Matsubara Kijirō, 'Shizuka na machi ga', pp. 99–101.
66 Maling, 'A Medical Student's Impressions', 15 September 1940.
67 Medical officers in Bristol cleared 700–800 beds for incoming military casualties, but they never arrived. Reid, *Bristol Blitz*, p. 11.

68 Bristol: Reported in the *Evening World*, and reprinted in *BSN*, p. 46 (also see H. Davies, 'Bombed in Four Hospitals', *BSN*, p. 59, where a man in a stretcher had eight nurses singing 'I've got sixpence' during an air raid). Liverpool: Leslie, 'This Was Your Victory'. Manchester: Anonymous, Air Raids, Manchester, 'Notes on the Effects of Air Raids on People in Manchester', p. 1 [10 January 1941].

69 Metcalfe, correspondence, 7 January 1941.

70 Takahashi Aiko, diary, 27 May 1945.

71 Itō Eiko, 'Shōidan tōka no naka de seimei o toritomete', *CK*, pp. 329–333.

72 Latchford, *Swansea Wartime Diary*, pp. 236 and 239 [20 February 1941].

73 Metcalfe, correspondence, 24 February 1941.

74 Buchanan, correspondence, 25 November 1940. Also see Maund, *Diary of a Bristol Woman*, 26–29 November 1940.

75 Maund, *Diary of a Bristol Woman*, 8 May 1942.

76 Beaven and Griffiths, 'The Blitz and Civilian Morale in Three Northern Cities'. However, one Mass Observer noted that the homeless 'seemed pathetically glad of any help given them, however ineffective, and were very disinclined to give trouble'. Anonymous, Air Raids, Manchester, 'Notes on the Effects of Air Raids on People in Manchester', p. 1 [10 January 1941].

77 Inaba Fuku, 'Shuki: isshun ni kita jigoku', *CK*, pp. 105–106.

78 Dorothy Hughes, diary, 24 December 1940.

79 Maloney, correspondence, p. 2.

80 Sadler, correspondence (letter to parents), 19 November 1940.

81 Katō Hideo, 'Kikansha ni kijū sōsha', *HK*, pp. 114–115.

82 Anne Shepperd, 'A Diary of the Blitz of London', p. 16.

83 Ōi Masao, 'Watashi wa mita', *NDK*, p. 37.

84 Bloomfield, *Wartime Memoirs*, 9 April 1941.

85 Hughes, diary, 28 January 1941. Shortages exposed hypocrisies in government nutrition advice: 'We used to be implored to eat more fruit', Dorothy noted, 'Now we are told it doesn't matter whether we have it or not'.

86 Latchford, *Swansea Wartime Diary*, p. 232 and 240 [11 and 21 February 1941].

87 Inoue Haruko and Fukubu Miyoko, 'Watashi no taiken', *NDK*, p. 139. Violet Maund gave up in her search for meat in Bristol during the war: Maund, *Diary of a Bristol Woman*, 19 February 1942.

88 Brode, 'The Leg of Mutton', *SB*, p. 86.

89 Metcalf, correspondence, 19 March 1941.

90 Elwood, diary, 1 September 1941.

91 Bertram Elwood noted that tobacconists in London would keep up their 'No Tobacco' signs while furtively selling hidden stock to regular customers; he later postulated the same to be true for alcohol in pubs. Elwood, diary, 5 and 11 September 1941. Dorothy Hughes noted that, in wartime Liverpool, shop assistants had become 'very off-hand' and indifferent to serving their customers. Hughes, diary, 7 November 1939.

92 Regan, diary, pp. 32–33 [September 1940].

93 On panic-buying in Coventry see Bloomfield, *Wartime Memoirs*, 2 September 1939, and on looting in the same, see Bonham, untitled memoir.

94 Monck, diary, 18 September 1940.
95 Tada Susumu, 'Kūshūka no keisatsukan', *KK*, p. 77. Among the looters, apparently, was Nibu Akiko, a dormitory mother (*ryōbo*) for evacuated children (see pp. 102–103, *KK*). Looting canned food after an air raid was dangerous, because the tins were heated and therefore liable to explode, burn one's hands, or set one's rucksack on fire.
96 Hares, 'A Broadmead Diary', p. 13.
97 Bonham, untitled memoir. 'One of the results of the Blitz was that so many shops and roads were ruined that food did not get through to Coventry in sufficient quantities. Add this to the shortage of water, it is easy to see why we were advised to evacuate women and children'.
98 Hollingsworth, diary, 19 November 1940. Water came back on roughly ten days after the blitz. Kirai Toshiko, 'Honō to ningen to', *TNK*, p. 20.
99 Bissell, untitled memoir.
100 Haslewood, 'The Blitz on London', 16 September 1940.
101 Fox, 'Diary of Events', 17 November 1940.
102 Maund, *Diary of a Bristol Woman*, 20 July 1942.
103 Suzuki Yoshiko, 'Onomoto mura yakuba no haikyūgakari shunin toshite', *SF*, p. 56. Onomoto Village's town hall in fact covered three of the outlying villages that supplied the Aizu-Wakamatsu urban area during the war.
104 Aojima Tokuji, 'Kūshū chokugo no shokryō haikyū gyōmu', *SK*, pp. 303–308.
105 Yamashita, *Leaves from an Autumn of Emergencies*; see articles in Cwiertka, *Food and War*.
106 Reid, *Bristol Blitz*, pp. 27–28.
107 Hollingsworth, diary, 20 January 1940. The 'Liberal' was Gladys' dance hall of choice, and she kept a record of her dance partners.
108 For example: Dorothy Hughes, diary, 16 November 1940, concerning two women evacuated to Wales from Liverpool, complaining about how boring it was – in particular, the lack of cinemas.
109 For a nice description of the sorts of amusements ordinary people enjoyed in regional cities, see Moriuchi Masashi, 'Shōwa shoki no taishū goraku', *IW*, p. 76.
110 Beaven and Griffiths, 'The Blitz and Civilian Morale in Three Northern Cities', pp. 195–203; on 'soft' Manchester, see Beaven and Griffiths, 'The Blitz, Civilian Morale, and the City', p. 77.
111 Murata Eizō, 'Senzen / senchū no yakkyū to watashi', *IW*, p. 77.
112 Kushner, 'Laughter as Materiel'; Orbaugh, *Propaganda Performed*.
113 Kay, 'Leeds Permanent Building Society', 8 September 1940. Searle, 'Plumstead Baths and a Tragic Birthday'.
114 Penrose, correspondence, 2 May 1991.
115 Kaneya Seiichi, 'Shōwa shonen koro no "kodomo no asobi"', *IW*, p. 78.
116 Endō Naoe, 'Joshi teishintai', p. 175.
117 Latchford, *Swansea Wartime Diary*, p. 238 [20 February 1941].
118 Furuya Hama, untitled memoir, *FD*, pp. 86–87.
119 Bramwell, correspondence, 17 November 1940.

120 Maund, *Diary of a Bristol Woman,* p. 99 [21 January 1941]; also cited in *BSN,* p. 15.
121 Kojima Haru, 'Hi no akuma no kyūen', *HaK,* p. 61.
122 Maling, 'A Medical Student's Impressions', 25 August 1940.
123 Endō Naoe, 'Joshi teishintai', p. 176.
124 Fagnani, 'On Christmas Steps', *BSN,* p. 24 [24 November 1940].
125 Latchford, *The Wartime Swansea Diary,* p. 241 [21 February 1941].
126 Cliff Lachem, quoted in Reid, *Bristol Blitz,* p. 8.
127 Fagnani, 'On Christmas Steps', *BSN,* p. 24 [24 November 1940].
128 Shiba Isa, 'Yakedasarete', p. 39; Nakayama, 'Wa ga ie wa yakareta', p. 47.
129 Hares, 'A Broadmead Diary', p. 17 [3–4 January 1941].
130 Bloomfield, *Wartime Memoirs,* 14 November 1940.
131 Fukazawa Kōji, 'Nikki: shōhi', *SK,* pp. 170–171.
132 Sadler, correspondence, 19 November 1940.
133 Thornton, correspondence, 17 November 1940.
134 Crosby, 'Memories of the First Coventry Blitz', p. 1.
135 Peat, news clipping, 1991.
136 Williams and Middleton, correspondence, 1990 or 1991.
137 Iriye Hisae, 'Sensō: 35-nen no kūhaku no onna toshite', p. 183.
138 On insects: Baker, *A City in Flames,* p. 39; Amatsu Tsuyako, 'Shōidan 78-ppatsu rakka', *HaK,* p. 14. Only with the postwar introduction of DDT, Tsuyako wrote, were the Japanese able to supress the flea outbreaks.
139 Ueno Kōsaku, 'Shitai shori ni atatte', *KK,* pp. 94–97.
140 Hollingsworth, diary, 18–24 November 1940.
141 Maund, *Diary of a Bristol Woman,* 26 November and 3–4 December 1940.
142 Ishigami Michie, 'Gareki no naka no chōshoku', *SK,* pp. 84–85.
143 Dorothy Hughes, diary, 12 November and 22–23 December 1940.
144 Kenneth Holmes, diary, 3–4 August 1944.
145 Takahashi Aiko, diary, 4 January 1944.
146 Dorothy Hughes, diary, 22 December 1940.
147 Inohara Mitsuko, diary, 15, 21 July 1945.

Chapter 4

1 Dorothy Hughes, diary, 20 April 1940. Three days later, the bus conductor 'stroked' Dorothy's hair – which was, of course, unsolicited. 'Really', she wrote 'I don't know what to do with people sometimes'. For her passage on crying, see 18 December 1940, and 'mum', 2 January 1940.
2 Dorothy Hughes, diary, 2 January 1941.
3 Dora Mockett, diary, date unclear, possibly 8 June 1941.
4 Takahashi Aiko, diary, 10 March 1945.
5 Kenneth Holmes, diary, 26 December 1944.
6 Dorothy Hughes, diary, 13 December 1939 and 15 January 1940.
7 Kobayashi Takako, 'Onna bakari no hito-ya', p. 42.
8 Bell, *London War Ours,* Chapter 4, 'Children and the Family'.
9 Bertram Elwood, diary, 15 September 1941.
10 Katayama Ryūtarō, untitled memoir, *FD,* pp. 69–70.

11 Penny Summerfield, *Reconstructing Women's Wartime Lives*, p. 46.
12 Ono Kazuo, 'Machi ga moete masse'. Bissell, untitled memoir.
13 Maund, *Diary of a Bristol Woman*, 20 October and 2 December 1941.
14 Hollingsworth, undated entry at the end of her 1940 diary.
15 Piper, 'Air Raid Accommodation', 17–18 October and 23–24 December 1940.
16 Yoshida Takeshi, 'Ikite iru yō na haha no kao', *CK*, p. 327.
17 Anonymous, Topic Folders: Air Raids, Coventry.
18 Imamura Hajime, untitled memoir, *FD*, p. 87.
19 Burkey, *Boyhood Blitz*, p.29.
20 Watanabe Teruko, 'Shi o kakugo shita toki', *NK*, pp. 302–304.
21 Simmonds, 'Beneath the Stairs', *BSN*, p. 52.
22 Rice, *Sand in My Shoes*, p. 80.
23 Kogami Kōichi, 'Kūshū chokugo no senro no tensa', *HaK*, p. 187.
24 Haslewood, 'The Blitz on London', 8 September 1940.
25 Mizutani Shin'ichi, diary, *NKS*, p. 89.
26 Violet Maund's account of an unclaimed child: *Diary of a Bristol Woman*, 30 April 1942.
27 Watanabe Shige,'26-nenme no akuma no odori', p. 630.
28 Monck, diary, 9 September 1940. Six days later, on 10 January, she was 'panic-stricken' about going back.
29 Skea, diary, 1 February 1940. Other women felt freer: 'A kiss is a chaste and exciting and rather daring experience', wrote one Manchester girl, 'we wander safely wherever we wish and it never crosses our mind that we shall lose the war.' Byrne, 'Memories and Extracts', *WW*.
30 Elwood, diary, 22 September 1941.
31 Inagaki Masami, *Mō hitotsu no Hansen fu – senchū no rakugaki kaeuta ni miru* [Different kinds of anti-war music – graffiti and parodied songs] (Tokyo: Nihon tosho sentā, 1994), pp. 41–48, 65–82; cited in and translated by Koshiro, *Imperial Eclipse*, p. 37.
32 Iwakuri Yasuko, 'Hyōshi no chigireta nikki no nōto kara', *CK*, p. 60.
33 Barnet, untitled memoir.
34 Kogawa Saburō, diary, *HaK*, pp. 214–222. Once the air raids began in earnest over Hachiōji from about 6 July 1945, however, his diary demonstrated a greater emphasis on the destruction of the city.
35 Ault, 'Memories of the blitz'.
36 Takatori Minoru, 'Dendōki fukitobu' [An electric generator blown into the air] and Nakajima Eiji, *KuK*, pp. 34, 36.
37 Maund, *Diary of a Bristol Woman*, 17 March 1942.
38 Bosworth, untitled memoir.
39 Miyada Katsuyo, 'Taga jinja he nigeru', *HaK*, pp. 12–13.
40 Thornton, correspondence, 28 October 1940.
41 Kawamura Masako, 'Hachiōji daikūshū no kizuato', *HaK*, p. 80.
42 Cockerill, correspondence, 15 January 1941.
43 Brodie, 'From a Headmaster's Diary', *BSN*, p. 22 [24 November 1940].
44 Gishibe Ayako, 'Shikabane o koete', *CK*, p. 430.
45 Bloomfield, *Wartime Memoirs*, 14 November 1940 and 16 September 1941.

46 Kobayashi Takako, 'Onna bakari no hito-ya', p. 43.
47 Piper, *A Century of Service*, p. 67.
48 Regan, diary, p. 2 [early September 1940].
49 Nakayama Teruo, 'Wa ga ie wa yakareta', *HK*, pp. 47–49.
50 Maund, *Diary of a Bristol Woman*, 20 March 1941.
51 Dora Mockett, diary, 3 September 1941 [image 180].
52 Hares, 'A Broadmead Diary', p. 14 [4–5 December 1940].
53 Maund, *Diary of a Bristol Woman*, 10 January and 29 June 1942.
54 Takimi Hiroyuki, 'Baketsu ippai no mizu', *HaK*, pp. 53–54.
55 Haslewood, 'The Blitz on London', 14 September 1940.
56 Kobayashi Takako, 'Onna bakari no hito-ya', p. 43.
57 Yamada Kikue, 'Itsu ni nattara te ga dete kuru no?', *HaK*, pp. 84–85.
58 Maling, 'A Medical Student's Impressions', 15 September 1940.
59 Harima Toki, 'Kūshū de shinda tte shō ga nai', *SG65*, p. 85. Concerning wartime midwives and obstetrics in Shizuoka, also see accounts by Murakami Shigeru and Ōmoji Katsuko in this section.
60 Hoshi Tomoki, 'Isho o yabutte', *SF*, p. 55.
61 Regan, diary, 15 September 1940.
62 Summerfield, *Women Workers in the Second World War*, and Calder, *The Myth of the Blitz*.
63 Reid, *Bristol Blitz*, pp. 48–49.
64 Anonymous, Air Raids, Birmingham: Notes from Mary Baker.
65 Anonymous, Air Raids, Coventry.
66 Miller, *British Literature of the Blitz*, Chapters 1 and 2.
67 Rice, *Sand in My Shoes*, pp. 16, 37.
68 Mitchell, *Thought Control in Prewar Japan*; Barshay, *State and Intellectual in Imperial Japan*.
69 Kabu Imuo, untitled memoir, *FD*, pp. 77–78.
70 Yoshida, 'Chichi wa jibun no ie yori jinushi no ie o mamotta', p. 334.
71 Murai Kasako, 'Kikigaki: Tomo no itai ni beni o sashite', *CK*, pp. 205–208.
72 Peirse, diary, 7 April 1944. She was much happier in Ilkley, Yorkshire: 'It was like Paradise being there now'. 14 April 1944.
73 Brode, memoir, *SB*, pp. 14, 23.
74 Fox, 'Diary of Events'.
75 Kaneda Kyūgorō, 'Hidaruma no beiki', *TDK* v. 2, p. 385.
76 Iguma Junjirō, diary, *HaK*, p. 204.
77 Searle, 'It Made a Lot of Sense to Kill Skilled Workers', p. 118.
78 Cleaver, 'Blitz Memories', p. 1.
79 Naga Yohei, untitled memoir, *FD*, p. 74.
80 Elliott, 'Mazawattee Pocket Diary, 1940', 7 September 1940.
81 Akagi Ryōzō and Nakajima Eiji, 'Yatto keihō kaijo', *KuK*, p. 35.
82 Toshima Mitsuharu, diary, *TNK*, pp. 149–150.
83 Bennett, 'The February War Charlesworth Bodies'.
84 Monck, diary, 11 December 1940.
85 Owen, correspondence.
86 Ronald Coles, quoted in Reid, *Bristol Blitz*, p. 37.
87 Akagi Ryōzō, 'Bakugeki tōka 336-ppatsu', in *KuK*, p. 41.

88 Gerteis, *Gender Struggles*.
89 Regan, diary, pp. 23–24 [September1940].
90 Yamashita Toshitsugu, untitled memoir, *FD*, p. 76.
91 Maund, *Diary of a Bristol Woman*, 7 December 1940.
92 Iriye Hisae, 'Sensō: 35-nen no kūhaku no onna toshite', *TNK*.
93 Buchanan, correspondence, 25 November 1940.
94 Takizawa Toki, 'Otto no rusu o mamoritsuzukete', p. 26.
95 Robins, diary, see entries from 2 to 27 September 1940.
96 Metcalfe, correspondence, 17 May 1941.
97 Rose, *Which People's War?*; Miller, *British Literature*, Chapter 3; Summer-field, *Women Workers*; Frühstück and Walthall, *Recreating Japanese Men*.
98 Lord, memoir, pp. 33, 35–36, 41.
99 Satō Ichio, 'Osanai koro kara heitai-san no shibō', *SF*, p. 48.
100 Ivy Barnes, untitled memoir, *MW*.
101 Peat, correspondence and news clipping, 9 May 1991.
102 Nakajima Shigeya, 'Hachiōji kūshū to shōbōdan', in *HaK*, p. 186.
103 Monck, diary, 10 September 1940.
104 Metcalfe, correspondence, 18 March 1941.
105 Gishibe Ayako, 'Shikabane o koete', *CK*, p. 429.
106 As related in Bertram Elwood's diary, 11 September 1941.
107 Randall, 'One Night of Hell', 3–4 May 1941, 1:45am.
108 Ozaki Aiko, 'Nakitomo no nōkan ni', in *CK*, pp. 164–165.
109 Fujii Tadatoshi, *Kokubō fujinkai*.
110 Piper, 'Air Raid Accommodation/Memoranda Minute Book', particularly entries for October 1940.
111 Bloomfield, *Wartime Memoirs*, 14 October 1940.
112 Kawano Yoshiko, '6-gatsu 9-ka: nikki kara', *NKS* 5, p.15.
113 Arai Takako, 'Mune ni ana ga aita', *TS* v. 2, pp. 47–48, emphasis in original text. Also see Miyake, 'Doubling Expectations', pp. 267–295.
114 Price, 'Spirit of Youth', *BSN*, p 48.
115 Koike Kinu, 'Kūshūgo', *NK*, p. 77.
116 Ogawa Takashi, diary, p. 21.
117 Peirse, diary, 22 September 1944.
118 Inoue Senri, untitled memoir, *FD*, pp. 71–72.
119 Donald, diary, 5 September 1940.
120 Miller, *British Literature*, p. 88.
121 Haslewood, 'The Blitz on London', 28 September 1940.
122 Alice (Mrs.), untitled memoir, *MW*.
123 Turner, untitled memoir, *MW*.
124 Elwood, diary, 8 September 1941.
125 Hughes, diary, 17 March 1941.
126 Calder, *The People's War*, p. 396.
127 Gordon, *The Evolution of Labor Relations in Japan*, pp. 257–298.
128 Morizaki Azuma, introduction, in *Isho*.
129 Takahashi Aiko, diary, 27 March 1943, 15 April 1945.
130 Hughes, diary, 19–20 March and 29 November 1941.

Conclusion

1 Hasegawa Tetsuo, 'Senchi kara no isho mo kaijin ni', *SG65*, pp. 44–45.
2 Yoshimi, *Grassroots Fascism*; Samuel Yamashita, *Daily Life in Wartime Japan*, pp. 11–34.
3 Cox, 'London War Diary', 10 February 1940.
4 Byrne, 'Memories and Extracts', *WW*.
5 Geoffrey Field, 'Social Patriotism', pp. 20–39; Ambaras, *Bad Youth*, pp. 166–181. See also Saitō Tsutomu's discussion of mobilised youth labour working to rule or walking off the floor in *Tōkyō-to gakuto kinrō dōin*, pp. 380–384.
6 Cripps, *The Struggle for Peace*, p. 38.
7 Eley, 'Finding the People's War', pp. 818–838.
8 E.P. Thomson, *Writing by Candlelight*. London: Merlin, 1980, p. 130; quoted in Noakes and Pattinson, 'Introduction', p. 11.
9 Noda Masaaki, *Sensō to zaiseki*.
10 Quoted in Powles, 'Abe Isoo', pp. 159–160.
11 Anderson, *Fascists, Communists, and the National Government*.
12 See discussion in Lukowitz, 'British Pacifists and Appeasement', pp. 115–127.
13 Quoted in Rempel, 'The Dilemmas of British Pacifists', p. D1214.
14 Overy, *The Bombing War*, p. 182.
15 Brodie, 'From a Headmaster's Diary', 1943, p. 23.
16 Yamashita Toshitsugu, untitled memoir, *FD*, p. 76.
17 Robins, diary, 23 September 1940.
18 Ronald Schaffer quoting Major General Frederick L. Anderson, in Schaffer, 'The Bombing Campaigns', p. 42.
19 Cottrell, correspondence, 18 November 1940.
20 Iketani Toyoko, 'Teki nagara utsukushii shōnen', p. 642.
21 Yamashita, *Leaves from an Autumn of Emergencies*, p. 89.
22 Pratt, 'War Diary', 9 August 1942.
23 Kimura Genzaemon, *Nicchū sensō shussei nikki*, 24 September 1937.
24 Hughes, diary, 23 November 1941.
25 Skea, diary, 23 October 1939. Also see 3 December 1939, when Skea insists on the humanity of German people.
26 Haslewood, 'The Blitz on London', 10 October 1940.
27 Latchford, *Swansea Wartime Diary*, p. 232 [11 February 1941].
28 Takahashi Aiko, diary, 10 June 1943.
29 Smith, diary, 2 July 1940 [pp. 12–13]. Such views were expressed in many British cities, including Liverpool, as Dorothy Hughes recorded in her diary: 'I think it's awful to think of Germans starving, and being led astray, even if they are our enemies'. Hughes, diary, 3 November 1939.
30 Tada Susumu, 'Kūshūka no keisatsukan', pp. 80–81.
31 Zwigenberg, *Hiroshima*.
32 Anonymous, 'An Editorial', pp. 1–4.
33 Havens, *Fire across the Sea*.

34 For a contemporary account by an activist, see Percival, 'The Other Way', pp. 7–8. For more on the historical use of these powers, see Townshend, *Making the Peace*.

35 Maund, *Diary of a Bristol Woman*, 11 November 1941.

36 Ball, *The Conservative Party*, pp. 103–108.

37 Tomihisa Taue, 'Nagasaki Peace Declaration 2013' [accessed 16 January 2014].

38 Elwood, diary, 1 September 1941.

39 Hollingsworth, undated entry at the end of her 1940 diary.

40 See the arguments in Taiheiyō sensō zenkoku kūbaku giseisha irei kyōkai, ed., *Heiwa no inori*.

41 Kobayashi Takako, 'Onna bakari no hito-ya', p. 45.

42 Glover, diary, 12 November 1941.

43 Kynaston, *Austerity Britain*, p. 21.

44 Some cities, such as Aomori and Nagoya, have put more in print by producing inexpensive journals. These can be difficult to obtain, however, and have a very limited circulation. For Tokyo, see *TDK*.

45 Owen, correspondence, probably 1991.

46 Dietmar Süss, *Death from the Skies*, p. 533.

47 Naylor, 'A Blind Man's War Experience', probably 1991.

48 Mockett, diary, 13 July 1941.

49 Yamagoe Yone, 'Shuki', *CK*, pp. 194–195.

50 Yamaki Mikiko, 'Sensō wa shi sono mono', *SF*, pp. 62–63.

51 Latchford, *Swansea Wartime Diary*, p. 240 [21 February 1941].

52 Dodman, correspondence, 21 November 1940.

53 Tillman, *Whirlwind*, p. 25, and Biddle, 'Dresden 1945', p. 428.

54 Biddle, *Rhetoric and Reality*.

55 Grayling, *Among the Dead Cities*, pp. 245–246.

56 Bloxham, 'Dresden as a War Crime', pp. 180–208.

57 Dower, *War without Mercy*.

58 Hamabe Mitsuru, 'E-nikki', 1945.

59 Quoted in Anastaplo, *Reflections on Life, Death, and the Constitution*, p. 84.

60 Elwood, diary, 13 October 1941.

61 Trent, 'Diary of the Admiralty Islands Campaign', 3 March 1944.

62 Fagnani, 'On Christmas Steps', *BSN*, p. 24 [25 November 1940].

63 Lieutenant Watanabe, diary, 17 March 1942.

64 Elwood, diary, 13 October 1941.

65 For more on the opposition to the use of the bomb, see Alperowitz, *The Decision to Use the Atomic Bomb*.

66 See Yamashita, *Leaves from an Autumn of Emergency* and *Daily Life in Wartime Japan*; Katarzyna Cwiertka, *Food and War*.

67 Hasegawa, *Racing the Enemy*; Koshiro, 'Racing the Enemy (review)'.

68 Hollingsworth, diary, 20 May 1940.

69 Satō Keiji, 'Shutsujin gakuto sōkōkai', *IW*, p. 81.

70 Koide Toshio, 'Nihonjin dōshi', p. 147.

Bibliography

Some of the short, undated, and unnamed manuscript memoirs in local British archives were originally collected for past memorial projects, particularly during the fifty-year anniversary of the first air raids over Britain, 1990–1991. I therefore acknowledge the hard work of those who studied the subject before me:

a. Coventry History Centre: Sue White of the Coventry Centre for Performing Arts
b. Hull History Centre: Tom Houlton, Hull historian, and Peter Adamson for BBC Radio Humberside.

Abbreviations for Collections

BL	British Library
CHC	Coventry History Centre
HHC	Hull History Centre
IWM	Imperial War Museum (London)
MCL	Manchester Central Library
LMA	London Metropolitan Archives
M-O	Mass Observation Archives, University of Sussex
OIPM	Osaka International Peace Museum
PC	Personal Correspondence/Collection

Abbreviations for Edited Volumes

AK   Aomori kūshū o kiroku suru kai, ed. *Jidai e no shōgen: Aomori kūshū 61–67 shūnen / taikensha no kiroku* [Testimony for the Ages: 61st to 67th Anniversaries of the Aomori Air Raids] v.17–21. Aomori: Self-published, 2006–2012.

BB   John Dike, ed. *Bristol Blitz Diary*. Bristol: Redcliffe, 1982 (BL).

BSN   Paul Shipley, ed. *Bristol Siren Nights*. Bristol: Redcliffe Press, 1943 (BL).

CK   Chiba-shi kūshū o kiroku suru kai, ed. *Chiba-shi kūshū no kiroku* [Records of the Chiba City Air Raids]. Chiba: Self-published, 1980.

FD   Etō Hide, ed. *Fukuoka daikūshū* [Fukuoka Air Raids]. Fukuoka: Nishi Nihon Shinbunsha, 1974.

GSK   Zenkoku sokai gakudō renraku kyōgikai, ed. *Gakudō sokai no kiroku* [Records of Student Evacuations]. Tokyo: Ōzorasha, 1994.

HK   Himeji kūshū o kataritsugu-kai, ed. *Himeji kūbaku no kiroku* [Records of the Bombing of Himeji], v.1–2. Himeji: Self-published, 1989.

HaK   Hachiōji-shi kyōdo shiryōkan, ed. *Hachiōji no kūshū to sensai no kiroku* [A Record of the Hachiōji Air Raids and War Damage], v.1–3. Hachiōji: Self-published, Hachiōji-shi kyōiku iinkai, 1985.

IW   Iwate kenritsu hakubutsukan, ed. *Jūgo no kurashi: senzen / senchū no Iwate* [Life on the Home Front: Pre-War and Wartime Iwate]. Morioka: Self-published, 1995.

KK   Kōfu-shi sensaishihen-san iinkai, ed. *Kōfu kūshū no kiroku* [Records of the Kōfu Air Raids]. Kōfu: Self-published, 1974.

KuK   Chūgoku shinbun Kure shisha, ed. *Kure kūshūki* [A Record of the Kure Air Raids]. Hiroshima: Chūgoku shinbunsha, 1979, 2nd edition.

MW   *Manchester at War*. Manchester: Self-published (MCL 942 733 Ma).

NDK   Hamada Ryūji, Mainichi shinbunsha, ed. *Nagoya daikūshū* [Nagoya Air Raids]. Tokyo: Mainichi shinbunsha, 1971.

NK   Minemura Tsuyoshi, ed. *Nagaoka kūshū: 60-nin no shōgen* [The Nagaoka Air Raids: Testimonies from 60 People]. Shiga: Kōkodō shoten, 2004.

NKS   Nagoya kūshū o kiroku suru kai, ed. *Nagoya kūshūshi* [Journal of the Nagoya Air Raids], v.1–8 (February 1977–August 1979).

SB   Anthony Bode, ed. *The Southampton Blitz*. Newbury: Countryside Books, 1982.

SF   Fukushima kenritsu hakubutsukan, ed. *Sensōka no Fukushima* [Fukushima at War]. Aizu-Wakamatsu: Self-published, 1996.

SGS   Shinagawa rekishikan, ed. *Shinagawa no gakudō shūdan sokai shiryōshū* [A Collection of Documents on the Mass Student Evacuations of Shinagawa Ward, Tokyo]. Tokyo: Self-published, 1988.

SG65   Shizuoka heiwa shiryōkan o tsukuru-kai, ed. *Sengo 65-nen no*
        tsuioku [Memories 65 Years after the War]. Shizuoka: Self-
        published, 2010.
SK   Shizuoka-shi kūshū o kiroku suru kai, ed. *Shizuoka-shi kūshū*
        no kiroku [Record of Shizuoka Air Raids]. Shizuoka: Self-
        Published, 1974.
STS   Satō Kiyo, ed. *Sensō to shomin, 1940–1949* [War and Ordinary
        People], v.3. Tokyo: Asahi shinbunsha, 1995.
TDK   Tōkyō daikūshū o kiroku suru kai, ed. *Tōkyō daikūshū /*
        sensaishi: Tomin no kūshū taiken kirokushū [The Air War on
        Tokyo / Record of War Damage: Records of Urban Citizens'
        Bombing Experiences], v.1–5. Tokyo: Self-published, 1975.
TK   Sasaki Hisaharu, ed. *Tsuchizaki-kō hibaku shimin kaigi*
        [Citizens' Association for Bombing Victims in the Port of
        Tsuchizaki], *Shōgen: Tsuchizaki kūshū* [Testimony: Tsuchizaki
        air raids]. Akita: Mumyō shuppan, 1992.
TNK   Takamatsu City, ed. *Takamatsu no kūshū: shuki-hen* [The
        Takamatsu Air Raids: Personal Records Edition]. Takamatsu:
        Self-published by municipal government, 1973.
TS   Ide Magoroku et al., eds. *Taiheiyō sensō to Shinshū* [Nagano
        and the Pacific War], v.1–3. Nagano: Issōsha shuppan, 2005.
WK   Wadatsumi-kai, ed. *Heiwa e no isho / ihinten: Senbotsu seinen to*
        no taiwa [Exhibition of Artefacts and Last Testaments for
        Peace: A Dialogue with Wartime Fallen Youth]. Tokyo: Self-
        published, 2002.
WW   *Women at War and Manchester Memories.* Manchester: Self-
        published (MCL: 940 5315 Wo (475)).

Primary Literature

Akagi Ryōzō. 'Yatto keihō kaijo' [At last, the all-clear] and 'Bakugeki tōka 336-
    ppatsu' [336 Bombs Dropped], in *KuK.*
Akiyama Shigeko. 'Mada mitsukaranai sobo' [My Paternal Grandmother Still
    Cannot Be Found], in *TNK.*
Albrighton (Mrs.). *Memoir of Coventry blitz,* 20 March 1990 (CHC, 1456/3).
Allen (Mrs.). 'The Beetroot', *BSN.*
Allison, E. K. *Correspondence* (HHC DMX/242/6).
Amatsu Tsuyako. 'Shōidan 78-ppatsu rakka' [Under 78 Incendiary Bombs], in
    HaK v.3.
Andō Toyoko. 'B-29 80-ki ga raishū' [80 B-29s Attack], in *KuK.*
Anonymous. Mass Observation Records (Air Raids and Evacuations):

    Air Raids, Coventry. Topic Folders (M-O, SxMOA1/2/25/8/T).
    Air Raids, Bradford. Topic Folders (M-O, SxMOA1/2/23/8/6).

Air Raids, Bristol. Topic Folders (M-O, SxMOA1/1/2/23/8/E).
Air Raids, Birmingham. Topic Folders (M-O, SxMOA1/1/2/23/8/E).
Air Raids, Manchester. Topic Folders, 'Notes on the Effects of Air Raids on People in Manchester' (SxMOA1/2/23/10/A).
'WRL Report 19, Ealing Spiritualist Church' (M-O, SxMOA1/2/S/1/A, TCS/1/A).
'Notes on evacuation of children' (M-O, SxMOA1/2/S/1/A, TCS/1/A).
'Further Instruction for Teachers and Helpers of School Parties', 31 August 1939 (M-O, SxMOA1/2/S/1/A, TCS/1/A).

'Memories of the War' (CHC, PA 1456/2).
'The Bad Days of the War' (CHC, 1456/4).
'Memories of the blitz' (CHC, 1656/3/1).
Unsigned letter, probably 1991 (HHC, DMX/242/5).
St. Thomas' Hospital memoir (LMA, H01/ST/4/086/003).
Aojima Tokuji. 'Kūshū chokugo no shokryō haikyū gyōmu' [The task of food distribution after air attacks], in SK.
Aoki Shige. 'Shizuoka yūbinkyoku enjō' [The Shizuoka Post Office in Flames], in SK.
Arai Takako, 'Mune ni ana ga aita: Joshi teishintaiin no kiroku' [A Hole in the Heart: Records of the Young Women's Volunteer Corps], in TS v.2.
Ault, Jo. 'Memories of the blitz' (CHC, PA 1456/5).
Baker, Esther. A City in Flames: A Firewoman's Recollections of the Hull Blitz. Beverley: Hutton Press, 1992.
Barnes, Ivy. Untitled memoir, in MW.
Barnet, E. (Mrs.). Untitled memoir (CHC PA 1456/8).
Beale, Joseph. 'Memories of the First Coventry Blitz' (CHC PA 1456/8).
Belsey, John and Elizabeth. Correspondence, in Harris, Blitz Diary.
Bennett (Mr.). 'The February War Charlesworth Bodies' (CHC PA 1456/4).
Berkeley, Ballard. Special Constable in London, in Joshua Levine, ed. Forgotten Voices of the Blitz and the Battle for Britain. London: Ebury Press, 2006.
Bissell (Mrs.). Untitled memoir (CHC PA 1456/12).
Bloomfield, Mary. 'War Stories' and Wartime Memoirs of Mary Bloomfield (IWM 77/177/1).
Bonham (Mrs.). Untitled memoir (CHC PA 1456/13).
Bosworth (nee Freke), Barbara. Untitled memoir (CHC PA 1450/14).
Bovill, Patricia Ann. Correspondence (HHC DMX/242/6).
Bramwell, John. Correspondence (CHC PA 1430/1/1).
Brittain, Vera. Testament of Youth: An Autobiographical Study of the Years 1900–1925. London: Victor Gollancz Ltd., 1940.
Brode, Anthony. Memoir, in SB.
Brode, Sylvia. 'The Leg of Mutton', in SB.
Brodie, Marjorie. Untitled memoir (CHC PA 1456/15).
Brodie, M. E. 'From a Headmaster's Diary', BSN.
Brownbill, C. Diary (IWM 88/49/1).
Bryan, Heather. 'War Memories', in MW.
Buchanan, Willy. Correspondence, 25 November 1940 (CHC PA2921/1).

Burkey, William B. *Boyhood Blitz*. Self-Published, 2012.

Byrne, Daphne. 'Memories and Extracts from a Land Girl's Diary, 1944–1945', in *WW*.

Castle, E., ed. *We're All in the Battle*. Coventry: City of Coventry, Self-Published, 1988 (CHC).

Cleaver, R. W. 'Blitz Memories' (CHC PA 1456/14).

Cockerill (Mrs.). Correspondence, 15 January 1941 (CHC PA 1274/1).

Coleman, M. (Mrs.). 'A Warden's Wife', *BSN*.

Coles, Marguerite E. 'Personal evacuation (with school children)' (letter, HHC DMX/242/4).

Compton, D. M. (Mrs.). Memoir (CHC PA 1656/18).

Cottrell, Dick. Correspondence (CHC, PA 1215/1).

Cox, Gwladys. 'London War Diary, 1939–1945' (IWM 86/46/1).

Craddock, W. 'St. Stephen's Boy's School, Diary 1940' (CHC PA 2945/1).

Cripps, Stafford. *The Struggle for Peace*. London: Victor Gollancz, 1936.

Crosby, T. ed. 'Memories of the First Coventry Blitz', 6 June 1990 (CHC PA 1456/21).

Daniel (nee Harper), Rita. Correspondence (HHC DMX/242/4).

Davies, A. E. (Mr.). Memoir, in *BB*.

Davies, H. 'Bombed in Four Hospitals', in *BSN*.

De Asis, Leocadio. *From Bataan to Tokyo: Diary of a Filipino Student in Wartime Japan, 1943–1944*, Grant K. Goodman, ed. Lawrence: University of Kansas Press, Center for East Asian Studies, 1979.

Dent, T. Correspondence, undated post-war memoir [probably 1991] (HHC DMX/242/6).

Dodman, Howard. Correspondence (CHC, PA 1464/1/1).

Donald, Patricia Maxine. Diary (IWM 89/14/1).

Dorrinton, J. W. Memoir, in *BB*.

Elliott, Joan. 'Mazawattee Pocket Diary, 1940' (IWM 72/33/1).

Elwood, Bertram. Diary (M-O).

Endō Naoe. 'Joshi teishintai' [The Young Women's Volunteer Units], in *SK*.

Fagnani, M. 'On Christmas Steps', in *BSN*.

Fox, Levi. 'Diary of Events' (CHC PA 2684/1/3/2).

Fuchikami Akira. 'Yakenokori no ki' [A record of burned remains], in *HaK* v.3.

Fujii Hiroshi, Fujii Aiko, and Koshinaka Tanitarō. 'Keibōdan no hibaku shori kara' [From Civil Defence Units contending with the blasts], in *TK*.

Fujimoto Kinuko. Diary, in *HaK* v.3.

Fukazawa Kōji. 'Nikki: shōhi' [Diary: extinguishing fires], in *SK*.

Furuya Hama. Untitled memoir, in *FD*.

Gishibe Ayako. 'Shikabane o koete' [Climbing over the bodies], in *CK*.

Glover, G. F. Diary (M-O).

Goodridge, Frederick. 'When Is It Going to Stop?' in *SB*.

Hamabe Mitsuru. 'E-nikki' [picture diary], 1945 (PC).

Hares, W. A. 'A Broadmead Diary', in *BSN*.

Harima Toki. 'Kūshū de shinda tte shō ga nai' [If we die in the raid, so be it], in *SG65*.

Harvey, Pamela. 'War Years', in *MW*.

Hasegawa Tetsuo. 'Senchi kara no isho mo kaijin ni' [A letter from the battlefield, lost in a burnt-out husk], in *SG65*.

Haslewood, I. S. 'The Blitz on London, 1940' (IWM 04/40/1).

Hirai Kiyoshi. Diary, in *WK*.

Hiraoka Tsutomu. 'Hayase chiku (Ondo) ni bakugeki' [Bombs in the Hayase area (Ondo)], in *KuK*.

Hollingsworth, Gladys A. 'Charles Lett's Diary 1940' (IWM 82/19/1).

Holmes, Kenneth. Diary (IWM, P129).

Hoshi Tomoki. 'Isho o yabutte' [Tearing up the letter of farewell], in *SF*.

Hughes, Dorothy, Diary.

Humphries, Eleanor. Diary (M-O).

Ichikawa Shōjirō. 'Wasurerarenai makka na hi' [An unforgettable red flame], in *HK*.

Iguma Junjirō. Diary, in *HaK* v.3.

Ikebe Toshiaki. 'Kūshū ni matowaru omoide' [Memories wrapped up in the bombing], in *AK* v.21.

Ikeda Kikue, 'Asa no bakufū' [An explosion's blast in the morning], in *TNK*.

Iketani Toyoko. 'Teki nagara utsukushii shōnen' [He's the enemy, but a beautiful lad], in *TDK* v.2.

Imamura Hajime. Untitled memoir, in *FD*.

Inaba Fuku. 'Shuki: isshun ni kita jigoku' [Notebook: Hell came in one second], in *CK*.

Inohara Mitsuko. 'Dōin nikki' (Mobilization diary), in *Tojōryō no shojotachi* [The girls of Tojō dormitory]. Osaka: Self-Published, 1991 (OIPM).

Inoue Haruko and Fukubu Miyoko. 'Watashi no taiken' [My experience], in *NDK*.

Inoue Masako. 'Kōshūkaidō wa hi no kawa' [The Kōshūkaidō was a river of fire], in *HaK* v.3.

Inoue Senri. Untitled memoir, in *FD*.

Inoue Tamiko. '1-jo gakusei no nikki yori' [From a diary by a girls' high school freshman], in *TDK* v.2.

Iriye Hisae. 'Sensō: 35-nen no kūhaku no onna toshite' [War: as a woman, 35 empty years], in *TNK*.

Ishigami Michie. 'Gareki no naka no chōshoku' [Breakfast in the ruins], in *SK*.

Ishikawa Chieko. 'Gakuto kinrō dōin nikki yori' [From the diary of a student labour conscript], in *CK*.

Itō [nee Takahashi] Eiko. 'Shōidan tōka no naka de seimei o toritomete' [My life was spared from the incendiary bombs], in *CK*.

Itoi Sayoko. 'B-29 80-ki ga raishū' [80 B-29s attack], in *KuK*.

Iwakuri (nee Tamura) Yasuko. 'Hyōshi no chigireta nikki no nōto kara' [Notes from a diary with a frayed cover], in *CK*.

Johnson, H. E. Correspondence, 10 April 1991 (HHC DMX/242/6).

Kabu Imuo. Untitled memoir, in *FD*.

Kahn, Dorothy Mary Isabel. 'Exercise Book' (IWM 88/10/1).

Kaneda Kyūgorō. 'Hidaruma no beiki (nikki yori)' [An American plane in a ball of fire (diary excerpt)], in *TDK* v.2.

Kaneyama Misao. 'Jitensha de nigete' [Fleeing by bicycle], in *TDK* v.2.

Katayama Ryūtarō. Untitled memoir, in *FD*.

Kent, D. H. 'Collins Diamond Diary 1941' (IWM 99/9/1).

Kanenaka Kimi. 'Dannen ni sagasedo (nikki yori)' [I searched as hard as I could (diary excerpt)], in *TNK* v.2.

Kaneya Seiichi. 'Shōwa shonen koro no "kodomo no asobi,"' in *IW*.

Katō Hideo. 'Kikansha ni kijū sōsha' [Strafed by machine guns in a train], in *HK*.

Kawahata Ichirō. 'Kūshū zengō no Katakura kaiwai no kurashi' [Life in Katakura before and after the air raids], in *HaK* v.3.

Kawamura Masako. 'Hachiōji daikūshū no kizuato' [Scars of the Hachiōji air raids], *HaK* v.3.

Kawano Yoshiko. '6-gatsu 9-ka: nikki kara' [9th June: from my diary], in *NKS* 5 (May 1978).

Kay, John. 'Leeds Permanent Building Society' [diary] (IWM 09/31/1).

Kimura Genzaemon. Nicchū sensō shussei nikki *[Sino-Japanese War service diary]*. Akita: Mumyō shuppan, 1982.

Kirai Toshiko. 'Honō to ningen to' [The people and the flames], in *TNK*.

Kobayashi Narimitsu. 'Nikki: shiritsu icchū no bakugeki' [Diary: Shizuoka City Middle School's bombing], in *SK*.

Kobayashi Takako. 'Onna bakari no hito-ya' [The women's night], in *HK*.

Kogami Kōichi. 'Kūshū chokugo no senro no tensa' [Inspecting the roads directly after an air raid], in *HaK* v.3.

Kogawa Kōtarō. 'Yami kara mo kuroi shōshitai' [Even in the dark, burned corpses], in *SK*.

Kogawa Saburō. Diary, in *HaK* v.3.

Koide Toshio. 'Nihonjin dōshi' [We're all Japanese], in *TDK* v.1.

Koike Kinu. 'Kūshūgo, haha wa musuko no na o sakebitsuzuketa' [After the air raid, a mother screamed for her son], in *NK*.

Kojima Haru, 'Hi no akuma no kyūen' [A feast for fire demons], in *HaK* v.3.

Kojima Yoshitaka. *Guriko nikki: boku no mita Taiheiyō sensō* [Glico diary: the Pacific War that I saw]. Tokyo: Gakuseisha, 1995.

Koide Keiko. 'Tachikirareta kokoro' [The feeling of being cut off], in *TDK* v.2.

Last, Nella. *Nella Last's War: The Second World War Diaries of a 'Housewife, 49'*. London: Profile Books, 2006.

Latchford, Laurie. *The Swansea Wartime Diary of Laurie Latchford, 1940–1941*, Kate Elliott Jones and Wendy Cope, ed. Newport: South Wales Record Society, 2010.

Leslie, S. C. 'This Was Your Victory', in *Bombers over Merseyside*. Liverpool: Daily Post and Echo, Ltd., 1943 [no pagination].

Lord, D. Memoir (IWM 91/19/1).

Maling, D. B. (Dr.). 'A Medical Student's Impressions of the Bombing of St. Thomas's in 1940' (LMA, H01/ST/4/086/002).

Maloney, R. (Mrs.). Correspondence (SxMOA1/2/23/10/A).

Matthews, Gwendoline. 'Memo' ['War Diary, 1939-'] (CHC PA 2928/1).

Matsubara Kijirō, 'Shizuka na machi ga' [The quiet town ...], *TNK*.

Matsubayashi Hana. 'Junshoku shita 8-mei no shiritsu byōin kangofu' [Eight nurses of Shizuoka municipal hospital who died in the line of duty], in *SG65*.

Matsuda Haruko, 'Fuhatsu no shōidan no oozutsu ga watashi no ie ni tsukisa-satta' [A dud firebomb ripped through our house], *NK*, p. 91

Matsui Ryūichirō, 'Chichi no nikki ni tōji o shinobu' [Remembering the war in dad's diary], *SK*.

Maund, Violet A. *Diary of a Bristol Woman, 1938–1945*. Ilfracombe, Devon: Arthur Stockwell, 1950 (IWM/BL).

Melkins, Mrs. 'A Child's Prayer', in *BSN*.

Merrill, Eva. *Looking Back: Reflections of a London Child on the War Years, 1939–1945*. Bloomington, IN: Author House, 2013.

Metcalfe, Olive. Correspondence (HHC C DICN/1/2).

Miyada Katsuyo, 'Taga-jinja e nigeru' [Fleeing to Taga Shrine], in *HaK* v.3.

Miyazawa Keikichi. Diary, *HaK* v.3.

Mizutani Shin'ichi. Diary, *NK*.
    Diary, *NKS* v.4 (Jan 1978).

Mizutani Teruko. 'Kōka no naka ni nao seimei arite' [There was life after the world burned], in *SG65*.

Mockett, Dora. 'Water Lily Stationary' [Diary] (HHC DIJG/1/3).

Mochizuki Masako, 'Dōkoku no hibi' [Days of lamentation], in *TNK*, v.2.

Monck, H. B. Diary (M-O).

Moriuchi Masashi. 'Shōwa shoki no taishū goraku' [Early Shōwa popular enter-tainment], in *IW*.

Morizaki Azuma, introduction, in Morizaki Minato, *Isho* [Final Testament]. Tokyo: Tosho shuppansha, 1971.

Muramatsu Naka. Untitled memoir, *FD*.

Murata Eizō. 'Senzen / senchū no yakkyū to watashi' [Pre-war / wartime baseball and myself], in *IW*.

Murai Kasako. 'Kikigaki: Tomo no itai ni beni o sashite' [Oral record: Putting lipstick on a friend's body], in *CK*.

Murphy, Edward. Letter, 6 May 1991 (HHC DMX/242/5).

Naga Yohei. Untitled memoir, in *FD*.

Nagi Katsumi. 'Go-shintai to tomo ni' [With the physical representation of our god], in *SK*.

Nakajima Kikue. Untitled memoir, in *KuK*.

Nakajima Shigeya. 'Hachiōji kūshū to shōbōdan' [The raids on Hachiōji and fire-fighting units], in *HaK*.

Nakayama Teruo, 'Wa ga ie wa yakareta' [Our house burned down], in *HK*.

Naylor, Ann. 'A Blind Man's War Experience', undated correspondence, prob-ably 1991 (HHC, DMX/242/4).

Narita Kazuko. 'Aomori no kūshū no kioku' [Memories of the Aomori air raid], *AK* v.21.

Narita Shigeru. Untitled memoir, in *NDK*.

Nibu Akiko. 'Sokai jidō o tsurete' [Leading the evacuees], in *KK*.

Noda Tsuru. 'Go-shin'ei o mamoru' [Defending the Imperial Portrait], in *SK*.

Nōso Masaichi. 'Ekichō toshite' [As a station manager], in *TNK*.

Nunobiki Junji. 'Shōidan no osoroshisa' [The terror of incendiaries], in *HaK* v.3.

Ogawa Takashi. Diary, in *NKS* 6.

Ōi Masao. 'Watashi wa mita' [I saw it], in *NDK*.

Okamoto Masao. 'Senshōdō nisshi' [Path to Victory Diary], in *TNK*.

Okamura Toshiyasu. 'Akai mōfubuki' [A red blizzard], in *SK*.

Ōmura Seitarō. 'Hi no umi' [A sea of flame], in *FD*.

Ono Kazuo. 'Machi ga moete masse' [The town is burning], in *TNK*.

Orwell, George. 'Looking Back on the Spanish Civil War', *New Road*. London: 1943.

Osborne (Mrs.). 'A Baker-Hero', *BSN*.

Owen, A. Correspondence, probably 1991 (HHC, DMX/242/6).

Ōyama Hidenori. Diary, in Akatsuka Yasuo, ed. *Ōsaka no gakudō sokai* [The mass student evacuation of Osaka]. Tokyo: Kurietibu 21, 1996.

Ozaki Aiko. 'Nakitomo no nōkan ni' [Dead friends into their coffins], in *CK*.

Peat, Raymond. Undated news interview and news clipping, probably 1991 (HHC DMX/242/6); correspondence, 7 May 1991 (HHC DMX/242/5).

Penrose, A. Correspondence (HHC DMX/242/3).

Perry, Colin. *Boy in the Blitz: The 1940 Diary of Colin Perry*. Stroud: Sutton Publishing, 2000.

Peirse, Edith Christabel. Diary (HHC DFPE/1/1/32; HHC DFPE/1/1/22).

Piper, C. A. 'Liverpool Unitarian Mission Air Raid Shelter Diary, 1940–1941' and 'Air Raid Accommodation / Memoranda Minute Book' (IWM Misc102/Item 1589).

A Century of Service: The Story of the Liverpool North End Domestic Mission Society's First Hundred Years, 1859–1959. Liverpool: Self-published, 1959.

Pratt, J. L. 'War Diary' (M-O).

Price, C. (Mr.). 'Spirit of Youth', in *BSN*.

Randall, A. E. 'One Night of Hell: Extract of AFS man, night of Merseyside's big Blitz, 3–4 May 1941' (IWM P76).

Regan, William Bernard. Untitled diary (IWM 88/10/1).

Reid, Helen. *Bristol Blitz: The Untold Story*. Bristol: Redcliffe, 1988.

Rice, Joan. *Sand in My Shoes: Coming of Age in the Second World War, A WAAF's Diary*. London: Harper Perennial, 2006.

Rich (Mr.). 'From a Bedminster Warden', in *BSN*.

Robins, G. (Mrs.). Diary (IWM 9/68/1).

Sadler, Marcus. Correspondence (CHC: PA 2914/1).

Sakai Jun. '"Sensō wa makeru" to iu uwasa' [Rumour has it 'we will lose the war'], in *SF*.

Sakazume Hiromi. 'Tōchan wa ikite ita' [My father was alive], in *TDK* v.1.

Sakurai Shizuko. 'Haka no naka no shōnetsu jigoku' [The flames of hell inside a grave], in *SK*.

Sano Tatsuo. 'Shizuoka ni hajimete kūshū ga atta hi' [The first day Shizuoka was bombed], in *SG65*.

Satō Fujie and Satō Makoto, 'Senaka ni bakudan no kizu o se-otte' [Carrying a wound from a bomb in my back], in *TK*.

Satō Ichio, 'Osanai koro kara heitai-san no shibō' [I wanted to be a soldier from an early age], in *SF*.

Satō Keiji. 'Shutsujin gakuto sōkōkai' [Rally for the student soldiers], in *IW*.

Searle, Ellen. 'Plumstead Baths and a Tragic Birthday', submitted to the BBC's 'WW2 People's War', 22 June 2004 [www.bbc.co.uk/history/ww2peoples war/stories/32/a2769032.shtml, accessed 12 July 2013].

Sekiya Tsuneo, 'Haha o seotte' [Carrying mom on my back], in *HaK* v.3.

Senuma Yukiko. 'Hachiōji kūshū to haha no shi' [The bombing of Hachiōji and my mother's death], in *HaK* v.3.

Shepperd, Anne. 'A Diary of the Blitz of London, 1940' (IWM 95/13/1).

Shiba Ei'ichi, 'Chokugeki o uketa kenchō' [The prefectural headquarters took a direct hit], in *SK*.

Shiba Isa. 'Yakedasarete' [Chased by Fire], in *HK* v.2.

Shinonori Mansaku. *Gakudō sokai no kiroku: Tōkyō / Jōbanmatsu shōgakkō* [A record of the student mass evacuation: Tokyo, the Jōbanmatsu Primary School]. Tokyo: Aoi tori sha, 1972.

Simmonds, A. (Mr.). 'Beneath the Stairs', in *BSN*.

Skea, Bessie. 'Countrywoman's Diary' (IWM 79/32/1).

Smith, Olivia. Diary (M-O).

Sonematsu Kazuko. Diary, in Kawasaki municipal government, ed. *Kawasaki-shi kūshū / sensai no kiroku* [A record of Kawasaki air raids and war damage]. Kawasaki: Self-published, 1978.

S. P. S. 'Hitler's Coming', in *BSN*.

Sugaya Sumi. 'Chi no naka no shi' [Blood-soaked death], in *TDK* v.2.

Sumiyoshi Konokichi. Diary, in *WK*.

Susuki Tetsuo. 'Shōidan ga rōjin no atama ni' [An incendiary bomb struck an elderly man's head], in *SK*.

Suzuki Yoshiko. 'Onomoto mura yakuba no haikyūgakari shunin toshite' [As the head of the rationing division of the Onomoto Village Hall], in *SF*.

Tada Susumu. 'Kūshūka no keisatsukan' [Policemen during an air raid], in *KK*.

Taiheiyō sensō zenkoku kūbaku giseisha irei kyōkai, ed. *Heiwa no inori: Ippan sensai irei no kiroku* [A prayer for peace: records of pacifying the spirits of ordinary people who suffered in the war]. Himeji: Himeji Department of Health and Welfare, 1995.

Takahashi Aiko. 'Kaisen kara no nikki' [A diary from the start of the war], in Agawa Hiroyuki, ed., *Shōwa sensō bungaku zenshū [Showa wartime literature collection]*. Tokyo: Shūeisha, 1972.

Takahashi Yoshiji. 'Shuki: Hizan o koete utsukushikatta hi no ame' [Notebook: Raining fire, a beauty that overcame the horror], in *CK*.

Takatori Minoru, 'Dendōki fukitobu' [An electric generator blown into the air], in *KuK*.

Takeuchi Toshitoyo. Untitled memoir, *NK*.

Takimi Hiroyuki, 'Baketsu ippai no mizu: sore wa osana kodomo-tachi no inochi no mizu datta' [A bucket of cold water: it was the water of life for little children], *HaK* v.3.

Takizawa Toki. 'Otto no rusu o mamoritsuzukete' [Looking after things for my husband], *HaK* v.3.

Tanaka Tatsumu. '300-hon no shōidan' [300 incendiary bombs], in *TK*.

Tanaka Osamu, 'Maruta no yō na shōshitai' [Burned corpses stacked like logs], *SK*.

Taylor, R. C. 'Diary, 1941' (LMA, P83/BAT/015).

Thornton, Joan. Correspondence (CHC PA1692/16/1; CHC 1692/17/2).

Tomihisa Taue. 'Nagasaki Peace Declaration 2013', www.city.nagasaki.lg.jp/peace/english/appeal/.

Toshima Mitsuharu. Diary, in *TNK*.

Trent, Charles V. 'Diary of the Admiralty Islands Campaign', 21 April 1944 (Carlisle, PA: US Military History Historical Center).

Tsuyuki Isao. 'Tekiki ni te o furu' [Waving a hand at an enemy plane], in *TDK* v.2.

Turner, Mabel. Correspondence (HHC, DMX/242/6).

Turner, Margaret. Untitled memoir, in *MW*.

Uekusa Shōsaburō. 'Shuki: Nigeru hito ni kenpei no binta ga tobu' [Notebook: MPs hit the refugees], in *CK*.

Ueno Kōsaku. 'Shitai shori ni atatte' [On the disposal of corpses], in *KK*.

Various interviewees. 'Futon kabutte nenbutsu tonae' [Throw a futon over your head and pray], in *TK*.

Walsh, Bill. Correspondence (HHC, DMX/242/4).

Ward, Hilda. Correspondence (HHC, DMX/242/5).

Lieutenant Watanabe [no first name given]. Diary (Quantico, VA: US Marine Corps Archives).

Watanabe [nee Igura] Masako. 'Honoo no machi' [Town of flame], *HaK* v.3.

Watanabe Masanori. 'Gesuikan no naka dde inochi hiroi' [I saved my life in a sewer], in *CK*.

Watanbe Shige. '26-nenme no akuma no odori' [The 26th year of the devil's dance], in *TDK* v.1.

Watanabe Teruko. 'Shi o kakugo shita toki, tasukete kureta no wa keikan datta' [When we had resolved to die, we were saved by a policeman], *NK*.

Weston (Mrs.). 'Laughter and Tears', *BSN*.

Wheal, Donald James. *World's End: Memoir of a Blitz Childhood*. London: Century Books, 2005.

Williams, S., and F. Middleton. Correspondence, 1990 or 1991 (HHC DMX/242/3).

Wookey, L. 'A Vision of St. Chad', *BSN*.

Yabe Masaaki. 'Shōidan chokugeki, muzan ni mo korosareta imoto' [My little sister was brutally killed by an incendiary's direct hit], in *SG65*.

Yagi Jun'ichi. Diary, in *HaK* v.3.

Yamada Kikue. 'Itsu ni nattara te ga dete kuru no?' [When will my hand grow back?], *HaK* v.3.

Yamagoe Yone, 'Shuki: "Onkuni no tame" to yū kotoba' [Notebook: When saying 'for the sake of the country'], in *CK*.

Yamaki Mikiko. 'Sensō wa shi sono mono' [War is death itself], in *SF*.

Yamamoto Shigeko. 'Bōgeki no kakoi no soto e' [Getting out of the bomber's net], in *HaK* v.3.

Yamashita Toshitsugu. Untitled memoir, in *FD*.

Yokono Kōichi and Asahina Masanori, 'Tsuiraku shita Amerika-hei, I & II' [A fallen American soldier, I & II], in *SG65*.

Yokouchi Tomi. 'Jigoku no soko de bōzen jishitsu' [Losing myself while staring blankly into the pit of Hell], in *KK*.

Yoshida Fusako. Diary, in Aoki Masami, *Senjika no shomin nikki* [Diaries of ordinary people at war]. Tokyo: Nihon tosho sentā, 1987.

Yoshida Takeshi, 'Ikite iru yō na haha no kao' [My mother's face, she looked alive], in *CK*.

Yoshida Yoshio, 'Chichi wa jibun no ie yori jinushi no ie o mamotta' [Dad protected his landlord's house more than his own home], in *NK.*
Yoshitake Teruyoshi. Memoir, in *FD.*

Secondary Literature

Addison, Paul and Jeremy A. Crang. *Firestorm: The Bombing of Dresden, 1945.* London: Pimlico, 2006.

Alperovitz, Gar. *The Decision to Use the Atomic Bomb.* New York: Vintage Books, 2001.

Ambaras, David. *Bad Youth: Juvenile Delinquency and the Politics of Everyday Life in Modern Japan.* Berkeley: University of California Press, 2006.

Anastaplo, George. *Reflections on Life, Death, and the Constitution.* Lexington: University of Kentucky Press, 2009.

Anderson, Gerald D. *Fascists, Communists, and the National Government: Civil Liberties in Great Britain, 1931–1937.* Columbia, MO: University of Missouri Press, 1983.

Anonymous. 'An Editorial', *Journal of Peace Research*, Vol. 1, No. 1 (1964).

Baker, Nicholson, *Human Smoke: The Beginnings of World War II, the End of Civilization.* London: Simon & Schuster UK, 2009.

Ball, Stuart. *The Conservative Party and British Politics, 1902–1951.* London: Longman Group Limited, 1995.

Barnhart, Michael. *Japan Prepares for Total War: The Search for Economic Security, 1919–1941.* Ithaca: Cornell University Press, 1988.

Barshay, Andrew. *State and Intellectual in Imperial Japan: The Public Man in Crisis.* Berkeley: University of California Press, 1988.

Beaven, Brad, and John Griffiths. 'The Blitz and Civilian Morale in Three Northern Cities, 1940–1942', *Northern History* 32:1 (1996): 195–203.

'The Blitz, Civilian Morale, and the City: Mass-Observation and Working-Class Culture in Britain, 1940–1941', *Urban History* 26:1 (May 1999): 71–88.

Bell, Amy. *London Was Ours: Diaries and Memoirs of the London Blitz.* London: I.B. Tauris, 2011.

'Landscapes of Fear: Wartime London, 1939–1945', *Journal of British Studies* 48 (January 2009): 153–175.

Biddle, Tami Davis. *Rhetoric and Reality in Air Warfare: The Evolution of British and Americans Ideas about Strategic Bombing, 1914–1945.* Princeton: Princeton University Press, 2004.

'Dresden 1945: Reality, History, and Memory', *The Journal of Military History* 72:2 (April 2008): 413–450.

Bloxham, David. 'Dresden as a War Crime', in Paul Addison and Jeremy Crang, eds., *Firestorm: The Bombing of Dresden, February 1945.* London: Pimlico, 2006.

Brown, Mike. *Evacuees: Evacuation in Wartime Britain, 1939–1945.* Thrupp: Sutton Publishing, 2005.

Byas, Hugh. *Government by Assassination.* New York: Alfred A. Knopf, 1942.

Calder, Angus. *The Myth of the Blitz*. London: Pimlico, 1992.

The People's War: Britain 1939–1945. London: Pimlico, 1992.

Cave, Peter, and Aaron William Moore. 'Historical Interrogations of Japanese Children amid Disaster and War, 1920–1945', *Japanese Studies* 36:3 (2016).

Coffey, Thomas M. *Iron Eagle: The Turbulent Life of General Curtis LeMay*. New York: Random House, 1986.

Collier, Basil. *The Defence of the United Kingdom*. London: The Naval Military Press, 2004.

Conte-Helm, Marie. *Japan and the North East of England: From 1862 to Present Day*. London: Athlone Press, 1989.

Crowley, James B. *Japan's Quest for Autonomy*. Princeton: Princeton University Press, 1967.

Cwiertka, Katarzyna, ed. *Food and War in Mid-Twentieth Century East Asia*. Farnham: Ashgate Press, 2013.

Dower, John W. *War without Mercy: Race & Power in the Pacific War*. New York, NY: Pantheon, 1987.

Duus, Peter. *The Abacus and the Sword: The Japanese Penetration of Korea*. Berkeley: University of California Press, 1998.

Eley, Geoff. 'Finding the People's War: Film, British Collective Memories and World War II', *The American Historical Review* 106:3 (2001): 818–838.

Field, Clive D. 'Puzzled People Revisited: Religious Believing and Belonging in Wartime Britain, 1939–1945', *20th Century British History* 19:4 (2008): 446–479.

Field, Geoffrey. 'Social Patriotism and the British Working Class: Appearance and Disappearance of a Tradition', *International Labor and Working Class History* 42 (1992): 20–39.

Fogel, Joshua, ed. *The Nanjing Massacre in History and Historiography*. Berkeley: University of California Press, 2000.

Frank, Richard B. *Downfall: The End of the Imperial Japanese Empire*. London: Penguin Books, 2001.

Frühstück, Sabine, and Anne Walthall, ed. *Recreating Japanese Men*. Berkeley: University of California Press, 2011.

Fujii Tadatoshi. *Kokubō fujinkai* [The National Women's Defense League]. Tokyo: Iwanami shoten, 1985.

Garon, Sheldon. *Beyond Our Means: Why American Spends While the World Saves*. Princeton: Princeton University Press, 2013.

Geraghty, T. *A North-East Coast Town, Ordeal and Triumph: The Story of Kingston upon Hull in the 1939–1945 Great War*. Hull: Kingston upon Hull Corporation, 1951.

Gerteis, Christopher. *Gender Struggles: Wage-Earning Women and Male-Dominated Unions in Postwar Japan*. Cambridge: Harvard East Asia Monographs, 2010.

Gillett, Edward, and Kenneth A. MacMahon, *A History of Hull*. Oxford University Press, 1980.

Gordon, Andrew. *The Evolution of Labor Relations in Japan: Heavy Industry, 1853–1955*. Cambridge: Harvard East Asia Monographs, 1985.

Grayling, A.C. *Among the Dead Cities*. London: Bloomsbury, 2007.

Gregor, Neil. 'A Schicksalsgemeinschaft? Allied Bombing, Civilian Morale, and Social Dissolution in Nuremberg, 1942–1945', *Historical Journal*, 43 (2000): 1051–1070.

Havens, Thomas R.H. *Fire across the Sea: The Vietnam War and Japan 1965–1975*. Princeton: Princeton University Press, 1987.

Harris, Carol. *Blitz Diary: Life under Fire in World War II*. London: The History Press, 2010.

Hasegawa Tsuyoshi. *Racing the Enemy: Stalin, Truman, and the Surrender of Japan*. Cambridge: Harvard University Press, 2005.

Hastings, Max. *Nemesis: The Battle for Japan, 1944–1945*. London: Harper Perennial, 2009.

Hewitt, Kenneth. 'Place Annihilation: Area Bombing and the Fate of Urban Places', *Annals of the Association of American Geographers* 73:2 (Jun., 1983): 257–284.

Hogan, Michael J., ed. *Hiroshima in History and Memory*. Cambridge University Press, 1996.

Hunter, Kate. 'More than an Archive of War: Intimacy and Manliness in the Letters of a Great War Soldier to the Woman He Loved, 1915–1919', *Gender and History* 25 (2013): 339–354.

Karacas, Cary. 'Place, Public Memory, and the Tokyo Air Raids', *Geographical Review* 100:4 (Oct., 2010): 521–537.

Kidd, Alan. *Manchester: A History*. Lancaster: Carnegie Publishing, 2006.

Koshiro Yukiko. *Imperial Eclipse: Japan's Strategic Thinking about Continental Asia before August 1945*. Ithaca: Cornell University Press, 2013.

'Racing the Enemy: Stalin, Truman, and the Surrender of Japan (review)', *The Journal of Japanese Studies*, vol. 33 no. 1 (2007): 211–216.

Kramer, Andrew E. 'Russia Shows What Happens When Terrorists' Families Are Targeted', *The New York Times*, 29 March 2016.

Kushner, Barak. *Men to Devils, Devils to Men: Japanese War Crimes and Chinese Justice*. Cambridge: Harvard University Press, 2015.

'Laughter as Materiel: The Mobilization of Comedy in Japan's Fifteen-Year War', The *International History Review*, volume xxvi, 2 (June 2004): 300–330.

Kynaston, David. *Austerity Britain, 1945–1951*. London: Bloomsbury, 2008.

Lary, Diana. *The Chinese People at War: Human Suffering and Social Transformation, 1937–1945*. Cambridge University Press, 2010.

Lee, Leo Ou-fan. *Shanghai Modern: The Flowering of a New Urban Culture in China, 1930–1945*. Cambridge: Harvard University Press, 1999.

Lowe, Keith. *Inferno: The Fiery Destruction of Hamburg, 1943*. London: Scribner, 2009.

Lukowitz. David C. 'British Pacifists and Appeasement: The Peace Pledge Union', *Journal of Contemporary History* 9:1 (January, 1974): 115–127.

McLeod, Hugh. *Religion and Society in England, 1850–1914*. New York: St. Martin's Press, 1996.

Metzler, Mark. *Lever of Empire: The International Gold Standard and the Crisis of Liberalism in Prewar Japan*. Berkeley: University of California Press, 2006.

Miller, Kristine A. *British Literature of the Blitz: Fighting the People's War*. London: Palgrave Macmillan, 2009.

Minear, Richard H. *Victors' Justice: Tokyo War Crimes Trial*. Ann Arbor: University of Michigan Press, 2001.

Mitchell, Richard H. *Thought Control in Prewar Japan*. Ithaca: Cornell University Press, 1976.

Mitter, Rana. *China's War with Japan, 1937–45: The Struggle for Survival*. London: Allen Lane, 2013.

Miyake Yoshiko. 'Doubling Expectations: Motherhood and Women's Factory Work under State Management, 1937–1945', in Gail Lee Bernstein, ed., *Recreating Japanese Women*, 1600–1945. Berkeley: University of California Press, 1991.

Moore, Aaron William. *Writing War: Soldiers Record the Japanese Empire*. Cambridge, MA: Harvard University Press, 2013.

Myers, Ramon H. 'Creating a Modern Enclave Economy: The Economic Integration of Japan, Manchuria, and North China, 1932–1945', in Peter Duus, Ramon Myers, and Mark Peattie, eds. *The Japanese Wartime Empire*, 1931–1945. Princeton: Princeton University Press, 1984.

Nakamura Takafusa, 'The Yen Bloc, 1931–1941', in Peter Duus, Ramon Myers, and Mark Peattie, eds. *The Japanese Wartime Empire, 1931–1945*. Princeton: Princeton University Press, 1984.

Neiman, Susan. *Evil in Modern Thought: An Alternative History of Philosophy*. Princeton, NJ: Princeton University Press, 2002.

Nish, Ian H. *The Anglo-Japanese Alliance: The Diplomacy of Two Island Empires 1894–1907*. London: Bloomsbury, 2012.
Alliance in Decline: A Study in Anglo-Japanese Relations, 1908–1923. London: Bloomsbury, 2012.

Noakes, Lucy, and Juliette Pattinson. 'Introduction: "Keep Calm and Carry on": The Cultural Memory of the Second World War in Britain', in Noakes and Pattinson, ed., *British Cultural Memory and the Second World War*. London: Bloomsbury, 2014.

Noda Masaaki. *Senshō to zaiseki* [War and responsibility]. Iwanami shoten, 1998.

Ohnuki-Tierney, Emiko. *Kamikaze, Cherry Blossoms, and Nationalisms: The Militarization of Aesthetics in Japanese History*. Chicago: University of Chicago Press, 2002.

Orbaugh, Sharalyn. *Propaganda Performed: Kamishibai in Japan's Fifteen Year War*. Leiden: Brill, 2015.

Overy, Richard. *The Bombing War: Europe, 1939–1945*. London: Allen Lane, 2013.

Pape, Robert A. *Bombing to Win: Air Power and Coercion in War*. Ithaca: Cornell University Press, 1996.

Percival, Robin. 'The Other Way', *Fortnight*, No. 123 (Mar. 19, 1976): 7–8.

Powles, Cyril H. 'Abe Isoo: The Utility Man', in Nobuya Bamba and John F. Howes, eds., *Pacifism in Japan: The Christian and Socialist Tradition*. Kyoto: Minerva Press, 1980.

Rempel, Richard A. 'The Dilemmas of British Pacifists during World War II', *The Journal of Modern History* 50:4 (December, 1978): D1213–D1229.

Rose, Sonya. *Which People's War? National Identity and Citizenship in Wartime Britain, 1939–1945*. Oxford: Oxford University Press, 2004.

Saitō Tsutomu. *Tōkyō-to gakuto kinrō dōin no kenkyū [Research on Tokyo student labour mobilization]*. Hachiōji: Nonburusha, 1999.

Schaffer, Ronald. 'The Bombing Campaigns in World War II: The European Theater', in Yuki Tanaka and Marilyn B. Young, eds., *Bombing Civilians: A Twentieth Century History*. New York: The New Press, 2009.

Schencking, J. *Charles. Making Waves: Politics, Propaganda, and the Emergence of the Imperial Japanese Navy, 1868–1922*. Stanford: Stanford University Press, 2005.

Searle, Thomas R. '"It Made a Lot of Sense to Kill Skilled Workers": The Firebombing of Tokyo in March 1945', *The Journal of Military History* 66:1 (Jan., 2002): 103–133.

Shields, John. 'The Battle of Britain: A Not So Narrow Margin', *Air Power Review* (Summer 2015): 182–197.

Shimazu, Naoko. *Japan, Race and Equality: The Racial Equality Proposal of 1919*. London: Routledge, 2002.

Smethurst, Richard J. *From Foot Soldier to Finance Minister: Takahashi Korekiyo, Japan's Keynes*. Cambridge: Harvard East Asian Monographs, 2009.

Strachan, Hew. 'Essay and Reflection: On Total War and Modern War', *The International History Review* 22:2 (Jun., 2000), 341–370.

Stranack, David. *Schools at War: A Story of Education, Evacuation, and Endurance in the Second World War*. Chichester: Phillimore, 2005.

Sugawara Katsuya, 'Great Bearer: Images of the U.S. in the Writings of the Air Raids', *Comparative Literature Studies* 41:4, East-West Issue (2004): 451–463.

Summerfield, Penny. *Reconstructing Women's Wartime Lives: Discourse and Subjectivity in Oral Histories of the Second World War*. Manchester: Manchester University Press, 1998.

Women Workers in the Second World War: Production and Patriarchy in Conflict. London: Routledge, 1989.

Süss, Dietmar. *Death from the Skies: How the British and Germans Survived Bombing in World War II, trans. Lesley Sharpe and Jeremy Noakes*. Oxford: Oxford University Press, 2013.

Tagaya Osamu. 'The Imperial Japanese Air Forces', in Robin Higham and Stephen J. Harris, eds. *Why Air Forces Fail: The Anatomy of Defeat*. Lexington: Kentucky University Press, 2006.

Taylor, Frederick. Dresden: *Tuesday 13 February 1945*. London: Bloomsbury, 2004.

Tillman, Barrett. *LeMay: A Biography*. London: Palgrave, 2007.

Whirlwind: The Air War against Japan, 1942–1945. New York, NY: Simon & Schuster, 2010.

Totani Yuma. *The Tokyo War Crimes Trial: The Pursuit of Justice in the Wake of World War II*. Cambridge: Harvard University Asia Center, 2008.

Townshend, Charles. *Making the Peace: Public Order and Public Security in Modern Britain*. Oxford: Oxford University Press, 1983.

Welshman, John. *Churchill's Children*. Oxford: Oxford University Press, 2010.

Werrel, Kenneth P. *Blankets of Fire: U.S. Bombers over Japan during World War II*. Washington, DC: Smithsonian Institution Press, 1996.

Yamashita Samuel Hideo. *Leaves from an Autumn of Emergencies*. Honolulu: University of Hawai'i Press, 2005.

Daily Life in Wartime Japan, 1940–1945. Lawrence: University of Kansas Press, 2016.

Yoshimi Yoshiaki. *Grassroots Fascism: The War Experience and the Japanese People*, trans. Ethan Mark. New York: Columbia University Press, 2015; *Kusa no ne no fashizumu: Nihon minshū no sensō taiken*. Tokyo: Tokyo daigaku shuppan-sha, 1987.

Young, Louise. *Beyond the Metropolis: Second Cities and Modern Life in Interwar Japan*. Berkeley: University of California Press, 2013.

Zwigenberg, Ran. *Hiroshima: The Origins of Global Memory Culture*. Cambridge: Cambridge University Press, 2016.

Index